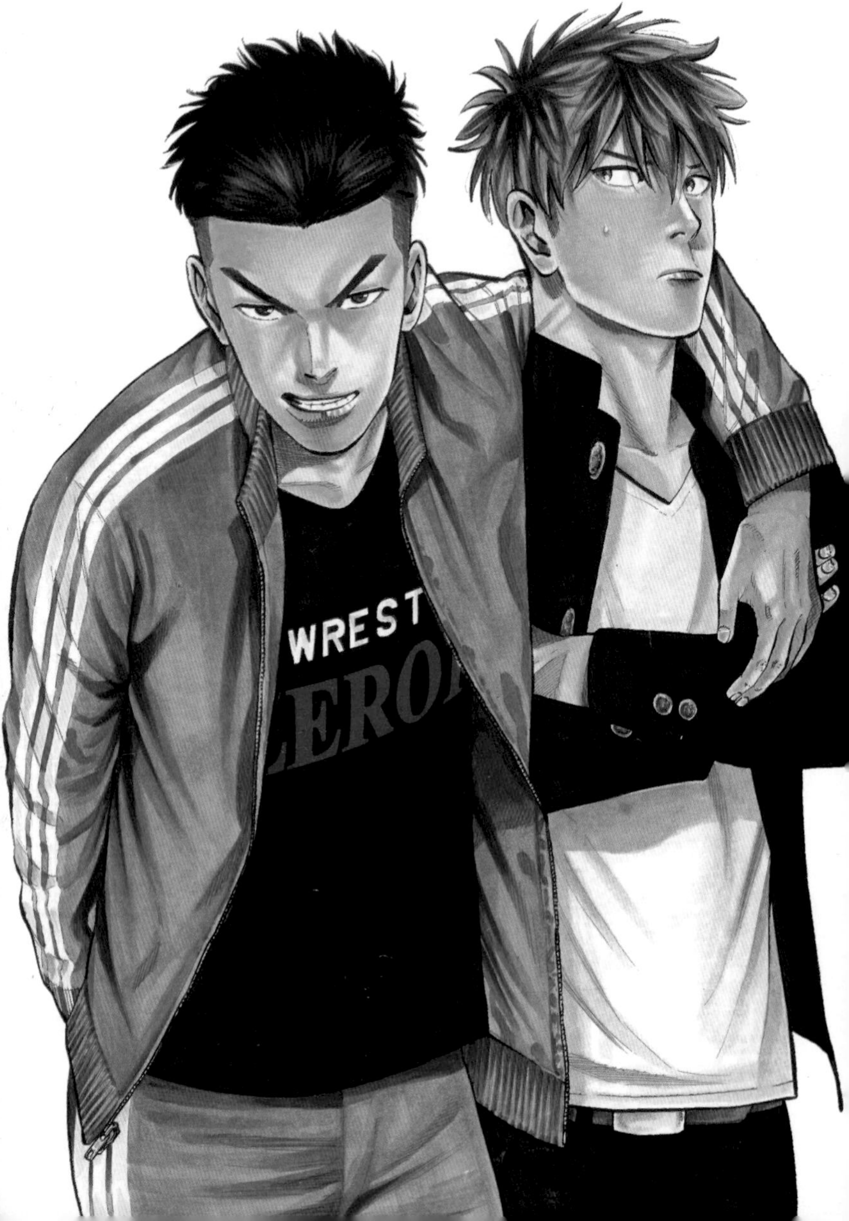
WREST
LERO

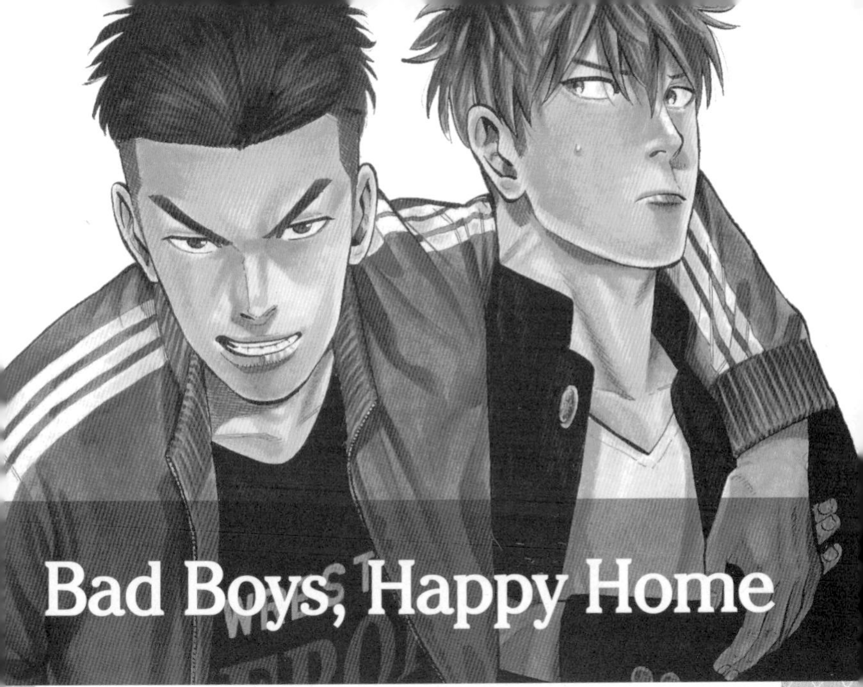

Bad Boys, Happy Home

Story by SHOOWA Art by Hiromasa Okujima volume 1

CONTENTS

SUBLIME

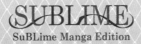

SuBLime Manga Edition

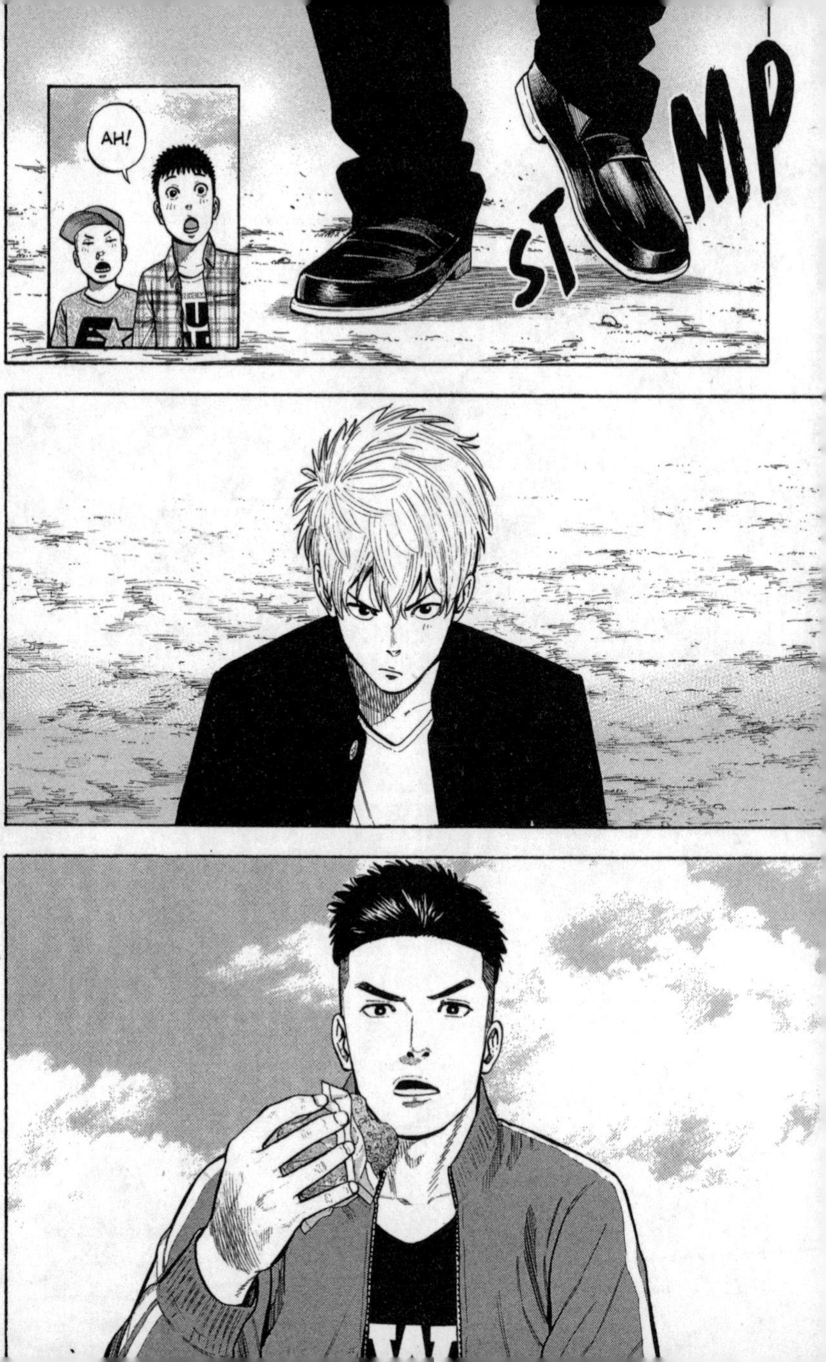
STOMP
AH!

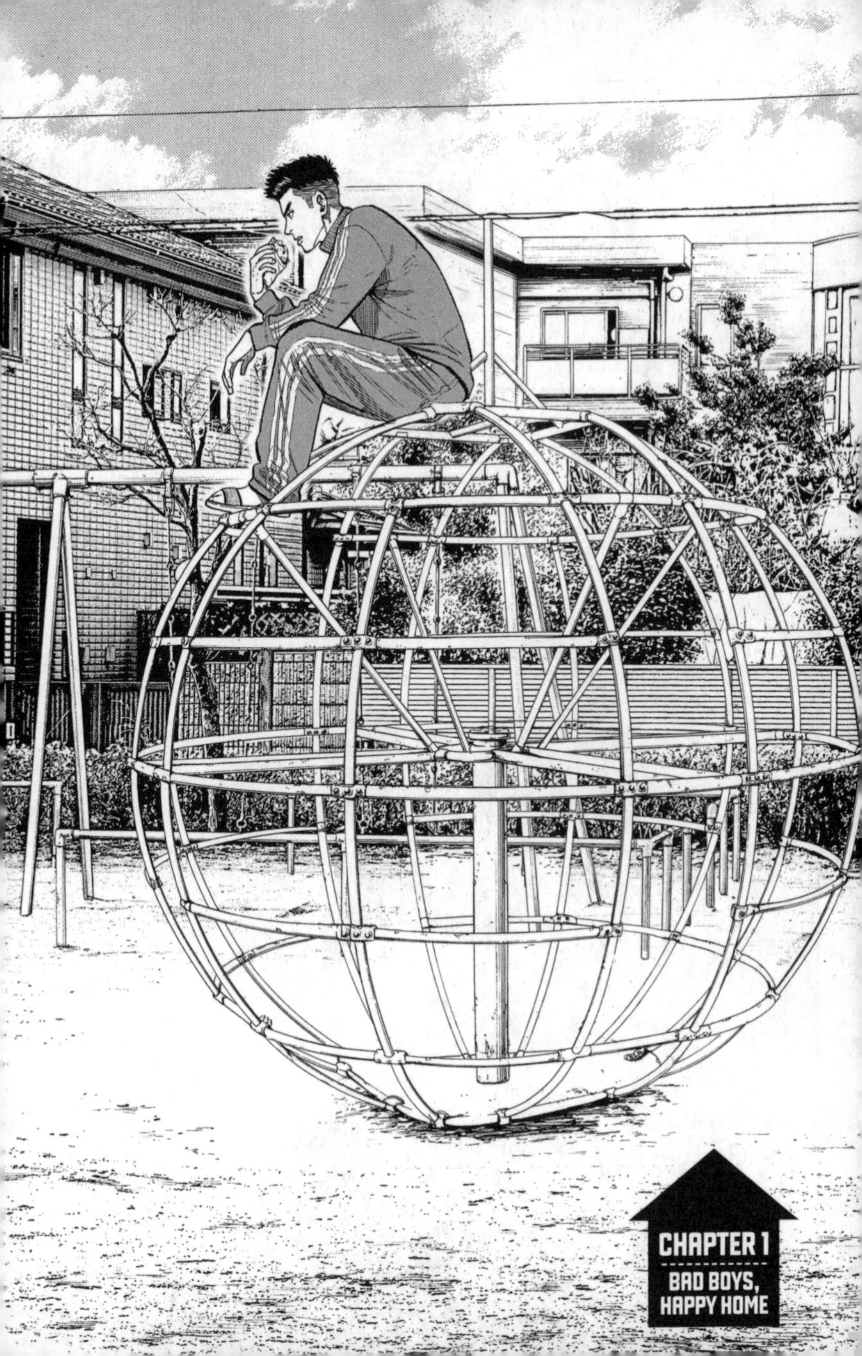
CHAPTER 1
BAD BOYS,
HAPPY HOME

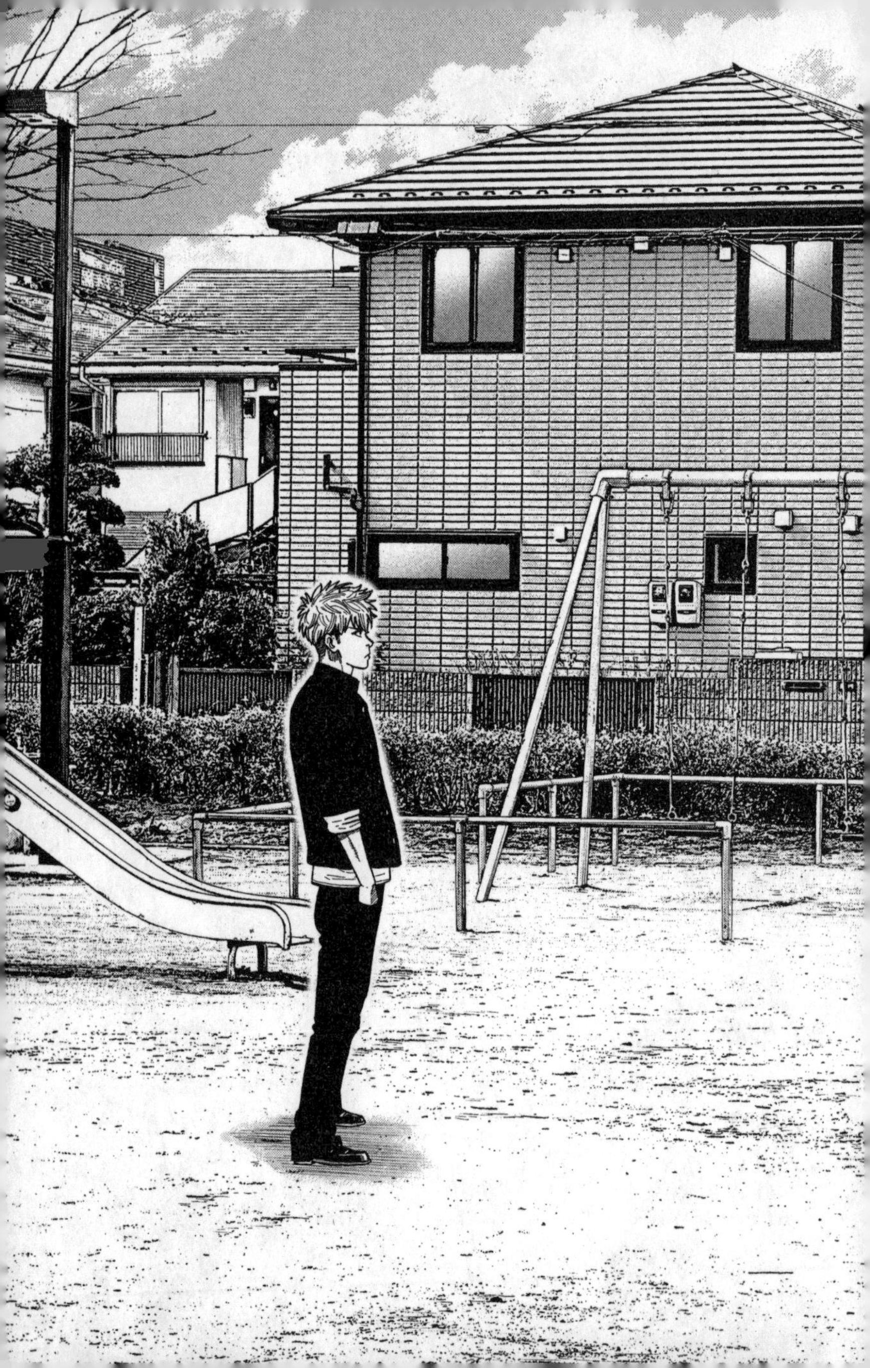

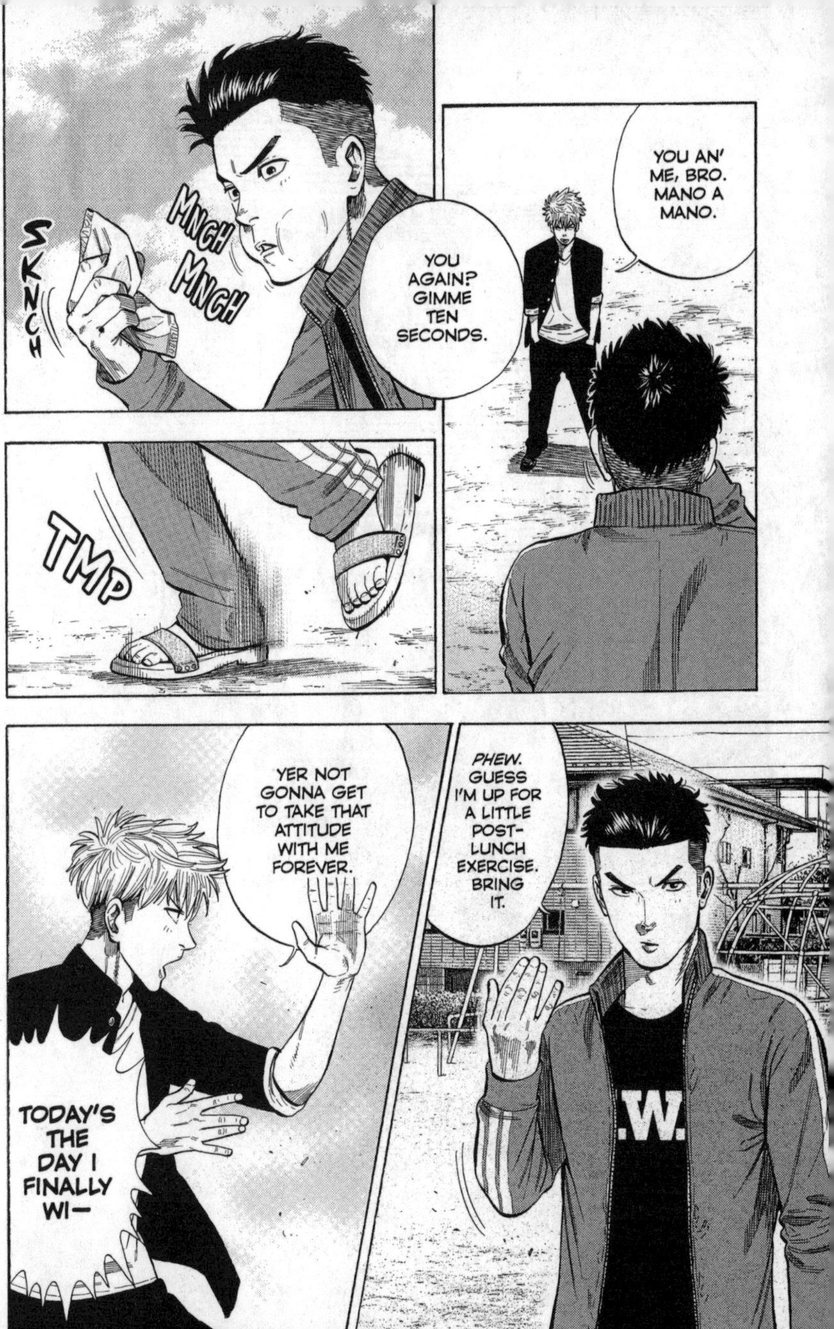
YOU AN' ME, BRO. MANO A MANO.
SKNCH
MNGH MNGH
YOU AGAIN? GIMME TEN SECONDS.
TMP
PHEW. GUESS I'M UP FOR A LITTLE POST-LUNCH EXERCISE. BRING IT.
YER NOT GONNA GET TO TAKE THAT ATTITUDE WITH ME FOREVER.
TODAY'S THE DAY I FINALLY WI—
.W.

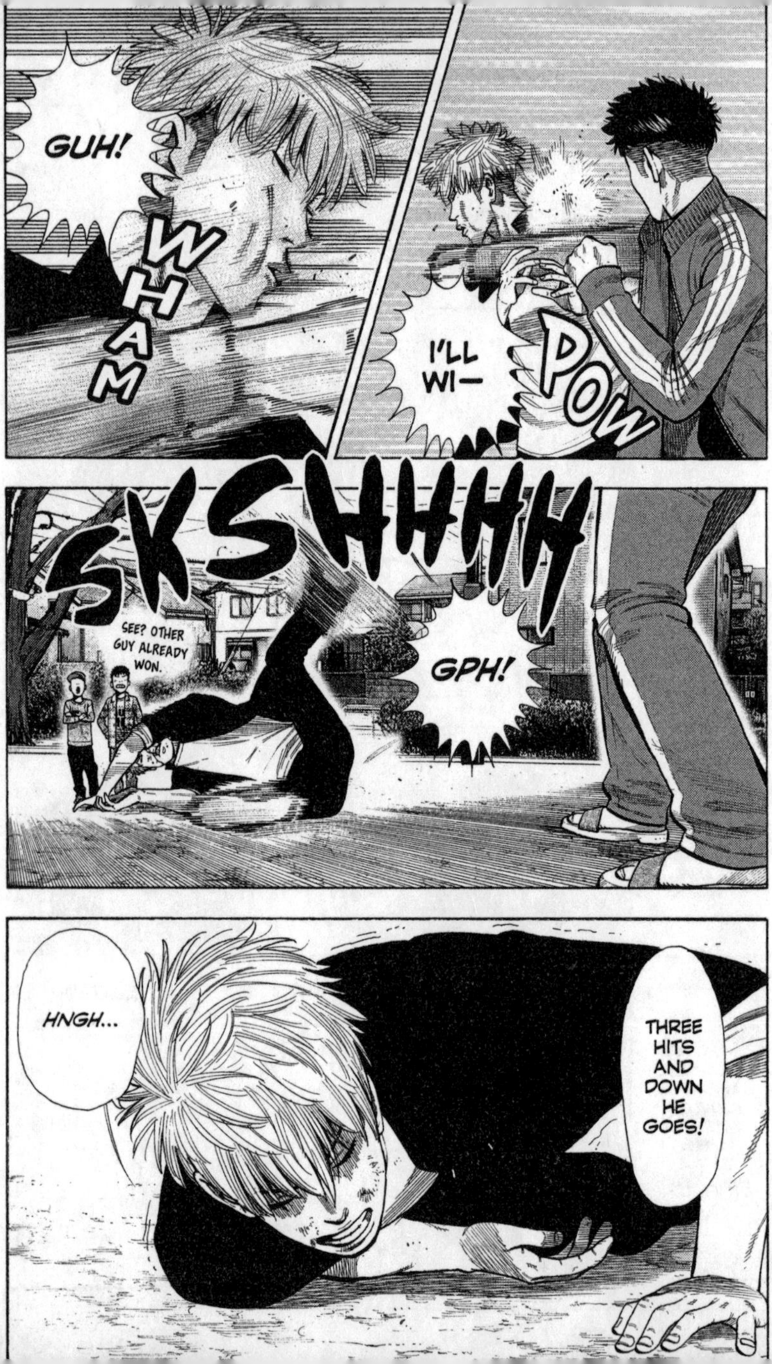
I'LL WI—
POW
GUH!
WHAM
SKSHHHH
GPH!
SEE? OTHER GUY ALREADY WON.
THREE HITS AND DOWN HE GOES!
HNGH...

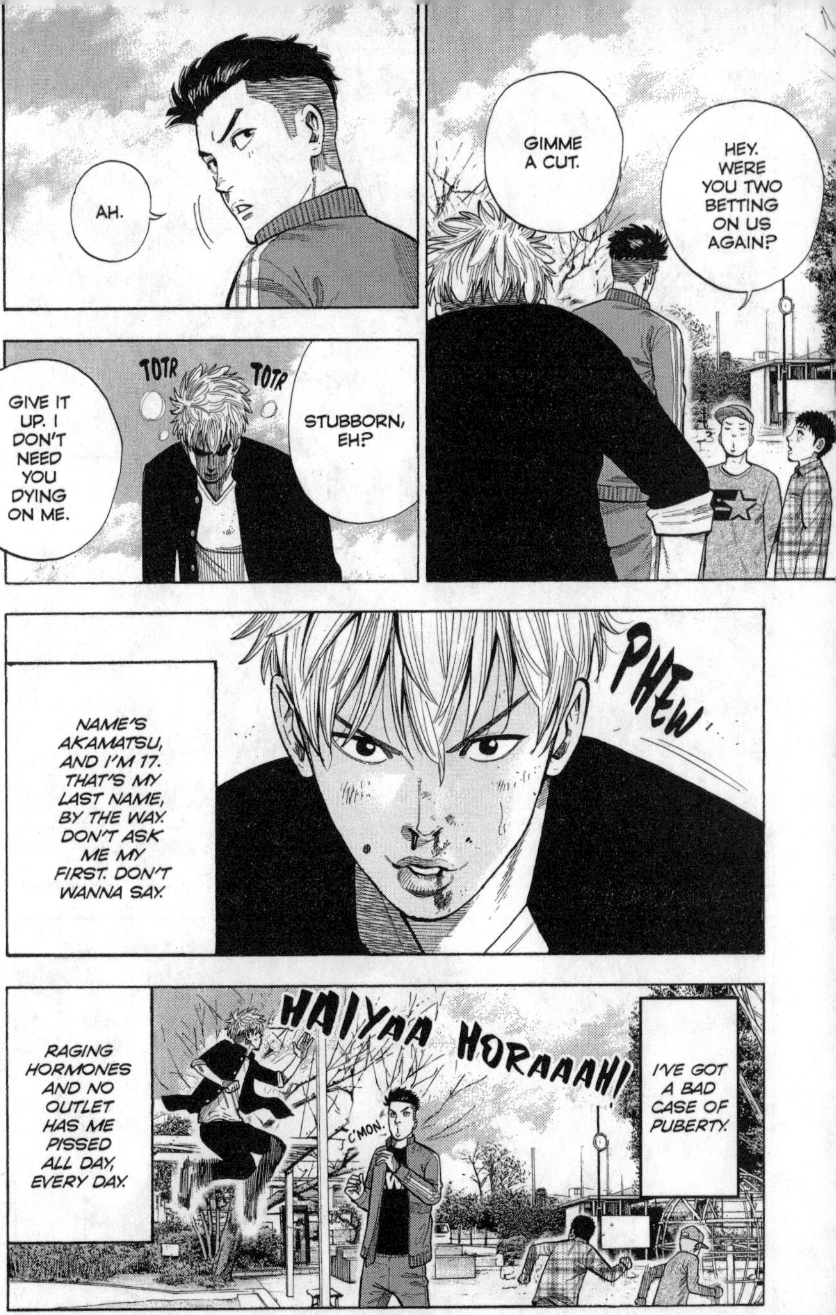
HEY. WERE YOU TWO BETTING ON US AGAIN?
GIMME A CUT.
AH.
TOTR
TOTR
STUBBORN, EH?
GIVE IT UP. I DON'T NEED YOU DYING ON ME.
PHEW
NAME'S AKAMATSU, AND I'M 17. THAT'S MY LAST NAME, BY THE WAY. DON'T ASK ME MY FIRST. DON'T WANNA SAY.
I'VE GOT A BAD CASE OF PUBERTY.
HORAAAH!
HAIYAA
C'MON.
RAGING HORMONES AND NO OUTLET HAS ME PISSED ALL DAY, EVERY DAY.

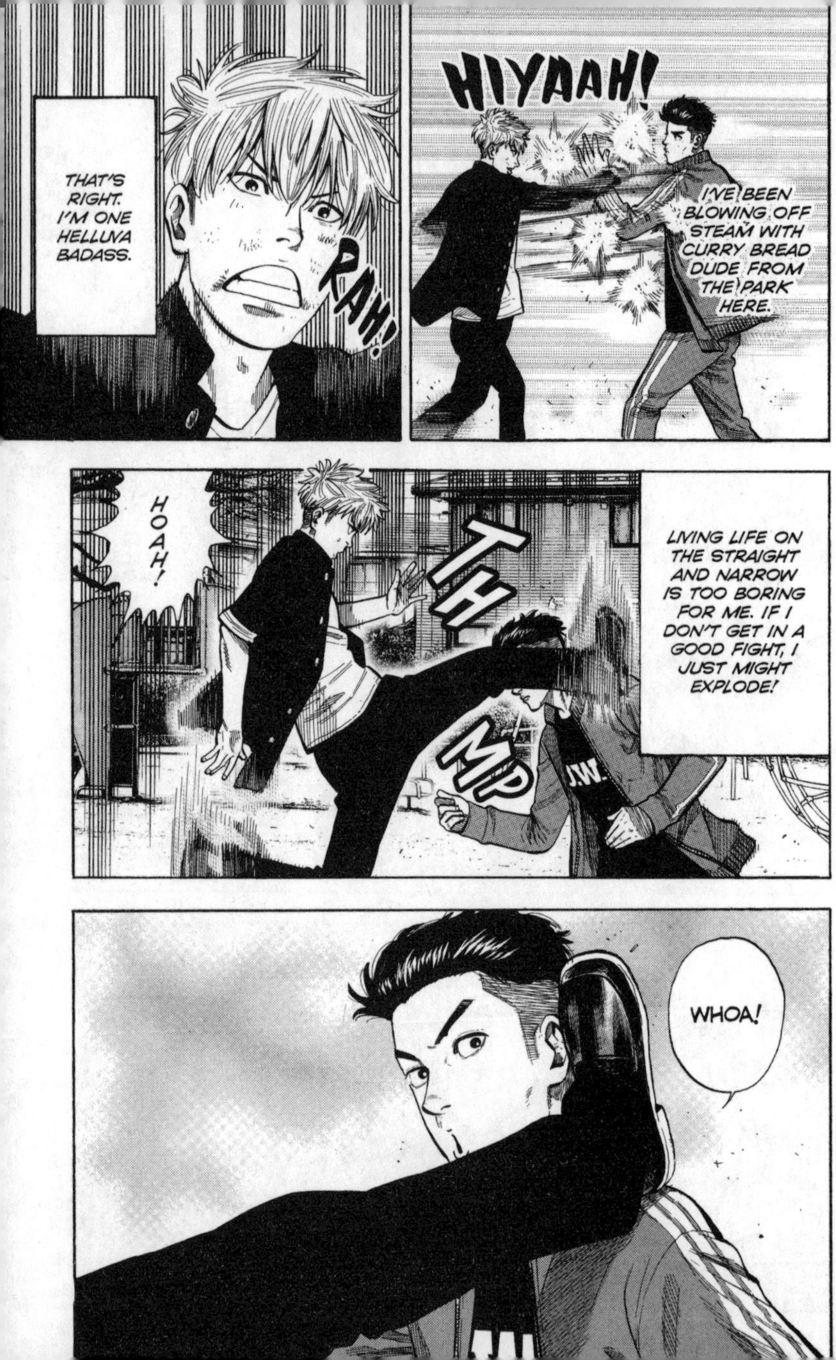
HIYAAH!
I'VE BEEN BLOWING OFF STEAM WITH CURRY BREAD DUDE FROM THE PARK HERE.
THAT'S RIGHT. I'M ONE HELLUVA BADASS.
RAH!
LIVING LIFE ON THE STRAIGHT AND NARROW IS TOO BORING FOR ME. IF I DON'T GET IN A GOOD FIGHT, I JUST MIGHT EXPLODE!
HOAH!
THMP
WHOA!

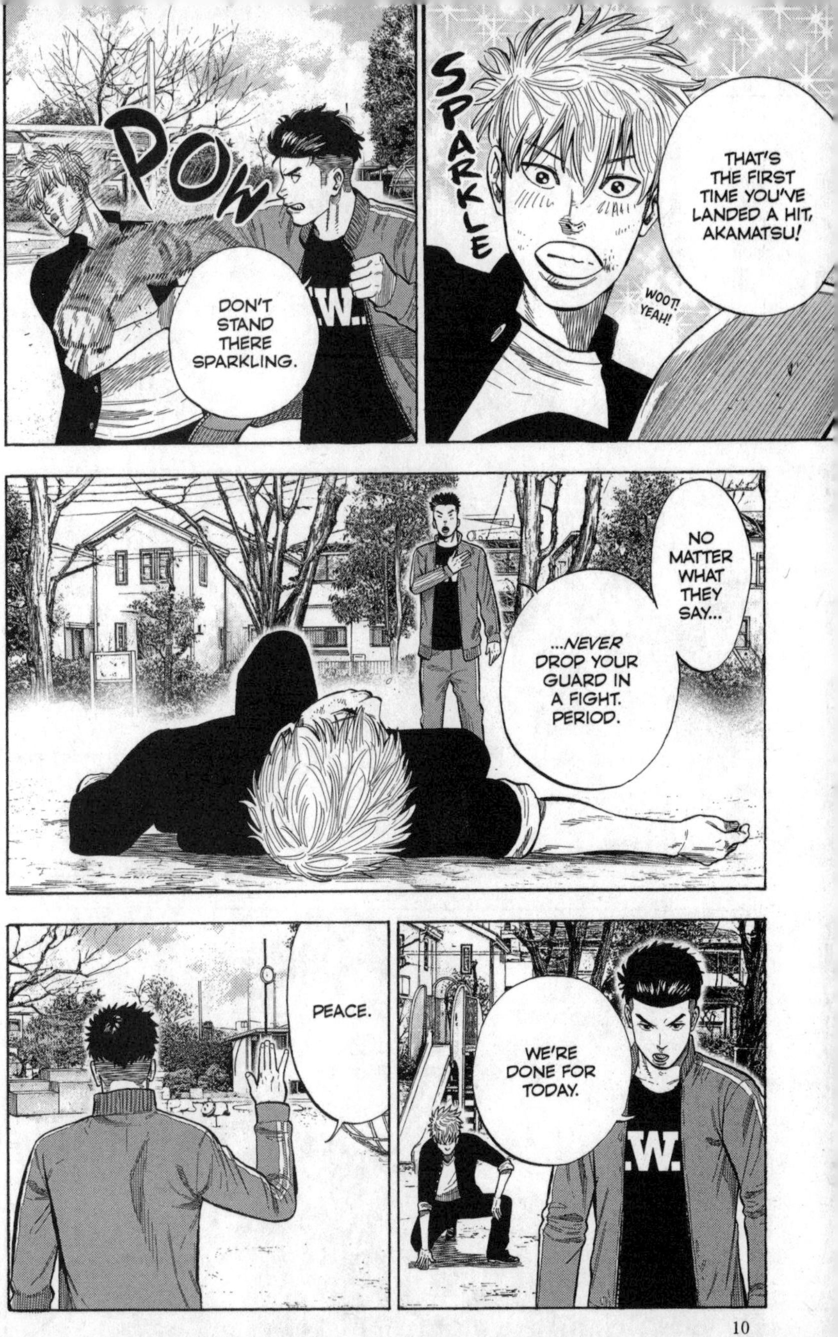
SPARKLE
THAT'S THE FIRST TIME YOU'VE LANDED A HIT, AKAMATSU!
WOOT! YEAH!
POW
DON'T STAND THERE SPARKLING.
NO MATTER WHAT THEY SAY...
...*NEVER* DROP YOUR GUARD IN A FIGHT. PERIOD.
WE'RE DONE FOR TODAY.
PEACE.

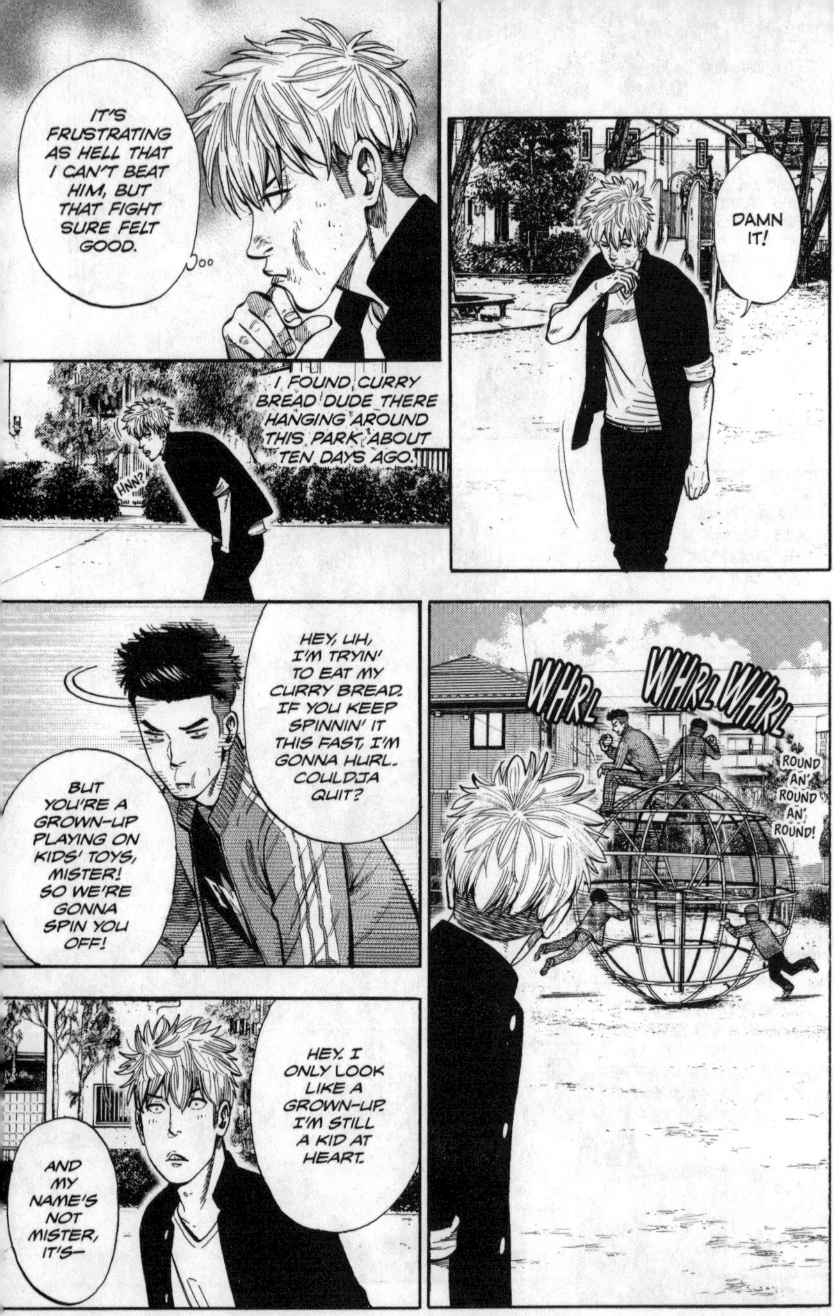
DAMN IT!
IT'S FRUSTRATING AS HELL THAT I CAN'T BEAT HIM, BUT THAT FIGHT SURE FELT GOOD.
I FOUND CURRY BREAD DUDE THERE HANGING AROUND THIS PARK ABOUT TEN DAYS AGO.
HNN?
WHRL
WHRL WHRL
ROUND AN' ROUND AN' ROUND!
HEY, UH, I'M TRYIN' TO EAT MY CURRY BREAD. IF YOU KEEP SPINNIN' IT THIS FAST, I'M GONNA HURL. COULDJA QUIT?
BUT YOU'RE A GROWN-UP PLAYING ON KIDS' TOYS, MISTER! SO WE'RE GONNA SPIN YOU OFF!
HEY. I ONLY LOOK LIKE A GROWN-UP. I'M STILL A KID AT HEART.
AND MY NAME'S NOT MISTER, IT'S—

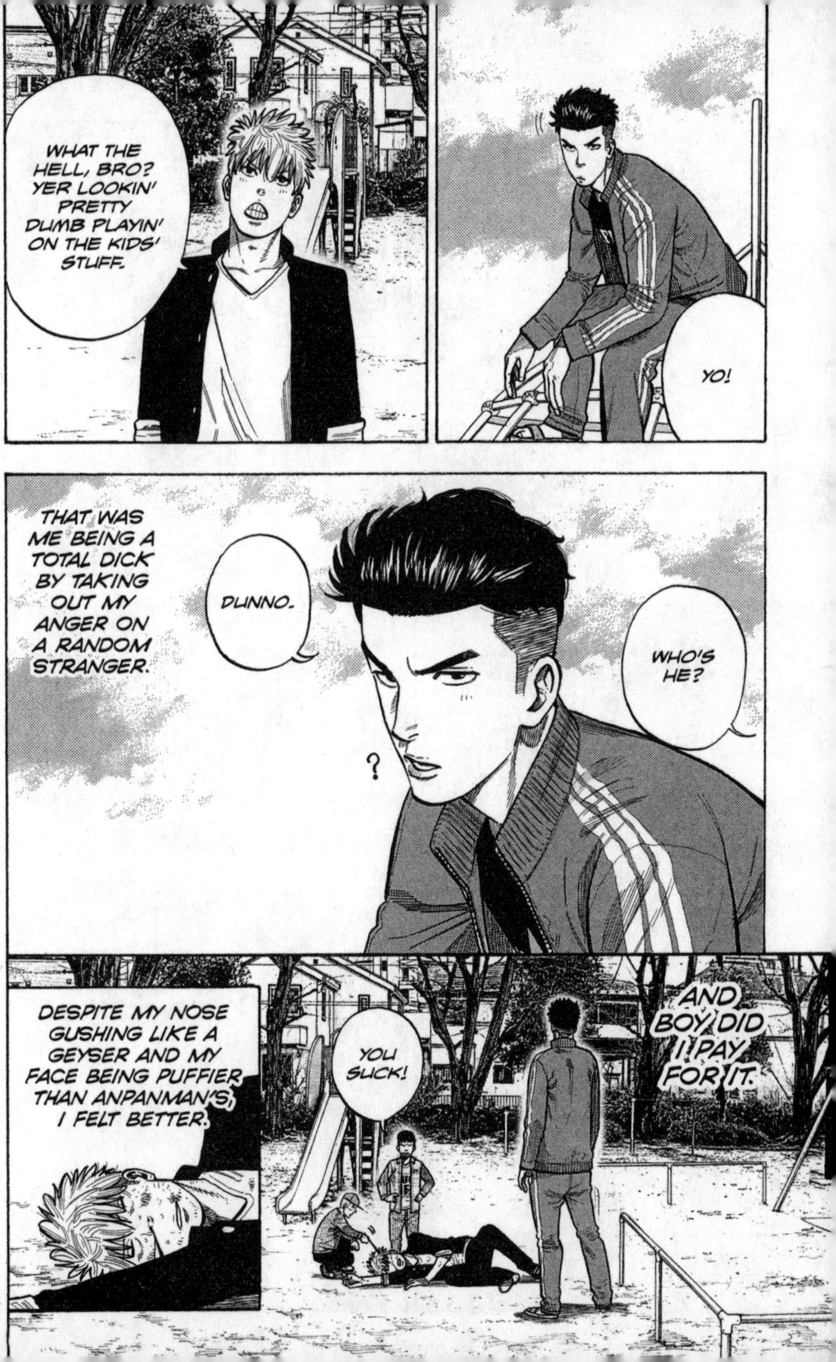
YO!
WHAT THE HELL, BRO? YER LOOKIN' PRETTY DUMB PLAYIN' ON THE KIDS' STUFF.
WHO'S HE?
DUNNO.
THAT WAS ME BEING A TOTAL DICK BY TAKING OUT MY ANGER ON A RANDOM STRANGER.
?
AND BOY DID I PAY FOR IT.
YOU SUCK!
DESPITE MY NOSE GUSHING LIKE A GEYSER AND MY FACE BEING PUFFIER THAN ANPANMAN'S, I FELT BETTER.

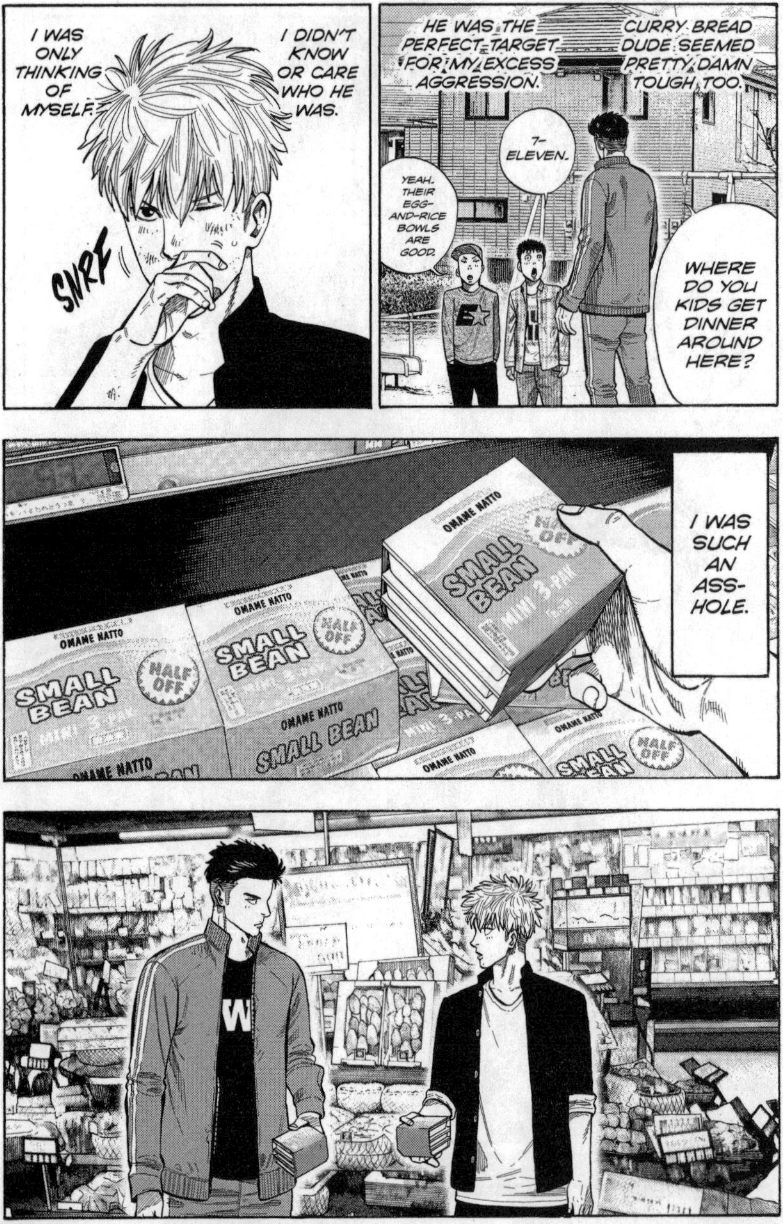

CURRY BREAD DUDE SEEMED PRETTY DAMN TOUGH TOO.
HE WAS THE PERFECT TARGET FOR MY EXCESS AGGRESSION.
WHERE DO YOU KIDS GET DINNER AROUND HERE?
7-ELEVEN.
YEAH. THEIR EGG-AND-RICE BOWLS ARE GOOD.
I DIDN'T KNOW OR CARE WHO HE WAS.
I WAS ONLY THINKING OF MYSELF.
SNRF
I WAS SUCH AN ASS-HOLE.
OMAME NATTO
SMALL BEAN
HALF OFF
MINI 3-PAK

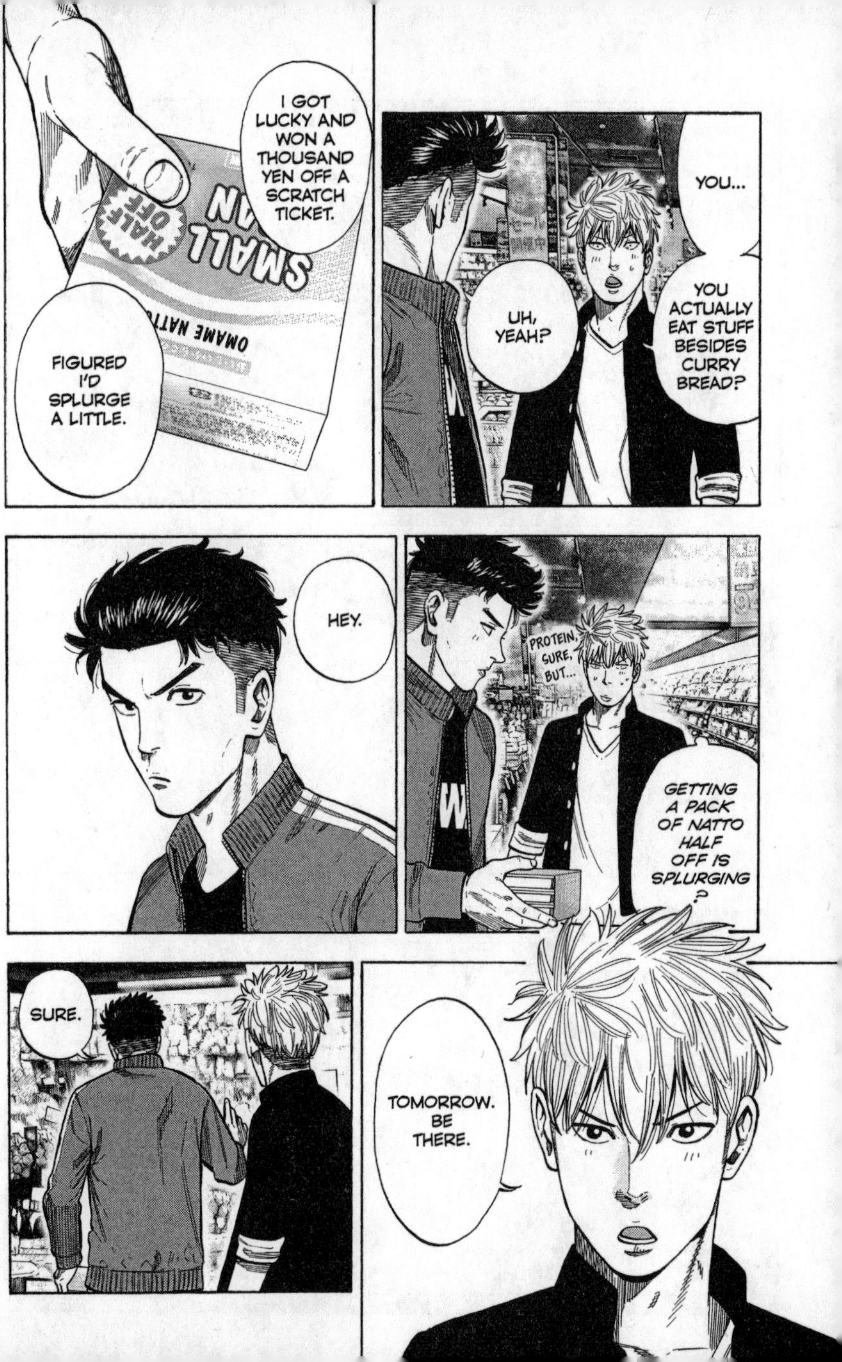
YOU...
YOU ACTUALLY EAT STUFF BESIDES CURRY BREAD?
UH, YEAH?
I GOT LUCKY AND WON A THOUSAND YEN OFF A SCRATCH TICKET.
FIGURED I'D SPLURGE A LITTLE.
PROTEIN, SURE, BUT...
GETTING A PACK OF NATTO HALF OFF IS SPLURGING?
HEY.
TOMORROW. BE THERE.
SURE.

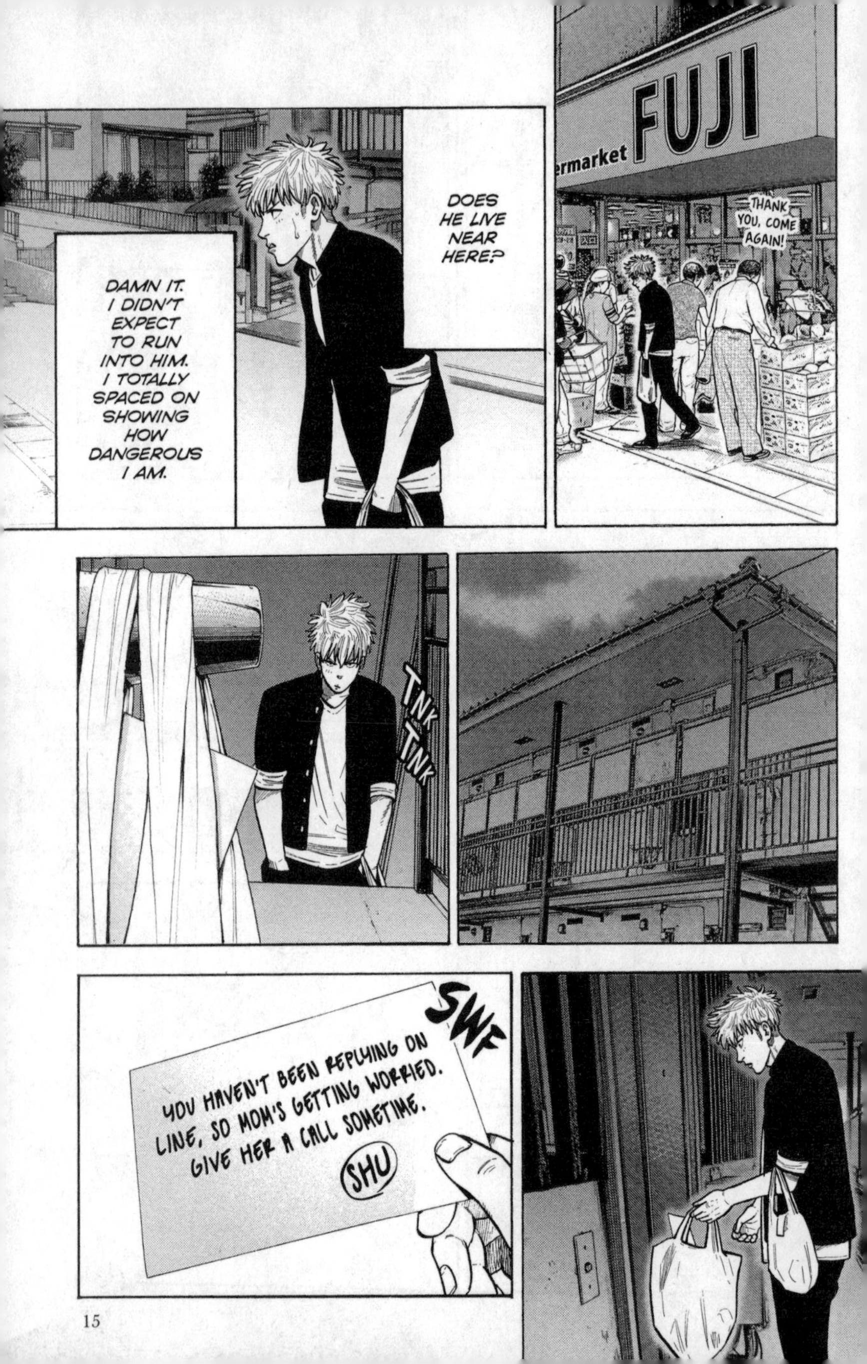
FUJI
ermarket
THANK YOU, COME AGAIN!
DOES HE LIVE NEAR HERE?
DAMN IT. I DIDN'T EXPECT TO RUN INTO HIM. I TOTALLY SPACED ON SHOWING HOW DANGEROUS I AM.
TNK TNK
SWF
YOU HAVEN'T BEEN REPLYING ON LINE, SO MOM'S GETTING WORRIED. GIVE HER A CALL SOMETIME.
SHU

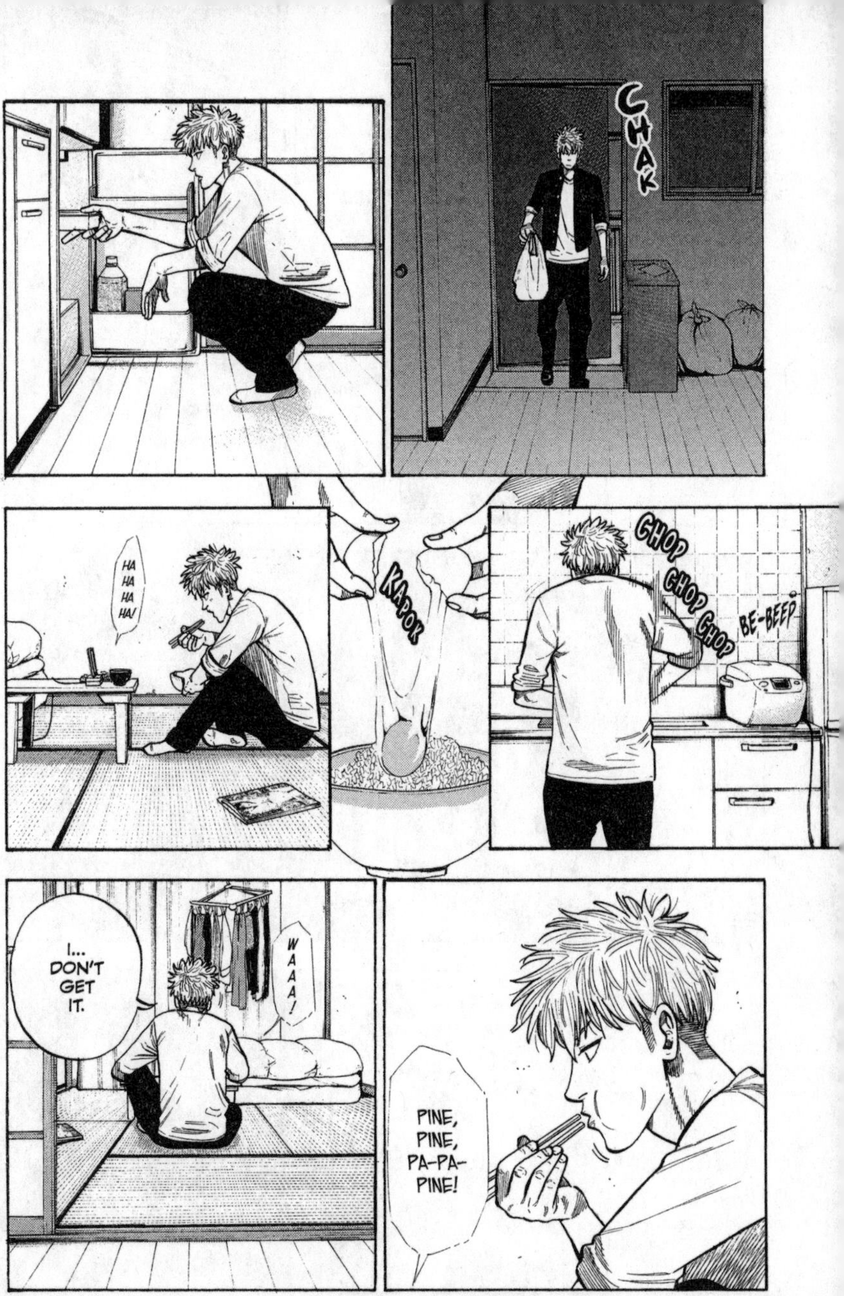
CHAK
CHOP CHOP CHOP
BE-BEEP
KAPOK
HA HA HA HA!
PINE, PINE, PA-PA-PINE!
WAAAA!
I... DON'T GET IT.

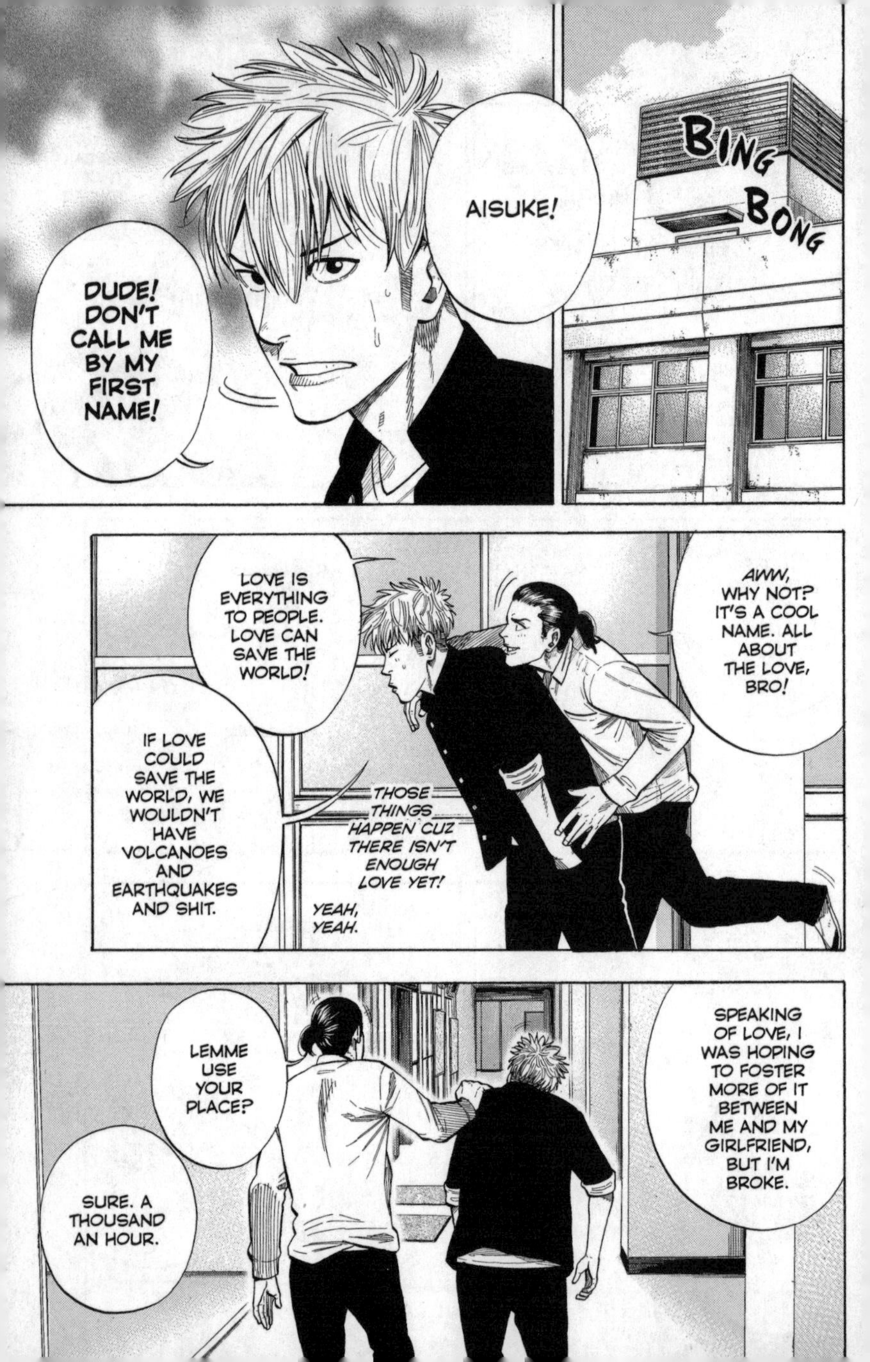
BING BONG
AISUKE!
DUDE! DON'T CALL ME BY MY FIRST NAME!
AWW, WHY NOT? IT'S A COOL NAME. ALL ABOUT THE LOVE, BRO!
LOVE IS EVERYTHING TO PEOPLE. LOVE CAN SAVE THE WORLD!
IF LOVE COULD SAVE THE WORLD, WE WOULDN'T HAVE VOLCANOES AND EARTHQUAKES AND SHIT.
THOSE THINGS HAPPEN CUZ THERE ISN'T ENOUGH LOVE YET!
YEAH, YEAH.
SPEAKING OF LOVE, I WAS HOPING TO FOSTER MORE OF IT BETWEEN ME AND MY GIRLFRIEND, BUT I'M BROKE.
LEMME USE YOUR PLACE?
SURE. A THOUSAND AN HOUR.

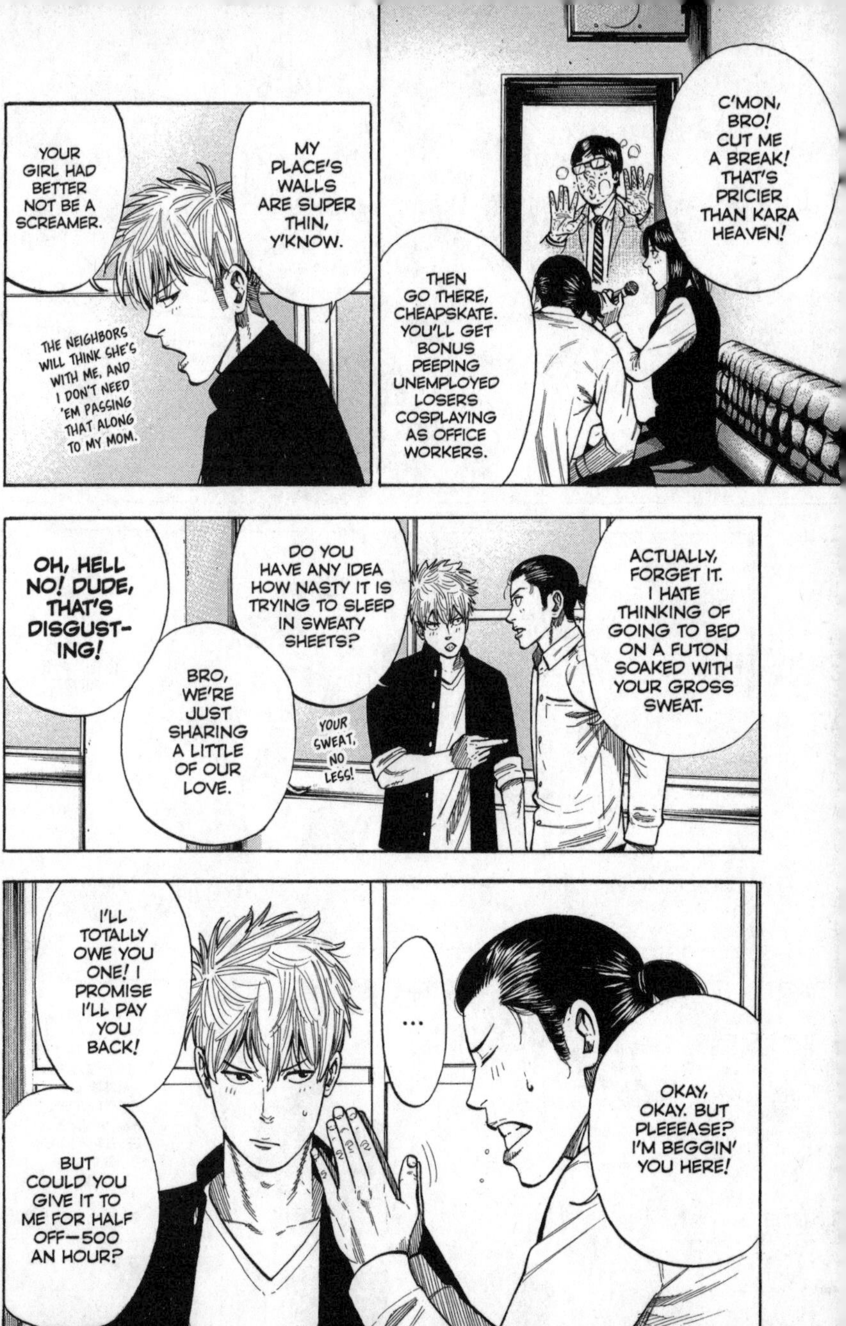
C'MON, BRO! CUT ME A BREAK! THAT'S PRICIER THAN KARA HEAVEN!
THEN GO THERE, CHEAPSKATE. YOU'LL GET BONUS PEEPING UNEMPLOYED LOSERS COSPLAYING AS OFFICE WORKERS.
MY PLACE'S WALLS ARE SUPER THIN, Y'KNOW.
YOUR GIRL HAD BETTER NOT BE A SCREAMER.
THE NEIGHBORS WILL THINK SHE'S WITH ME, AND I DON'T NEED 'EM PASSING THAT ALONG TO MY MOM.
ACTUALLY, FORGET IT. I HATE THINKING OF GOING TO BED ON A FUTON SOAKED WITH YOUR GROSS SWEAT.
DO YOU HAVE ANY IDEA HOW NASTY IT IS TRYING TO SLEEP IN SWEATY SHEETS?
BRO, WE'RE JUST SHARING A LITTLE OF OUR LOVE.
OH, HELL NO! DUDE, THAT'S DISGUST-ING!
YOUR SWEAT, NO LESS!
OKAY, OKAY. BUT PLEEEASE? I'M BEGGIN' YOU HERE!
...
I'LL TOTALLY OWE YOU ONE! I PROMISE I'LL PAY YOU BACK!
BUT COULD YOU GIVE IT TO ME FOR HALF OFF—500 AN HOUR?

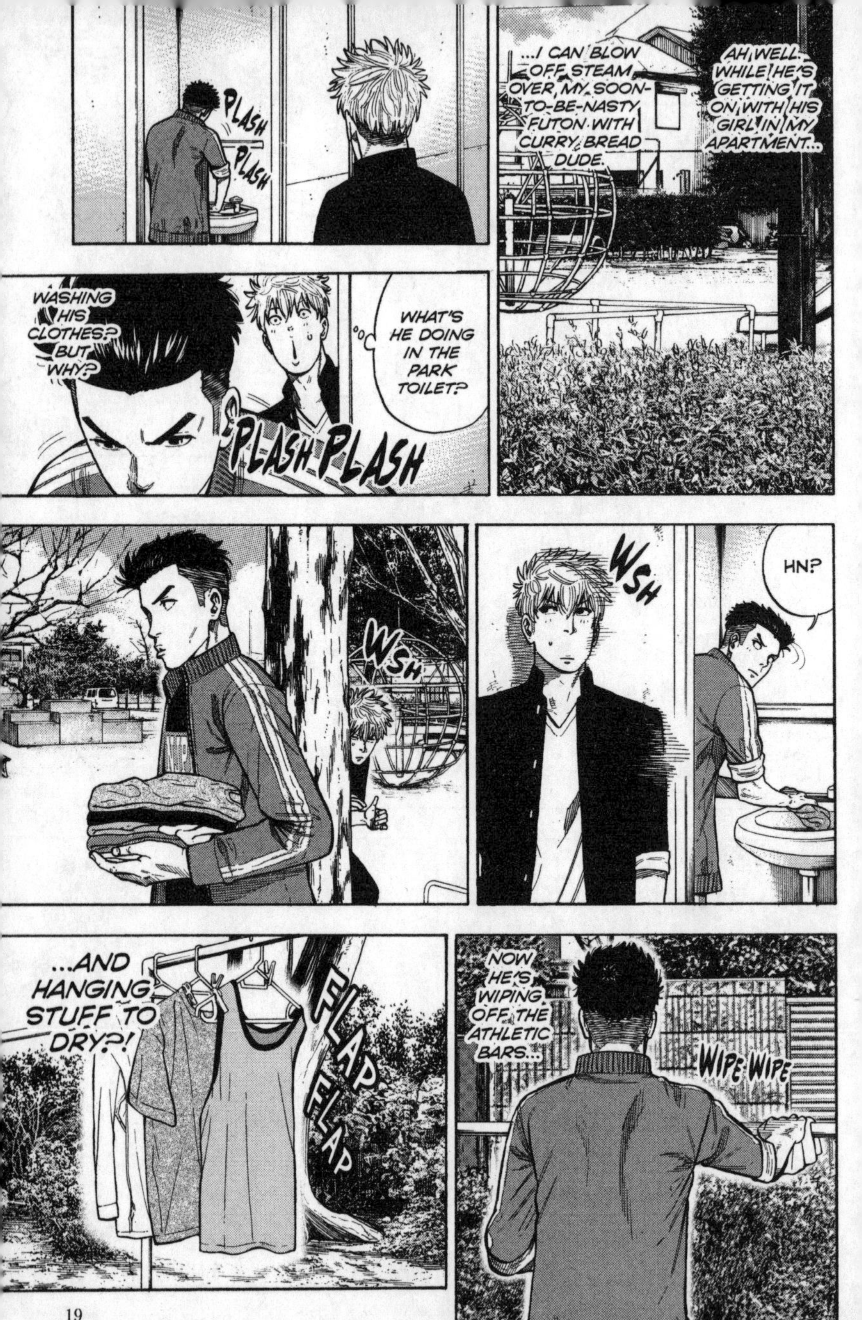
AH WELL. WHILE HE'S GETTING IT ON WITH HIS GIRL IN MY APARTMENT...
...I CAN BLOW OFF STEAM OVER MY SOON-TO-BE-NASTY FUTON WITH CURRY BREAD DUDE.
PLASH
PLASH
WHAT'S HE DOING IN THE PARK TOILET?
WASHING HIS CLOTHES? BUT WHY?
PLASH PLASH
HN?
WSH
WSH
NOW HE'S WIPING OFF THE ATHLETIC BARS...
WIPE WIPE
...AND HANGING STUFF TO DRY?!
FLAP FLAP

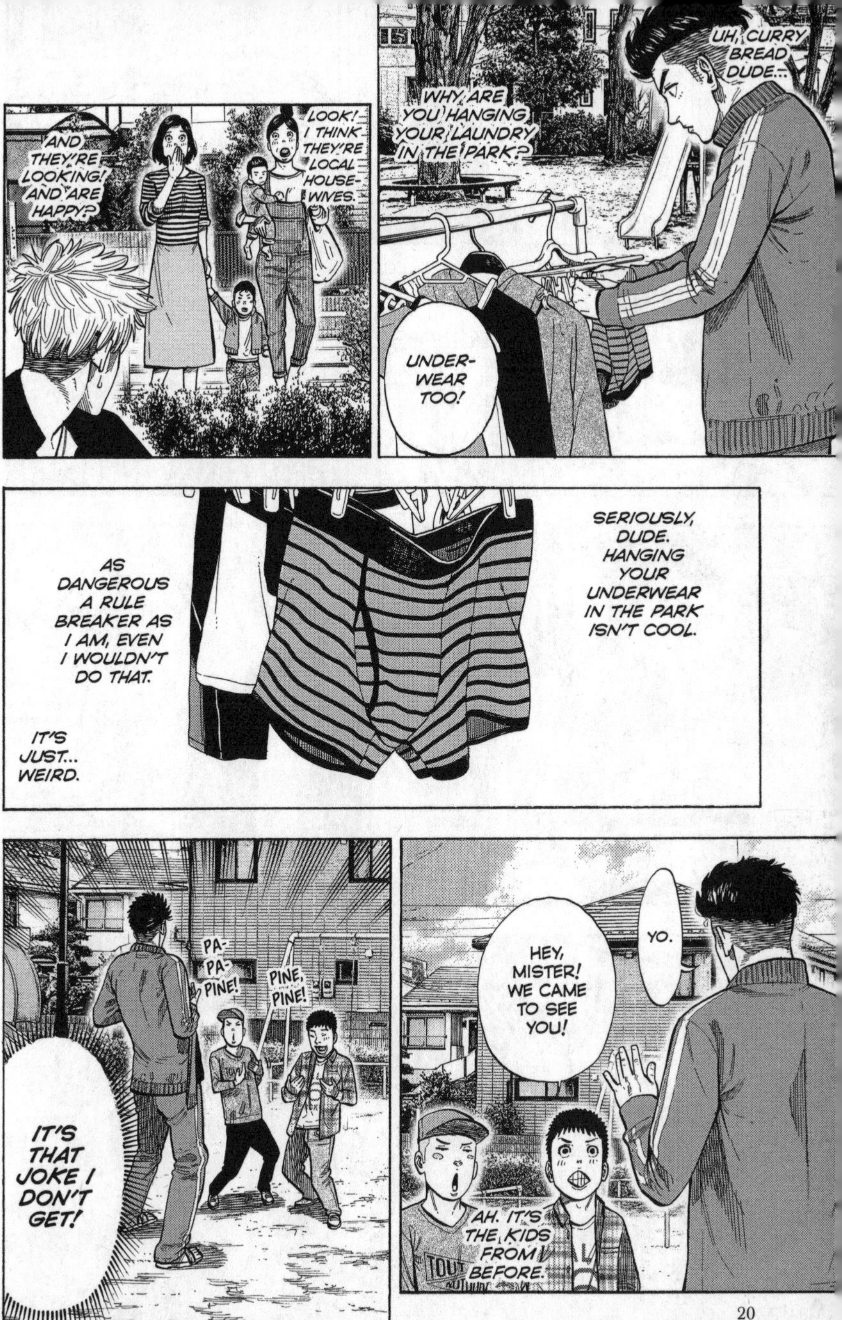
UH, CURRY BREAD DUDE...
WHY ARE YOU HANGING YOUR LAUNDRY IN THE PARK?
UNDER-WEAR TOO!
LOOK! I THINK THEY'RE LOCAL HOUSE-WIVES.
AND THEY'RE LOOKING! AND ARE HAPPY?
SERIOUSLY, DUDE. HANGING YOUR UNDERWEAR IN THE PARK ISN'T COOL.
AS DANGEROUS A RULE BREAKER AS I AM, EVEN I WOULDN'T DO THAT.
IT'S JUST... WEIRD.
YO.
HEY, MISTER! WE CAME TO SEE YOU!
AH. IT'S THE KIDS FROM BEFORE.
PA-PA-PINE!
PINE, PINE!
IT'S THAT JOKE I DON'T GET!

SERIOUSLY, CURRY BREAD DUDE. ARE YOU A CREEPER ON TOP OF BEING A TOUGH GUY?

BUT, FOR SOME REASON, THIS FEELS WAY MORE...DOMESTIC THAN CREEPY.

SINCE HE'S NOT HERE YET, I'LL BE BACK IN A SEC.

'KAY! WE'LL WATCH YOUR LAUNDRY.

LOWSAN

RED HOT CHILI PEPPERS IN JAPAN

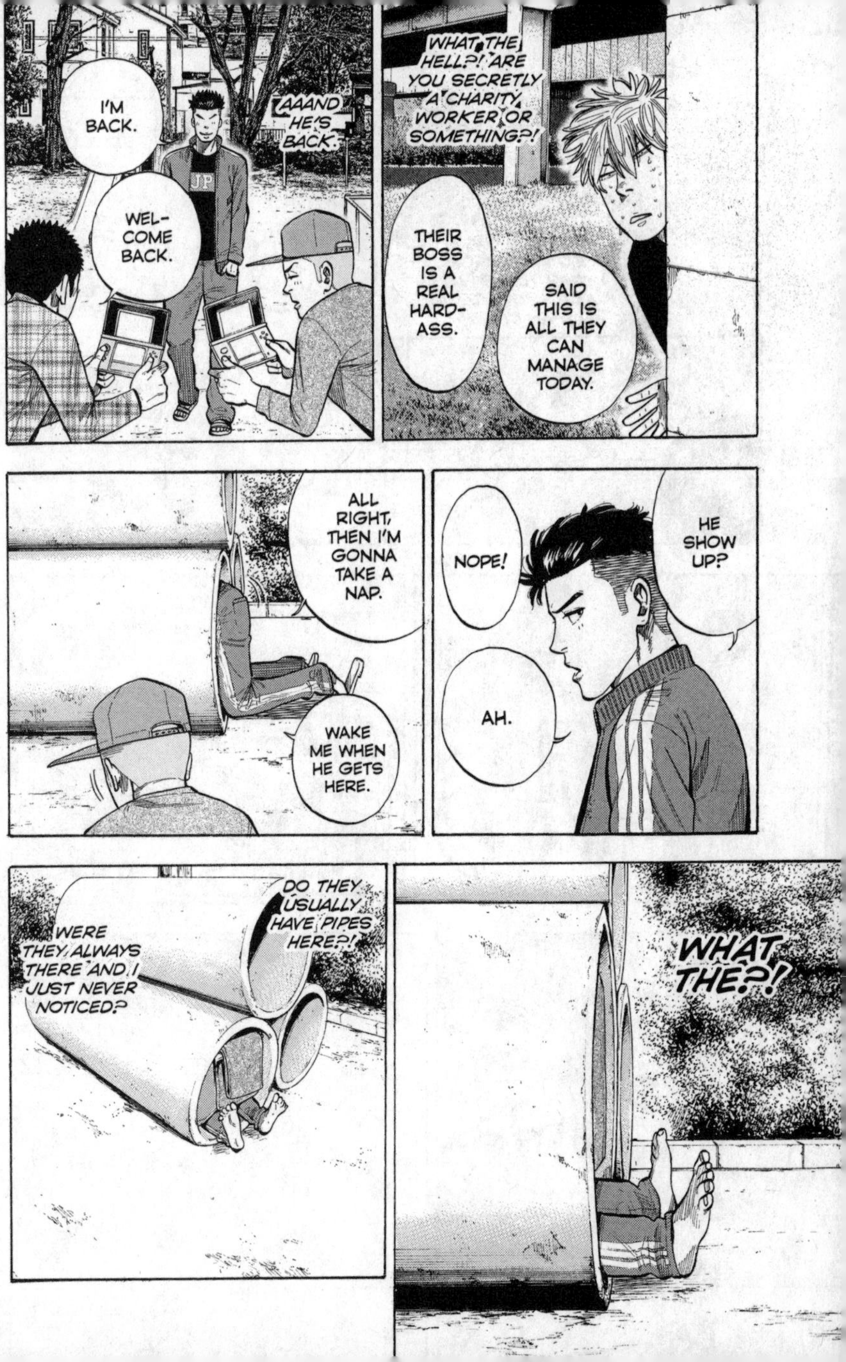
WHAT THE HELL?! ARE YOU SECRETLY A CHARITY WORKER OR SOMETHING?!
SAID THIS IS ALL THEY CAN MANAGE TODAY.
THEIR BOSS IS A REAL HARD-ASS.
I'M BACK.
AAAND HE'S BACK.
WEL-COME BACK.
HE SHOW UP?
NOPE!
AH.
ALL RIGHT, THEN I'M GONNA TAKE A NAP.
WAKE ME WHEN HE GETS HERE.
WHAT THE?!
DO THEY USUALLY HAVE PIPES HERE?!
WERE THEY ALWAYS THERE AND I JUST NEVER NOTICED?

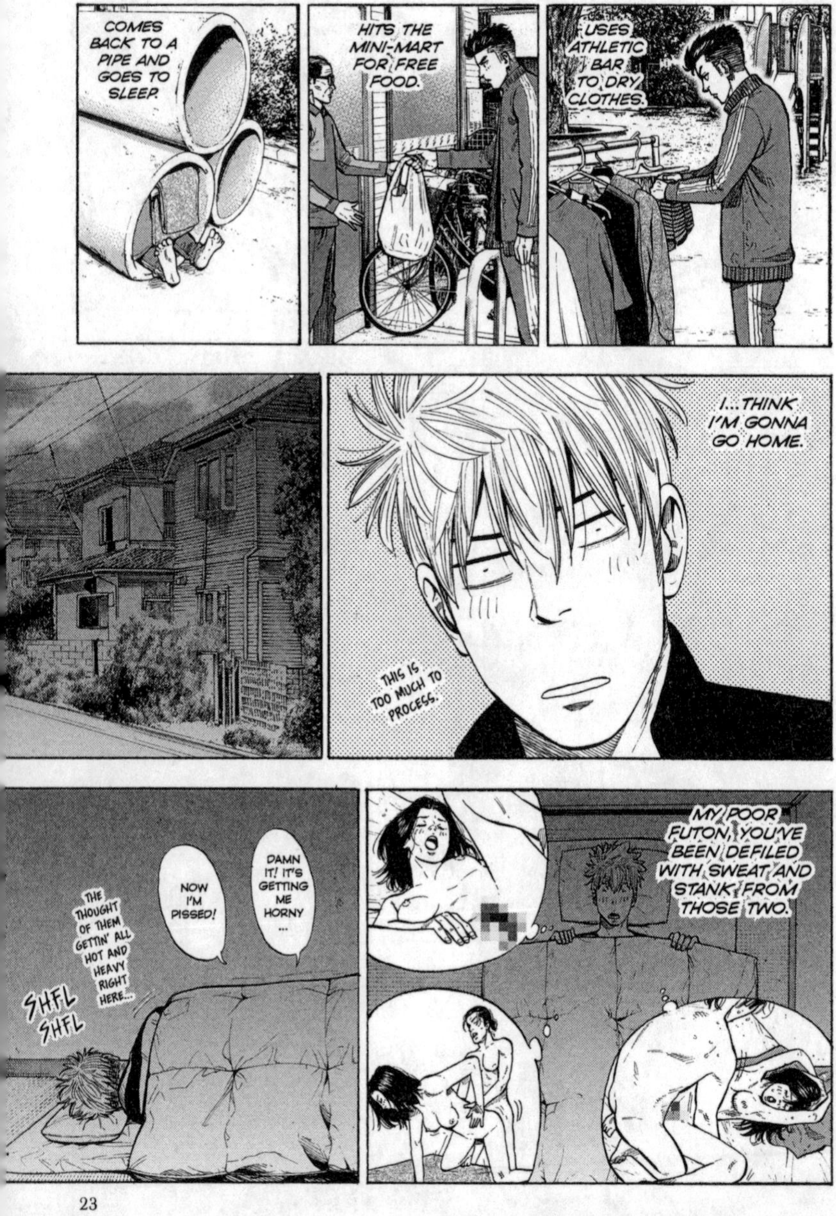
USES ATHLETIC BAR TO DRY CLOTHES.
HITS THE MINI-MART FOR FREE FOOD.
COMES BACK TO A PIPE AND GOES TO SLEEP.
I...THINK I'M GONNA GO HOME.
THIS IS TOO MUCH TO PROCESS.
MY POOR FUTON, YOU'VE BEEN DEFILED WITH SWEAT AND STANK FROM THOSE TWO.
DAMN IT! IT'S GETTING ME HORNY ...
NOW I'M PISSED!
THE THOUGHT OF THEM GETTIN' ALL HOT AND HEAVY RIGHT HERE...
SHFL SHFL

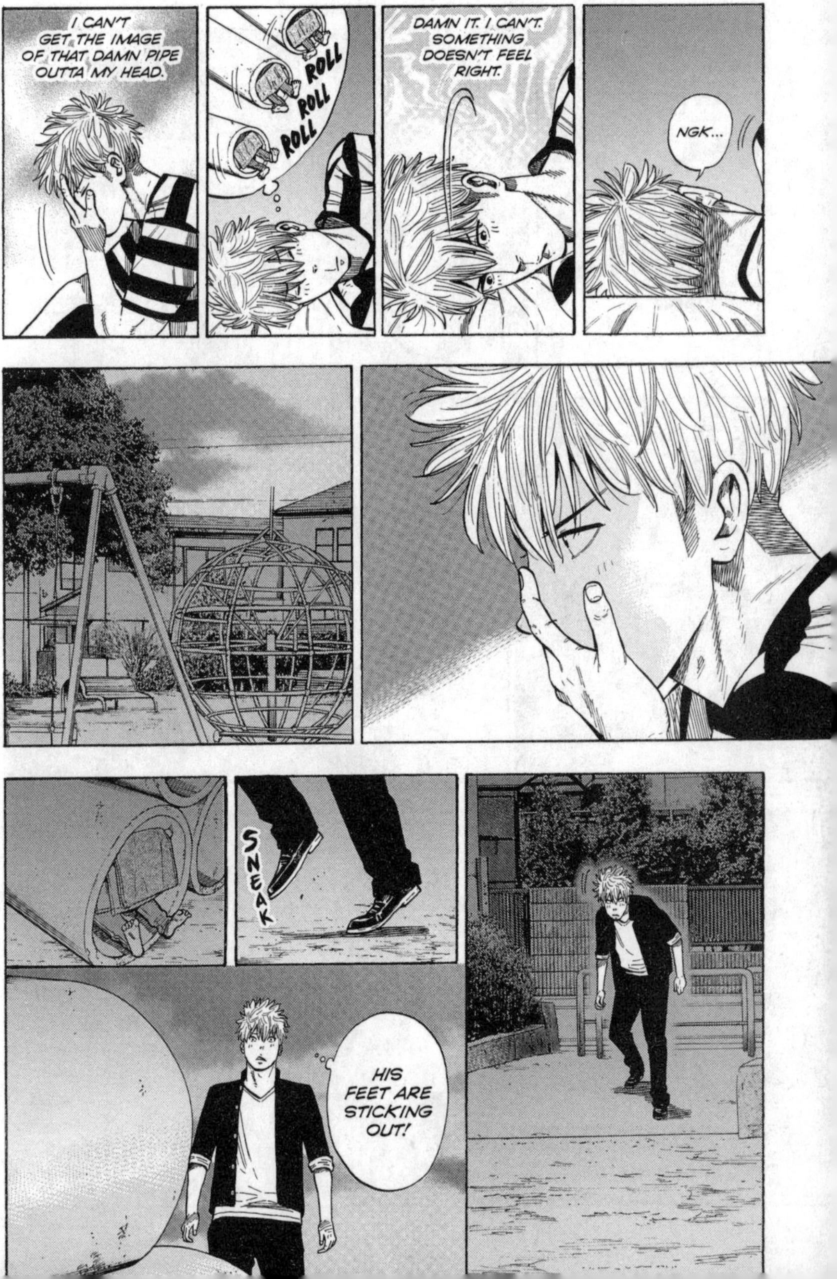
NGK...
DAMN IT. I CAN'T. SOMETHING DOESN'T FEEL RIGHT.
ROLL
ROLL
ROLL
I CAN'T GET THE IMAGE OF THAT DAMN PIPE OUTTA MY HEAD.
SNEAK
HIS FEET ARE STICKING OUT!

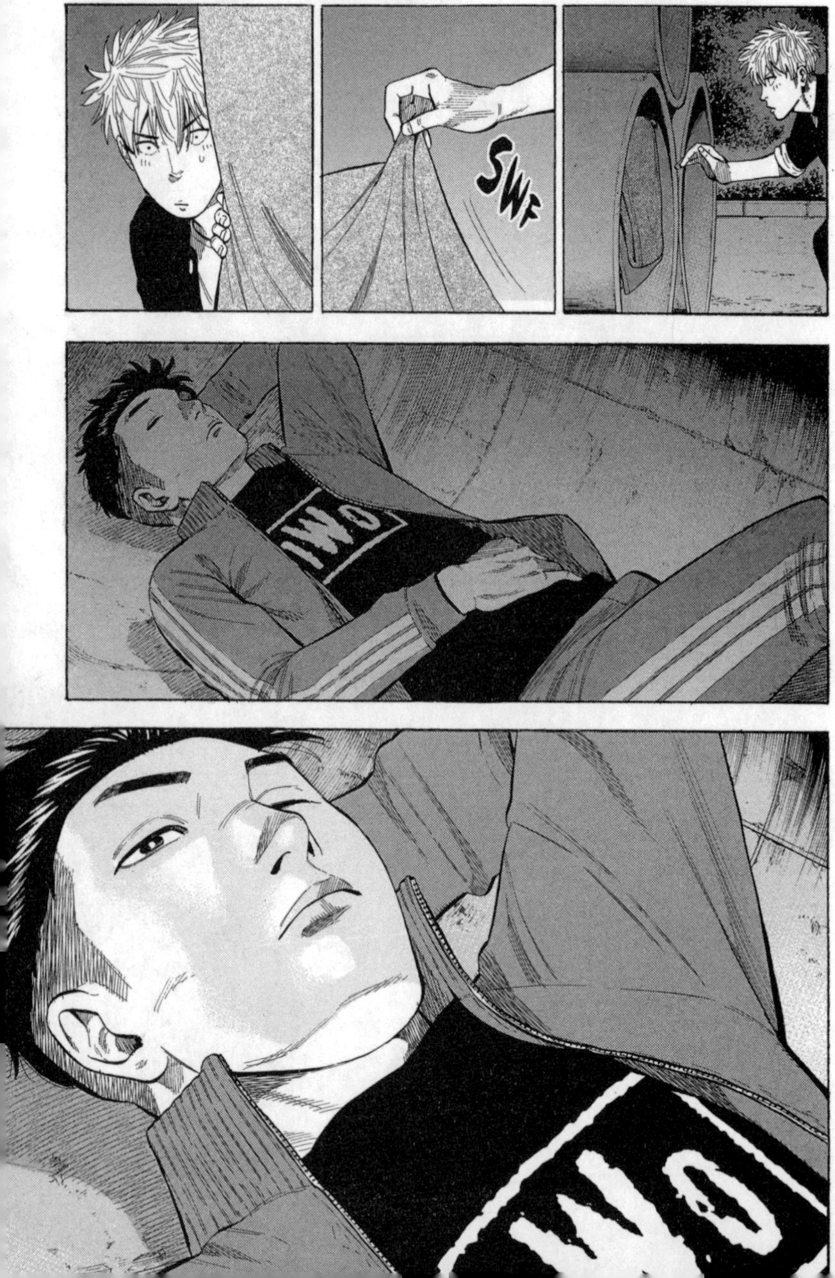
SWF

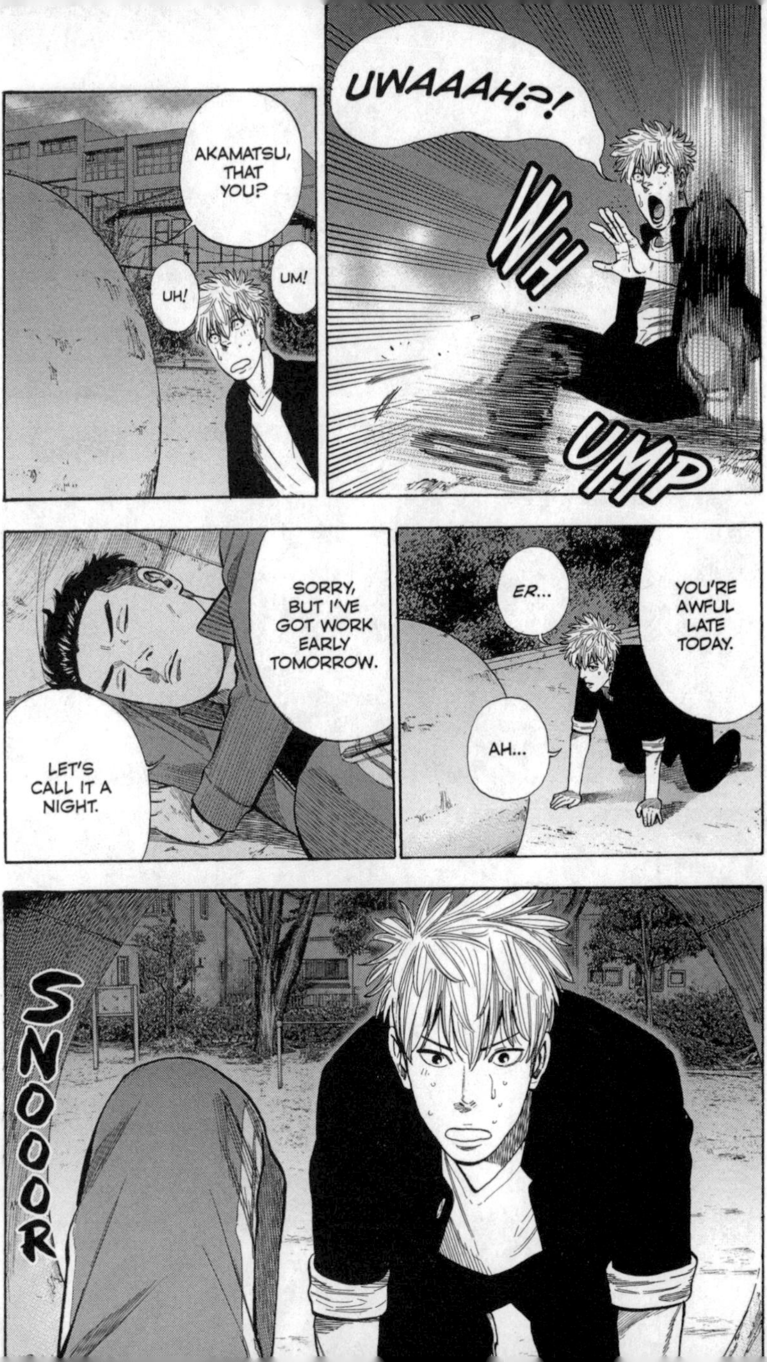
UWAAAH?!
WHUMP
AKAMATSU, THAT YOU?
UM!
UH!
YOU'RE AWFUL LATE TODAY.
ER...
AH...
SORRY, BUT I'VE GOT WORK EARLY TOMORROW.
LET'S CALL IT A NIGHT.
SNOOOR

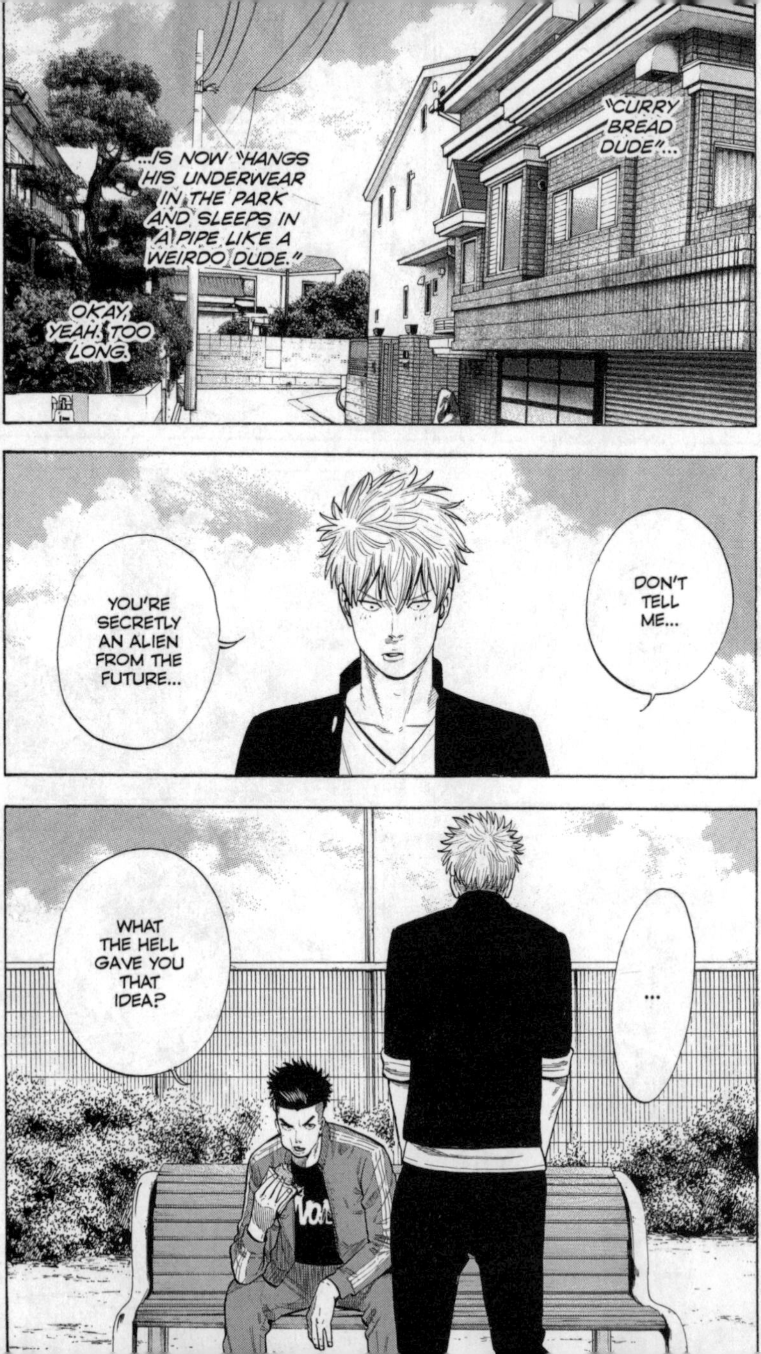
"CURRY BREAD DUDE"...
...IS NOW "HANGS HIS UNDERWEAR IN THE PARK AND SLEEPS IN A PIPE LIKE A WEIRDO DUDE."
OKAY, YEAH. TOO LONG.
DON'T TELL ME...
YOU'RE SECRETLY AN ALIEN FROM THE FUTURE...
...
WHAT THE HELL GAVE YOU THAT IDEA?

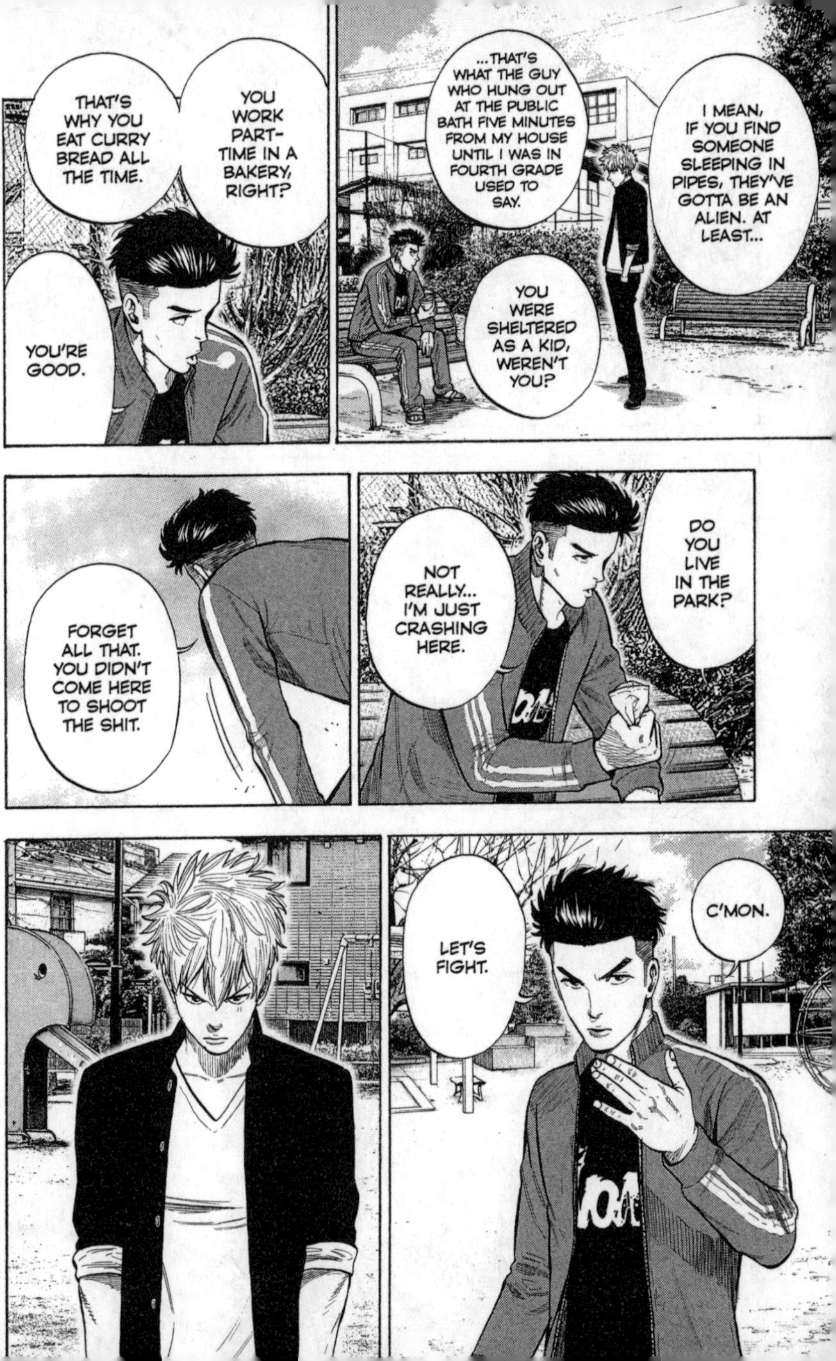
I MEAN, IF YOU FIND SOMEONE SLEEPING IN PIPES, THEY'VE GOTTA BE AN ALIEN. AT LEAST...
...THAT'S WHAT THE GUY WHO HUNG OUT AT THE PUBLIC BATH FIVE MINUTES FROM MY HOUSE UNTIL I WAS IN FOURTH GRADE USED TO SAY.
YOU WERE SHELTERED AS A KID, WEREN'T YOU?
YOU WORK PART-TIME IN A BAKERY, RIGHT?
THAT'S WHY YOU EAT CURRY BREAD ALL THE TIME.
YOU'RE GOOD.
DO YOU LIVE IN THE PARK?
NOT REALLY... I'M JUST CRASHING HERE.
FORGET ALL THAT. YOU DIDN'T COME HERE TO SHOOT THE SHIT.
C'MON.
LET'S FIGHT.

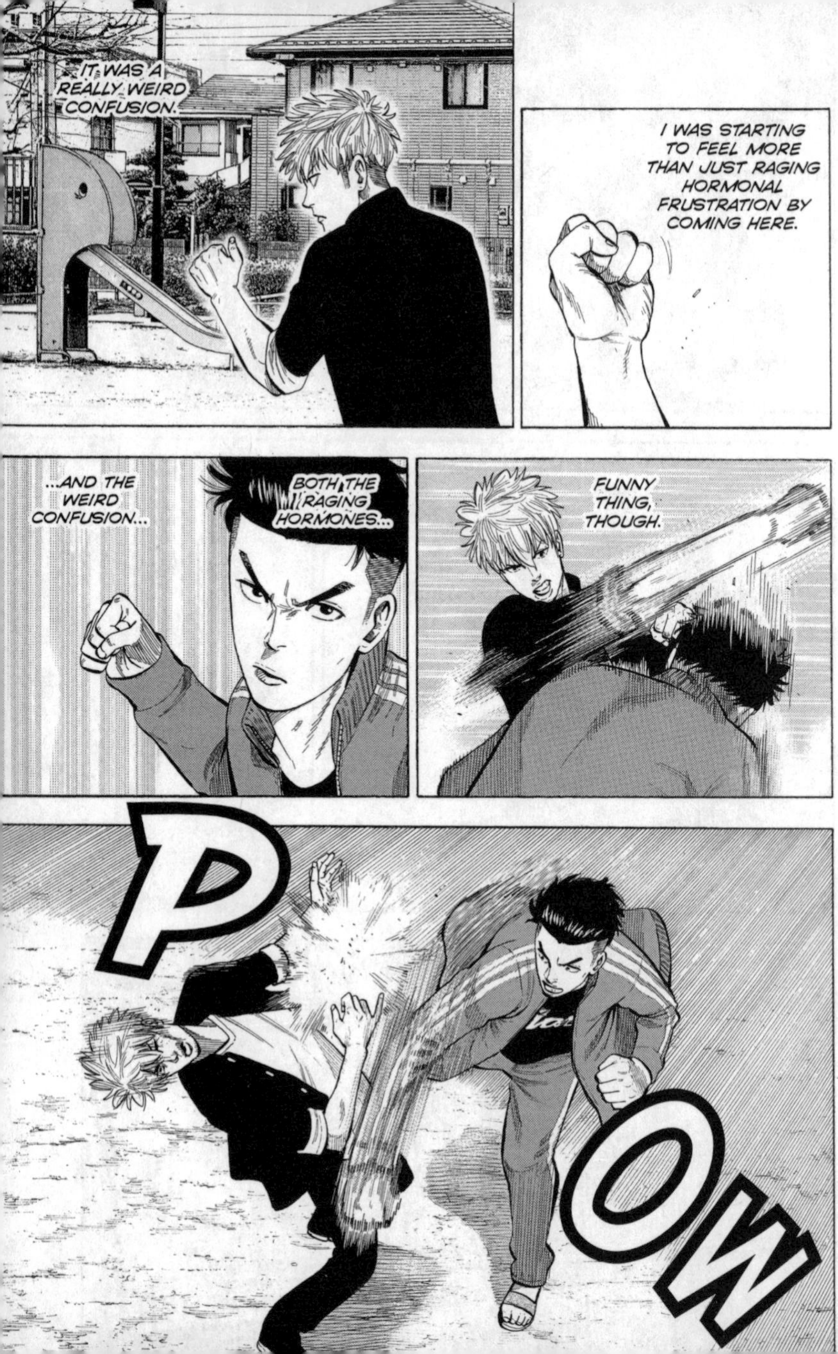
I WAS STARTING TO FEEL MORE THAN JUST RAGING HORMONAL FRUSTRATION BY COMING HERE.
IT WAS A REALLY WEIRD CONFUSION.
FUNNY THING, THOUGH.
BOTH THE RAGING HORMONES...
...AND THE WEIRD CONFUSION...
POW

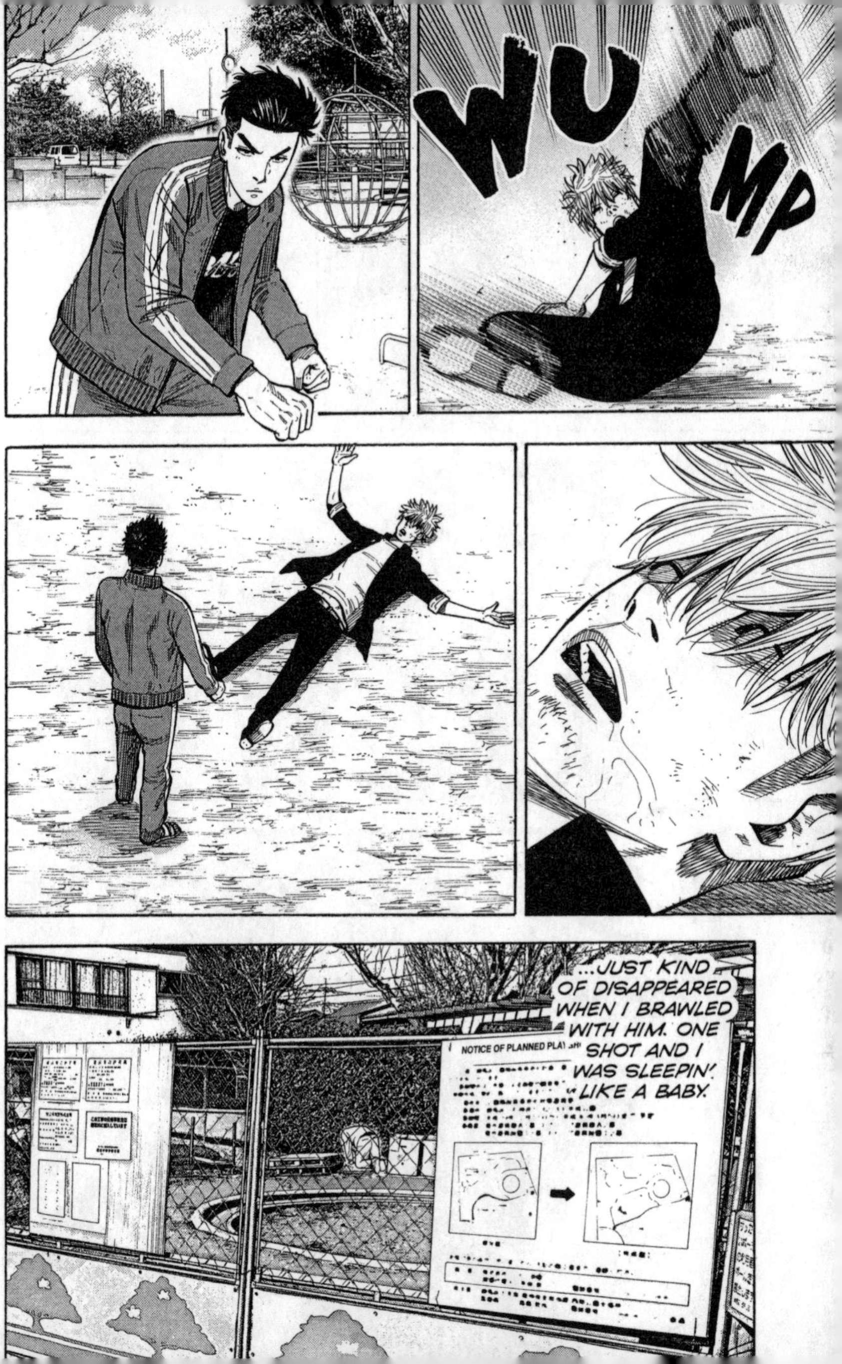
WUMP
...JUST KIND OF DISAPPEARED WHEN I BRAWLED WITH HIM. ONE SHOT AND I WAS SLEEPIN'. LIKE A BABY.
NOTICE OF PLANNED PLAY

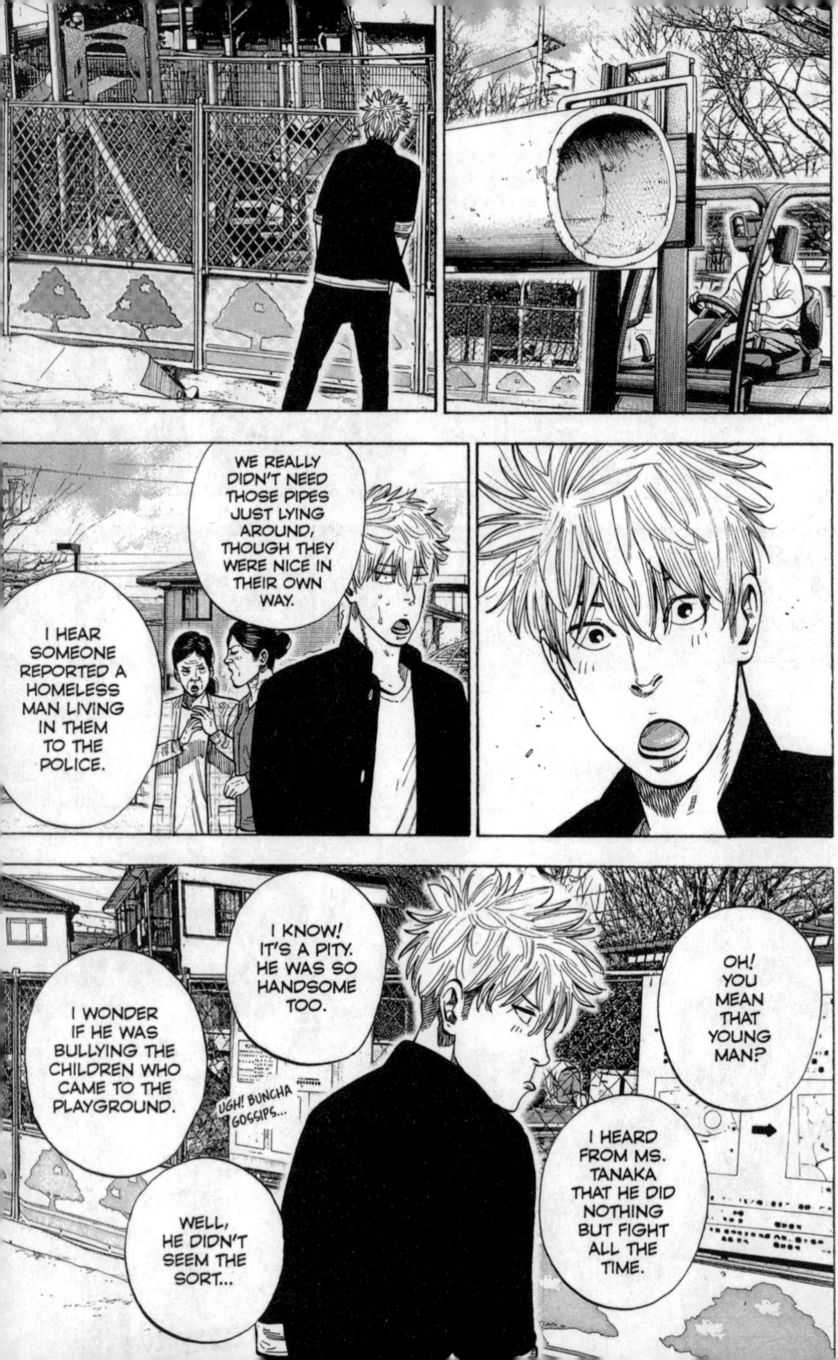
WE REALLY DIDN'T NEED THOSE PIPES JUST LYING AROUND, THOUGH THEY WERE NICE IN THEIR OWN WAY.
I HEAR SOMEONE REPORTED A HOMELESS MAN LIVING IN THEM TO THE POLICE.
OH! YOU MEAN THAT YOUNG MAN?
I KNOW! IT'S A PITY. HE WAS SO HANDSOME TOO.
I HEARD FROM MS. TANAKA THAT HE DID NOTHING BUT FIGHT ALL THE TIME.
I WONDER IF HE WAS BULLYING THE CHILDREN WHO CAME TO THE PLAYGROUND.
WELL, HE DIDN'T SEEM THE SORT...
UGH! BUNCHA GOSSIPS...

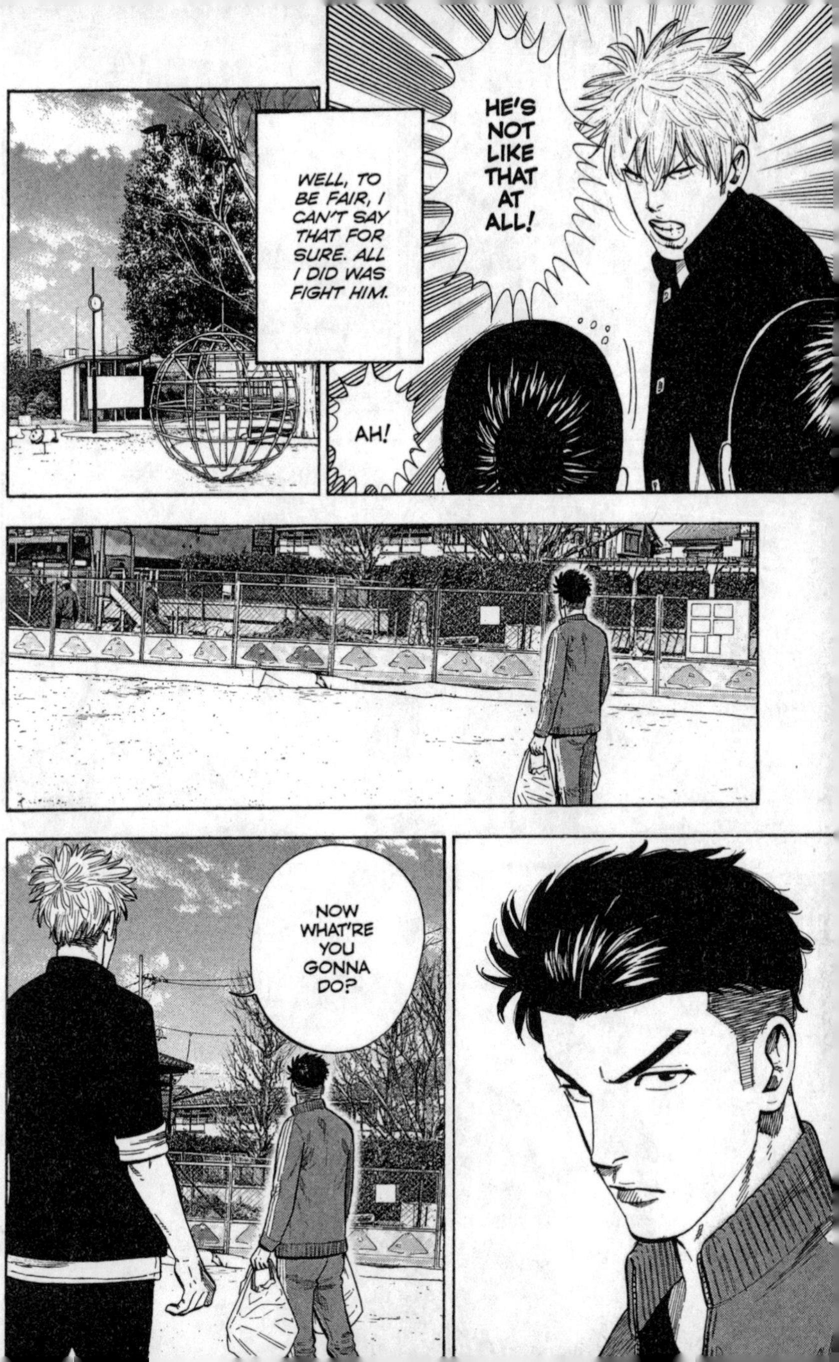
HE'S NOT LIKE THAT AT ALL!
AH!
WELL, TO BE FAIR, I CAN'T SAY THAT FOR SURE. ALL I DID WAS FIGHT HIM.
NOW WHAT'RE YOU GONNA DO?

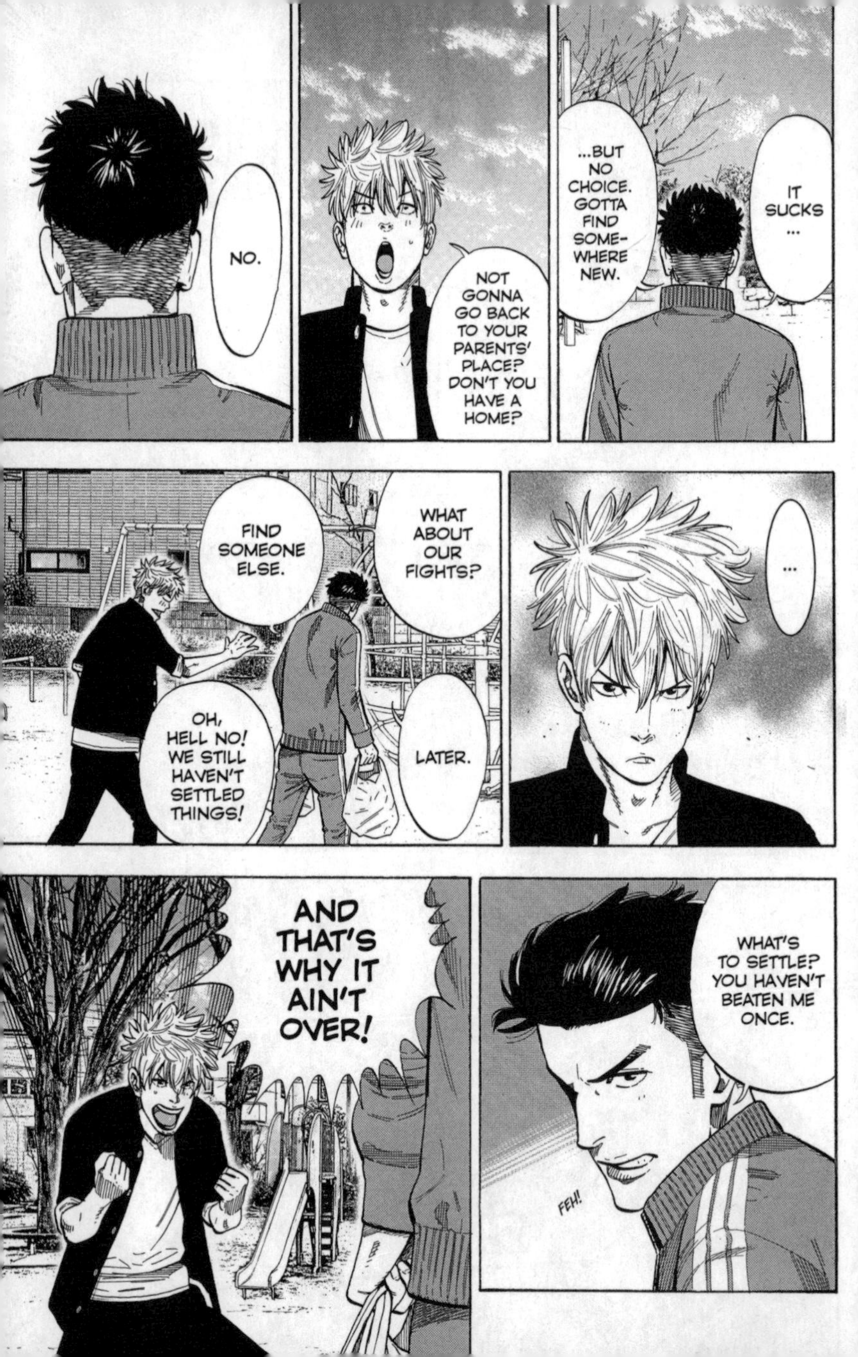
IT SUCKS ...
...BUT NO CHOICE. GOTTA FIND SOME-WHERE NEW.
NOT GONNA GO BACK TO YOUR PARENTS' PLACE? DON'T YOU HAVE A HOME?
NO.
...
WHAT ABOUT OUR FIGHTS?
FIND SOMEONE ELSE.
LATER.
OH, HELL NO! WE STILL HAVEN'T SETTLED THINGS!
WHAT'S TO SETTLE? YOU HAVEN'T BEATEN ME ONCE.
FEH!
AND THAT'S WHY IT AIN'T OVER!

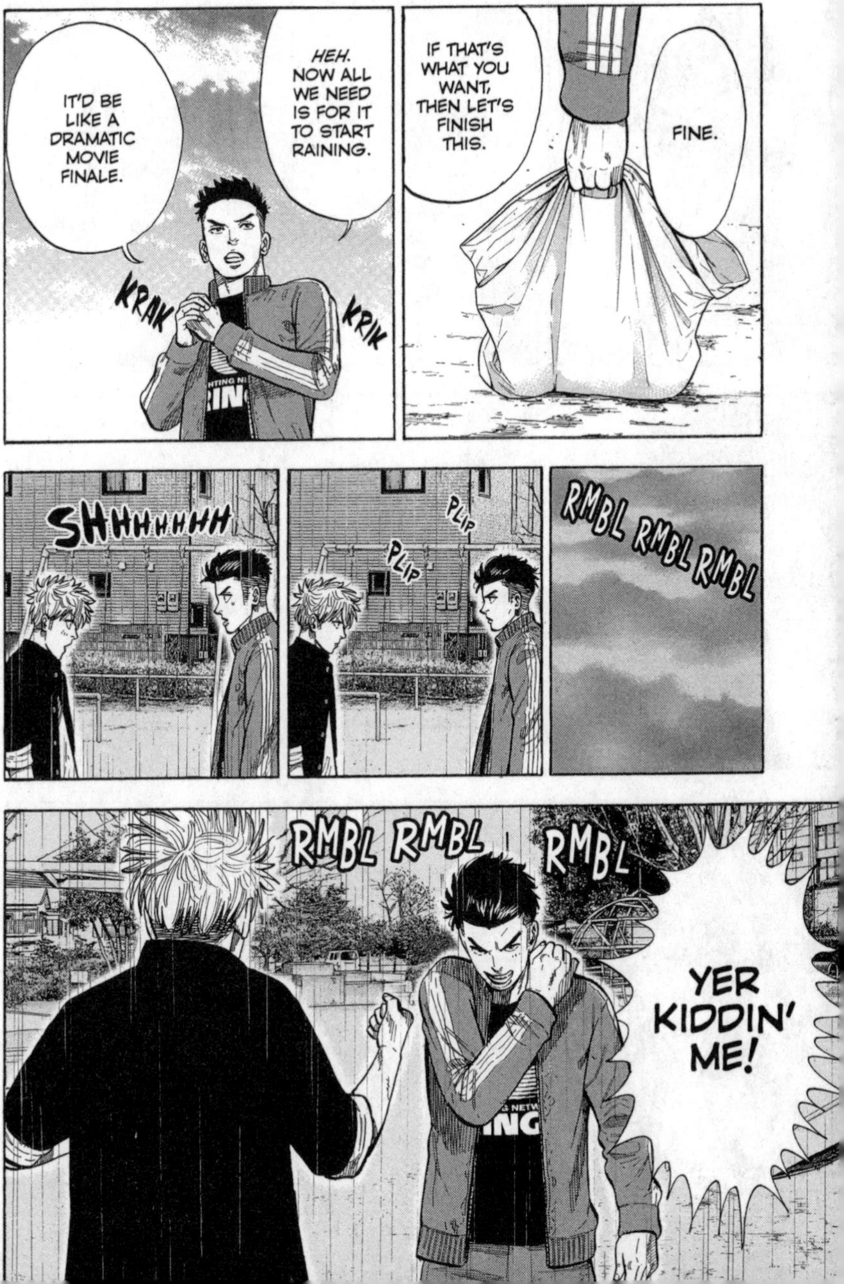
FINE.
IF THAT'S WHAT YOU WANT, THEN LET'S FINISH THIS.
HEH. NOW ALL WE NEED IS FOR IT TO START RAINING.
IT'D BE LIKE A DRAMATIC MOVIE FINALE.
KRIK
KRAK
RMBL RMBL RMBL
PLIP
PLIP
SHHHHHHH
RMBL RMBL RMBL
YER KIDDIN' ME!

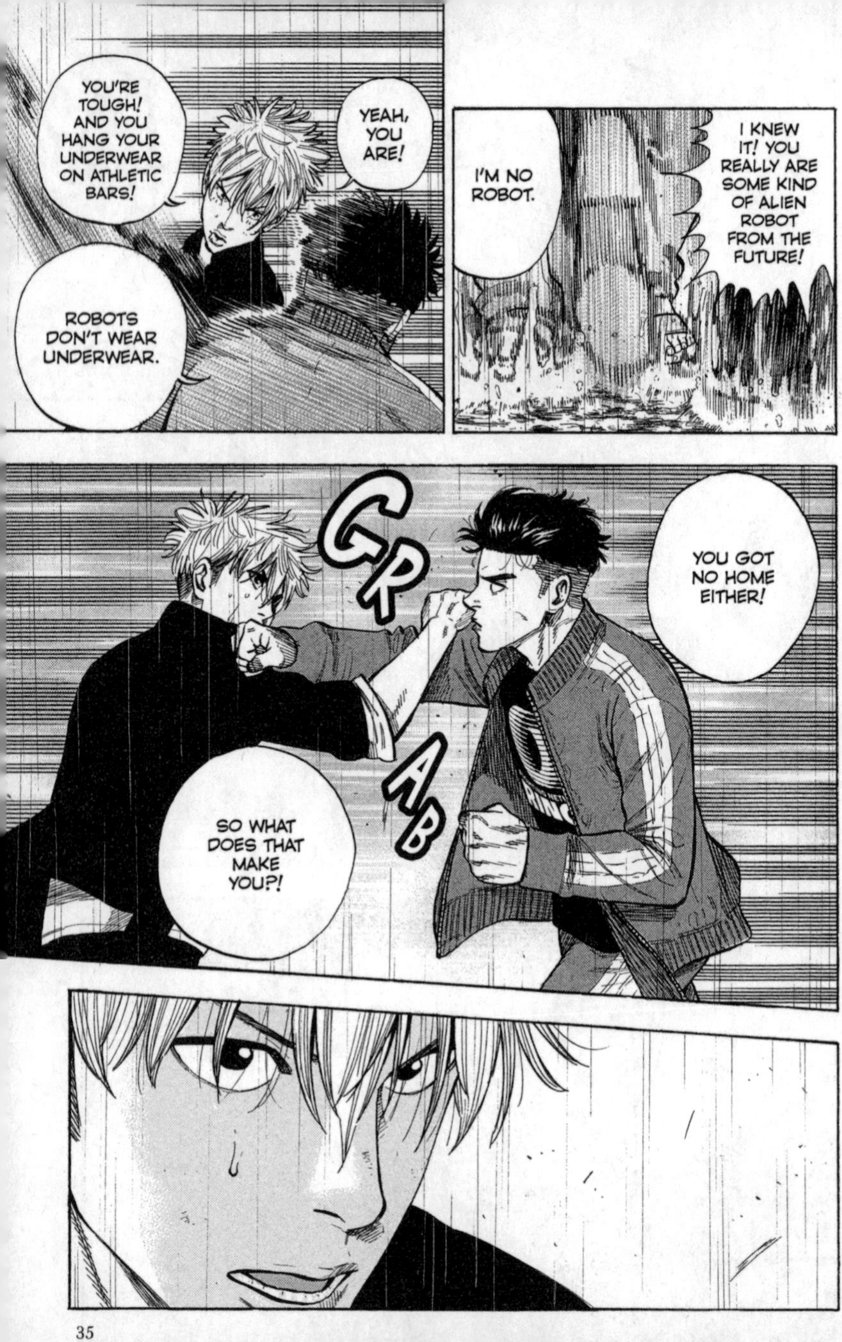
I KNEW IT! YOU REALLY ARE SOME KIND OF ALIEN ROBOT FROM THE FUTURE!
I'M NO ROBOT.
YEAH, YOU ARE!
YOU'RE TOUGH! AND YOU HANG YOUR UNDERWEAR ON ATHLETIC BARS!
ROBOTS DON'T WEAR UNDERWEAR.
YOU GOT NO HOME EITHER!
GRAB
SO WHAT DOES THAT MAKE YOU?!

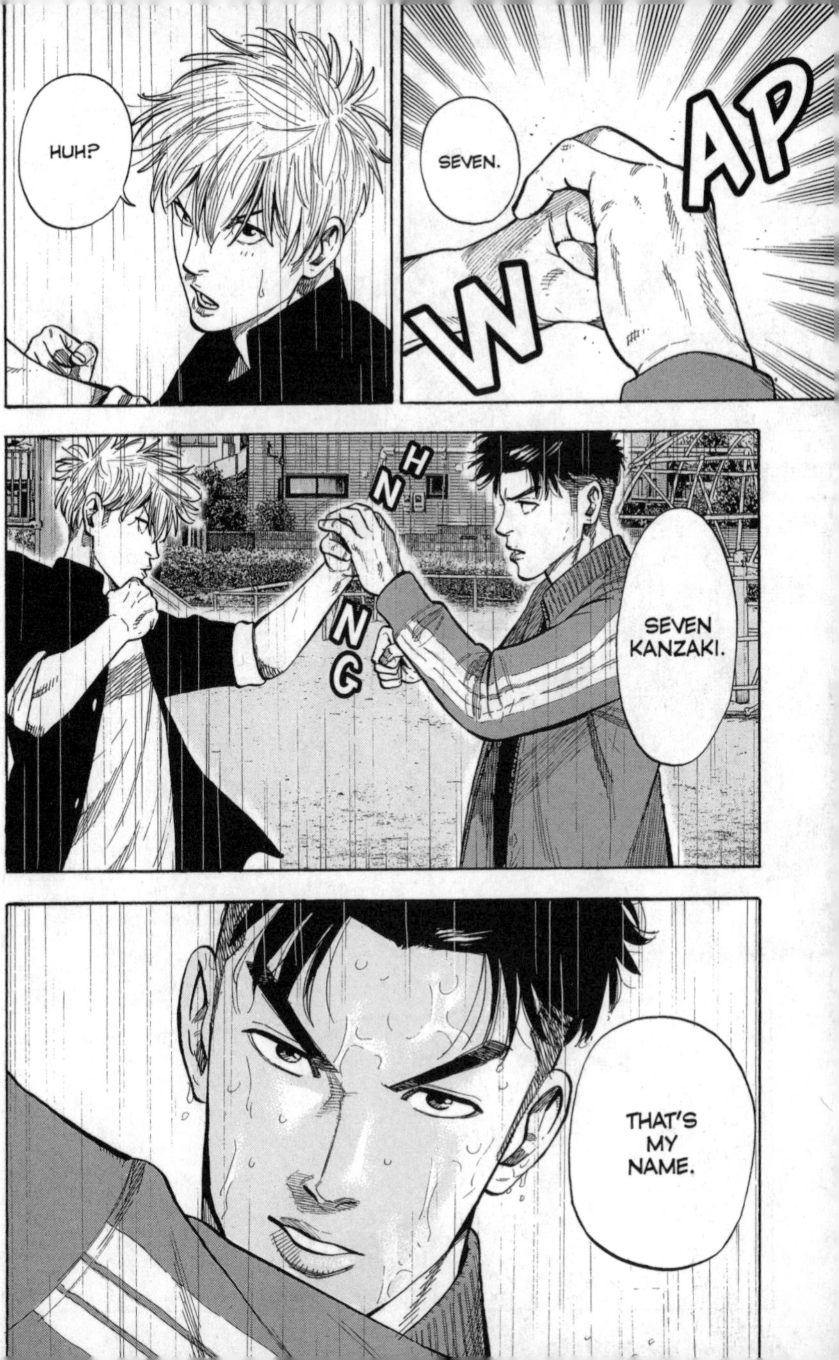
SEVEN.
WAP
HUH?
HNNG
SEVEN KANZAKI.
THAT'S MY NAME.

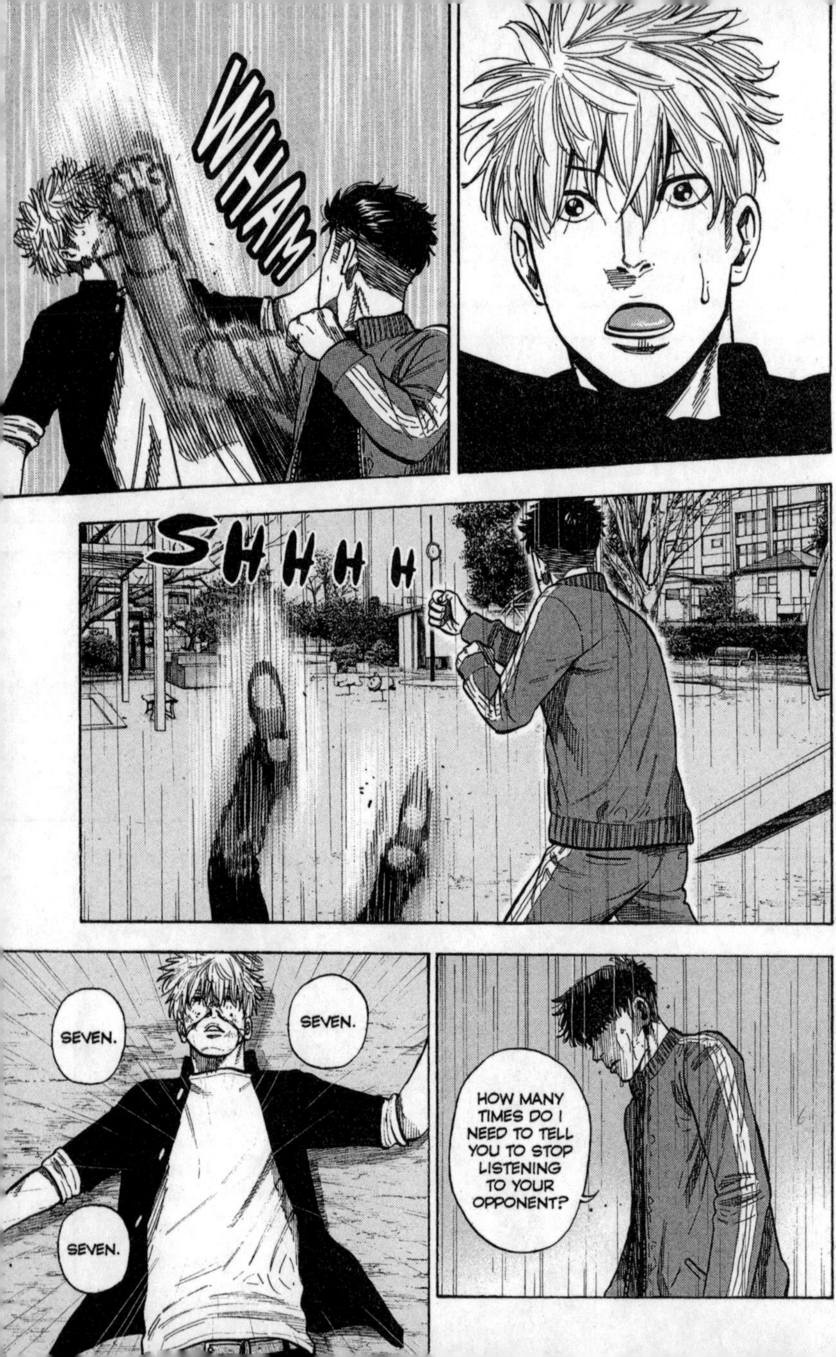
WHAM
SHHHH
HOW MANY TIMES DO I NEED TO TELL YOU TO STOP LISTENING TO YOUR OPPONENT?
SEVEN.
SEVEN.
SEVEN.

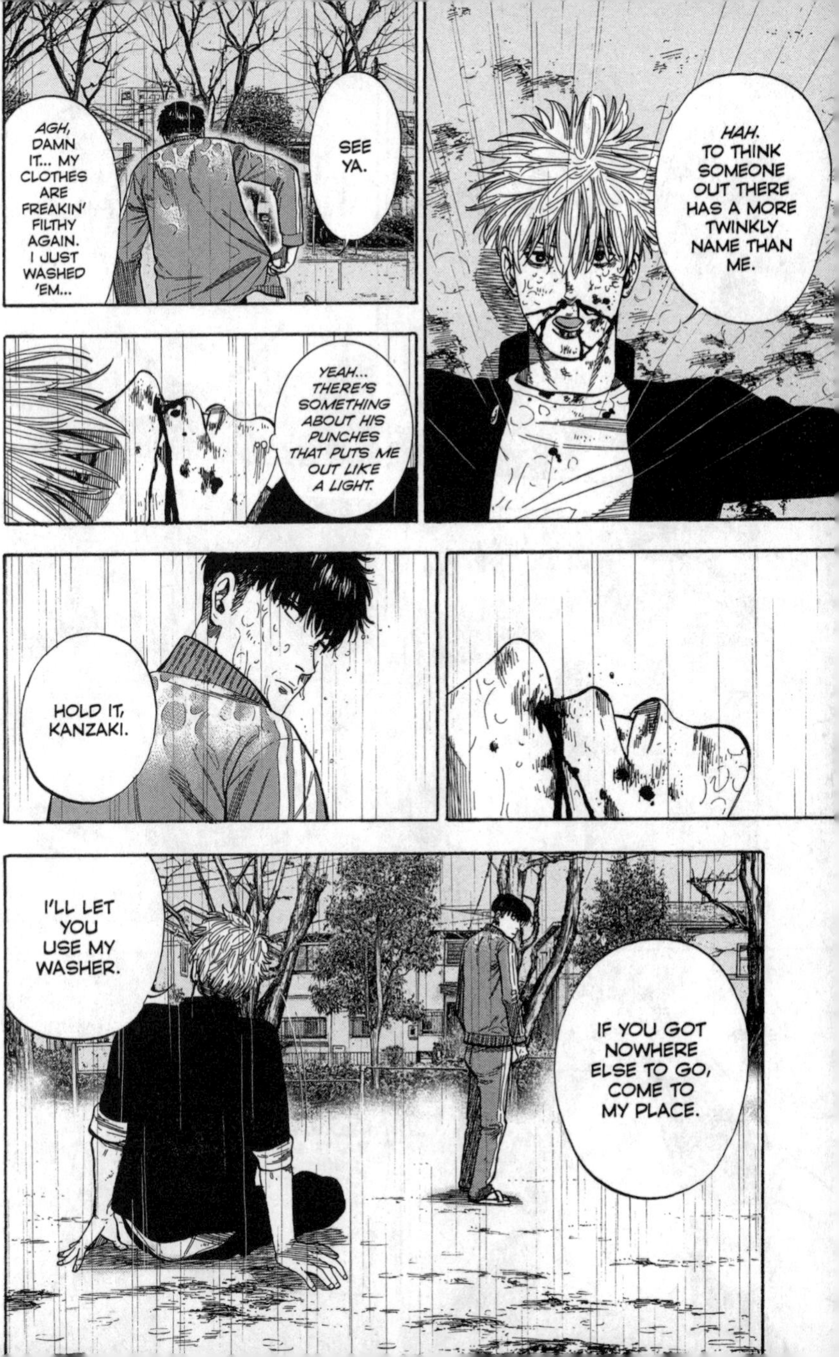
HAH. TO THINK SOMEONE OUT THERE HAS A MORE TWINKLY NAME THAN ME.
SEE YA.
AGH, DAMN IT... MY CLOTHES ARE FREAKIN' FILTHY AGAIN. I JUST WASHED 'EM...
YEAH... THERE'S SOMETHING ABOUT HIS PUNCHES THAT PUTS ME OUT LIKE A LIGHT.
HOLD IT, KANZAKI.
IF YOU GOT NOWHERE ELSE TO GO, COME TO MY PLACE.
I'LL LET YOU USE MY WASHER.

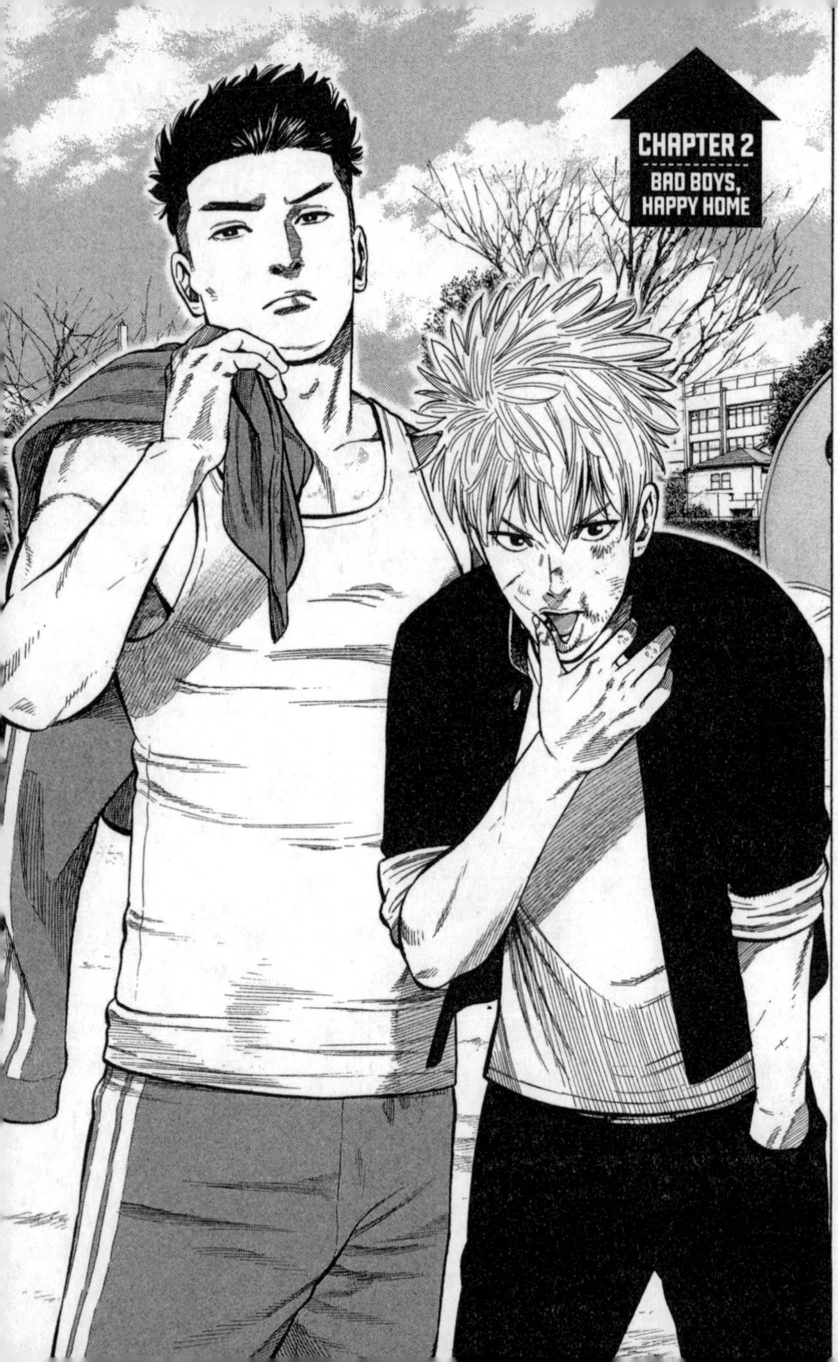
CHAPTER 2
BAD BOYS, HAPPY HOME

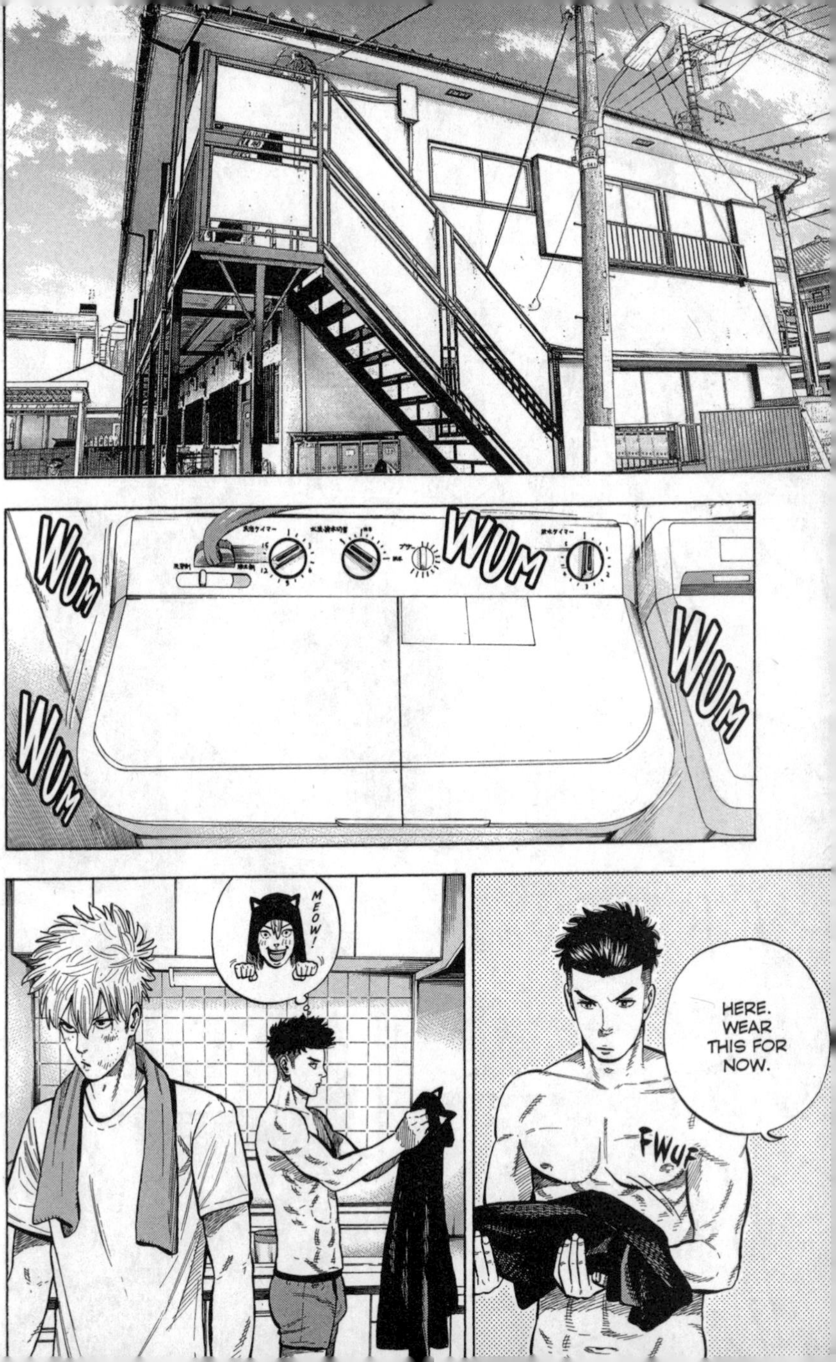
WUM
WUM
WUM
WUM
FWUF
HERE. WEAR THIS FOR NOW.
MEOW!

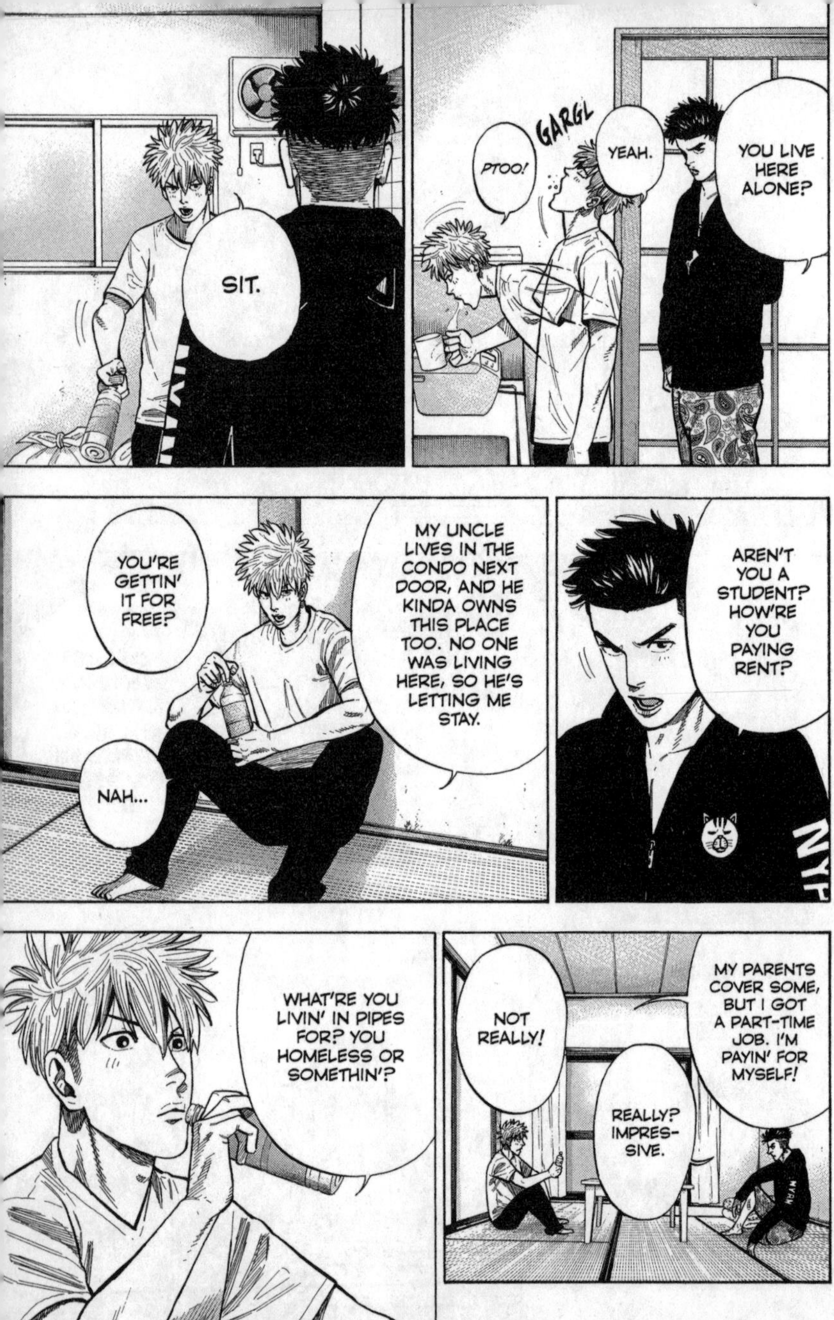
YOU LIVE HERE ALONE?
YEAH.
GARGL
PTOO!
SIT.
AREN'T YOU A STUDENT? HOW'RE YOU PAYING RENT?
MY UNCLE LIVES IN THE CONDO NEXT DOOR, AND HE KINDA OWNS THIS PLACE TOO. NO ONE WAS LIVING HERE, SO HE'S LETTING ME STAY.
YOU'RE GETTIN' IT FOR FREE?
NAH...
MY PARENTS COVER SOME, BUT I GOT A PART-TIME JOB. I'M PAYIN' FOR MYSELF!
REALLY? IMPRES-SIVE.
NOT REALLY!
WHAT'RE YOU LIVIN' IN PIPES FOR? YOU HOMELESS OR SOMETHIN'?

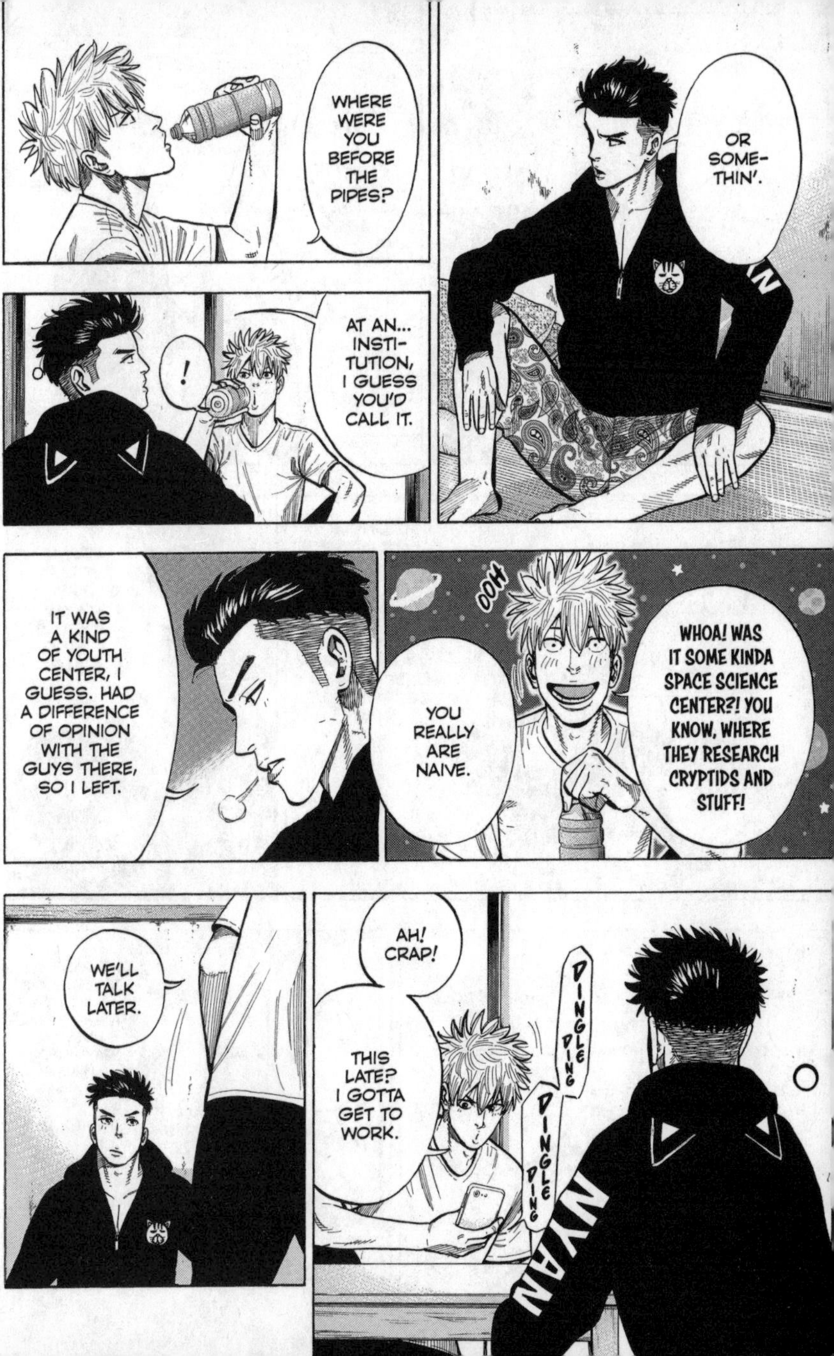
OR SOME-THIN'.
WHERE WERE YOU BEFORE THE PIPES?
AT AN... INSTI-TUTION, I GUESS YOU'D CALL IT.
!
OOH
WHOA! WAS IT SOME KINDA SPACE SCIENCE CENTER?! YOU KNOW, WHERE THEY RESEARCH CRYPTIDS AND STUFF!
YOU REALLY ARE NAIVE.
IT WAS A KIND OF YOUTH CENTER, I GUESS. HAD A DIFFERENCE OF OPINION WITH THE GUYS THERE, SO I LEFT.
DINGLE DING
DINGLE DING
AH! CRAP!
THIS LATE? I GOTTA GET TO WORK.
NYAN
WE'LL TALK LATER.

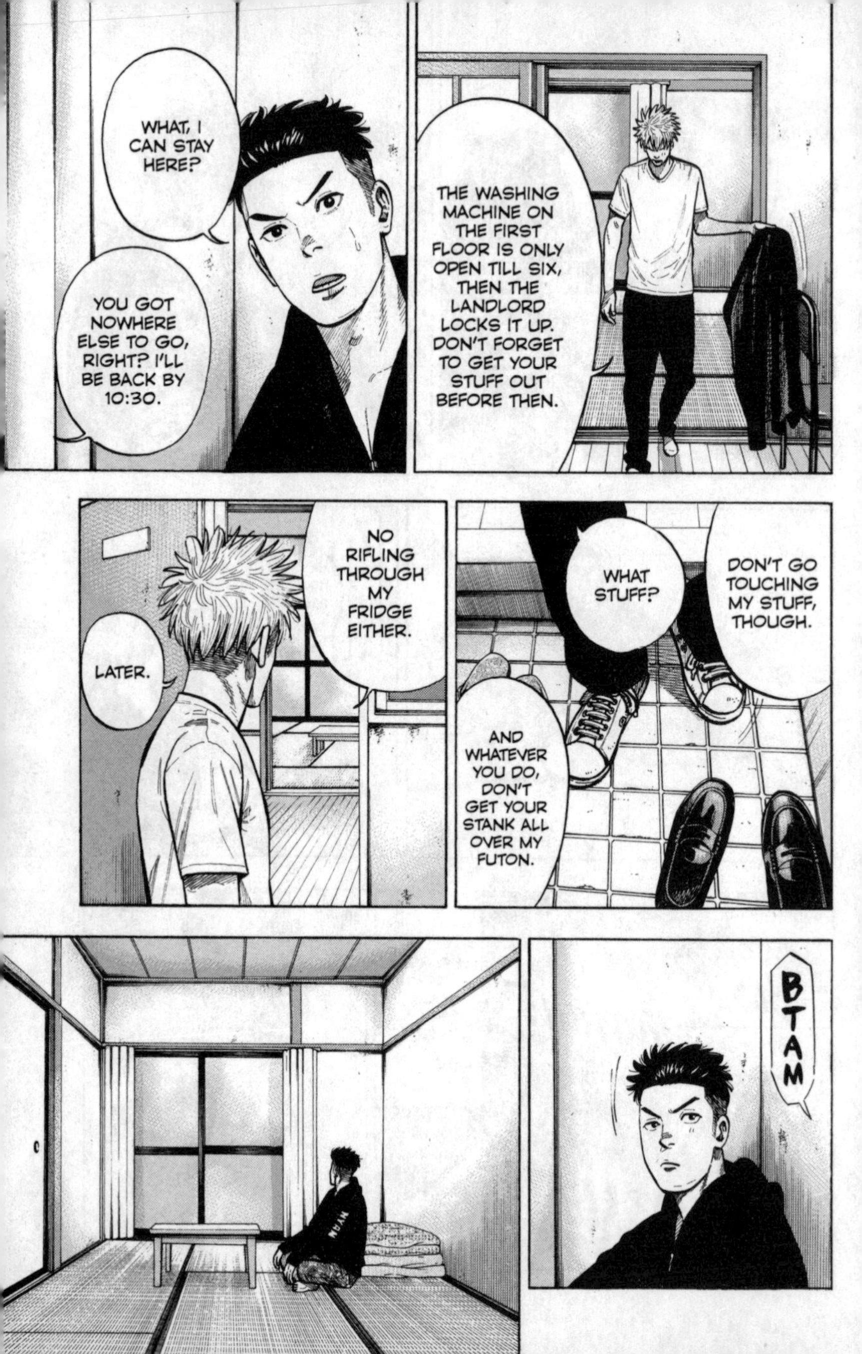
THE WASHING MACHINE ON THE FIRST FLOOR IS ONLY OPEN TILL SIX, THEN THE LANDLORD LOCKS IT UP. DON'T FORGET TO GET YOUR STUFF OUT BEFORE THEN.
WHAT, I CAN STAY HERE?
YOU GOT NOWHERE ELSE TO GO, RIGHT? I'LL BE BACK BY 10:30.
DON'T GO TOUCHING MY STUFF, THOUGH.
WHAT STUFF?
AND WHATEVER YOU DO, DON'T GET YOUR STANK ALL OVER MY FUTON.
NO RIFLING THROUGH MY FRIDGE EITHER.
LATER.
BTAM

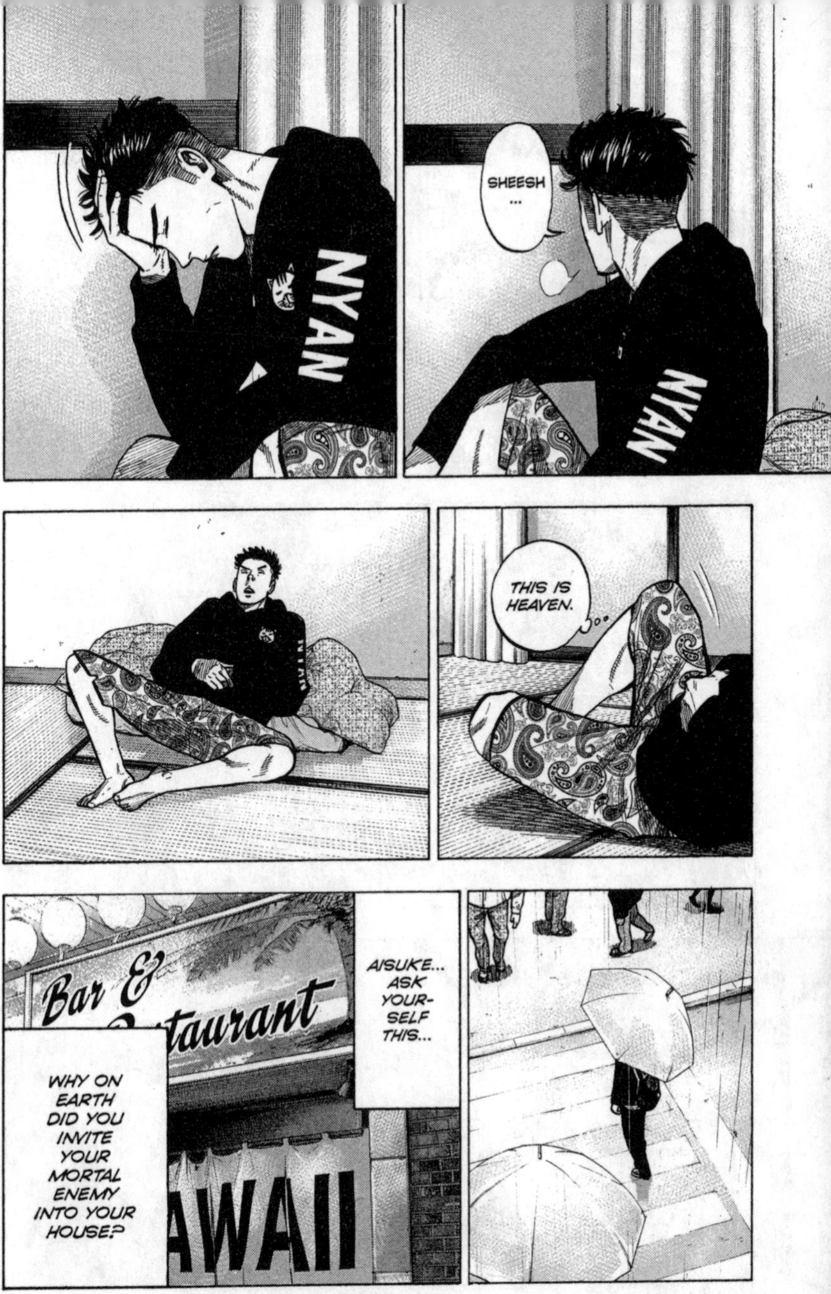
SHEESH ...
NYAN
NYAN
THIS IS HEAVEN.
AISUKE... ASK YOURSELF THIS...
WHY ON EARTH DID YOU INVITE YOUR MORTAL ENEMY INTO YOUR HOUSE?
Bar &
taurant
AWAII

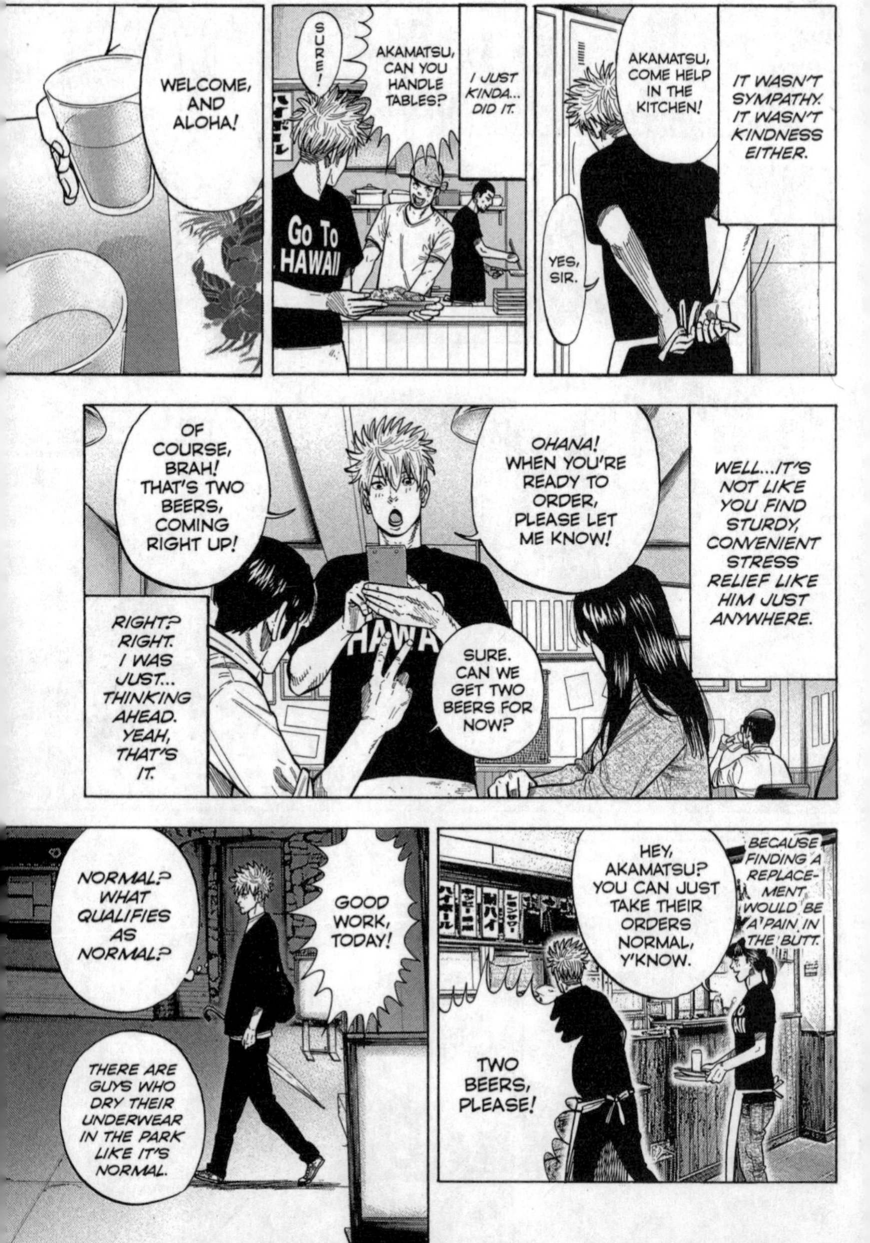
IT WASN'T SYMPATHY. IT WASN'T KINDNESS EITHER.
AKAMATSU, COME HELP IN THE KITCHEN!
YES, SIR.
I JUST KINDA... DID IT.
AKAMATSU, CAN YOU HANDLE TABLES?
SURE!
Go To HAWAII
WELCOME, AND ALOHA!
WELL...IT'S NOT LIKE YOU FIND STURDY, CONVENIENT STRESS RELIEF LIKE HIM JUST ANYWHERE.
OHANA! WHEN YOU'RE READY TO ORDER, PLEASE LET ME KNOW!
SURE. CAN WE GET TWO BEERS FOR NOW?
OF COURSE, BRAH! THAT'S TWO BEERS, COMING RIGHT UP!
RIGHT? RIGHT. I WAS JUST... THINKING AHEAD. YEAH, THAT'S IT.
BECAUSE FINDING A REPLACEMENT WOULD BE A PAIN IN THE BUTT.
HEY, AKAMATSU? YOU CAN JUST TAKE THEIR ORDERS NORMAL, Y'KNOW.
TWO BEERS, PLEASE!
GOOD WORK, TODAY!
NORMAL? WHAT QUALIFIES AS NORMAL?
THERE ARE GUYS WHO DRY THEIR UNDERWEAR IN THE PARK LIKE IT'S NORMAL.

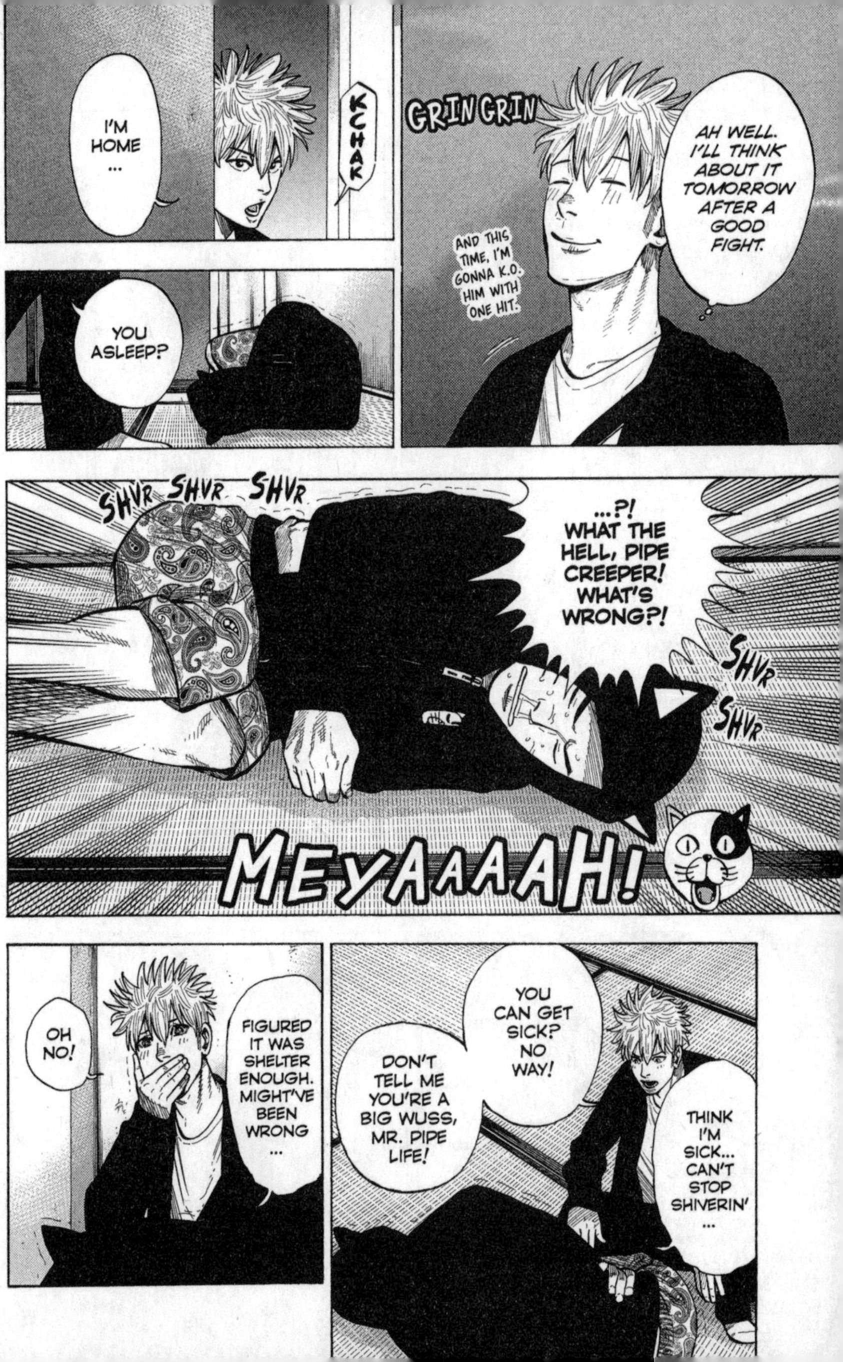
AH WELL. I'LL THINK ABOUT IT TOMORROW AFTER A GOOD FIGHT.
GRIN GRIN
AND THIS TIME, I'M GONNA K.O. HIM WITH ONE HIT.
KCHAK
I'M HOME ...
YOU ASLEEP?
SHVR
SHVR
...?! WHAT THE HELL, PIPE CREEPER! WHAT'S WRONG?!
SHVR SHVR SHVR
MEYAAAAAH!
THINK I'M SICK... CAN'T STOP SHIVERIN' ...
YOU CAN GET SICK? NO WAY!
DON'T TELL ME YOU'RE A BIG WUSS, MR. PIPE LIFE!
FIGURED IT WAS SHELTER ENOUGH. MIGHT'VE BEEN WRONG ...
OH NO!

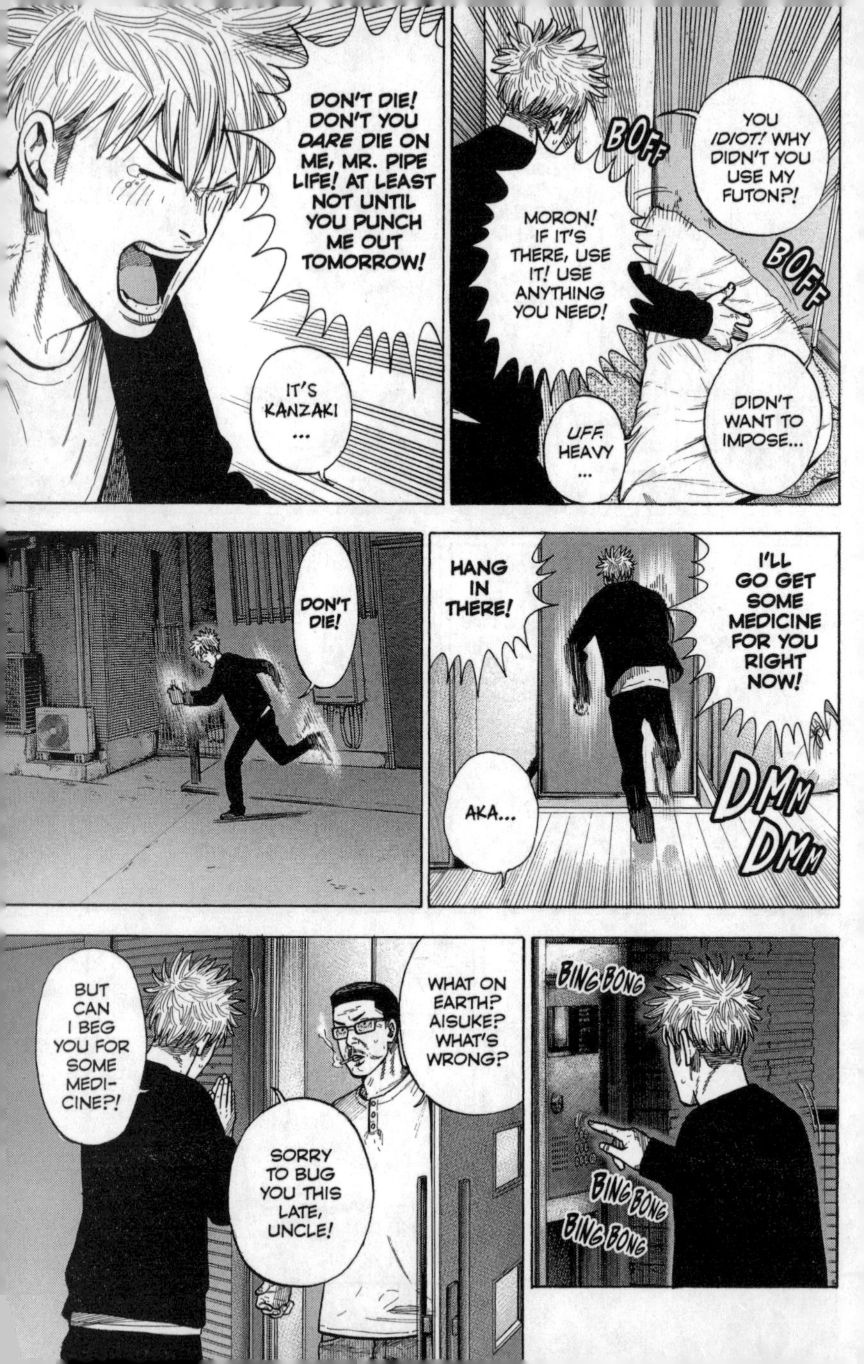
BOFF
YOU IDIOT! WHY DIDN'T YOU USE MY FUTON?!
MORON! IF IT'S THERE, USE IT! USE ANYTHING YOU NEED!
BOFF
DIDN'T WANT TO IMPOSE...
UFF. HEAVY ...
DON'T DIE! DON'T YOU DARE DIE ON ME, MR. PIPE LIFE! AT LEAST NOT UNTIL YOU PUNCH ME OUT TOMORROW!
IT'S KANZAKI ...
I'LL GO GET SOME MEDICINE FOR YOU RIGHT NOW!
HANG IN THERE!
DMM DMM
AKA...
DON'T DIE!
BING BONG
BING BONG
BING BONG
WHAT ON EARTH? AISUKE? WHAT'S WRONG?
SORRY TO BUG YOU THIS LATE, UNCLE!
BUT CAN I BEG YOU FOR SOME MEDICINE?!

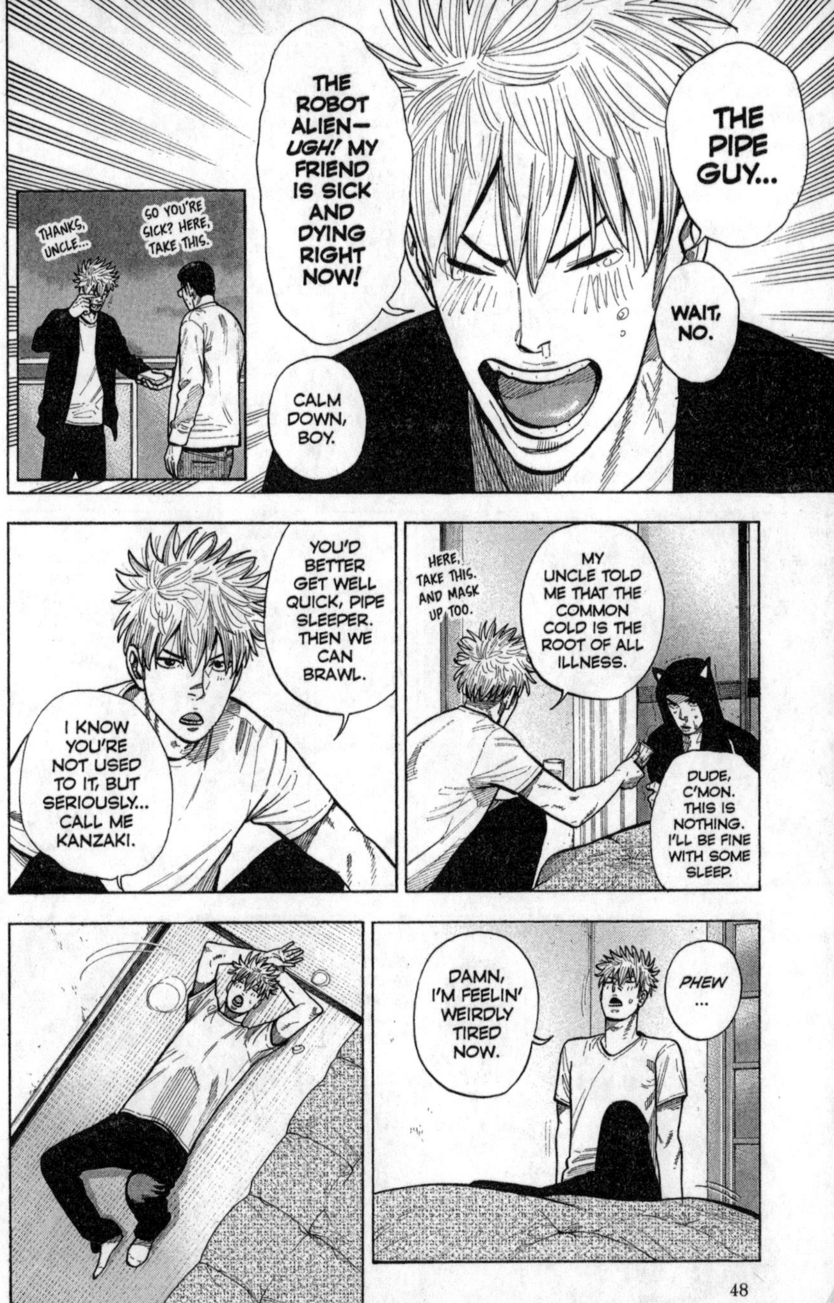
THE PIPE GUY...
WAIT, NO.
THE ROBOT ALIEN—*UGH!* MY FRIEND IS SICK AND DYING RIGHT NOW!
CALM DOWN, BOY.
SO YOU'RE SICK? HERE, TAKE THIS.
THANKS, UNCLE...
MY UNCLE TOLD ME THAT THE COMMON COLD IS THE ROOT OF ALL ILLNESS.
HERE, TAKE THIS. AND MASK UP, TOO.
DUDE, C'MON. THIS IS NOTHING. I'LL BE FINE WITH SOME SLEEP.
YOU'D BETTER GET WELL QUICK, PIPE SLEEPER. THEN WE CAN BRAWL.
I KNOW YOU'RE NOT USED TO IT, BUT SERIOUSLY... CALL ME KANZAKI.
PHEW ...
DAMN, I'M FEELIN' WEIRDLY TIRED NOW.

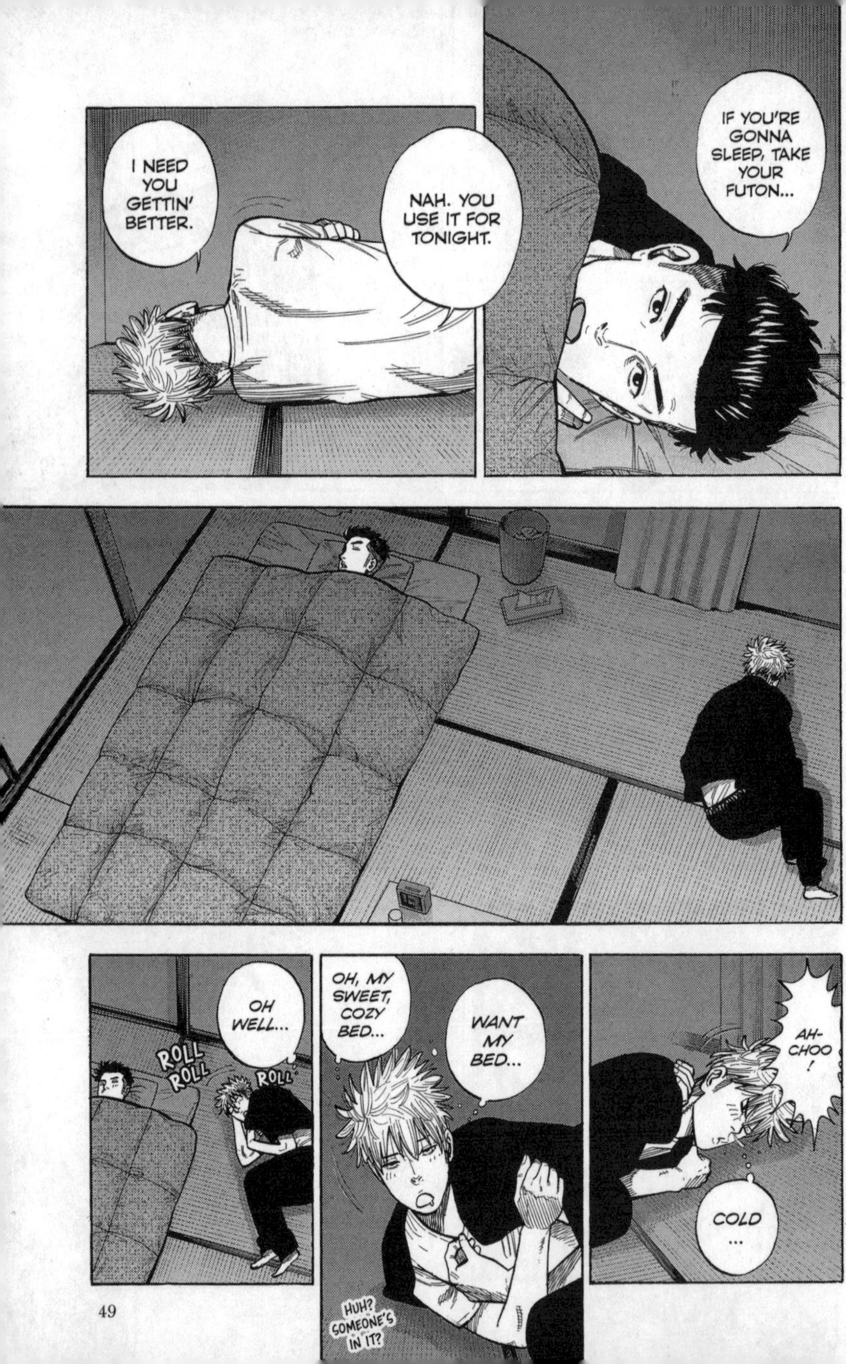
IF YOU'RE GONNA SLEEP, TAKE YOUR FUTON...
NAH. YOU USE IT FOR TONIGHT.
I NEED YOU GETTIN' BETTER.
AH-CHOO!
COLD...
WANT MY BED...
OH, MY SWEET, COZY BED...
HUH? SOMEONE'S IN IT?
OH WELL...
ROLL ROLL
ROLL

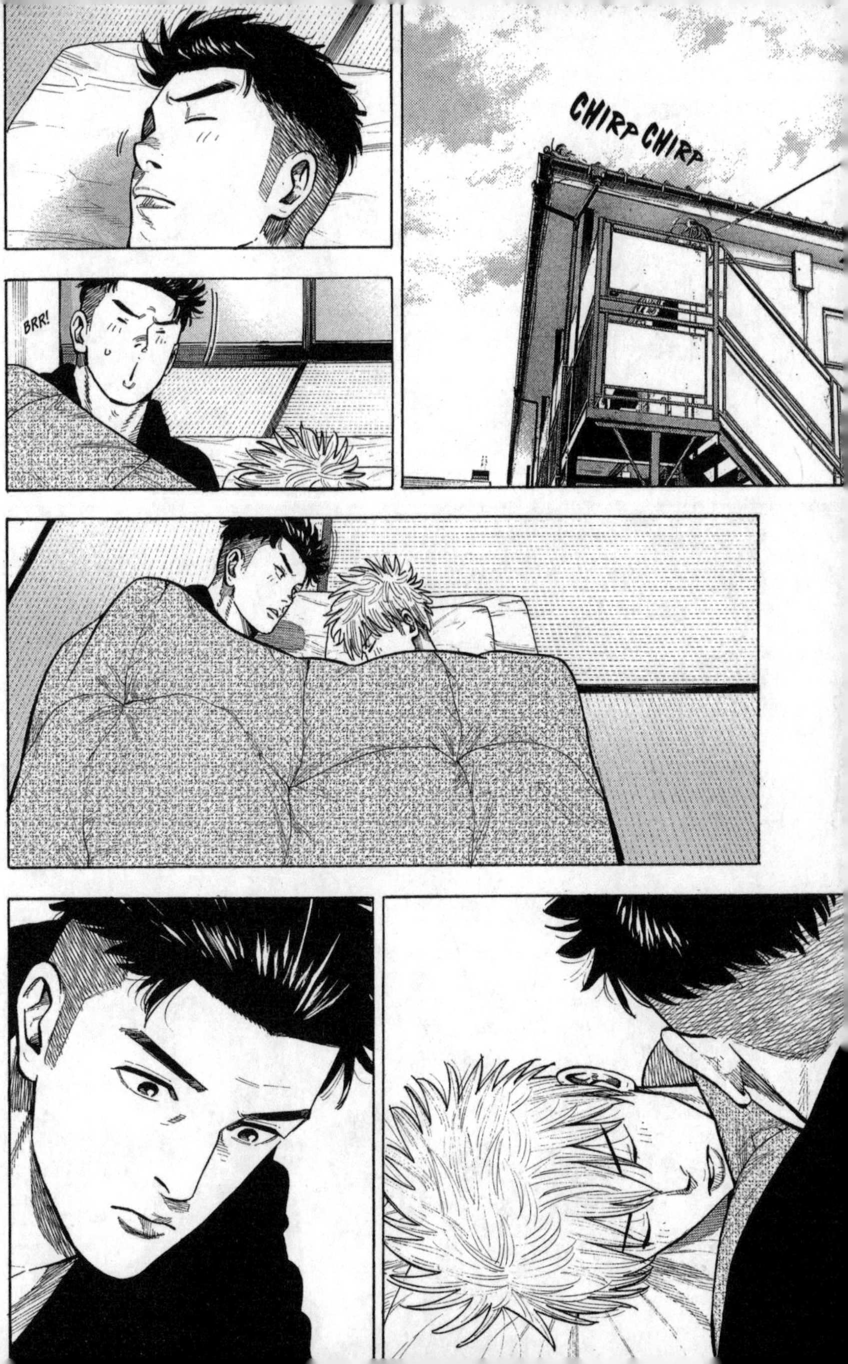
CHIRP CHIRP
BRR!

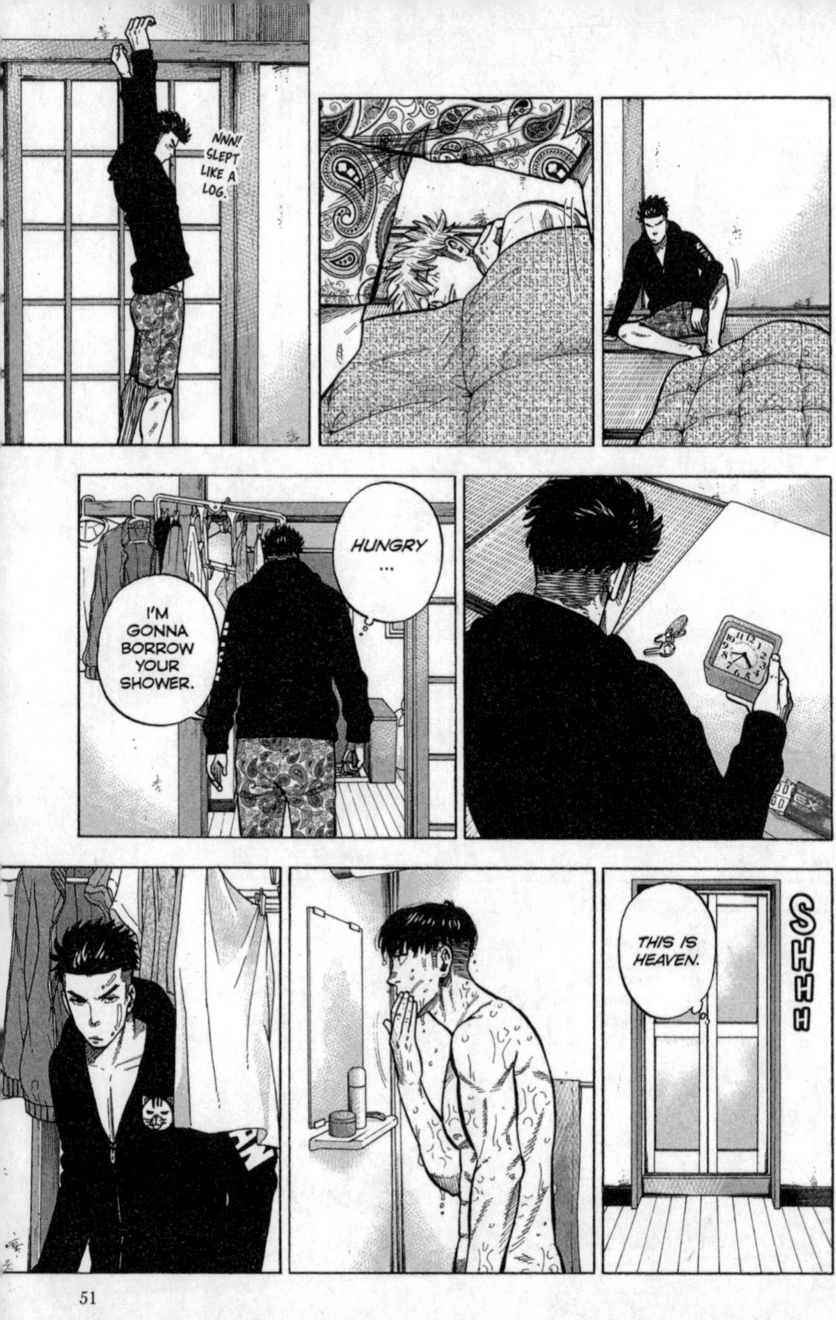
NNN! SLEPT LIKE A LOG.
HUNGRY ...
I'M GONNA BORROW YOUR SHOWER.
SHHHH
THIS IS HEAVEN.

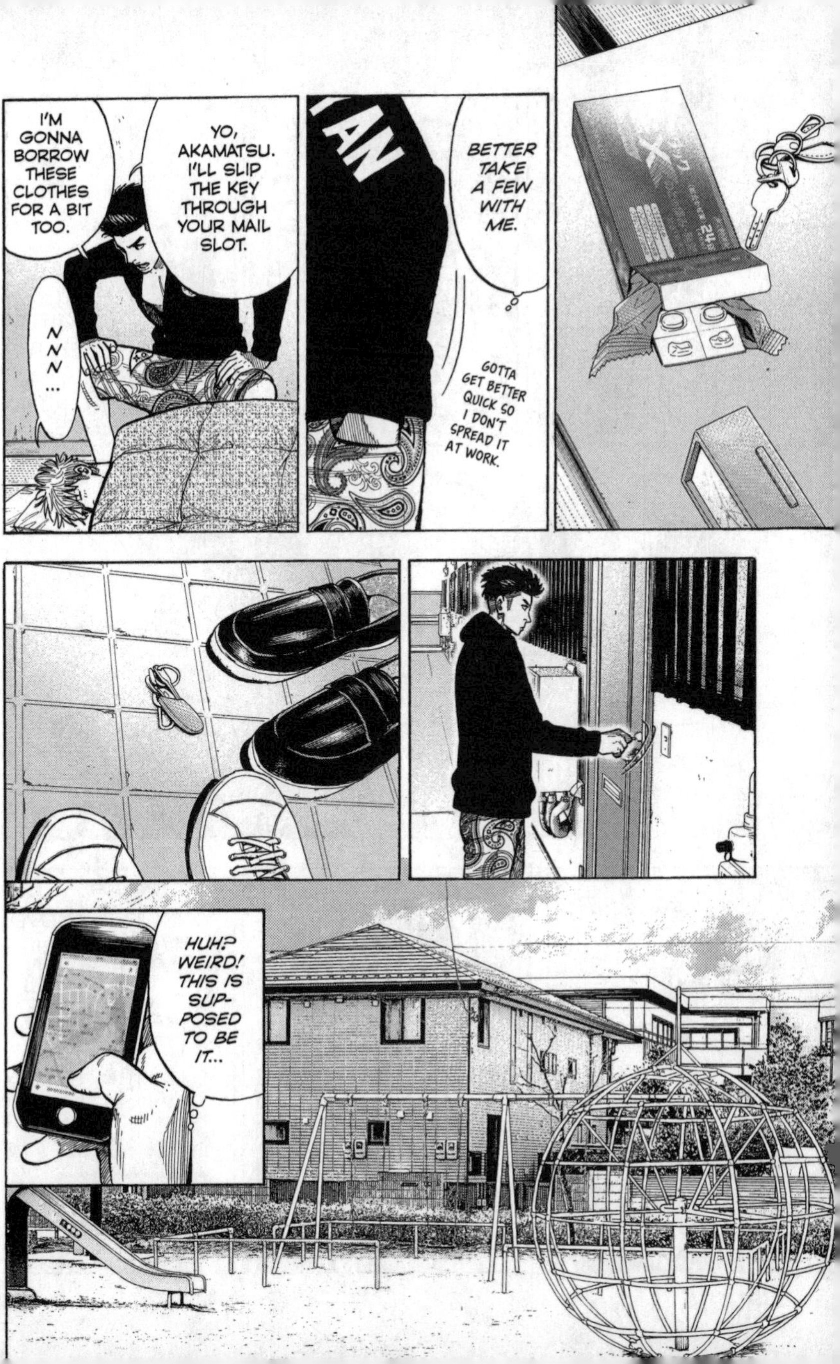
BETTER TAKE A FEW WITH ME.
GOTTA GET BETTER QUICK SO I DON'T SPREAD IT AT WORK.
YO, AKAMATSU. I'LL SLIP THE KEY THROUGH YOUR MAIL SLOT.
I'M GONNA BORROW THESE CLOTHES FOR A BIT TOO.
NNN...
HUH? WEIRD! THIS IS SUP-POSED TO BE IT...

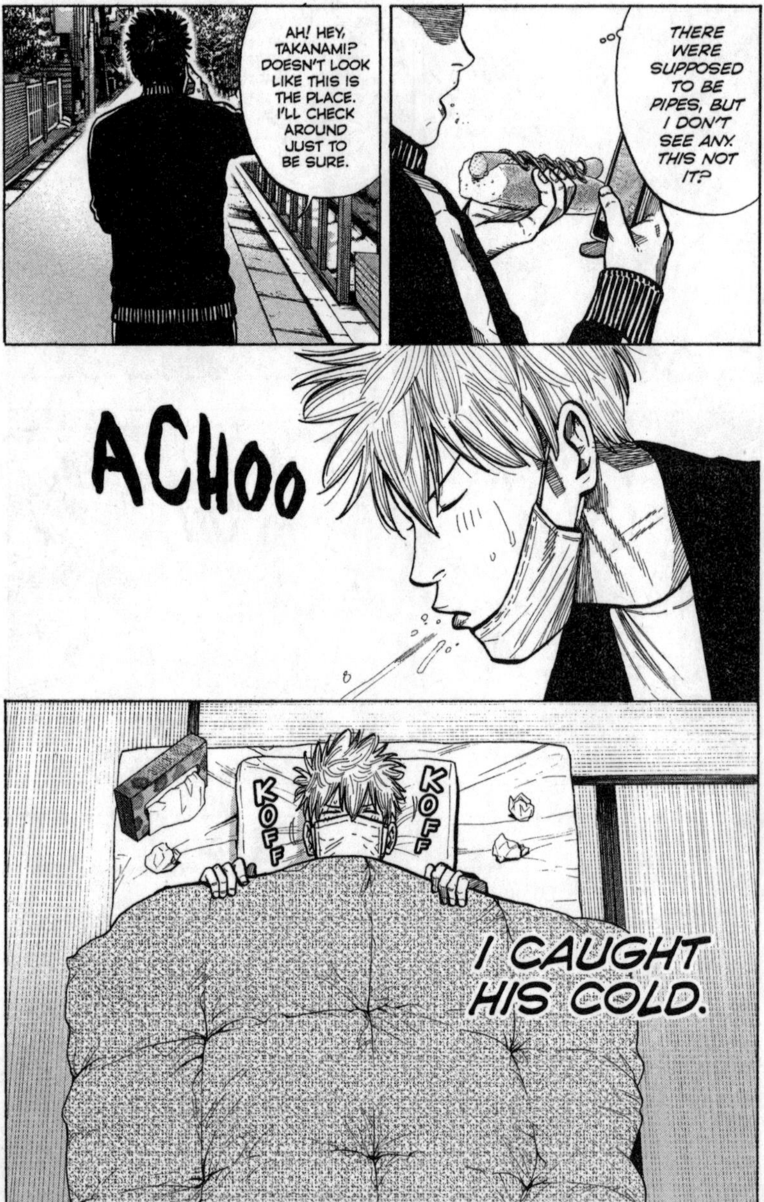
THERE WERE SUPPOSED TO BE PIPES, BUT I DON'T SEE ANY. THIS NOT IT?
AH! HEY, TAKANAMI? DOESN'T LOOK LIKE THIS IS THE PLACE. I'LL CHECK AROUND JUST TO BE SURE.
ACHOO
KOFF
KOFF
I CAUGHT HIS COLD.

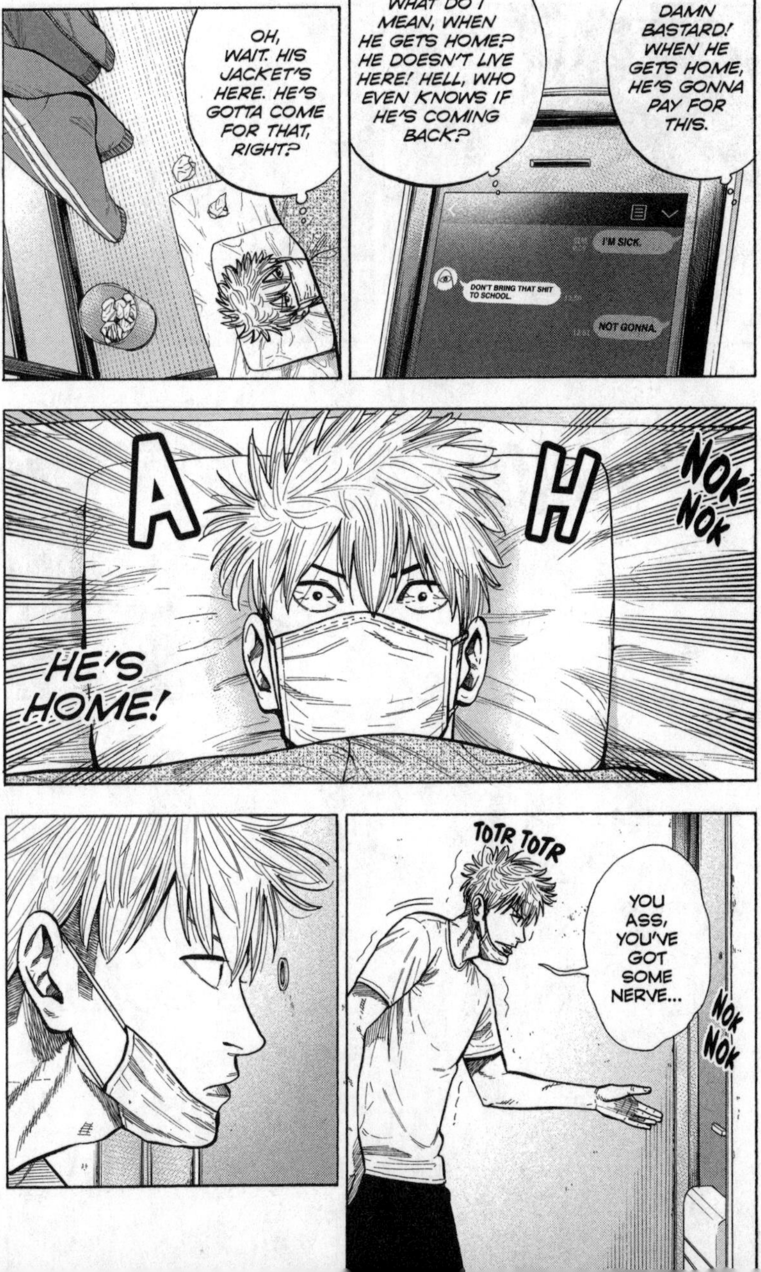
DAMN BASTARD! WHEN HE GETS HOME, HE'S GONNA PAY FOR THIS.
WAIT, WHAT DO I MEAN, WHEN HE GETS HOME? HE DOESN'T LIVE HERE! HELL, WHO EVEN KNOWS IF HE'S COMING BACK?
I'M SICK.
DON'T BRING THAT SHIT TO SCHOOL.
NOT GONNA.
OH, WAIT. HIS JACKET'S HERE. HE'S GOTTA COME FOR THAT, RIGHT?
NOK NOK
A
H
HE'S HOME!
TOTR TOTR
YOU ASS, YOU'VE GOT SOME NERVE...
NOK NOK

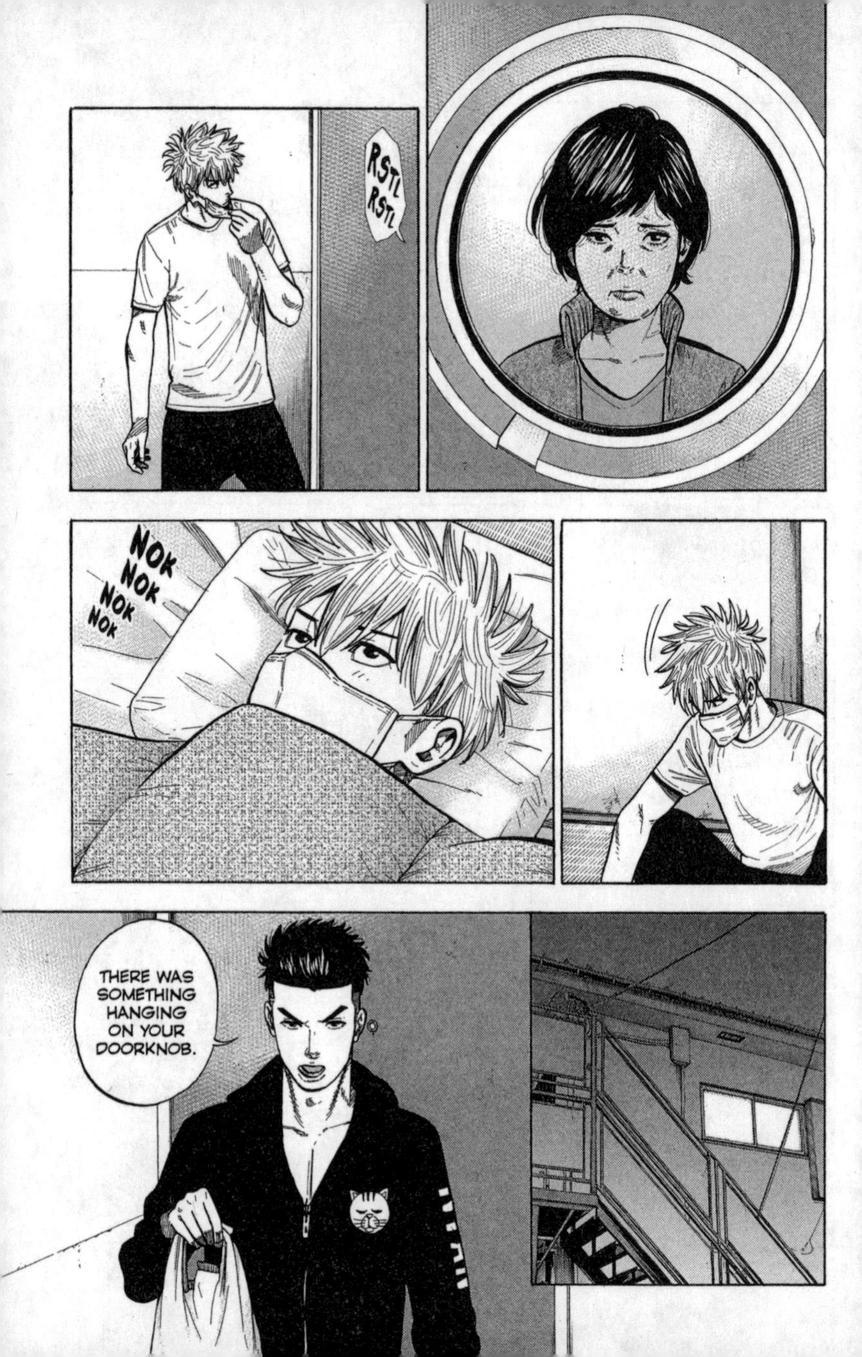
RSTL RSTL
NOK NOK NOK NOK
THERE WAS SOMETHING HANGING ON YOUR DOORKNOB.

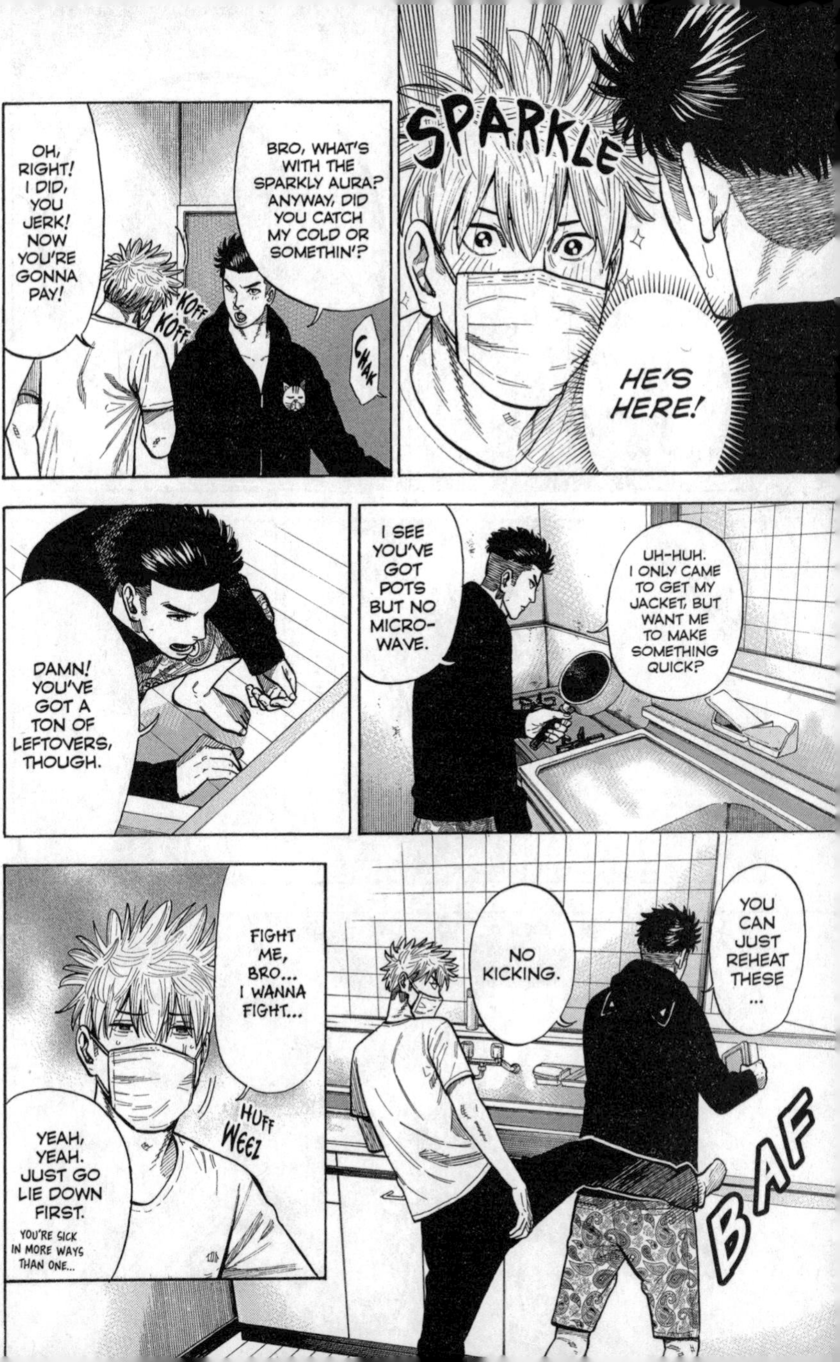
SPARKLE
HE'S HERE!
BRO, WHAT'S WITH THE SPARKLY AURA? ANYWAY, DID YOU CATCH MY COLD OR SOMETHIN'?
CHAK
KOFF KOFF
OH, RIGHT! I DID, YOU JERK! NOW YOU'RE GONNA PAY!
UH-HUH. I ONLY CAME TO GET MY JACKET, BUT WANT ME TO MAKE SOMETHING QUICK?
I SEE YOU'VE GOT POTS BUT NO MICRO-WAVE.
DAMN! YOU'VE GOT A TON OF LEFTOVERS, THOUGH.
YOU CAN JUST REHEAT THESE...
NO KICKING.
BAF
FIGHT ME, BRO... I WANNA FIGHT...
HUFF WEEZ
YEAH, YEAH. JUST GO LIE DOWN FIRST.
YOU'RE SICK IN MORE WAYS THAN ONE...

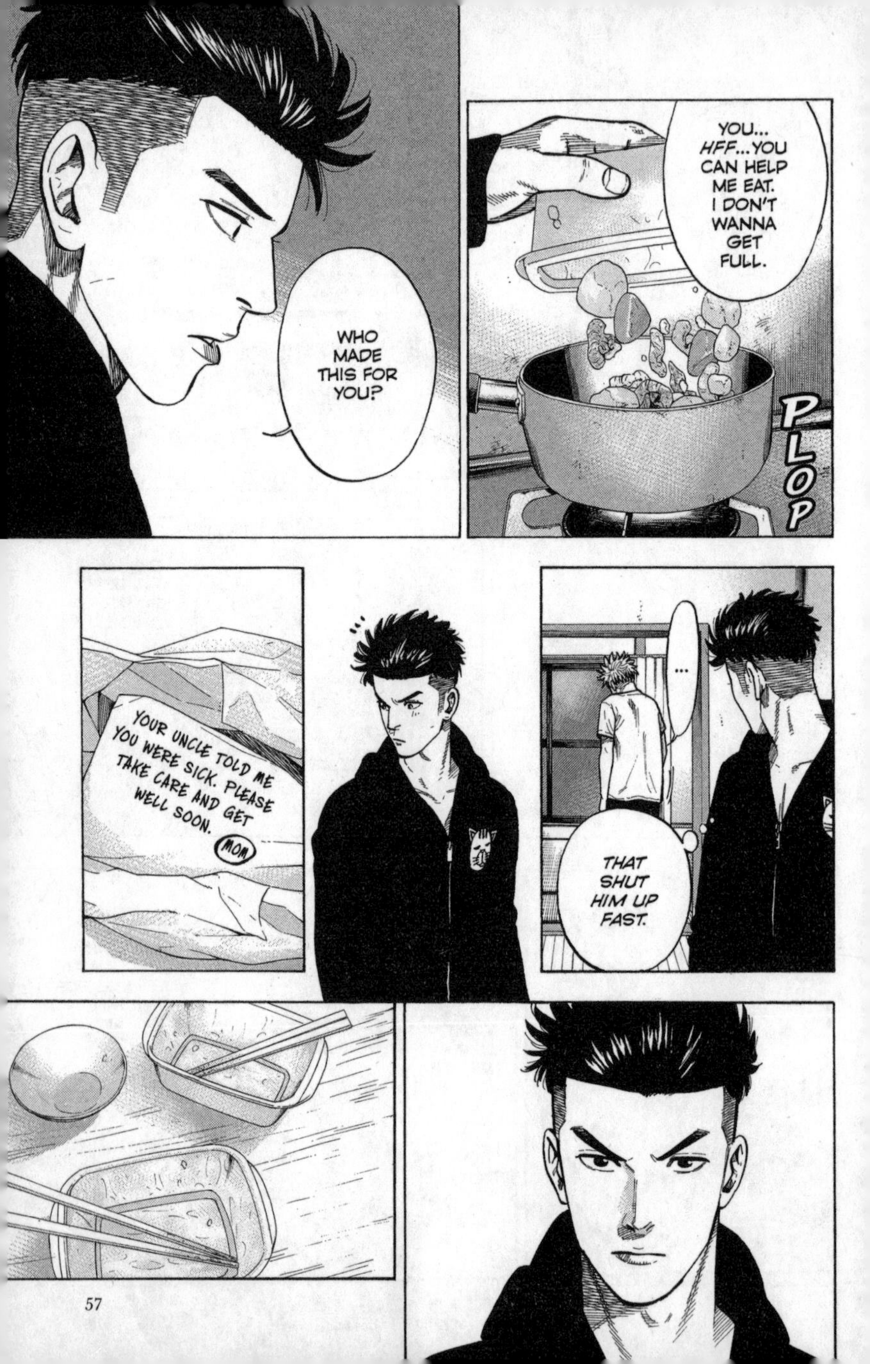
YOU... HFF...YOU CAN HELP ME EAT. I DON'T WANNA GET FULL.
PLOP
WHO MADE THIS FOR YOU?
...
THAT SHUT HIM UP FAST.
YOUR UNCLE TOLD ME YOU WERE SICK. PLEASE TAKE CARE AND GET WELL SOON.
MOM

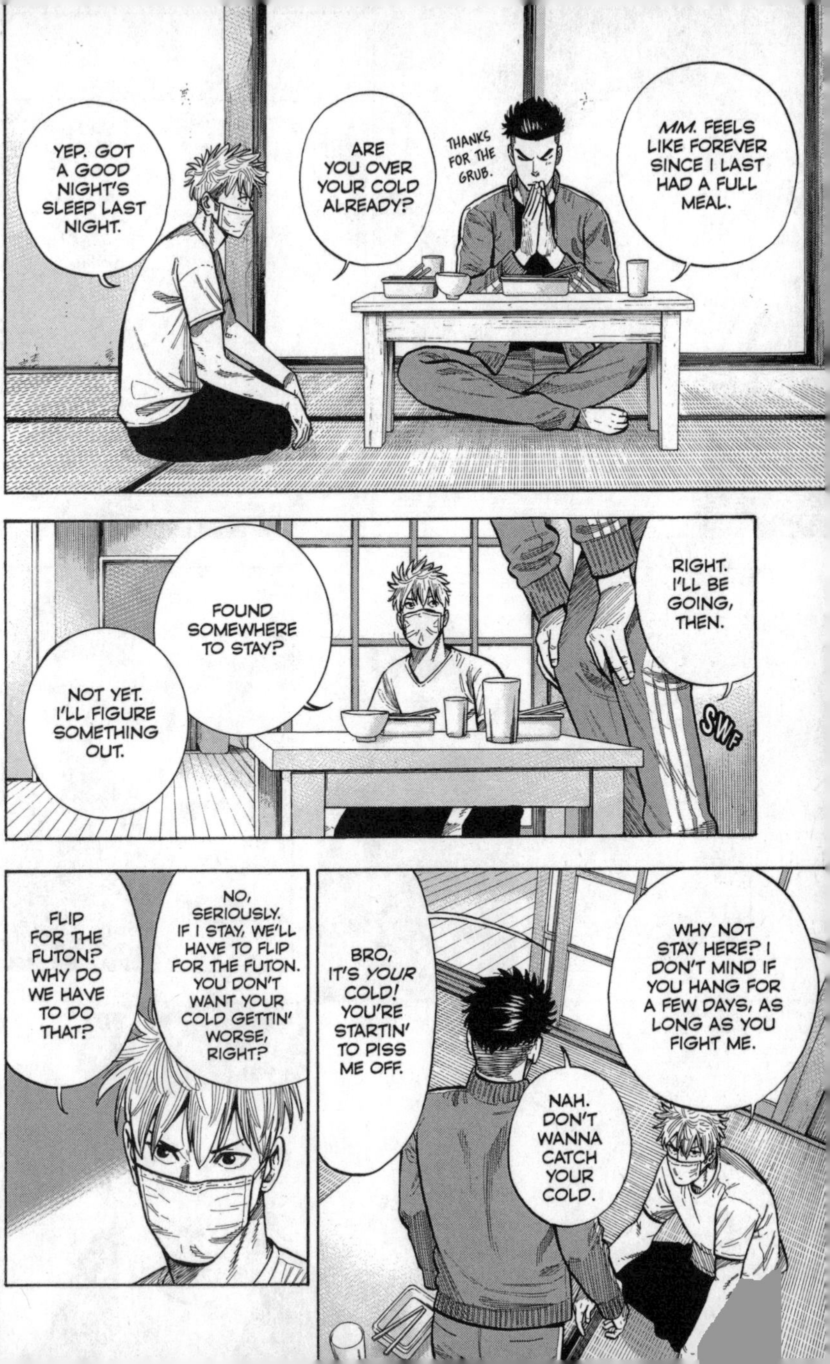
MM. FEELS LIKE FOREVER SINCE I LAST HAD A FULL MEAL.
THANKS FOR THE GRUB.
ARE YOU OVER YOUR COLD ALREADY?
YEP. GOT A GOOD NIGHT'S SLEEP LAST NIGHT.
RIGHT. I'LL BE GOING, THEN.
SWF
FOUND SOMEWHERE TO STAY?
NOT YET. I'LL FIGURE SOMETHING OUT.
WHY NOT STAY HERE? I DON'T MIND IF YOU HANG FOR A FEW DAYS, AS LONG AS YOU FIGHT ME.
NAH. DON'T WANNA CATCH YOUR COLD.
BRO, IT'S *YOUR* COLD! YOU'RE STARTIN' TO PISS ME OFF.
NO, SERIOUSLY. IF I STAY, WE'LL HAVE TO FLIP FOR THE FUTON. YOU DON'T WANT YOUR COLD GETTIN' WORSE, RIGHT?
FLIP FOR THE FUTON? WHY DO WE HAVE TO DO THAT?

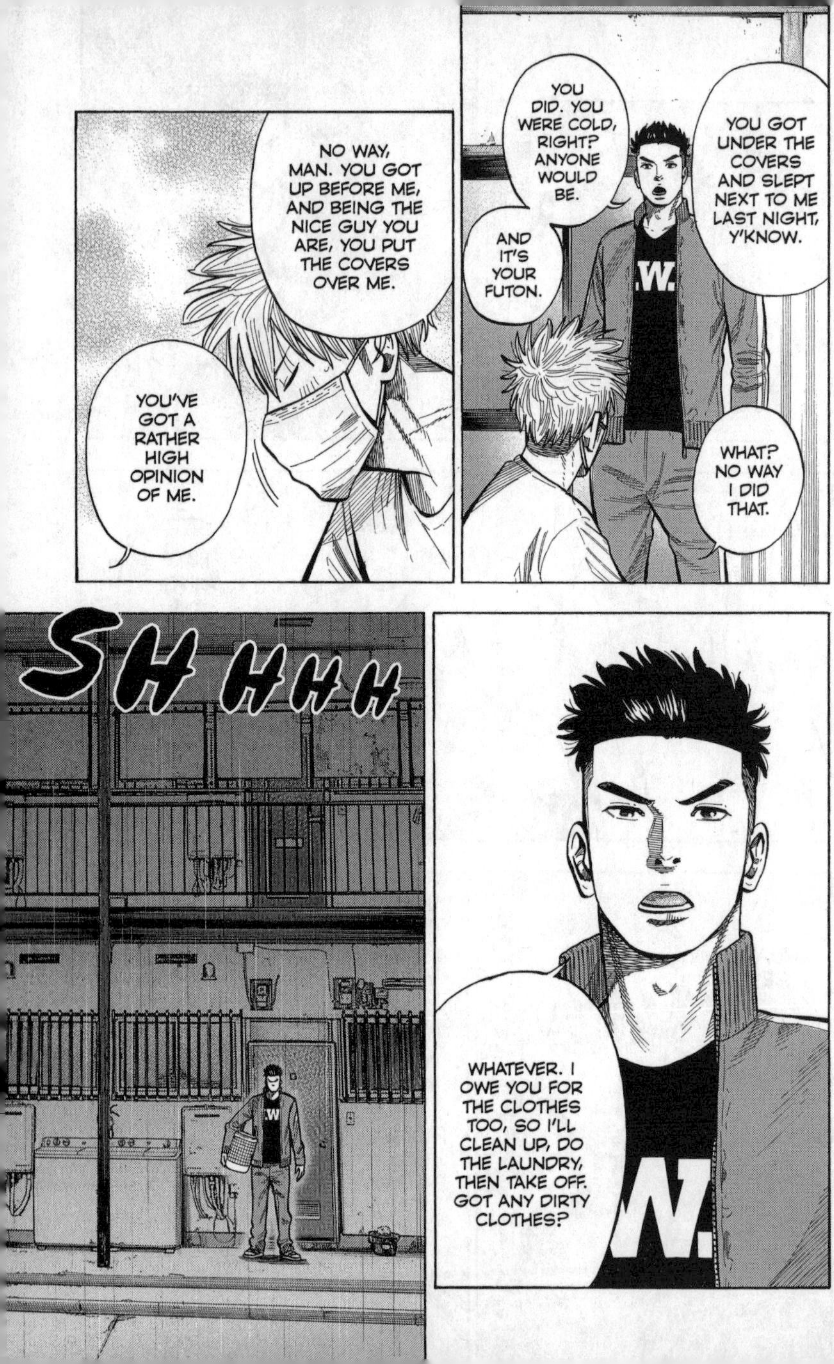
YOU GOT UNDER THE COVERS AND SLEPT NEXT TO ME LAST NIGHT, Y'KNOW.
WHAT? NO WAY I DID THAT.
YOU DID. YOU WERE COLD, RIGHT? ANYONE WOULD BE.
AND IT'S YOUR FUTON.
NO WAY, MAN. YOU GOT UP BEFORE ME, AND BEING THE NICE GUY YOU ARE, YOU PUT THE COVERS OVER ME.
YOU'VE GOT A RATHER HIGH OPINION OF ME.
WHATEVER. I OWE YOU FOR THE CLOTHES TOO, SO I'LL CLEAN UP, DO THE LAUNDRY, THEN TAKE OFF. GOT ANY DIRTY CLOTHES?
SHHHH

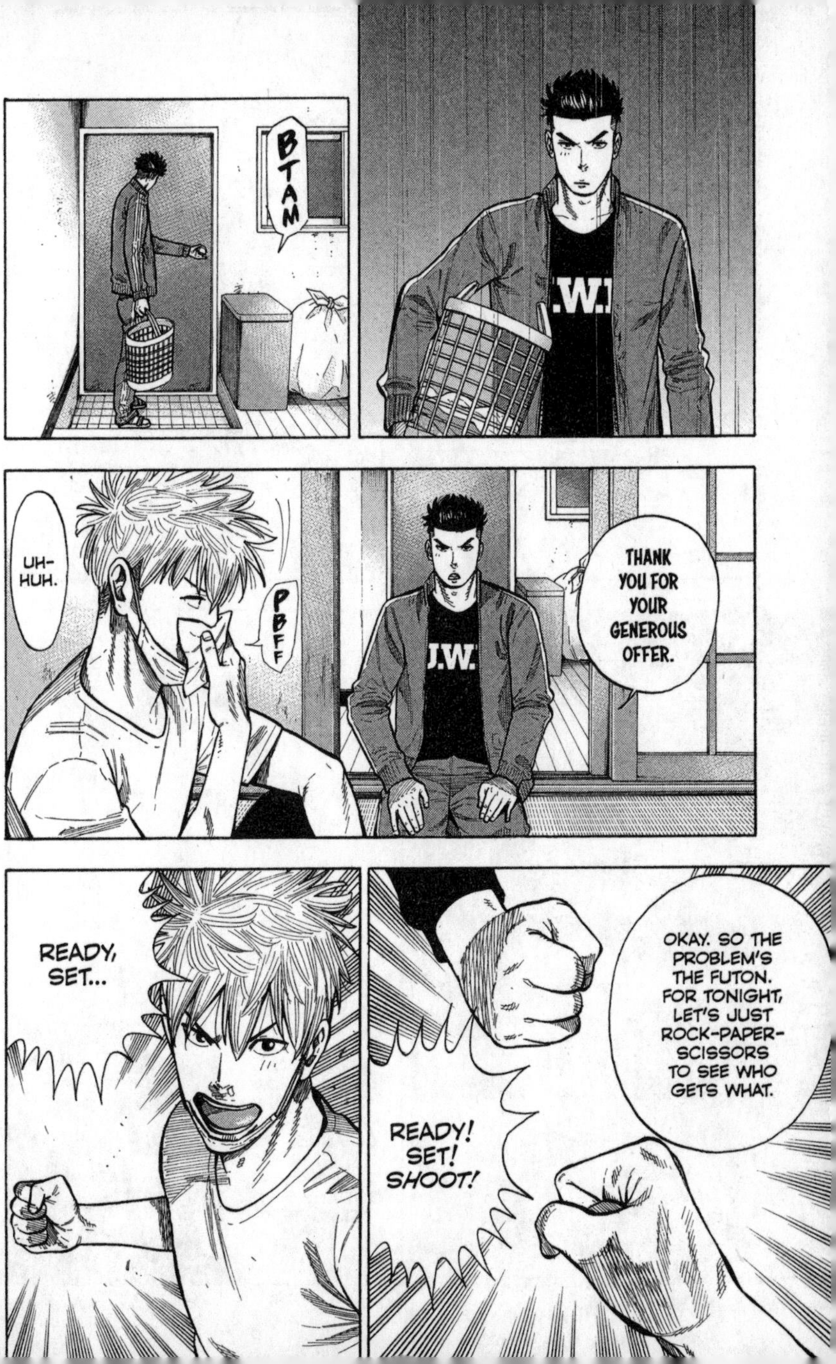
BTAM
THANK YOU FOR YOUR GENEROUS OFFER.
PBFF
UH-HUH.
OKAY. SO THE PROBLEM'S THE FUTON. FOR TONIGHT, LET'S JUST ROCK-PAPER-SCISSORS TO SEE WHO GETS WHAT.
READY! SET! SHOOT!
READY, SET...

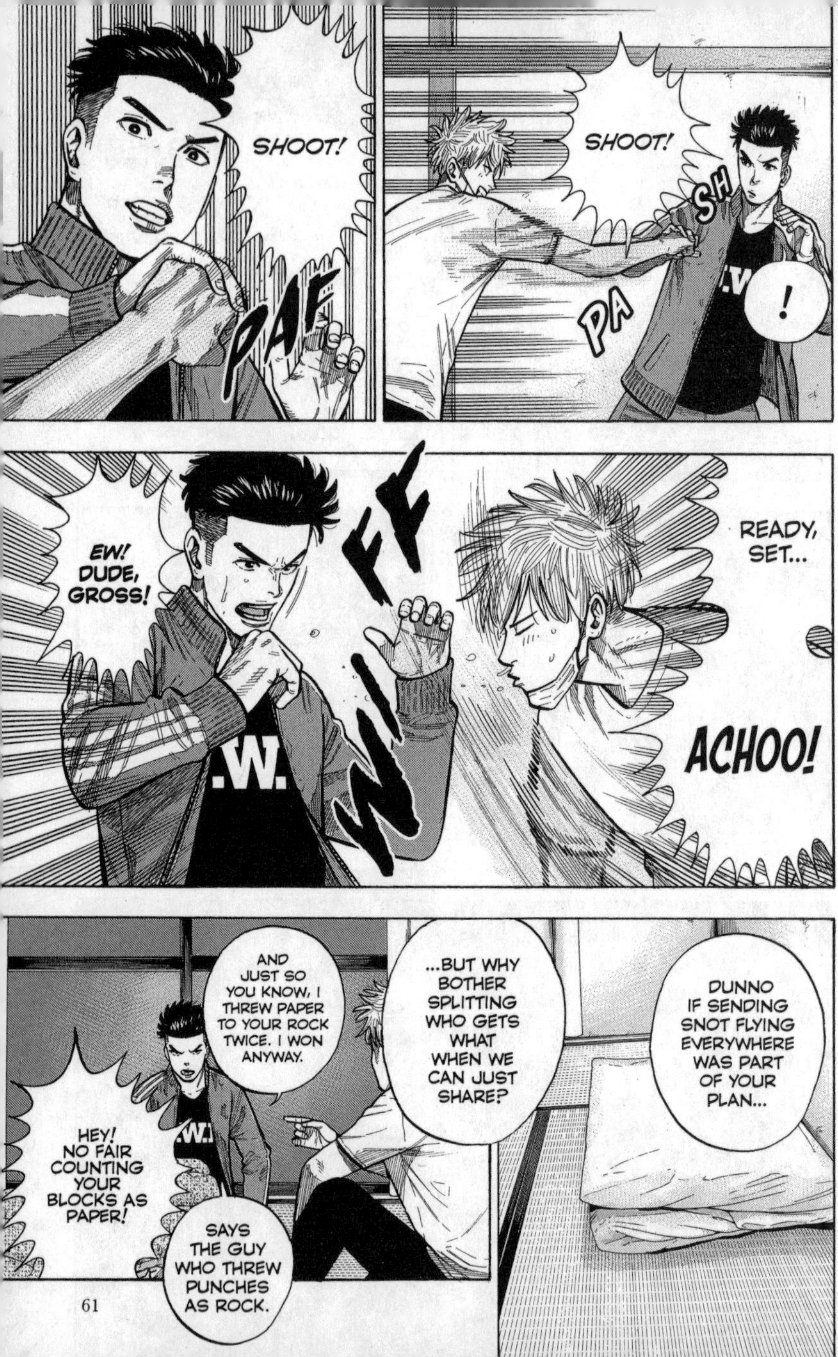
SHOOT!
SH
PA
!
SHOOT!
PAF
READY, SET...
ACHOO!
WHFF
EW! DUDE, GROSS!
DUNNO IF SENDING SNOT FLYING EVERYWHERE WAS PART OF YOUR PLAN...
...BUT WHY BOTHER SPLITTING WHO GETS WHAT WHEN WE CAN JUST SHARE?
AND JUST SO YOU KNOW, I THREW PAPER TO YOUR ROCK TWICE. I WON ANYWAY.
HEY! NO FAIR COUNTING YOUR BLOCKS AS PAPER!
SAYS THE GUY WHO THREW PUNCHES AS ROCK.

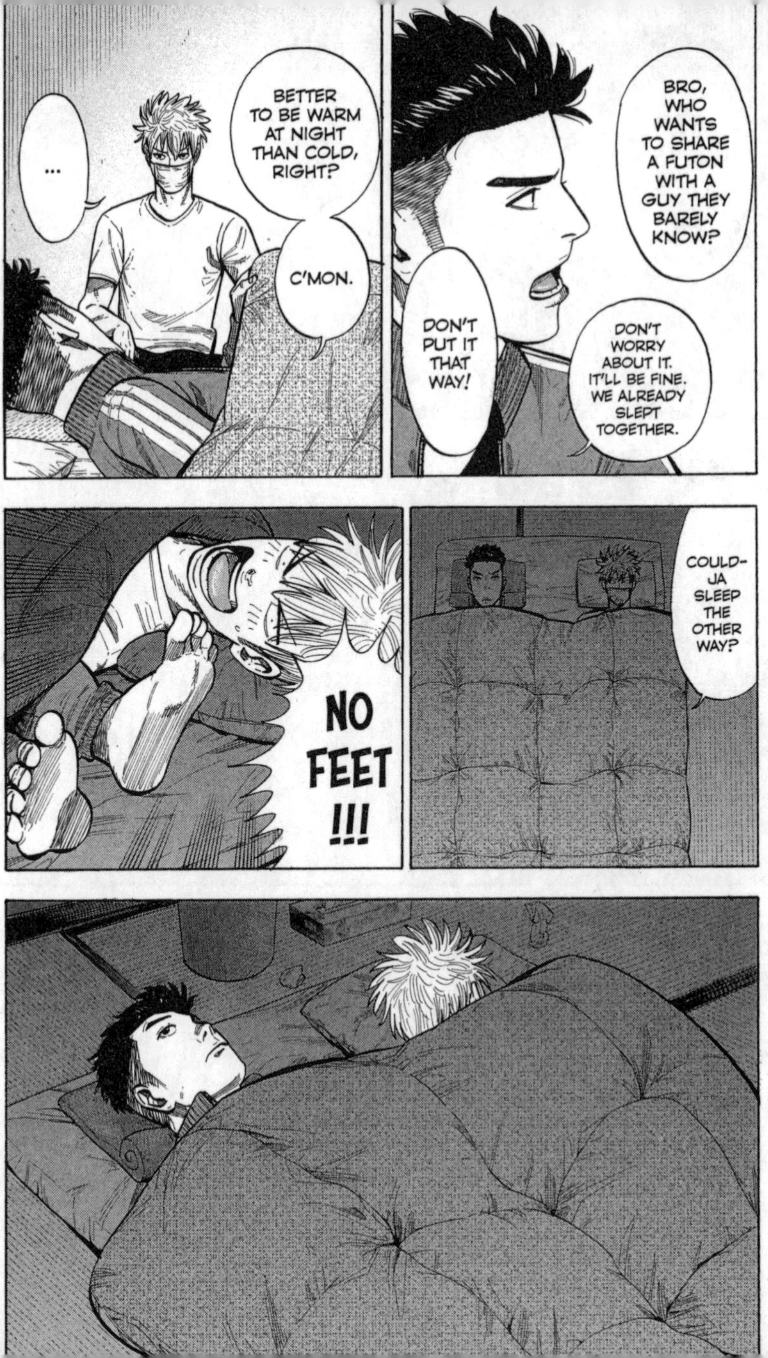
BRO, WHO WANTS TO SHARE A FUTON WITH A GUY THEY BARELY KNOW?
DON'T WORRY ABOUT IT. IT'LL BE FINE. WE ALREADY SLEPT TOGETHER.
DON'T PUT IT THAT WAY!
BETTER TO BE WARM AT NIGHT THAN COLD, RIGHT?
C'MON.
...
COULD-JA SLEEP THE OTHER WAY?
NO FEET !!!

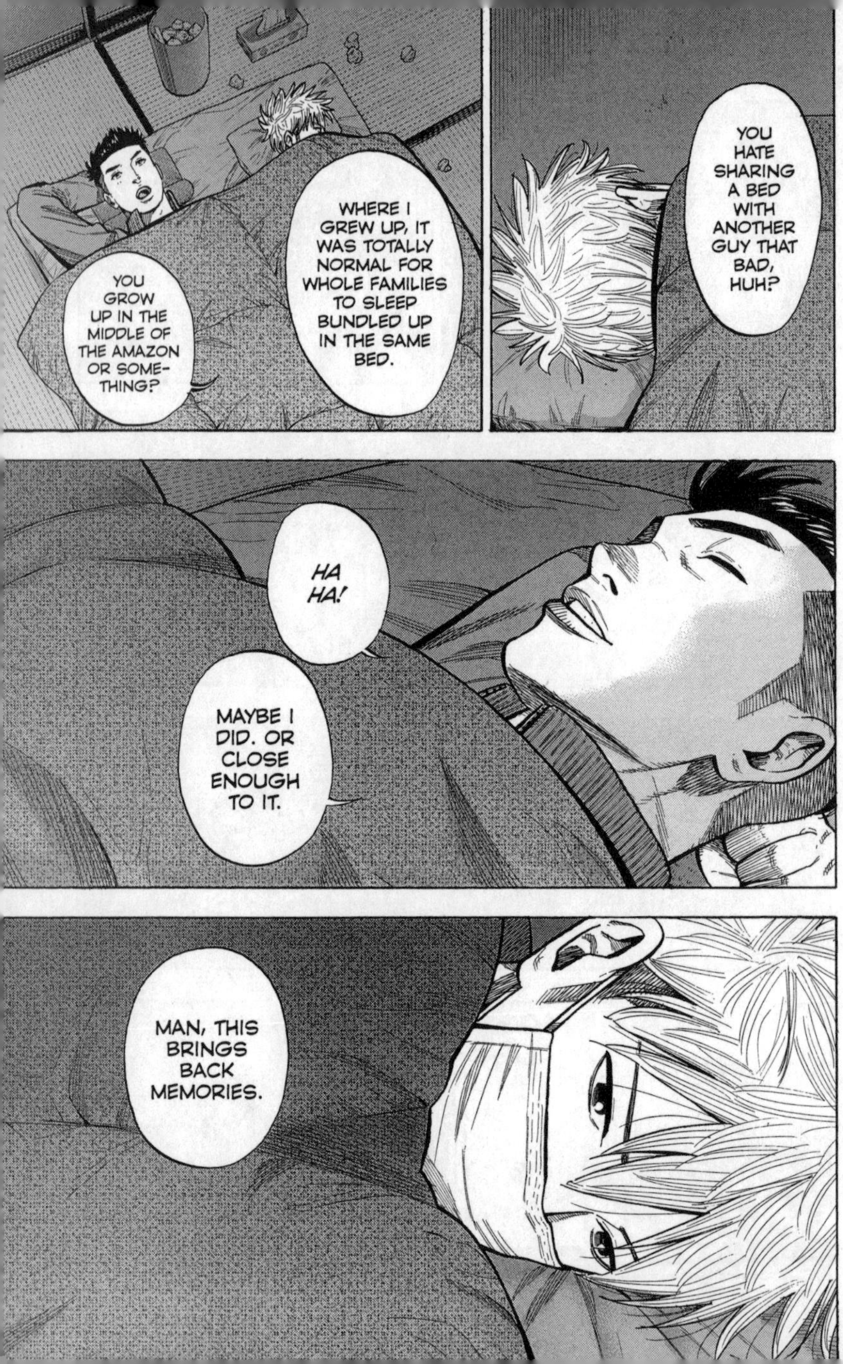
YOU HATE SHARING A BED WITH ANOTHER GUY THAT BAD, HUH?
WHERE I GREW UP, IT WAS TOTALLY NORMAL FOR WHOLE FAMILIES TO SLEEP BUNDLED UP IN THE SAME BED.
YOU GROW UP IN THE MIDDLE OF THE AMAZON OR SOME-THING?
HA HA!
MAYBE I DID. OR CLOSE ENOUGH TO IT.
MAN, THIS BRINGS BACK MEMORIES.

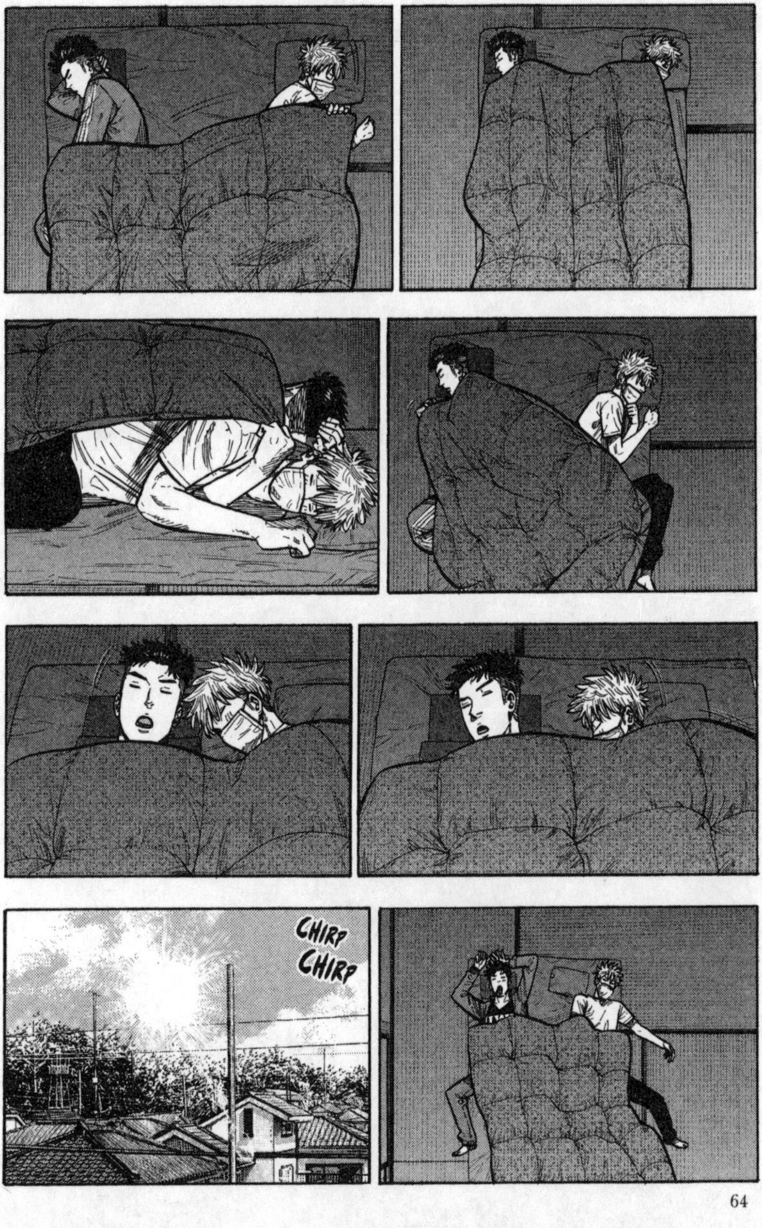
CHIRP
CHIRP

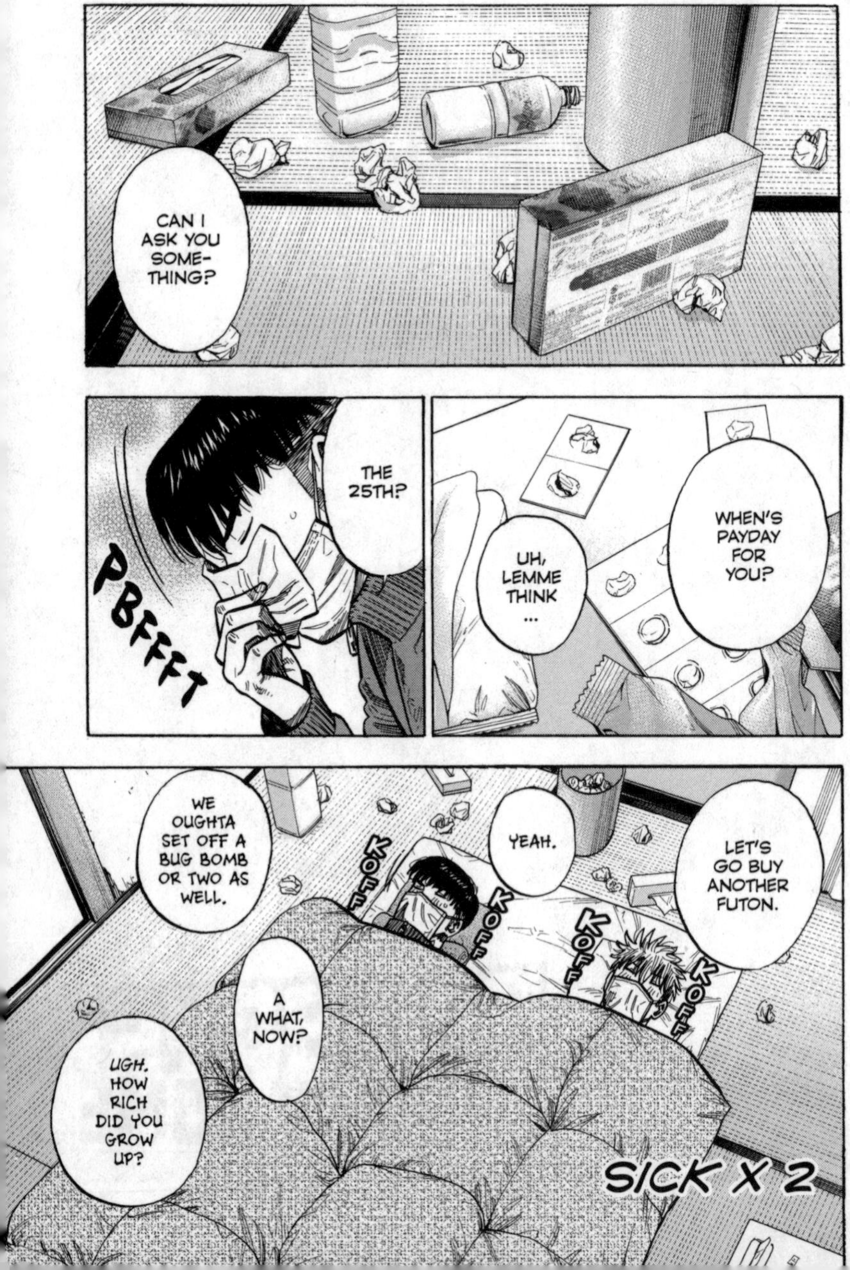
CAN I ASK YOU SOME-THING?
WHEN'S PAYDAY FOR YOU?
UH, LEMME THINK ...
THE 25TH?
PBFFFT
LET'S GO BUY ANOTHER FUTON.
YEAH.
WE OUGHTA SET OFF A BUG BOMB OR TWO AS WELL.
KOFF
KOFF
KOFF
KOFF
KOFF
A WHAT, NOW?
UGH. HOW RICH DID YOU GROW UP?
SICK X 2

BAD BOYS
HAPPY HOME

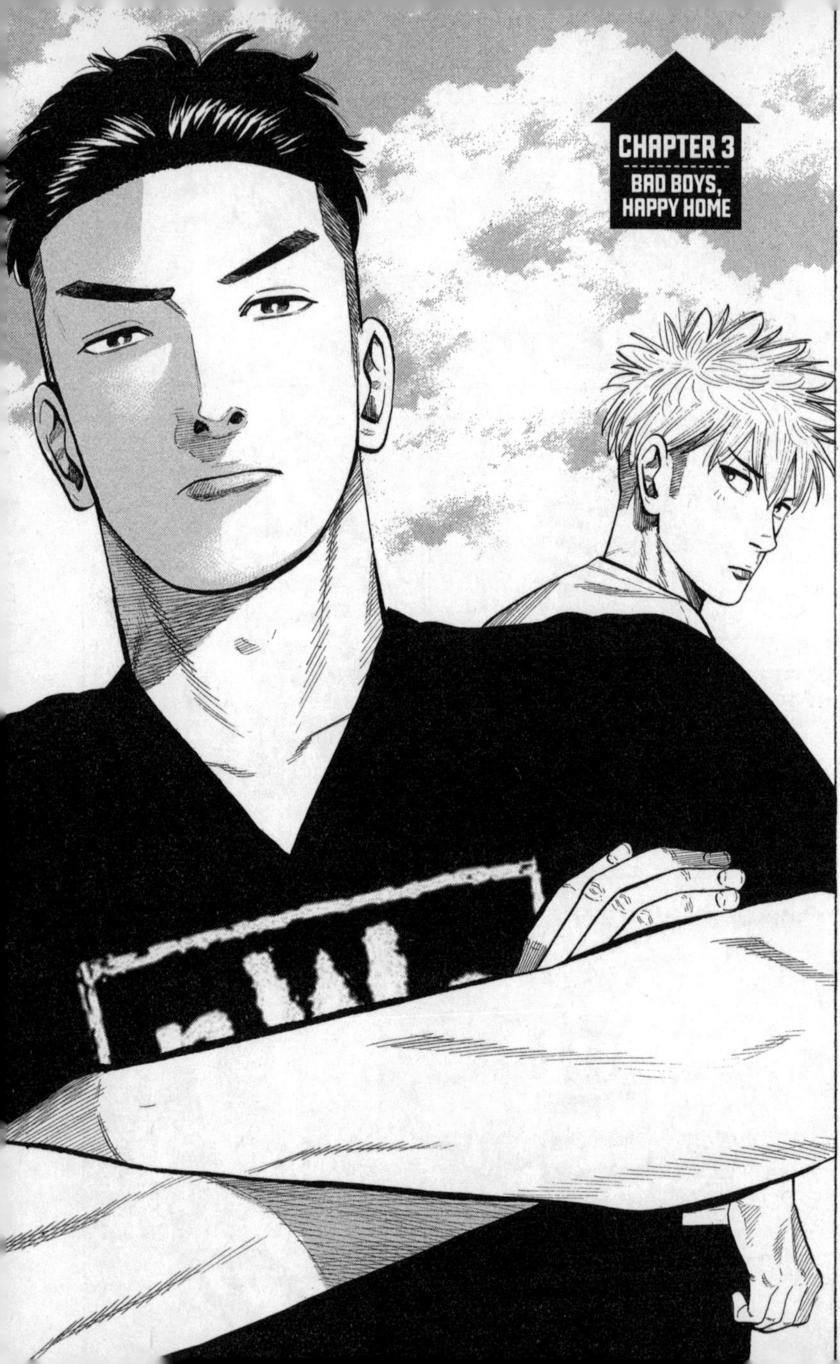
CHAPTER 3
BAD BOYS, HAPPY HOME

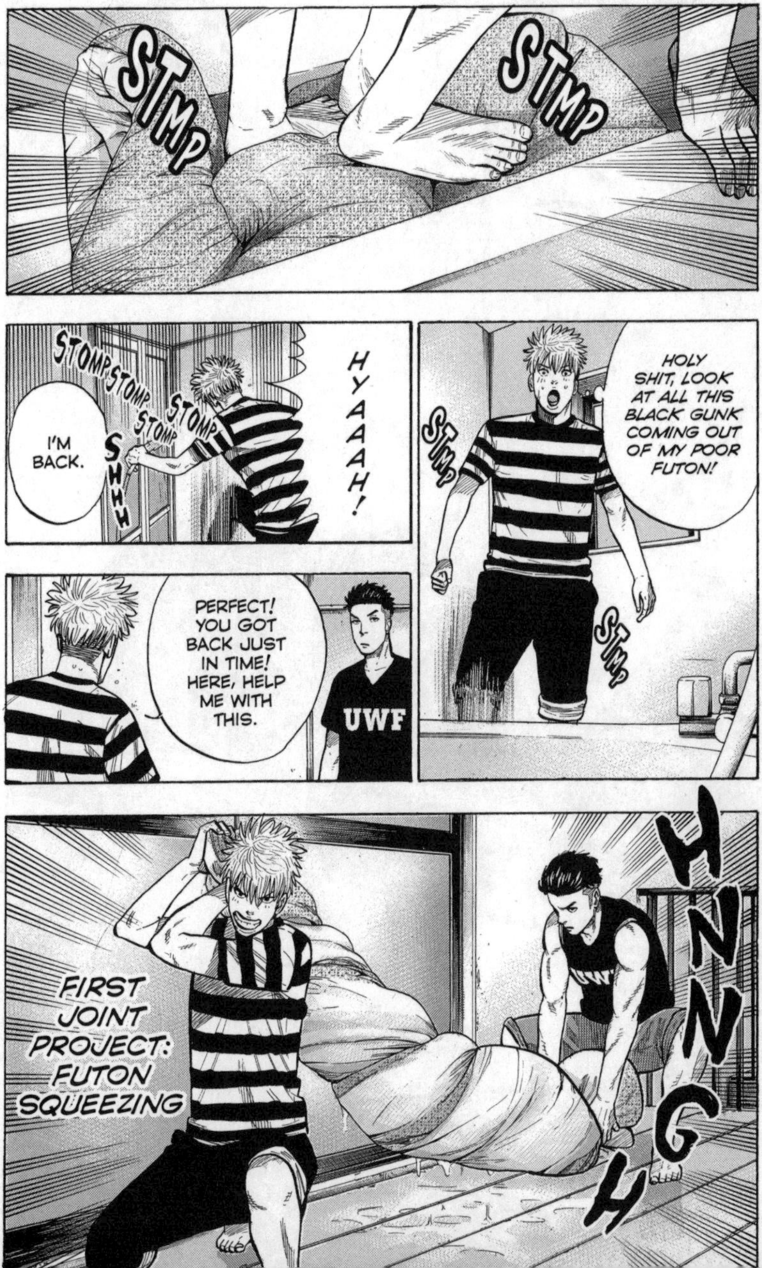
STMP
STMP
HOLY SHIT, LOOK AT ALL THIS BLACK GUNK COMING OUT OF MY POOR FUTON!
STMP
STMP
HYAAAAH!
STOMP STOMP STOMP STOMP STOMP
SHHH
I'M BACK.
PERFECT! YOU GOT BACK JUST IN TIME! HERE, HELP ME WITH THIS.
UWF
HNNGHH
FIRST JOINT PROJECT: FUTON SQUEEZING

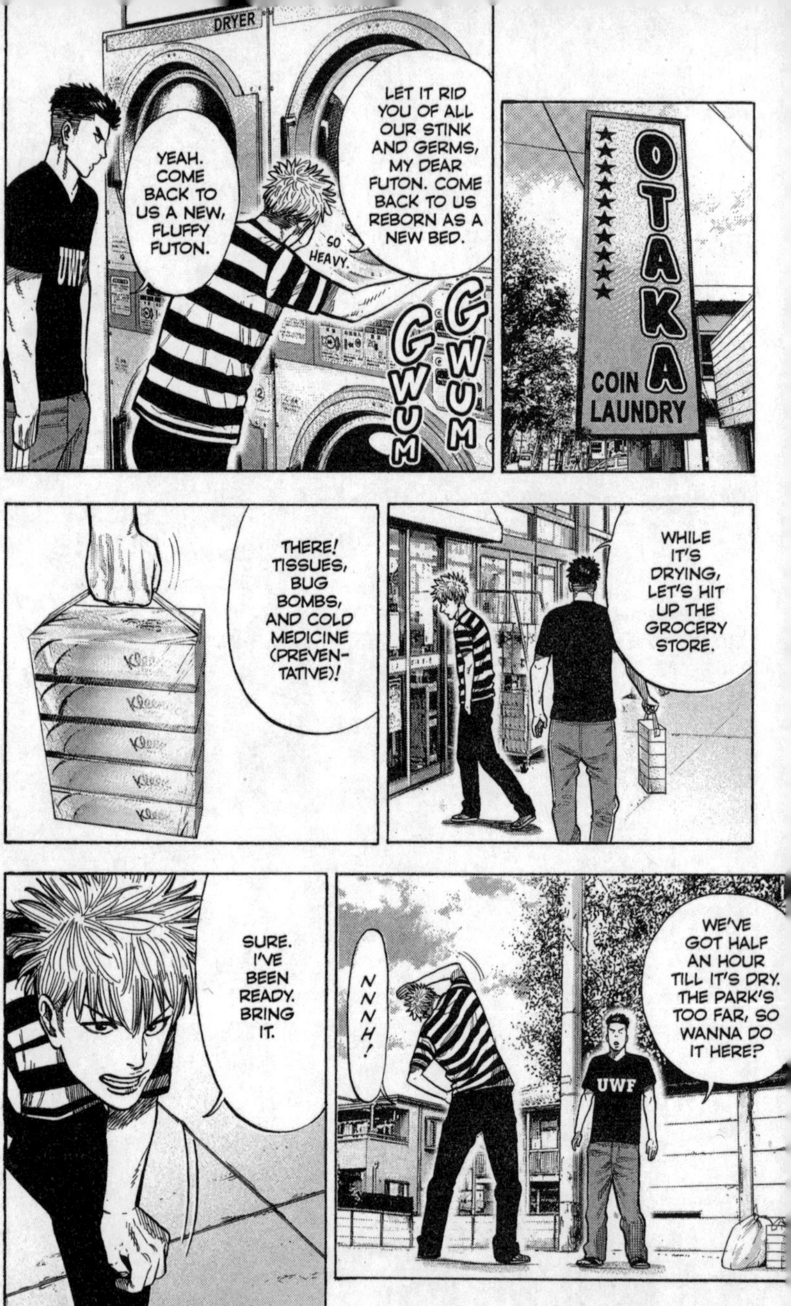
OTAKA
COIN LAUNDRY
DRYER
LET IT RID YOU OF ALL OUR STINK AND GERMS, MY DEAR FUTON. COME BACK TO US REBORN AS A NEW BED.
SO HEAVY.
GWUM
GWUM
YEAH. COME BACK TO US A NEW, FLUFFY FUTON.
WHILE IT'S DRYING, LET'S HIT UP THE GROCERY STORE.
THERE! TISSUES, BUG BOMBS, AND COLD MEDICINE (PREVENTATIVE)!
WE'VE GOT HALF AN HOUR TILL IT'S DRY. THE PARK'S TOO FAR, SO WANNA DO IT HERE?
UWF
NNNH!
SURE. I'VE BEEN READY. BRING IT.

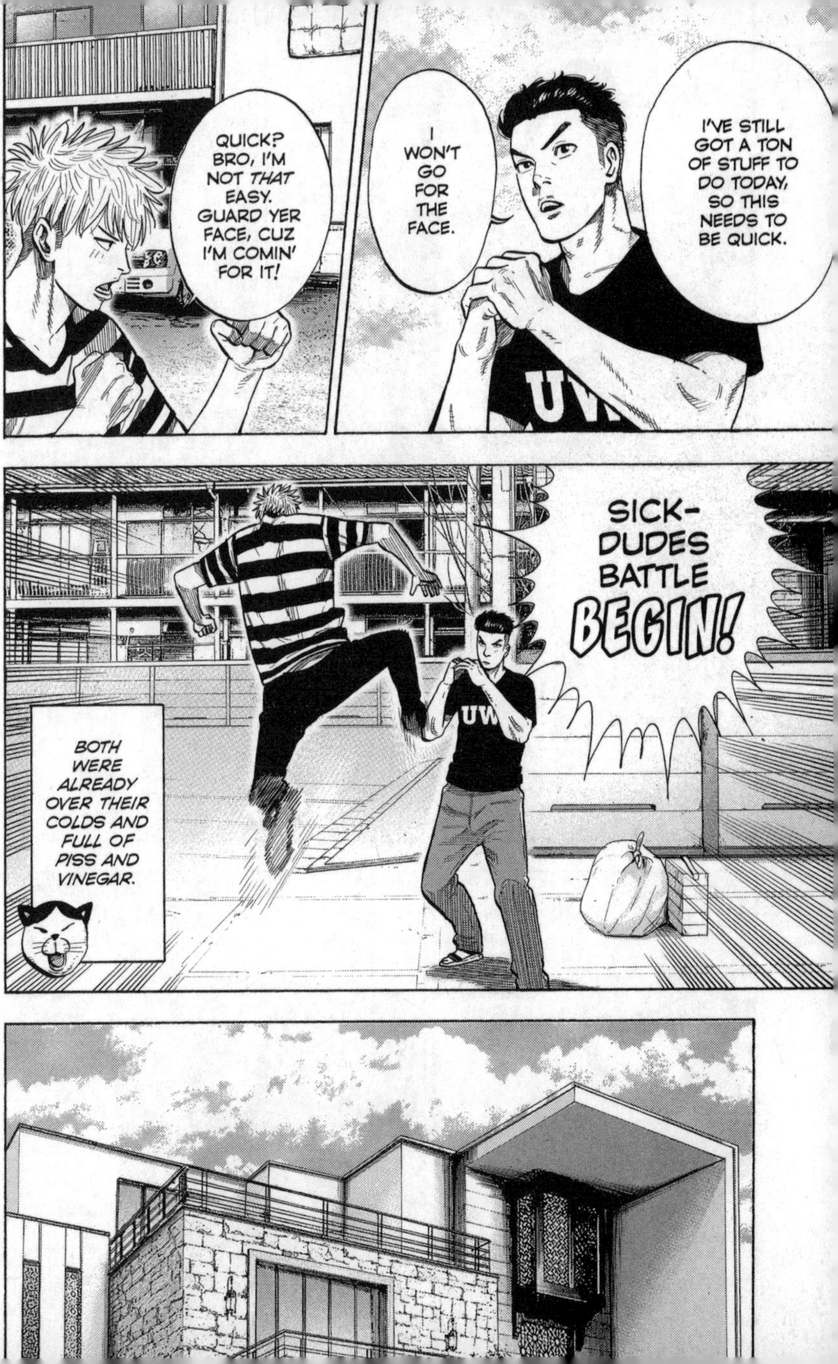
I'VE STILL GOT A TON OF STUFF TO DO TODAY, SO THIS NEEDS TO BE QUICK.
I WON'T GO FOR THE FACE.
QUICK? BRO, I'M NOT *THAT* EASY. GUARD YER FACE, CUZ I'M COMIN' FOR IT!
SICK-DUDES BATTLE BEGIN!
BOTH WERE ALREADY OVER THEIR COLDS AND FULL OF PISS AND VINEGAR.

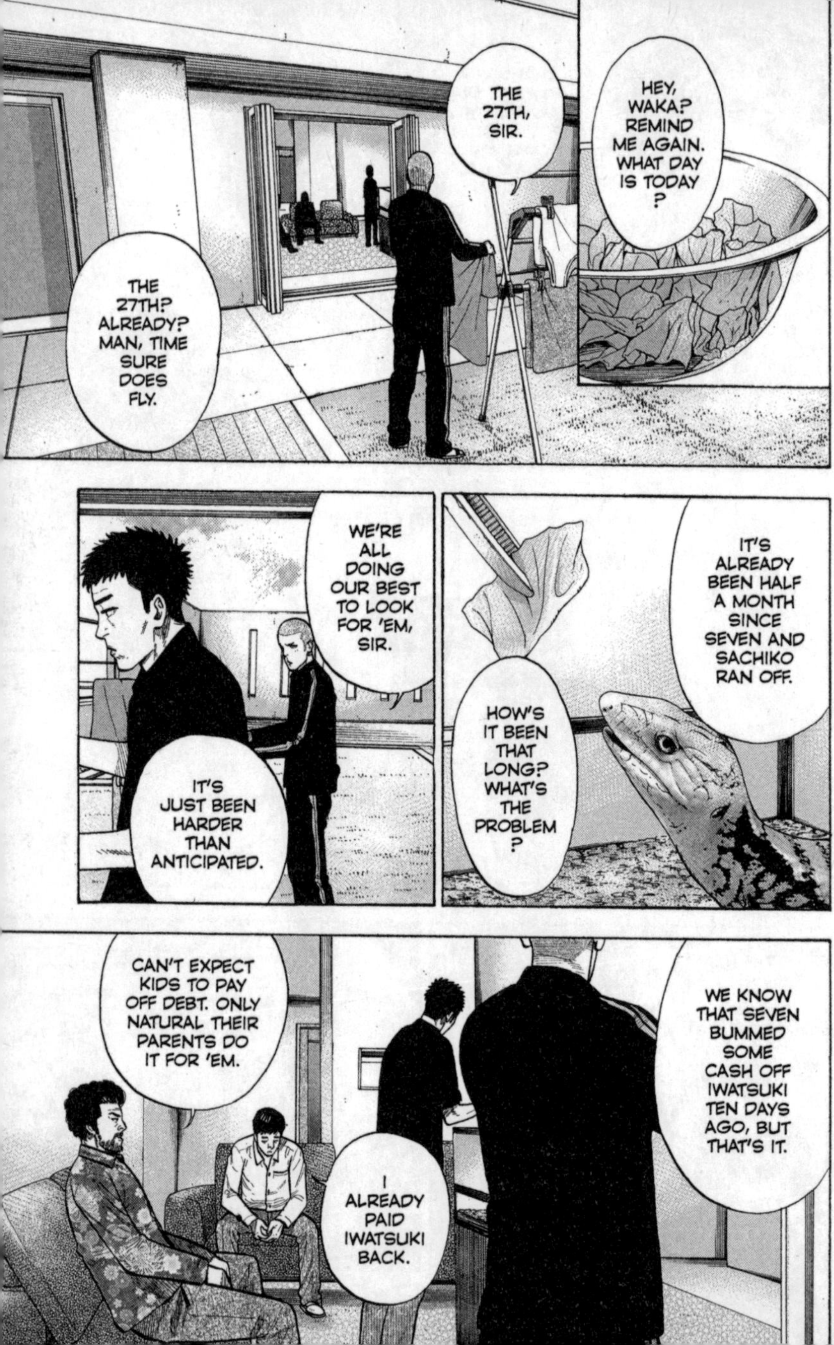
HEY, WAKA? REMIND ME AGAIN. WHAT DAY IS TODAY?
THE 27TH, SIR.
THE 27TH? ALREADY? MAN, TIME SURE DOES FLY.
IT'S ALREADY BEEN HALF A MONTH SINCE SEVEN AND SACHIKO RAN OFF.
HOW'S IT BEEN THAT LONG? WHAT'S THE PROBLEM?
WE'RE ALL DOING OUR BEST TO LOOK FOR 'EM, SIR.
IT'S JUST BEEN HARDER THAN ANTICIPATED.
WE KNOW THAT SEVEN BUMMED SOME CASH OFF IWATSUKI TEN DAYS AGO, BUT THAT'S IT.
CAN'T EXPECT KIDS TO PAY OFF DEBT. ONLY NATURAL THEIR PARENTS DO IT FOR 'EM.
I ALREADY PAID IWATSUKI BACK.

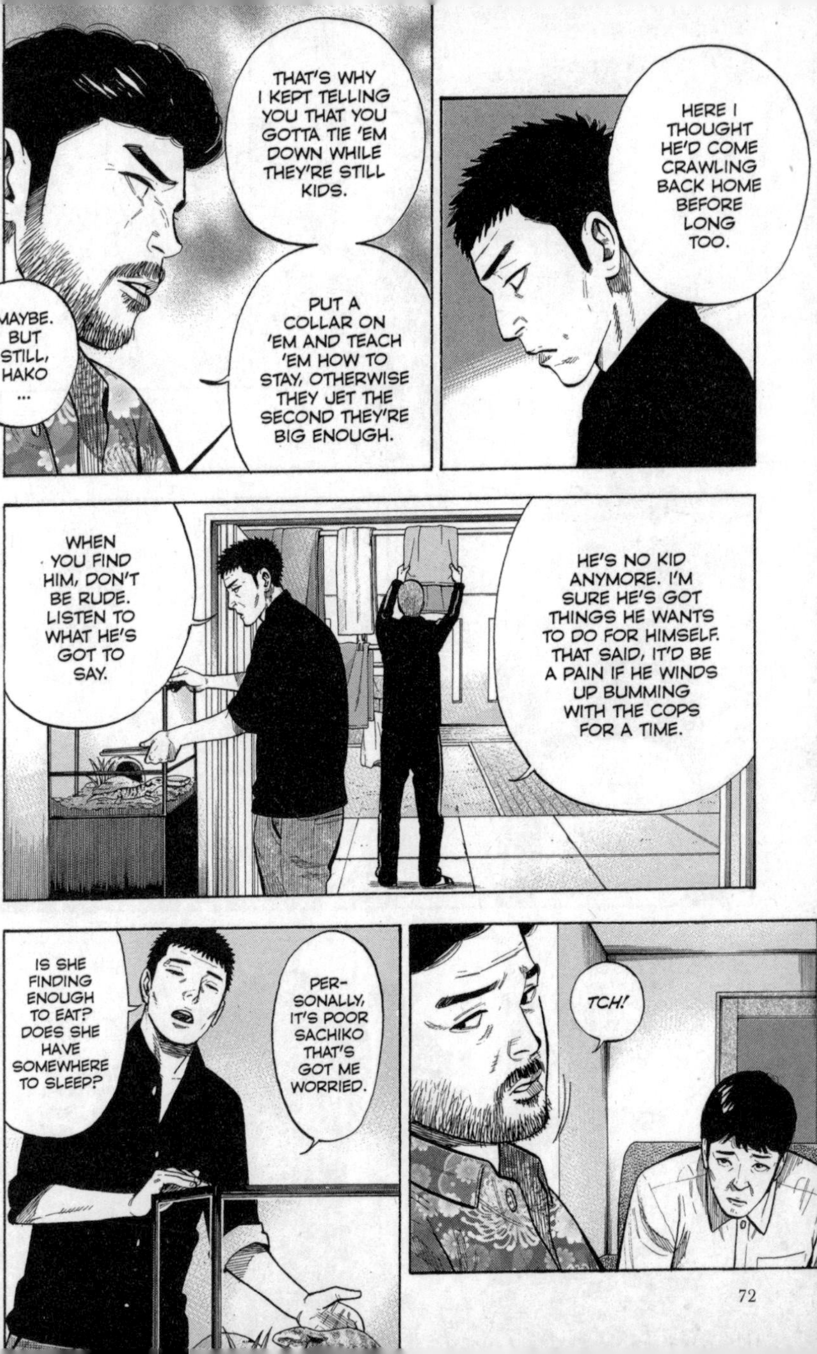
HERE I THOUGHT HE'D COME CRAWLING BACK HOME BEFORE LONG TOO.
THAT'S WHY I KEPT TELLING YOU THAT YOU GOTTA TIE 'EM DOWN WHILE THEY'RE STILL KIDS.
PUT A COLLAR ON 'EM AND TEACH 'EM HOW TO STAY, OTHERWISE THEY JET THE SECOND THEY'RE BIG ENOUGH.
MAYBE. BUT STILL, HAKO ...
HE'S NO KID ANYMORE. I'M SURE HE'S GOT THINGS HE WANTS TO DO FOR HIMSELF. THAT SAID, IT'D BE A PAIN IF HE WINDS UP BUMMING WITH THE COPS FOR A TIME.
WHEN YOU FIND HIM, DON'T BE RUDE. LISTEN TO WHAT HE'S GOT TO SAY.
TCH!
PER-SONALLY, IT'S POOR SACHIKO THAT'S GOT ME WORRIED.
IS SHE FINDING ENOUGH TO EAT? DOES SHE HAVE SOMEWHERE TO SLEEP?

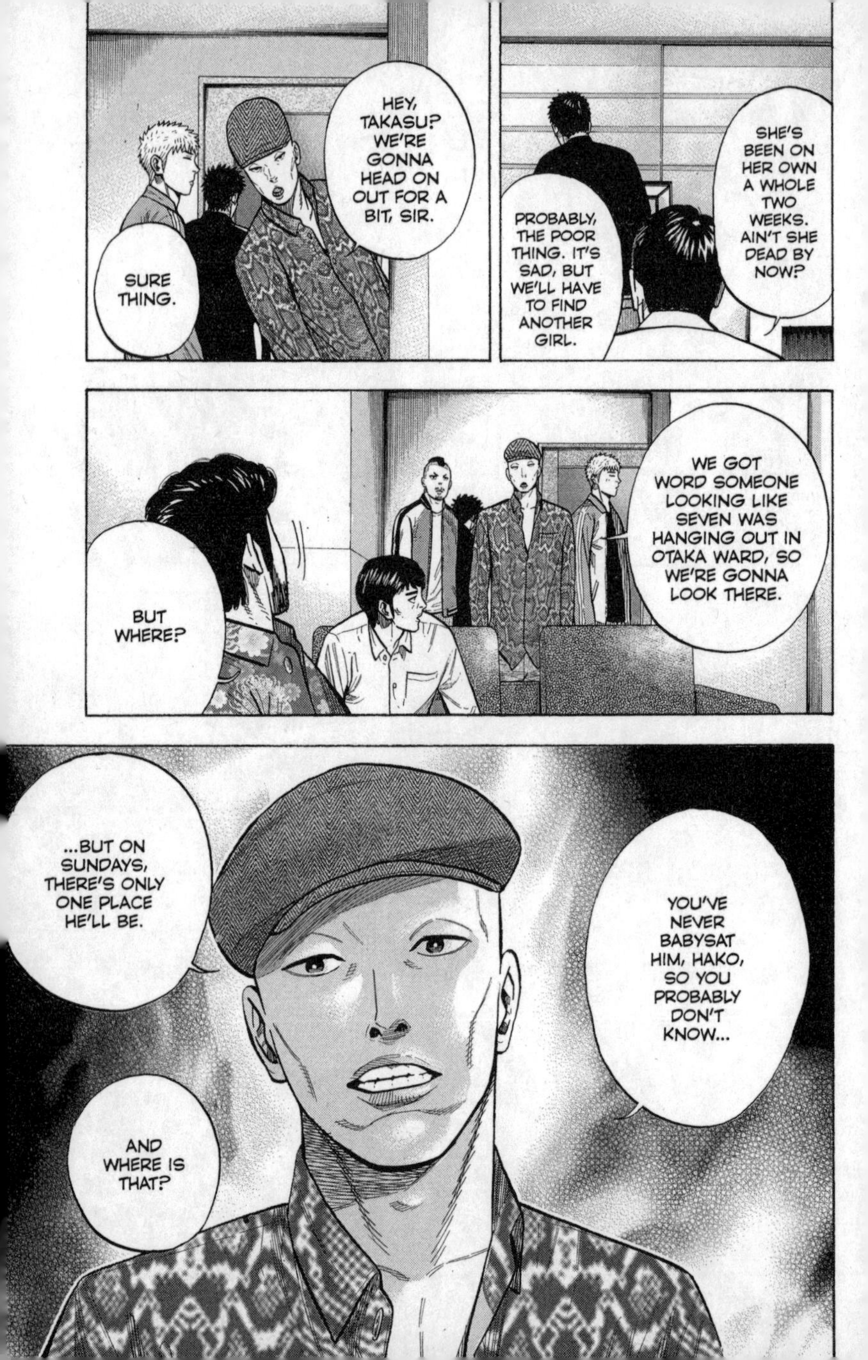
SHE'S BEEN ON HER OWN A WHOLE TWO WEEKS. AIN'T SHE DEAD BY NOW?
PROBABLY, THE POOR THING. IT'S SAD, BUT WE'LL HAVE TO FIND ANOTHER GIRL.
HEY, TAKASU? WE'RE GONNA HEAD ON OUT FOR A BIT, SIR.
SURE THING.
WE GOT WORD SOMEONE LOOKING LIKE SEVEN WAS HANGING OUT IN OTAKA WARD, SO WE'RE GONNA LOOK THERE.
BUT WHERE?
YOU'VE NEVER BABYSAT HIM, HAKO, SO YOU PROBABLY DON'T KNOW...
...BUT ON SUNDAYS, THERE'S ONLY ONE PLACE HE'LL BE.
AND WHERE IS THAT?

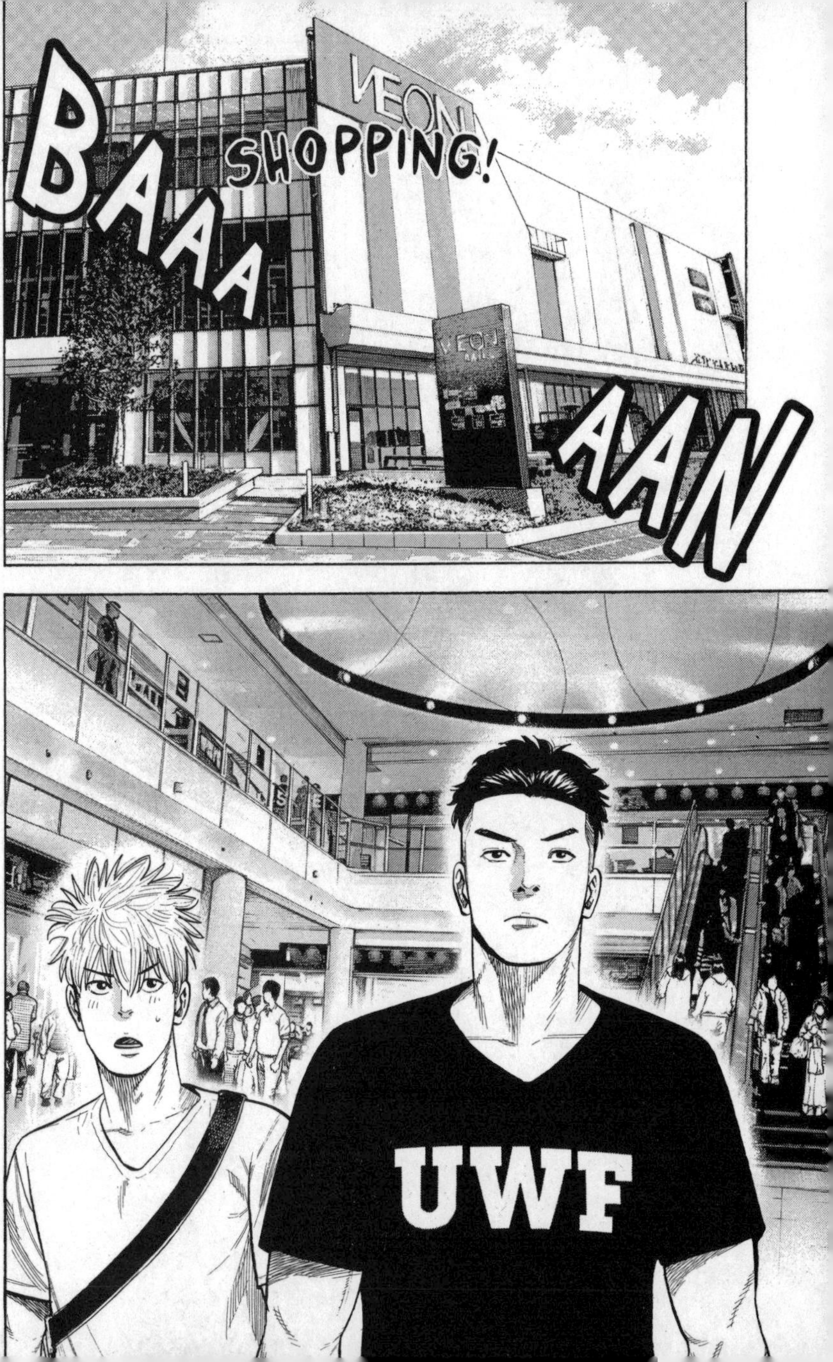
VEON
BAAA
SHOPPING!
AAN
UWF

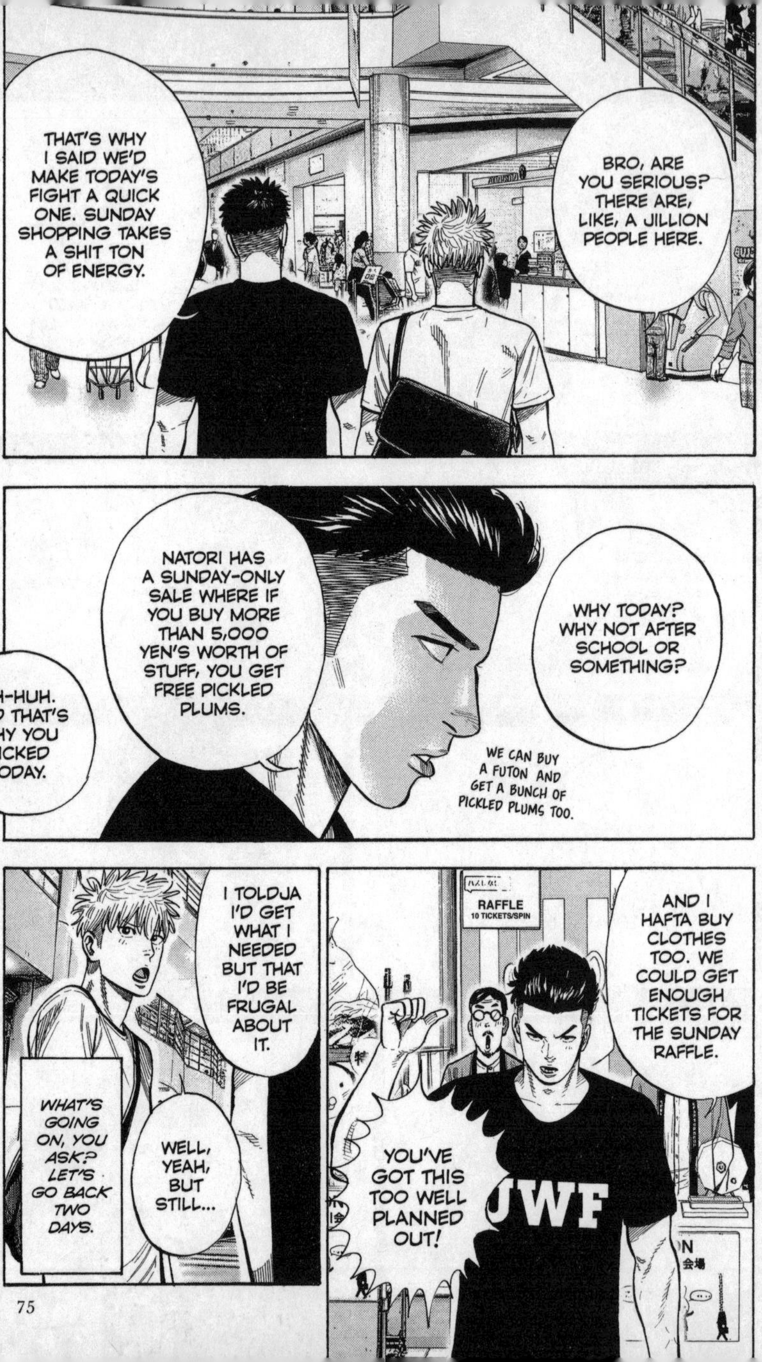
BRO, ARE YOU SERIOUS? THERE ARE, LIKE, A JILLION PEOPLE HERE.
THAT'S WHY I SAID WE'D MAKE TODAY'S FIGHT A QUICK ONE. SUNDAY SHOPPING TAKES A SHIT TON OF ENERGY.
WHY TODAY? WHY NOT AFTER SCHOOL OR SOMETHING?
NATORI HAS A SUNDAY-ONLY SALE WHERE IF YOU BUY MORE THAN 5,000 YEN'S WORTH OF STUFF, YOU GET FREE PICKLED PLUMS.
WE CAN BUY A FUTON AND GET A BUNCH OF PICKLED PLUMS TOO.
UH-HUH. AND THAT'S WHY YOU PICKED TODAY.
RAFFLE
10 TICKETS/SPIN
AND I HAFTA BUY CLOTHES TOO. WE COULD GET ENOUGH TICKETS FOR THE SUNDAY RAFFLE.
YOU'VE GOT THIS TOO WELL PLANNED OUT!
UWF
I TOLDJA I'D GET WHAT I NEEDED BUT THAT I'D BE FRUGAL ABOUT IT.
WELL, YEAH, BUT STILL...
WHAT'S GOING ON, YOU ASK? LET'S GO BACK TWO DAYS.

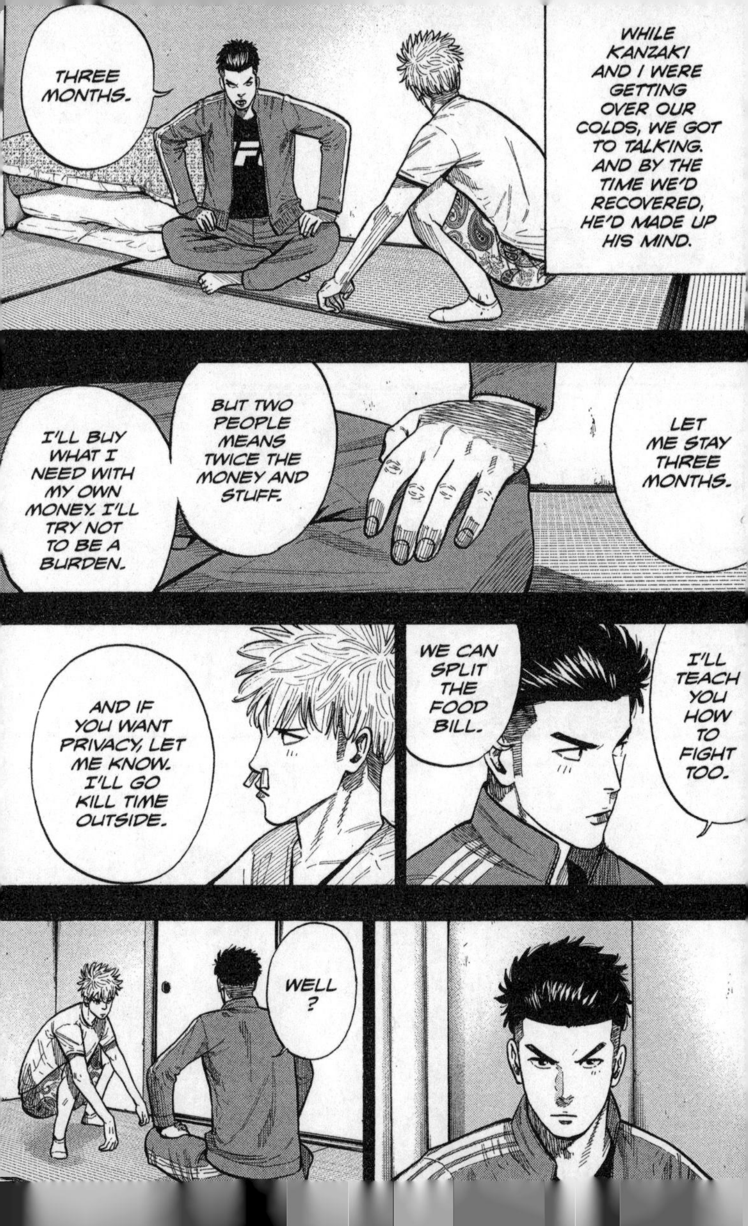
WHILE KANZAKI AND I WERE GETTING OVER OUR COLDS, WE GOT TO TALKING. AND BY THE TIME WE'D RECOVERED, HE'D MADE UP HIS MIND.
THREE MONTHS.
LET ME STAY THREE MONTHS.
BUT TWO PEOPLE MEANS TWICE THE MONEY AND STUFF.
I'LL BUY WHAT I NEED WITH MY OWN MONEY. I'LL TRY NOT TO BE A BURDEN.
I'LL TEACH YOU HOW TO FIGHT TOO.
WE CAN SPLIT THE FOOD BILL.
AND IF YOU WANT PRIVACY, LET ME KNOW. I'LL GO KILL TIME OUTSIDE.
WELL?

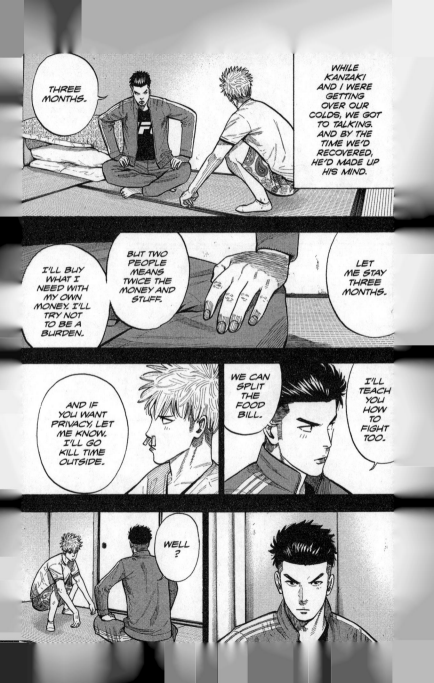

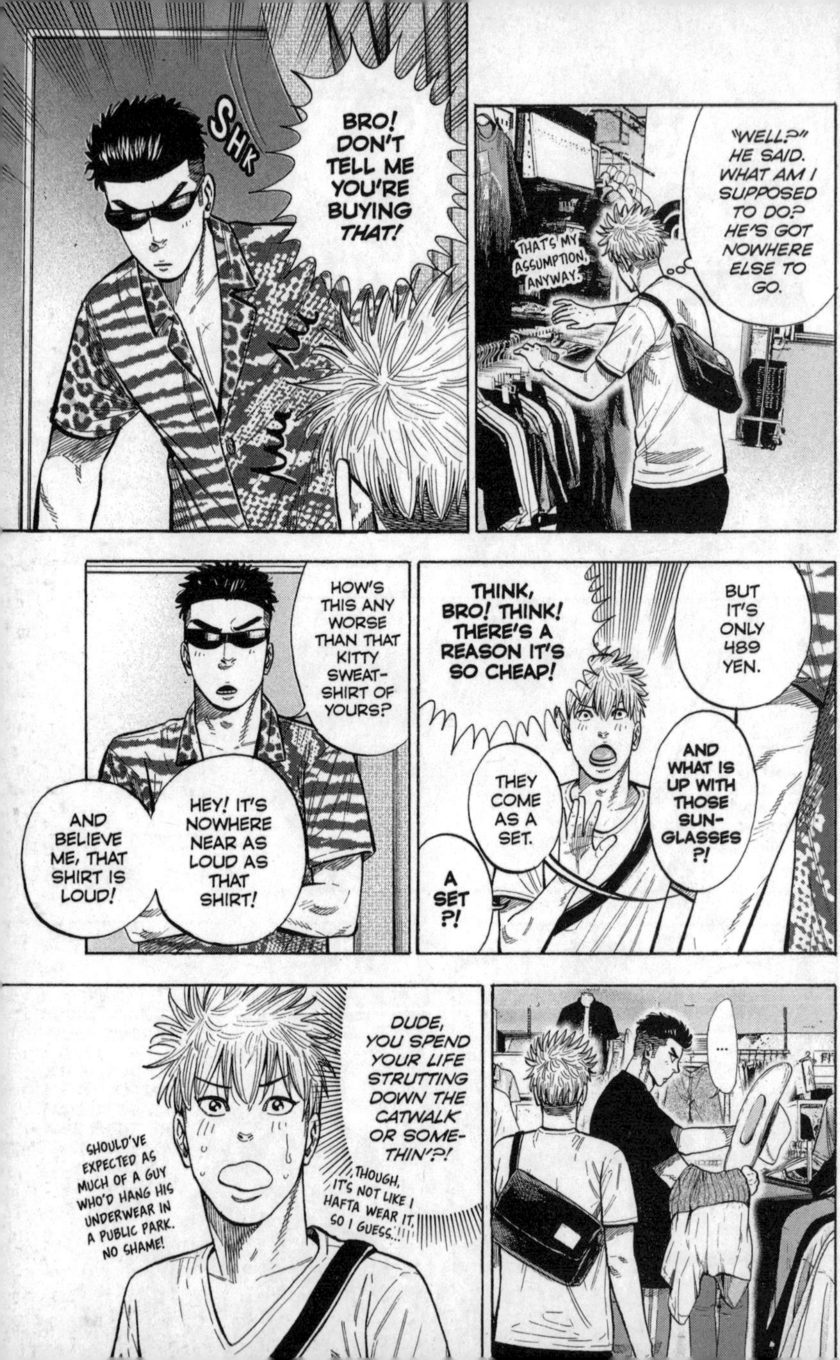
"WELL?" HE SAID. WHAT AM I SUPPOSED TO DO? HE'S GOT NOWHERE ELSE TO GO.
THAT'S MY ASSUMPTION, ANYWAY.
SHK
BRO! DON'T TELL ME YOU'RE BUYING *THAT!*
BUT IT'S ONLY 489 YEN.
THINK, BRO! THINK! THERE'S A REASON IT'S SO CHEAP!
AND WHAT IS UP WITH THOSE SUN-GLASSES ?!
THEY COME AS A SET.
A SET ?!
HOW'S THIS ANY WORSE THAN THAT KITTY SWEAT-SHIRT OF YOURS?
HEY! IT'S NOWHERE NEAR AS LOUD AS THAT SHIRT!
AND BELIEVE ME, THAT SHIRT IS LOUD!
...
DUDE, YOU SPEND YOUR LIFE STRUTTING DOWN THE CATWALK OR SOME-THIN'?!
THOUGH, IT'S NOT LIKE I HAFTA WEAR IT, SO I GUESS...
SHOULD'VE EXPECTED AS MUCH OF A GUY WHO'D HANG HIS UNDERWEAR IN A PUBLIC PARK. NO SHAME!

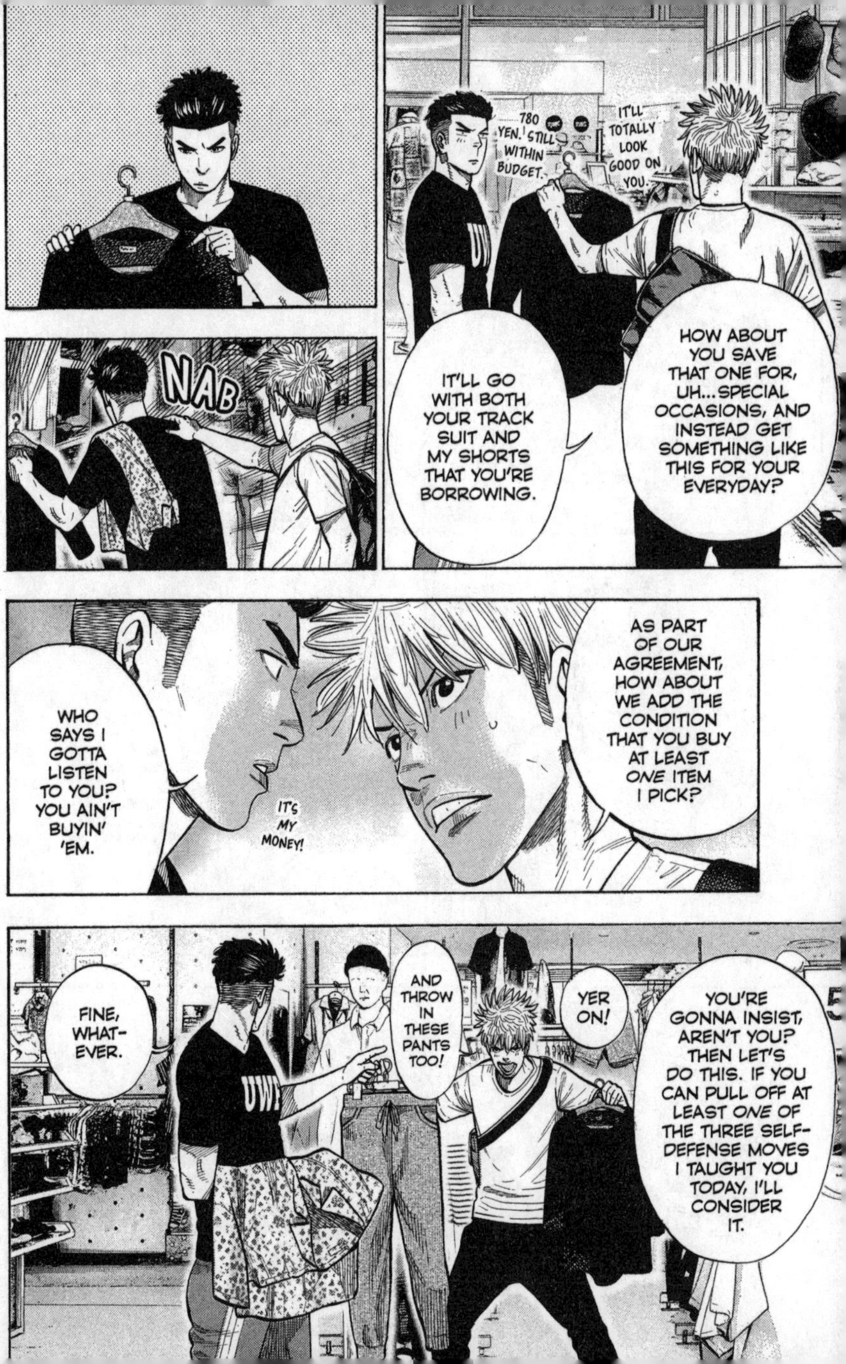
IT'LL TOTALLY LOOK GOOD ON YOU.
780 YEN. STILL WITHIN BUDGET.
HOW ABOUT YOU SAVE THAT ONE FOR, UH...SPECIAL OCCASIONS, AND INSTEAD GET SOMETHING LIKE THIS FOR YOUR EVERYDAY?
IT'LL GO WITH BOTH YOUR TRACK SUIT AND MY SHORTS THAT YOU'RE BORROWING.
NAB
AS PART OF OUR AGREEMENT, HOW ABOUT WE ADD THE CONDITION THAT YOU BUY AT LEAST *ONE* ITEM I PICK?
IT'S MY MONEY!
WHO SAYS I GOTTA LISTEN TO YOU? YOU AIN'T BUYIN' 'EM.
YOU'RE GONNA INSIST, AREN'T YOU? THEN LET'S DO THIS. IF YOU CAN PULL OFF AT LEAST *ONE* OF THE THREE SELF-DEFENSE MOVES I TAUGHT YOU TODAY, I'LL CONSIDER IT.
YER ON!
AND THROW IN THESE PANTS TOO!
FINE, WHATEVER.

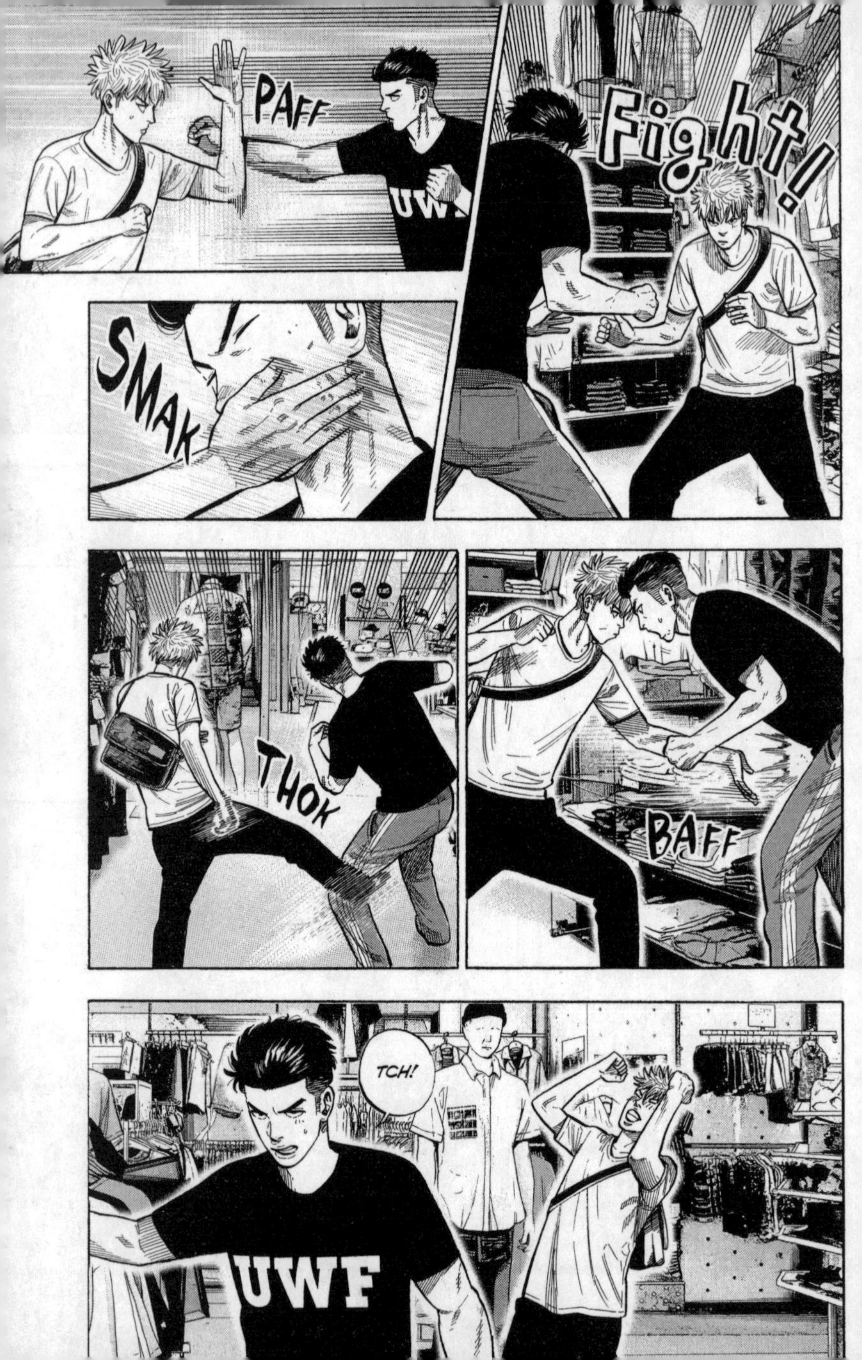
Fight!
PAFF
SMAK
BAFF
THOK
TCH!
UWF

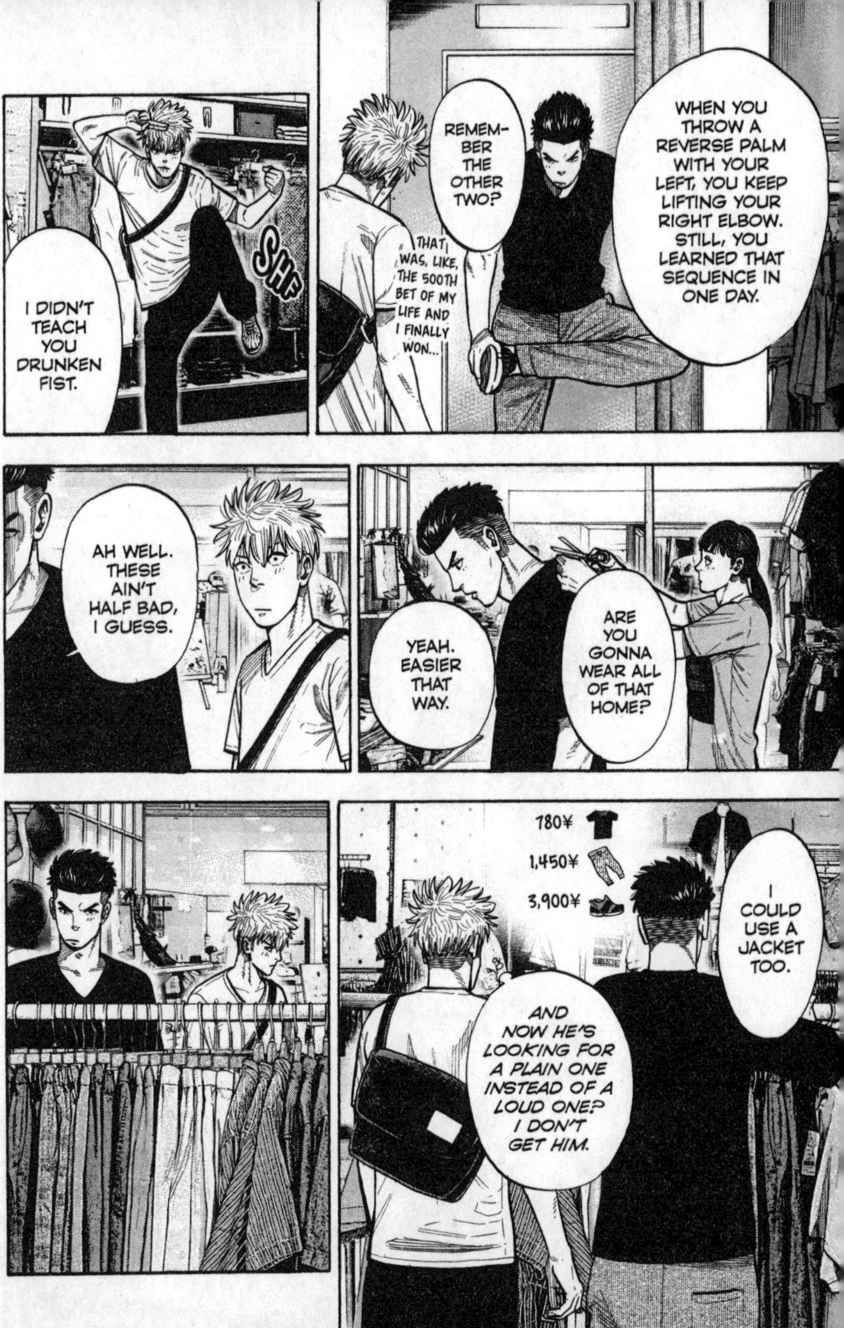
WHEN YOU THROW A REVERSE PALM WITH YOUR LEFT, YOU KEEP LIFTING YOUR RIGHT ELBOW. STILL, YOU LEARNED THAT SEQUENCE IN ONE DAY.
REMEMBER THE OTHER TWO?
THAT WAS, LIKE, THE 500TH BET OF MY LIFE AND I FINALLY WON...
SHF
I DIDN'T TEACH YOU DRUNKEN FIST.
ARE YOU GONNA WEAR ALL OF THAT HOME?
YEAH. EASIER THAT WAY.
AH WELL. THESE AIN'T HALF BAD, I GUESS.
I COULD USE A JACKET TOO.
780¥
1,450¥
3,900¥
AND NOW HE'S LOOKING FOR A PLAIN ONE INSTEAD OF A LOUD ONE? I DON'T GET HIM.

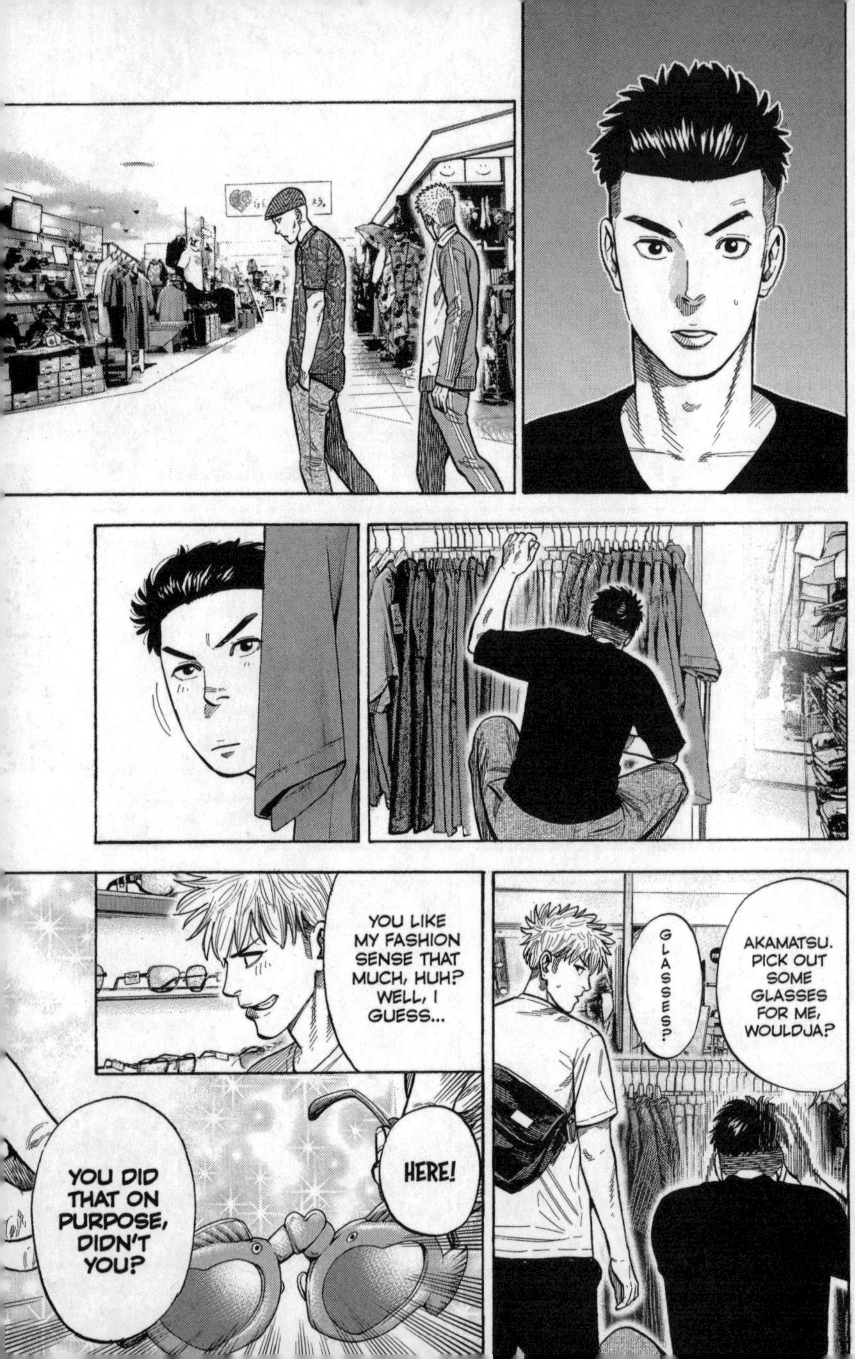
AKAMATSU. PICK OUT SOME GLASSES FOR ME, WOULDJA?
GLASSES?
YOU LIKE MY FASHION SENSE THAT MUCH, HUH? WELL, I GUESS...
HERE!
YOU DID THAT ON PURPOSE, DIDN'T YOU?

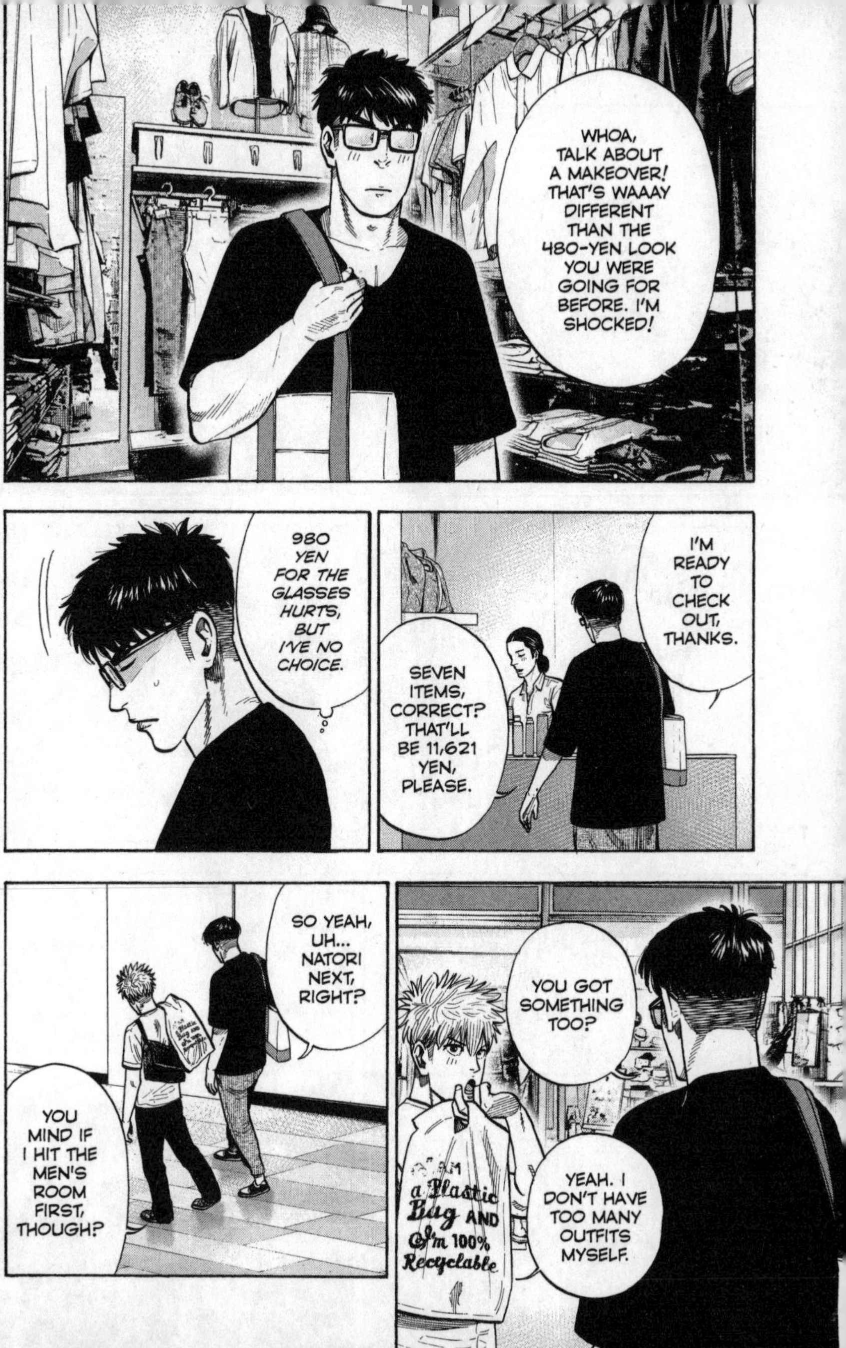
WHOA, TALK ABOUT A MAKEOVER! THAT'S WAAAY DIFFERENT THAN THE 480-YEN LOOK YOU WERE GOING FOR BEFORE. I'M SHOCKED!
I'M READY TO CHECK OUT, THANKS.
SEVEN ITEMS, CORRECT? THAT'LL BE 11,621 YEN, PLEASE.
980 YEN FOR THE GLASSES HURTS, BUT I'VE NO CHOICE.
YOU GOT SOMETHING TOO?
YEAH. I DON'T HAVE TOO MANY OUTFITS MYSELF.
a Plastic Bag AND I'm 100% Recyclable
SO YEAH, UH... NATORI NEXT, RIGHT?
YOU MIND IF I HIT THE MEN'S ROOM FIRST, THOUGH?

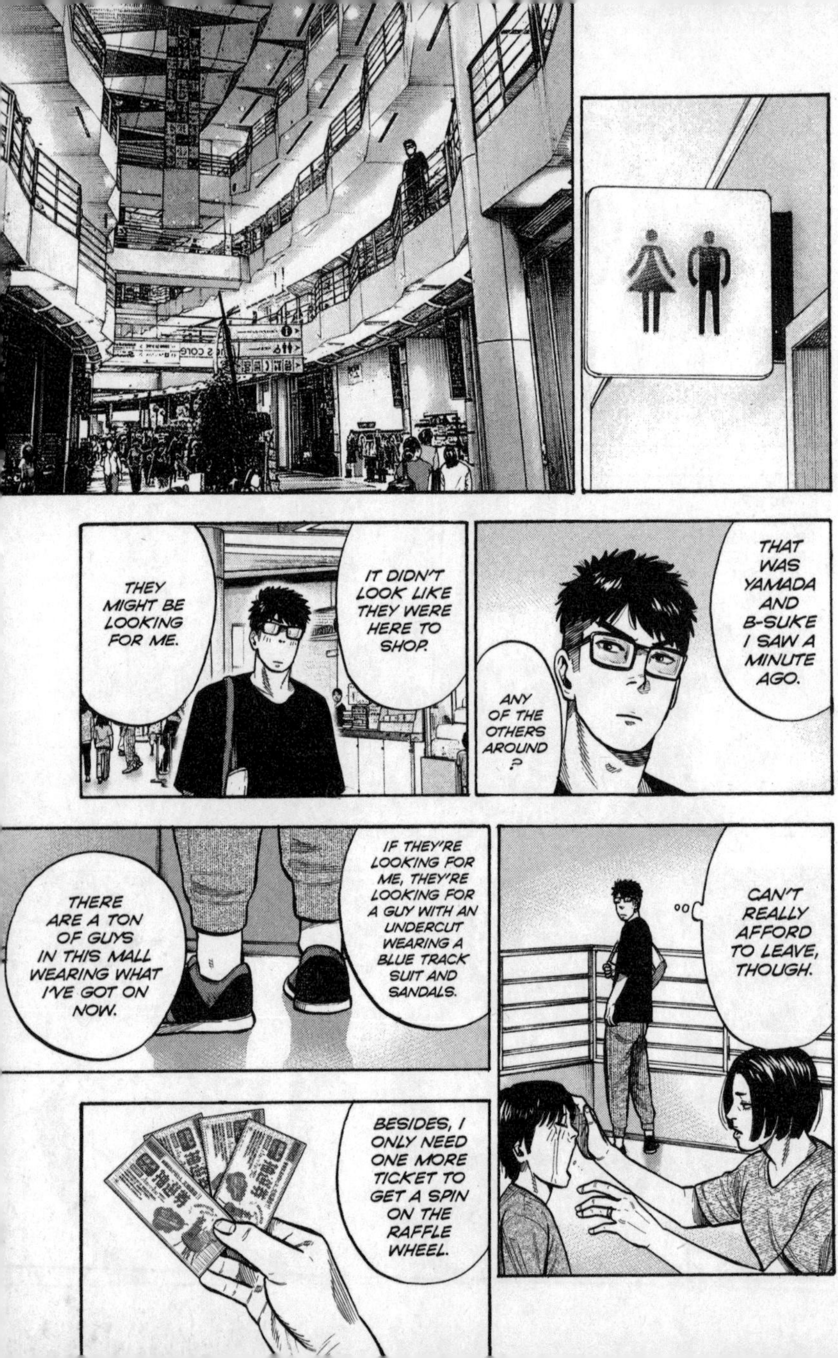
THAT WAS YAMADA AND B-SUKE I SAW A MINUTE AGO.
ANY OF THE OTHERS AROUND?
IT DIDN'T LOOK LIKE THEY WERE HERE TO SHOP.
THEY MIGHT BE LOOKING FOR ME.
CAN'T REALLY AFFORD TO LEAVE, THOUGH.
IF THEY'RE LOOKING FOR ME, THEY'RE LOOKING FOR A GUY WITH AN UNDERCUT WEARING A BLUE TRACK SUIT AND SANDALS.
THERE ARE A TON OF GUYS IN THIS MALL WEARING WHAT I'VE GOT ON NOW.
BESIDES, I ONLY NEED ONE MORE TICKET TO GET A SPIN ON THE RAFFLE WHEEL.

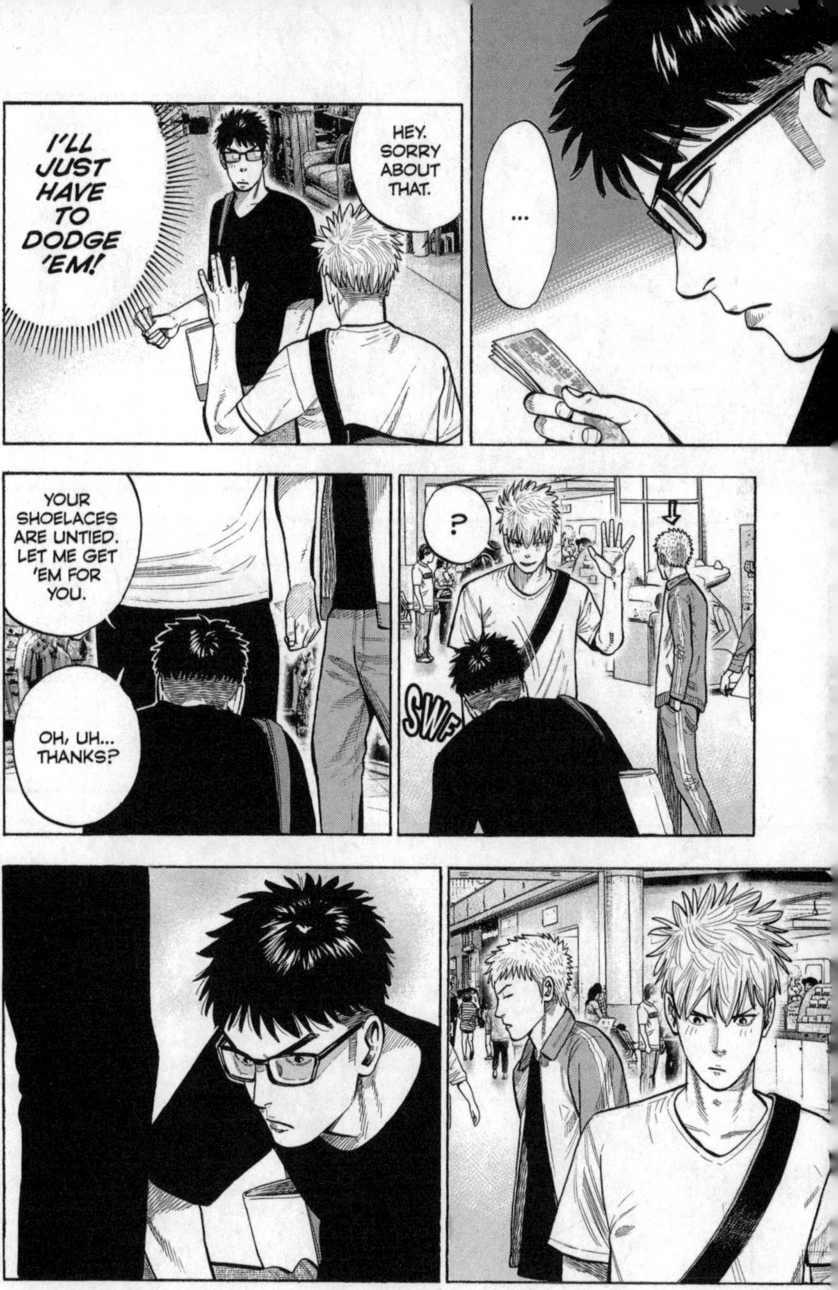
...
HEY. SORRY ABOUT THAT.
I'LL JUST HAVE TO DODGE 'EM!
?
SWF
YOUR SHOELACES ARE UNTIED. LET ME GET 'EM FOR YOU.
OH, UH... THANKS?

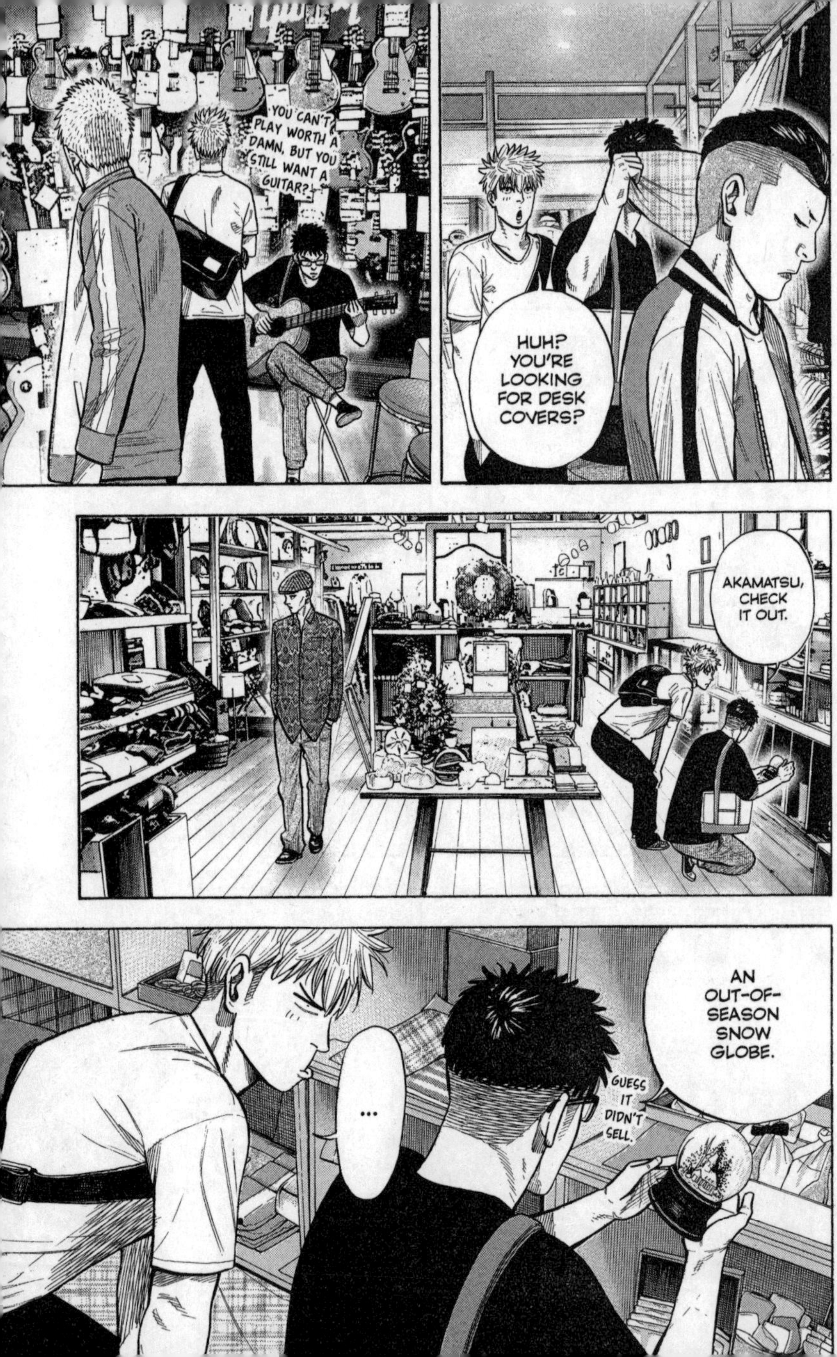
HUH? YOU'RE LOOKING FOR DESK COVERS?
YOU CAN'T PLAY WORTH A DAMN, BUT YOU STILL WANT A GUITAR?
AKAMATSU, CHECK IT OUT.
AN OUT-OF-SEASON SNOW GLOBE.
GUESS IT DIDN'T SELL.
...

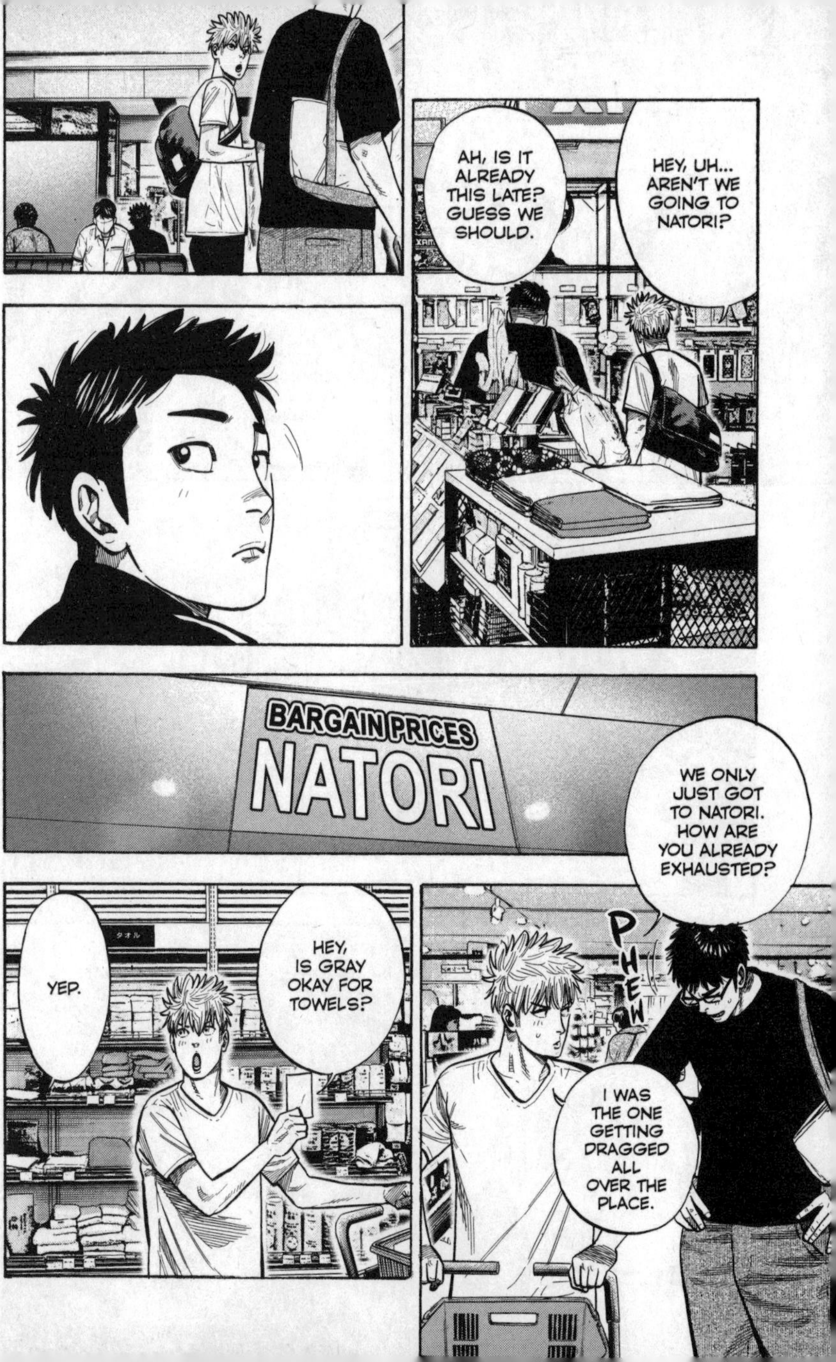
HEY, UH... AREN'T WE GOING TO NATORI?
AH, IS IT ALREADY THIS LATE? GUESS WE SHOULD.
BARGAIN PRICES
NATORI
WE ONLY JUST GOT TO NATORI. HOW ARE YOU ALREADY EXHAUSTED?
PHEW
I WAS THE ONE GETTING DRAGGED ALL OVER THE PLACE.
HEY, IS GRAY OKAY FOR TOWELS?
タオル
YEP.

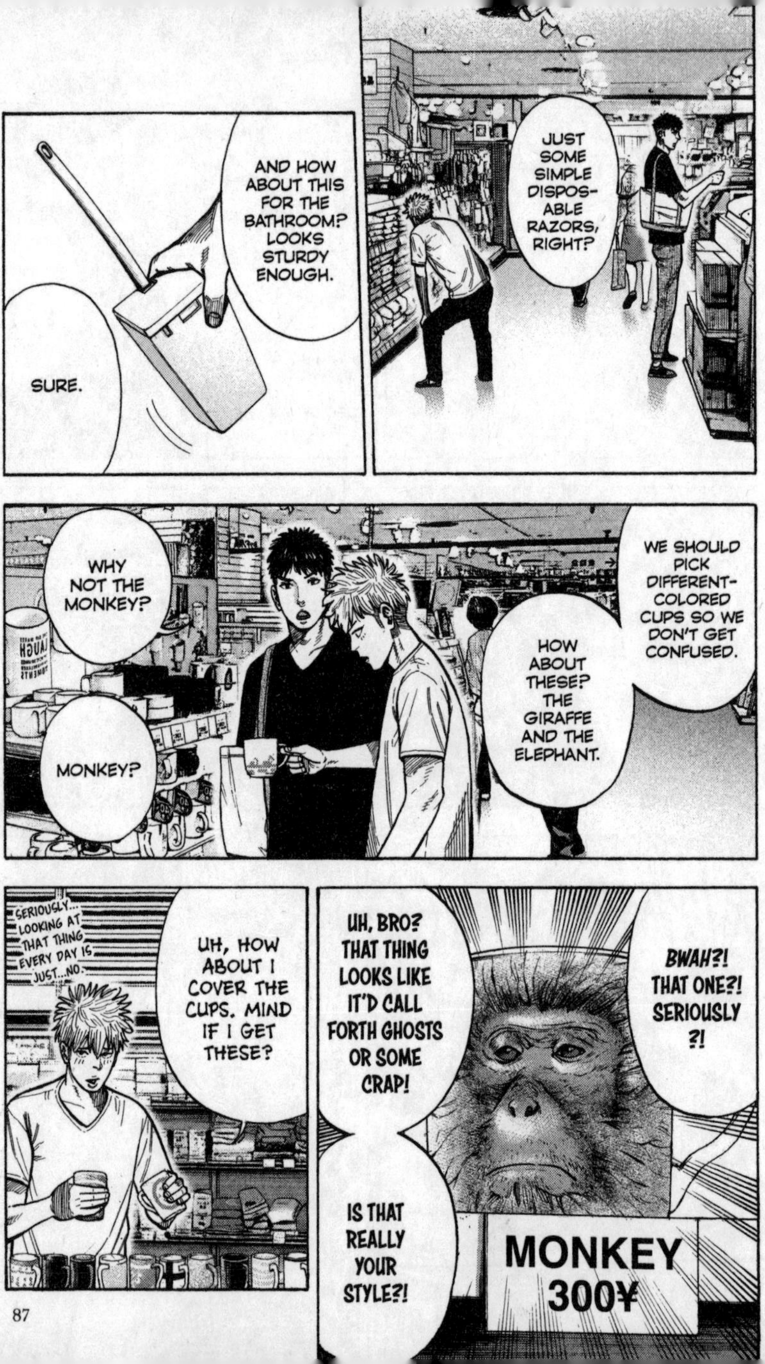

JUST SOME SIMPLE DISPOS-ABLE RAZORS, RIGHT?
AND HOW ABOUT THIS FOR THE BATHROOM? LOOKS STURDY ENOUGH.
SURE.
WE SHOULD PICK DIFFERENT-COLORED CUPS SO WE DON'T GET CONFUSED.
HOW ABOUT THESE? THE GIRAFFE AND THE ELEPHANT.
WHY NOT THE MONKEY?
MONKEY?
BWAH?! THAT ONE?! SERIOUSLY ?!
UH, BRO? THAT THING LOOKS LIKE IT'D CALL FORTH GHOSTS OR SOME CRAP!
IS THAT REALLY YOUR STYLE?!
MONKEY 300¥
UH, HOW ABOUT I COVER THE CUPS. MIND IF I GET THESE?
SERIOUSLY... LOOKING AT THAT THING EVERY DAY IS JUST...NO.

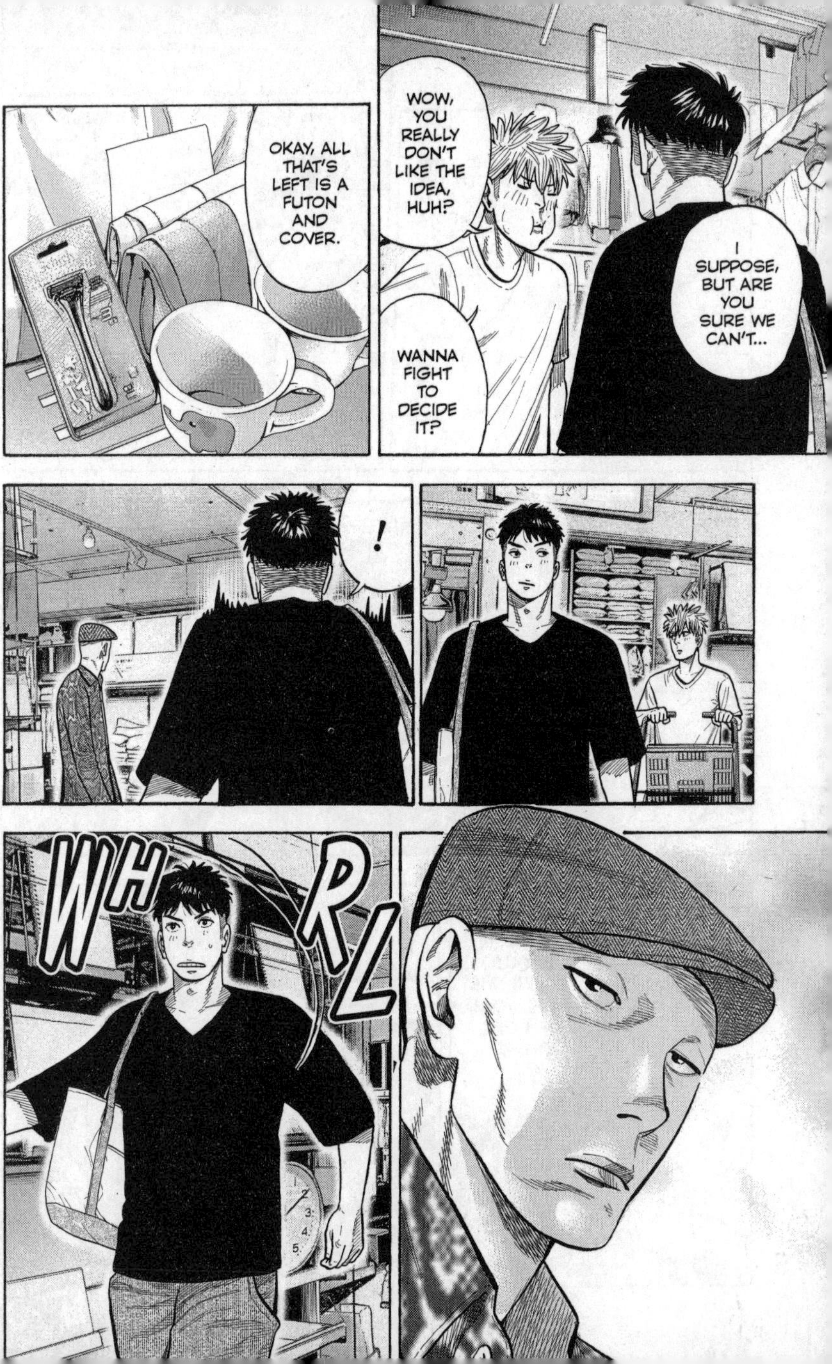
I SUPPOSE, BUT ARE YOU SURE WE CAN'T...
WOW, YOU REALLY DON'T LIKE THE IDEA, HUH?
WANNA FIGHT TO DECIDE IT?
OKAY, ALL THAT'S LEFT IS A FUTON AND COVER.
!
WHRL

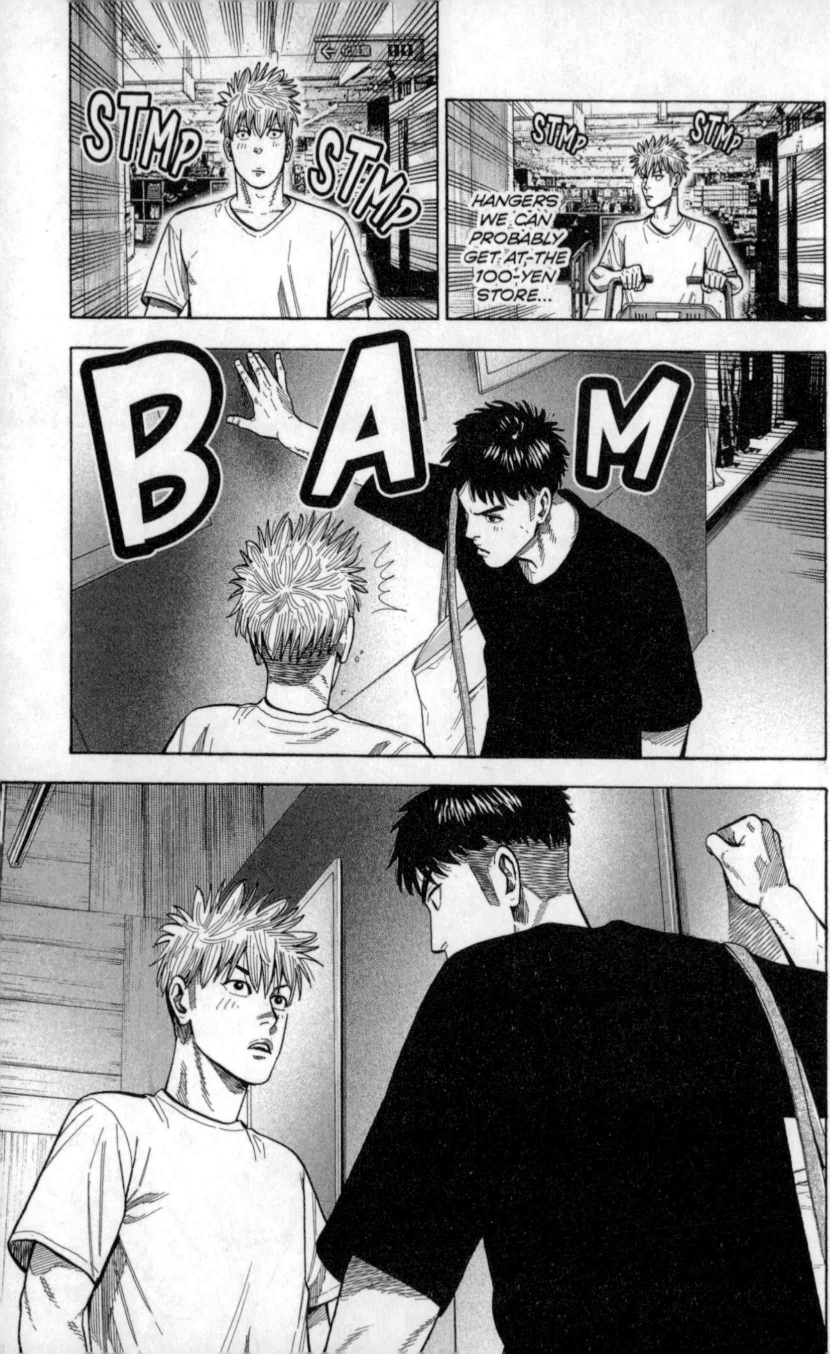
STMP
STMP
HANGERS WE CAN PROBABLY GET AT THE 100-YEN STORE...
STMP
STMP
BAM

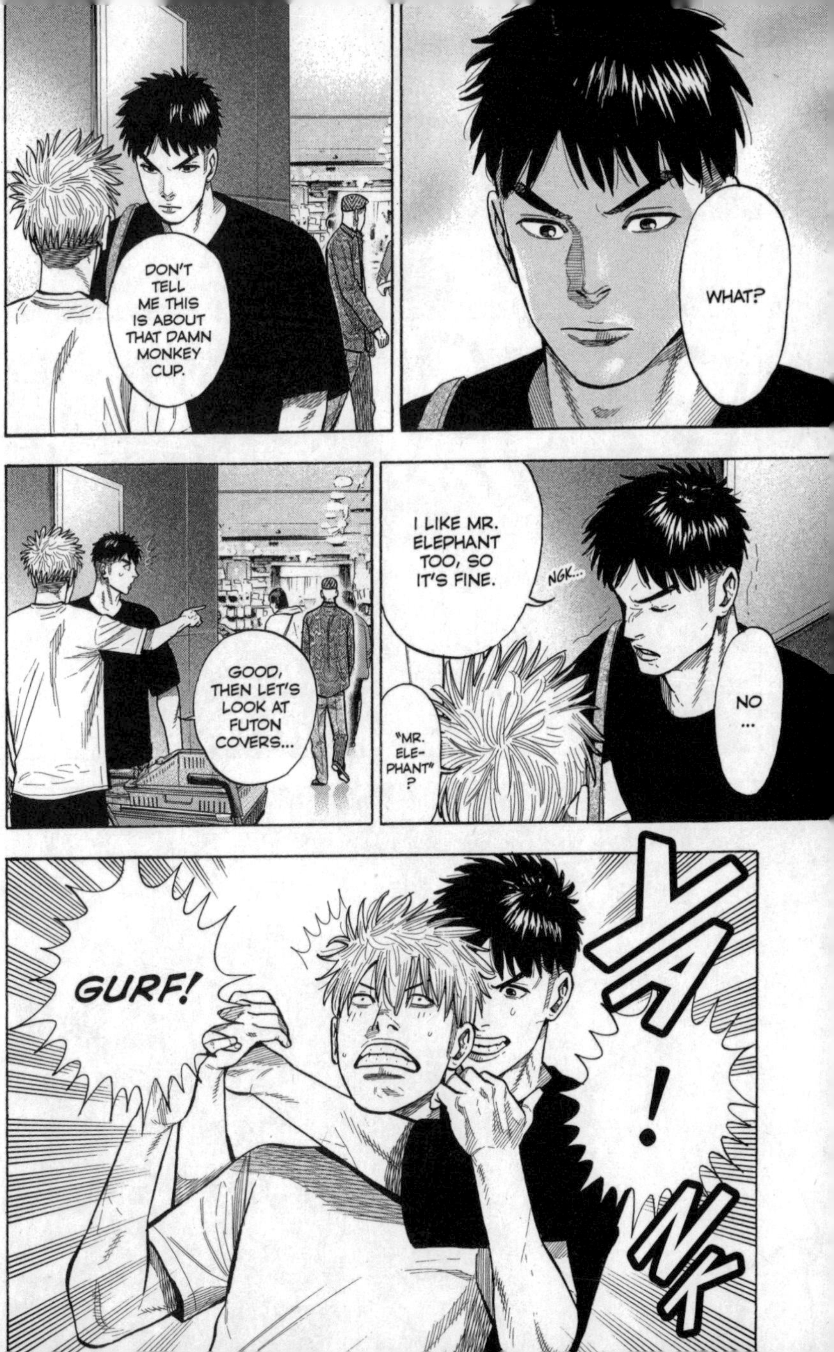
WHAT?
DON'T TELL ME THIS IS ABOUT THAT DAMN MONKEY CUP.
I LIKE MR. ELEPHANT TOO, SO IT'S FINE.
NGK...
NO ...
"MR. ELEPHANT"?
GOOD, THEN LET'S LOOK AT FUTON COVERS...
YANK!
GURF!

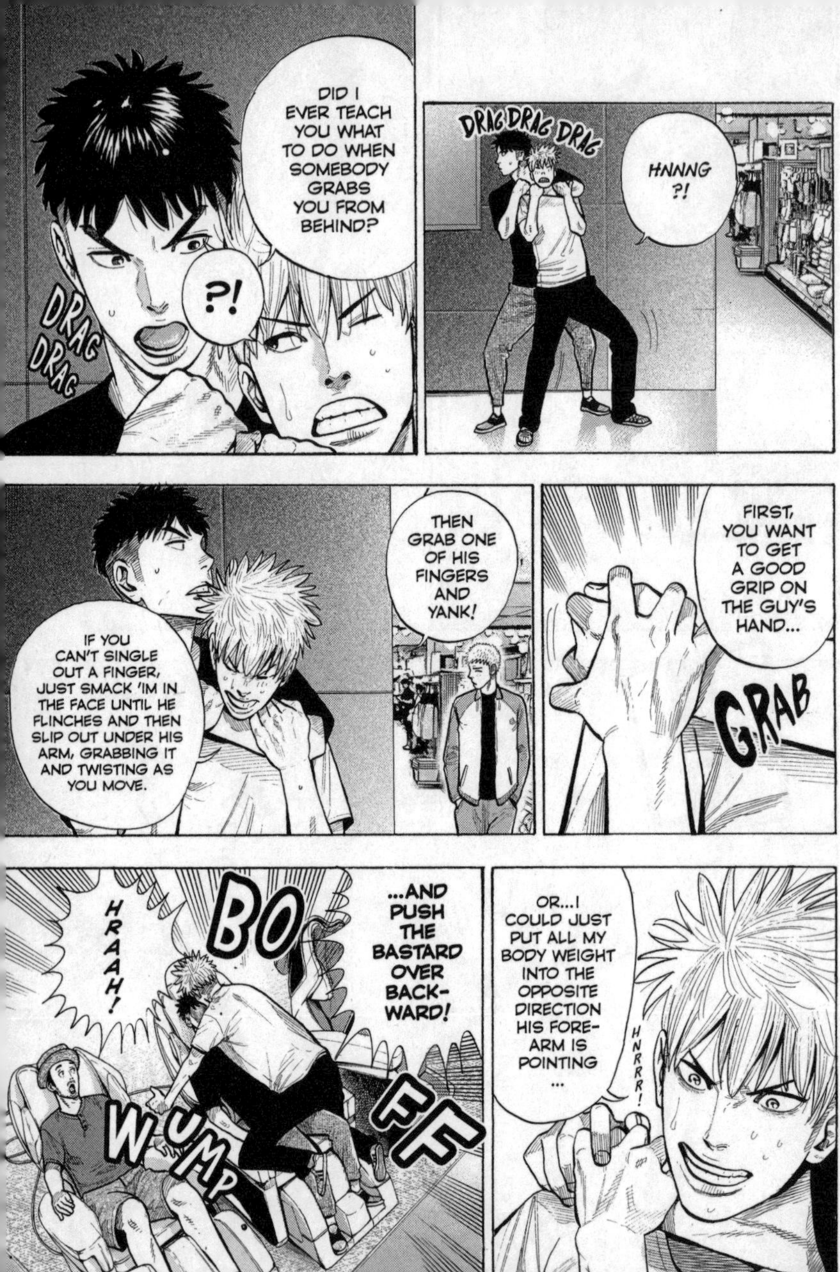
DRAG DRAG DRAG
HNNNG ?!
DID I EVER TEACH YOU WHAT TO DO WHEN SOMEBODY GRABS YOU FROM BEHIND?
?!
DRAG DRAG
FIRST, YOU WANT TO GET A GOOD GRIP ON THE GUY'S HAND...
GRAB
THEN GRAB ONE OF HIS FINGERS AND YANK!
IF YOU CAN'T SINGLE OUT A FINGER, JUST SMACK 'IM IN THE FACE UNTIL HE FLINCHES AND THEN SLIP OUT UNDER HIS ARM, GRABBING IT AND TWISTING AS YOU MOVE.
OR...I COULD JUST PUT ALL MY BODY WEIGHT INTO THE OPPOSITE DIRECTION HIS FORE-ARM IS POINTING ...
HNRRR!
...AND PUSH THE BASTARD OVER BACK-WARD!
HRAAAH!
BOFF
WUMP

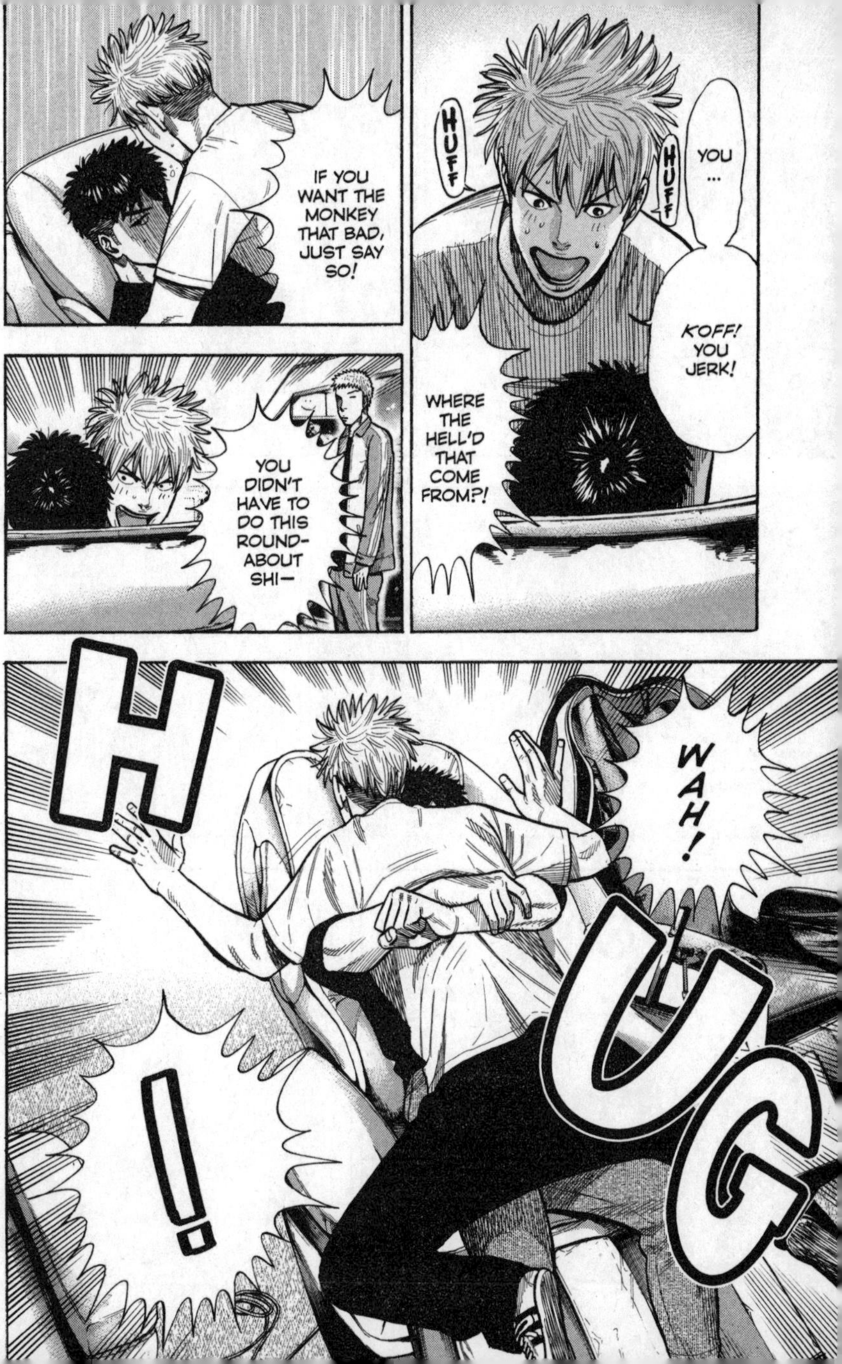
HUFF
HUFF
YOU ...
KOFF! YOU JERK!
WHERE THE HELL'D THAT COME FROM?!
IF YOU WANT THE MONKEY THAT BAD, JUST SAY SO!
YOU DIDN'T HAVE TO DO THIS ROUND-ABOUT SHI—
WAH!
HUG!

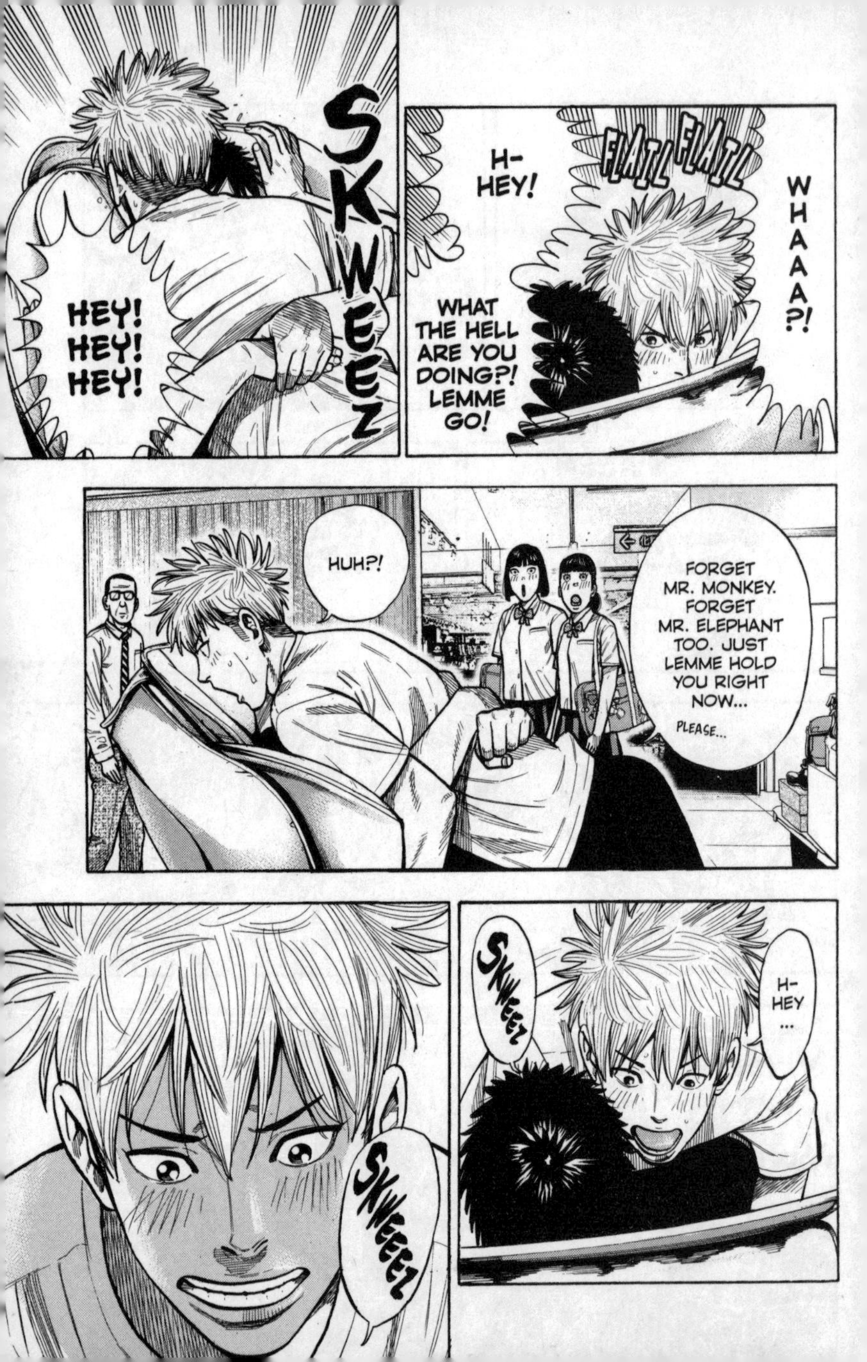
FLATL FLATL
WHAAAA?!
H-HEY!
WHAT THE HELL ARE YOU DOING?! LEMME GO!
SKWEEZ
HEY! HEY! HEY!
FORGET MR. MONKEY. FORGET MR. ELEPHANT TOO. JUST LEMME HOLD YOU RIGHT NOW...
PLEASE...
HUH?!
H-HEY...
SKWEEZ
SKWEEEZ

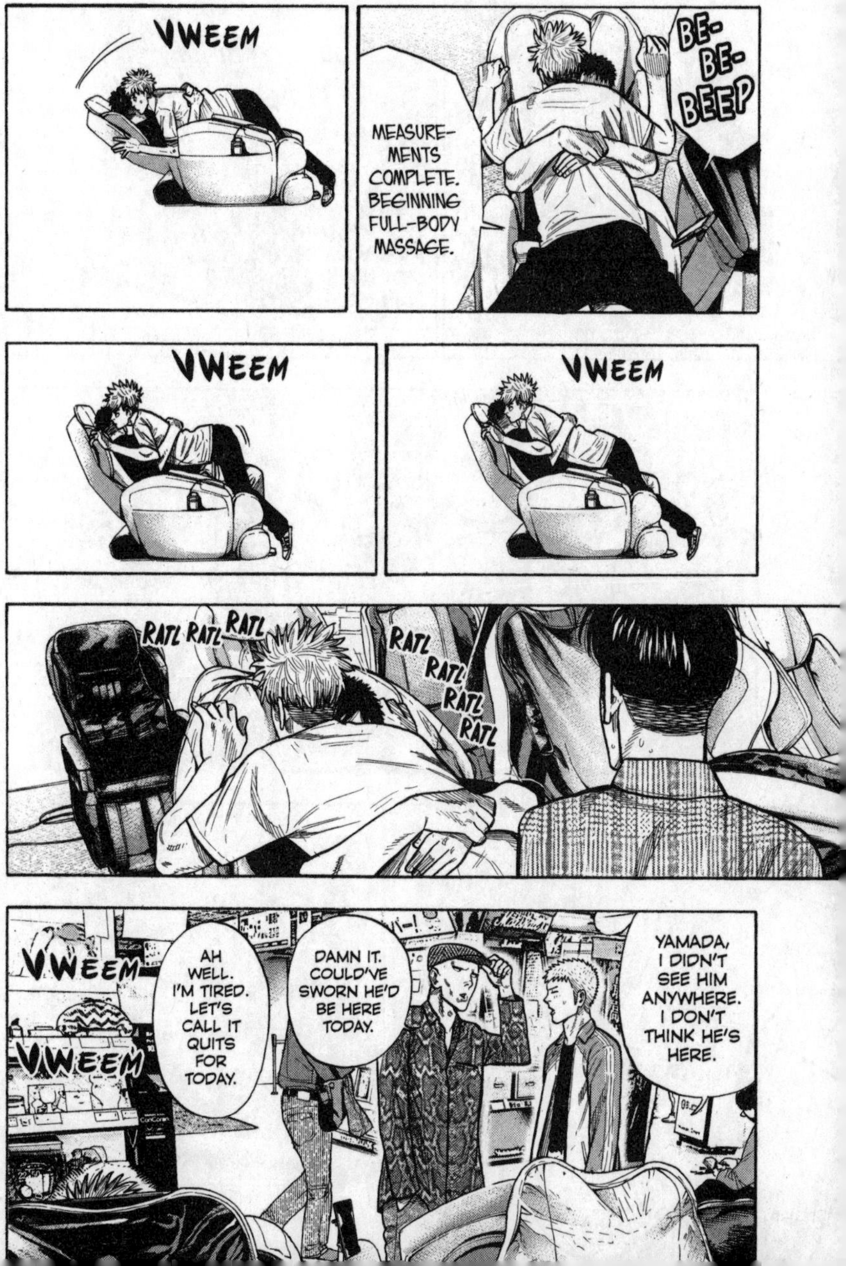
BE-
BE-
BEEP
MEASUREMENTS COMPLETE. BEGINNING FULL-BODY MASSAGE.
VWEEM
VWEEM
VWEEM
RATL RATL RATL
RATL
RATL
RATL
RATL
YAMADA, I DIDN'T SEE HIM ANYWHERE. I DON'T THINK HE'S HERE.
DAMN IT. COULD'VE SWORN HE'D BE HERE TODAY.
AH WELL. I'M TIRED. LET'S CALL IT QUITS FOR TODAY.
VWEEM
VWEEM

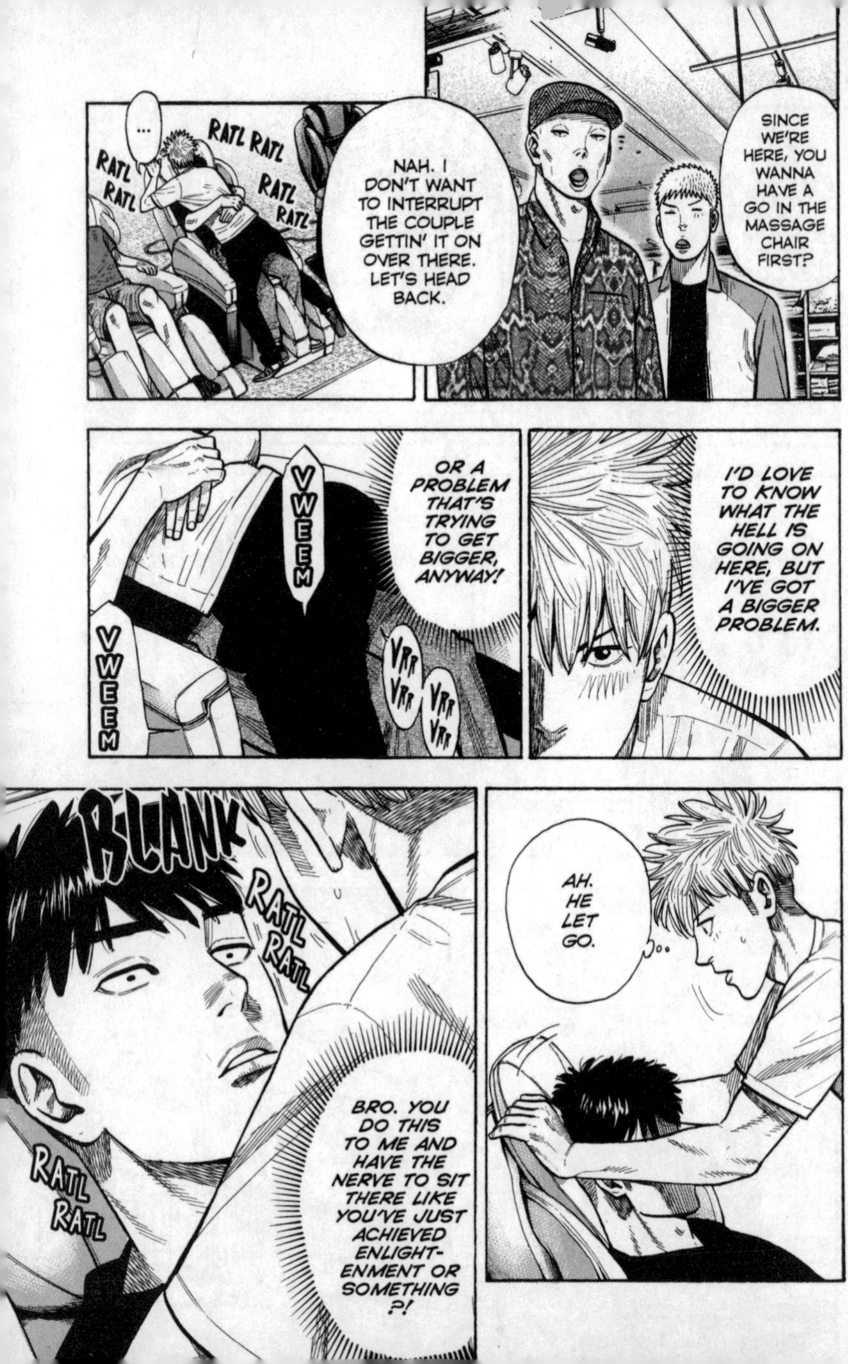
SINCE WE'RE HERE, YOU WANNA HAVE A GO IN THE MASSAGE CHAIR FIRST?
NAH. I DON'T WANT TO INTERRUPT THE COUPLE GETTIN' IT ON OVER THERE. LET'S HEAD BACK.
...
RATL RATL
RATL RATL
RATL RATL
RATL RATL
I'D LOVE TO KNOW WHAT THE HELL IS GOING ON HERE, BUT I'VE GOT A BIGGER PROBLEM.
OR A PROBLEM THAT'S TRYING TO GET BIGGER, ANYWAY!
VWEEM
VRR VRR
VRR VRR
VWEEM
AH. HE LET GO.
BLANK
RATL RATL
BRO. YOU DO THIS TO ME AND HAVE THE NERVE TO SIT THERE LIKE YOU'VE JUST ACHIEVED ENLIGHT-ENMENT OR SOMETHING ?!
RATL RATL

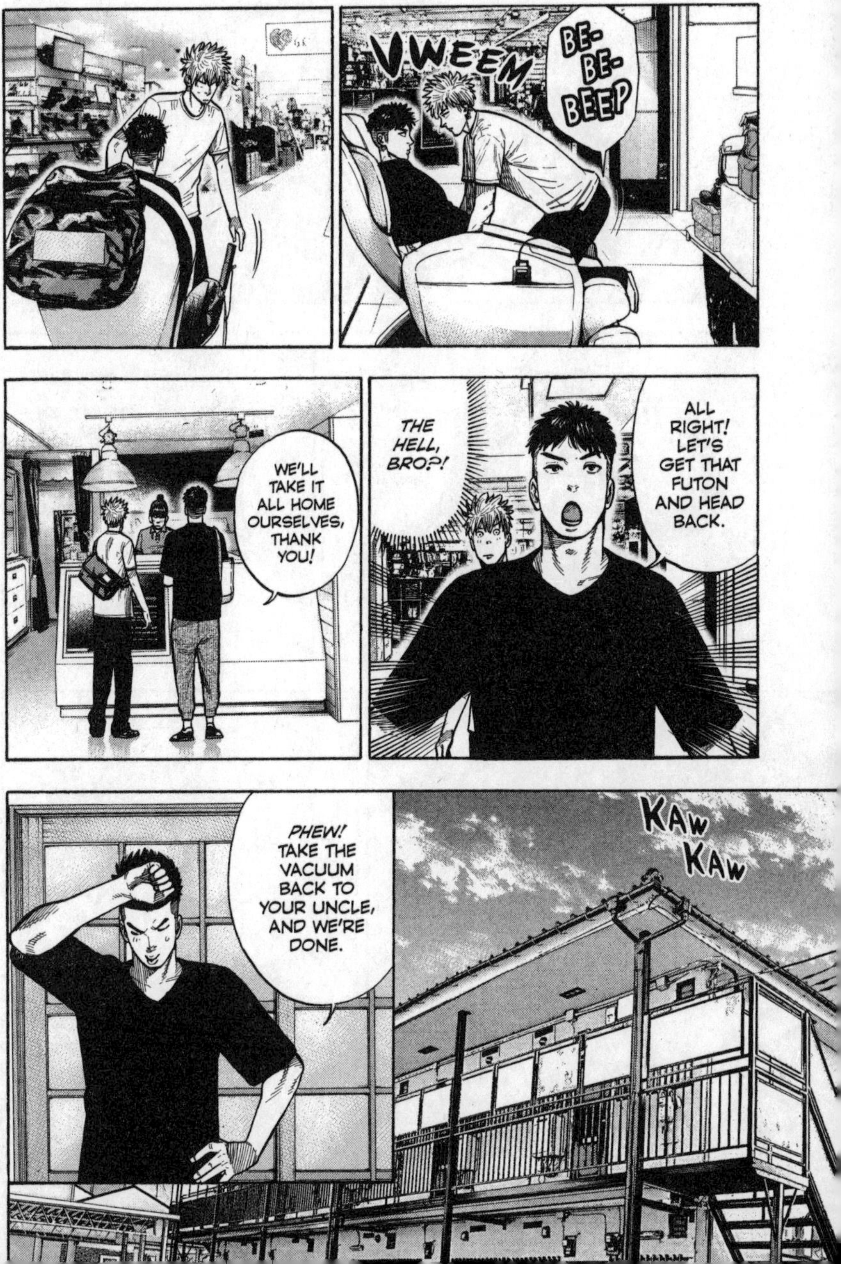
BE-BE-BEEP
VWEEM
ALL RIGHT! LET'S GET THAT FUTON AND HEAD BACK.
THE HELL, BRO?!
WE'LL TAKE IT ALL HOME OURSELVES, THANK YOU!
KAW KAW
PHEW! TAKE THE VACUUM BACK TO YOUR UNCLE, AND WE'RE DONE.

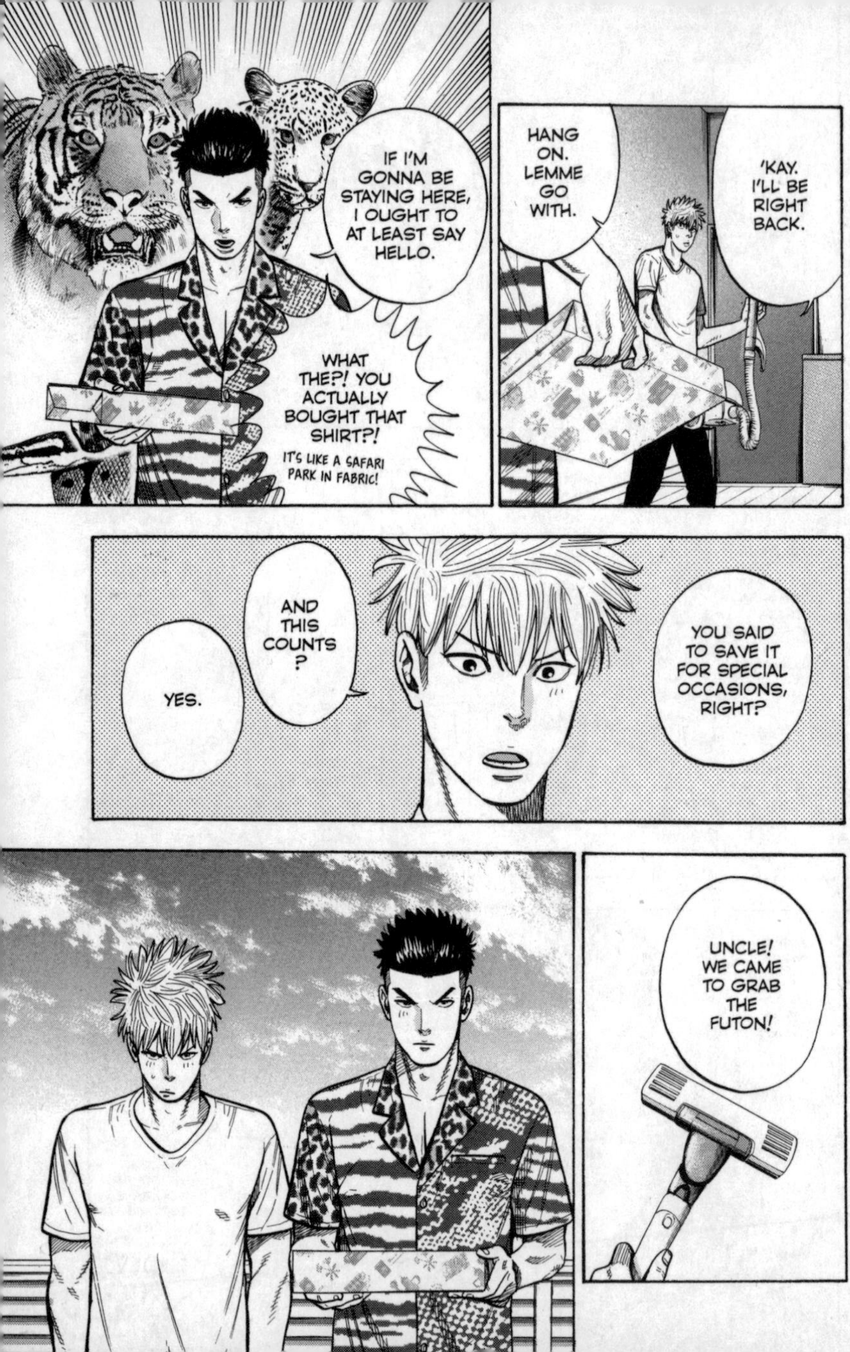
'KAY. I'LL BE RIGHT BACK.
HANG ON. LEMME GO WITH.
IF I'M GONNA BE STAYING HERE, I OUGHT TO AT LEAST SAY HELLO.
WHAT THE?! YOU ACTUALLY BOUGHT THAT SHIRT?!
IT'S LIKE A SAFARI PARK IN FABRIC!
YOU SAID TO SAVE IT FOR SPECIAL OCCASIONS, RIGHT?
AND THIS COUNTS?
YES.
UNCLE! WE CAME TO GRAB THE FUTON!

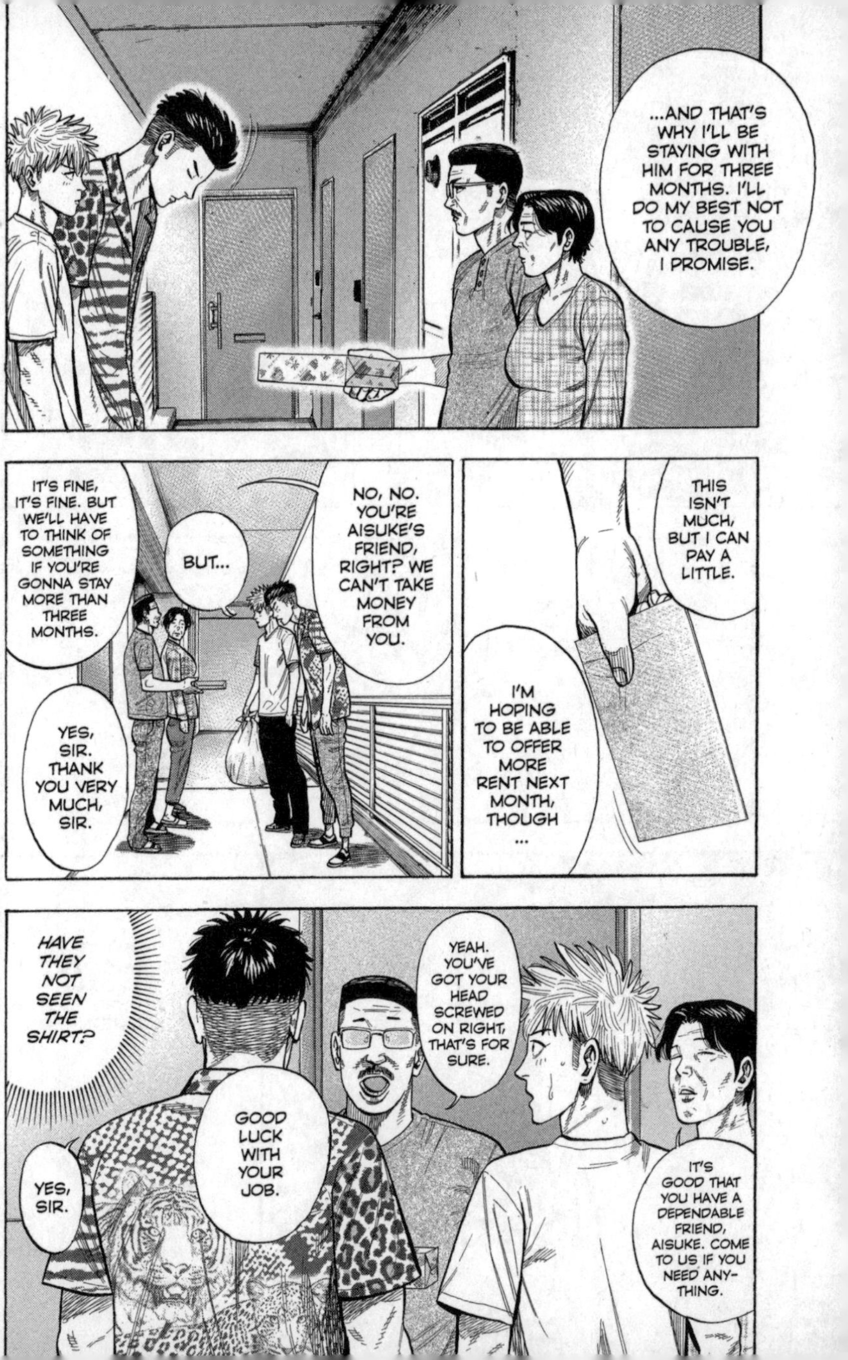
...AND THAT'S WHY I'LL BE STAYING WITH HIM FOR THREE MONTHS. I'LL DO MY BEST NOT TO CAUSE YOU ANY TROUBLE, I PROMISE.
THIS ISN'T MUCH, BUT I CAN PAY A LITTLE.
I'M HOPING TO BE ABLE TO OFFER MORE RENT NEXT MONTH, THOUGH ...
NO, NO. YOU'RE AISUKE'S FRIEND, RIGHT? WE CAN'T TAKE MONEY FROM YOU.
BUT...
IT'S FINE, IT'S FINE. BUT WE'LL HAVE TO THINK OF SOMETHING IF YOU'RE GONNA STAY MORE THAN THREE MONTHS.
YES, SIR. THANK YOU VERY MUCH, SIR.
YEAH. YOU'VE GOT YOUR HEAD SCREWED ON RIGHT, THAT'S FOR SURE.
IT'S GOOD THAT YOU HAVE A DEPENDABLE FRIEND, AISUKE. COME TO US IF YOU NEED ANY-THING.
GOOD LUCK WITH YOUR JOB.
YES, SIR.
HAVE THEY NOT SEEN THE SHIRT?

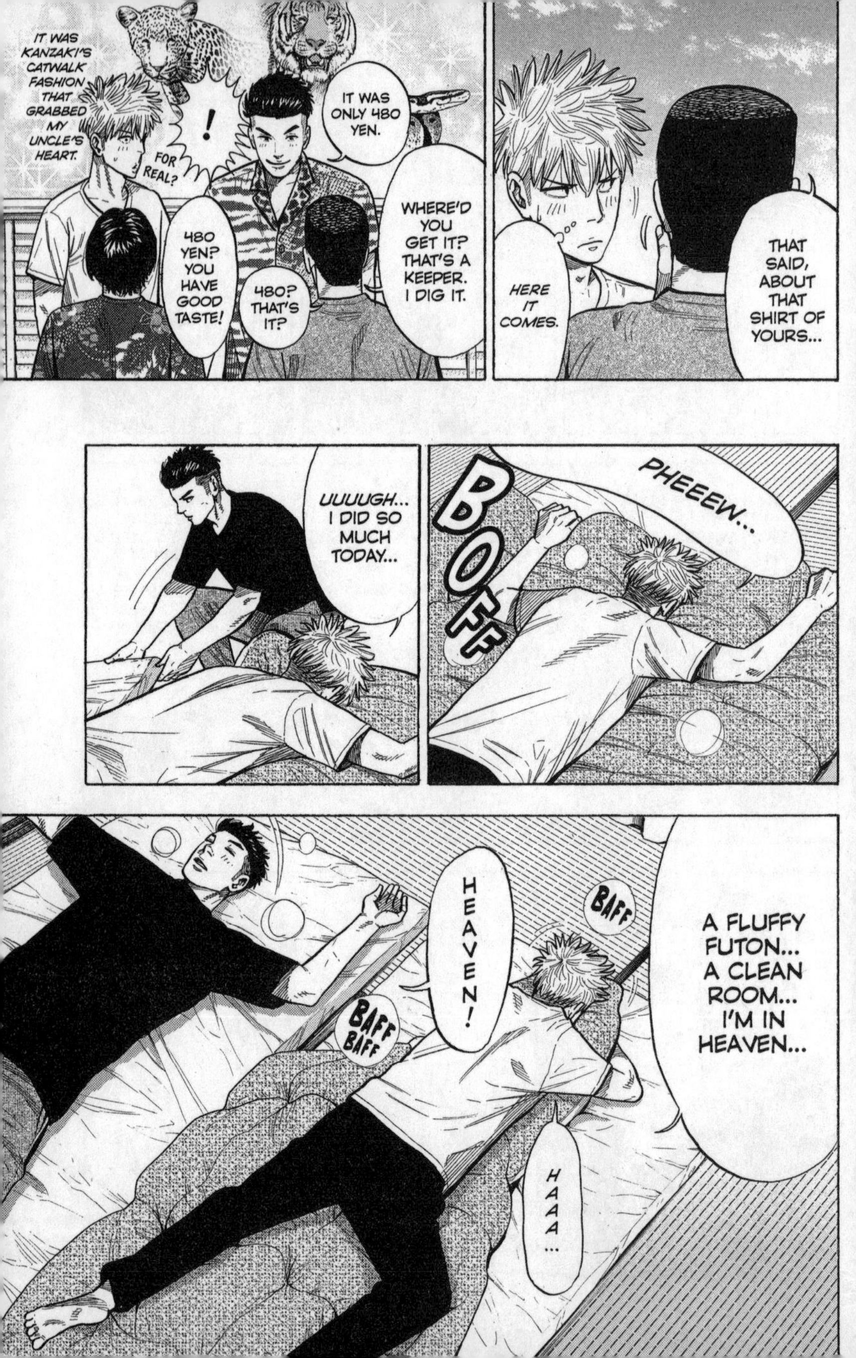
THAT SAID, ABOUT THAT SHIRT OF YOURS...
HERE IT COMES.
WHERE'D YOU GET IT? THAT'S A KEEPER. I DIG IT.
IT WAS ONLY 480 YEN.
480? THAT'S IT?
!
FOR REAL?
480 YEN? YOU HAVE GOOD TASTE!
IT WAS KANZAKI'S CATWALK FASHION THAT GRABBED MY UNCLE'S HEART.
PHEEEW...
BOFF
UUUUGH... I DID SO MUCH TODAY...
A FLUFFY FUTON... A CLEAN ROOM... I'M IN HEAVEN...
BAFF
HEAVEN!
HAAA...
BAFF BAFF

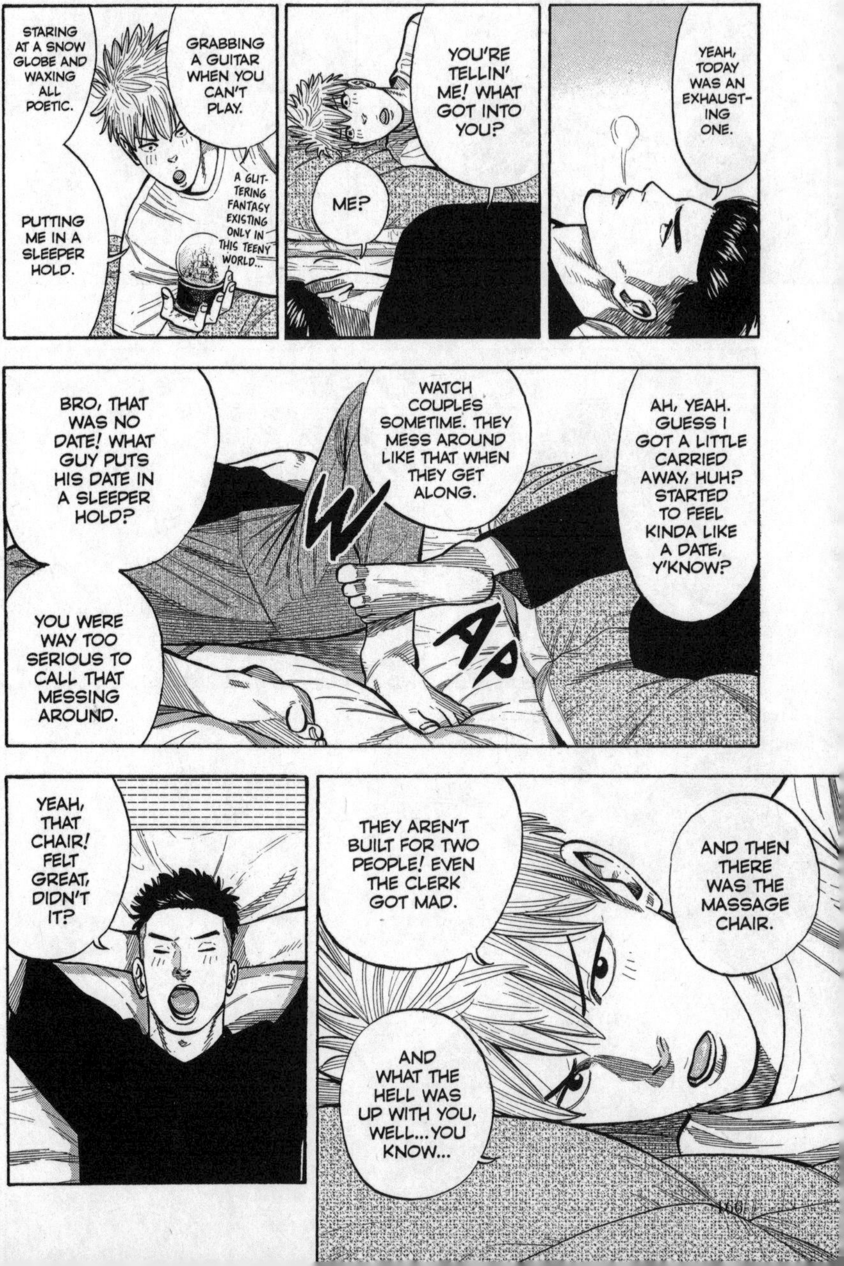
YEAH, TODAY WAS AN EXHAUST-ING ONE.
YOU'RE TELLIN' ME! WHAT GOT INTO YOU?
ME?
GRABBING A GUITAR WHEN YOU CAN'T PLAY.
STARING AT A SNOW GLOBE AND WAXING ALL POETIC.
A GLIT-TERING FANTASY EXISTING ONLY IN THIS TEENY WORLD...
PUTTING ME IN A SLEEPER HOLD.
AH, YEAH. GUESS I GOT A LITTLE CARRIED AWAY, HUH? STARTED TO FEEL KINDA LIKE A DATE, Y'KNOW?
WATCH COUPLES SOMETIME. THEY MESS AROUND LIKE THAT WHEN THEY GET ALONG.
BRO, THAT WAS NO DATE! WHAT GUY PUTS HIS DATE IN A SLEEPER HOLD?
YOU WERE WAY TOO SERIOUS TO CALL THAT MESSING AROUND.
WAP
AND THEN THERE WAS THE MASSAGE CHAIR.
THEY AREN'T BUILT FOR TWO PEOPLE! EVEN THE CLERK GOT MAD.
AND WHAT THE HELL WAS UP WITH YOU, WELL...YOU KNOW...
YEAH, THAT CHAIR! FELT GREAT, DIDN'T IT?

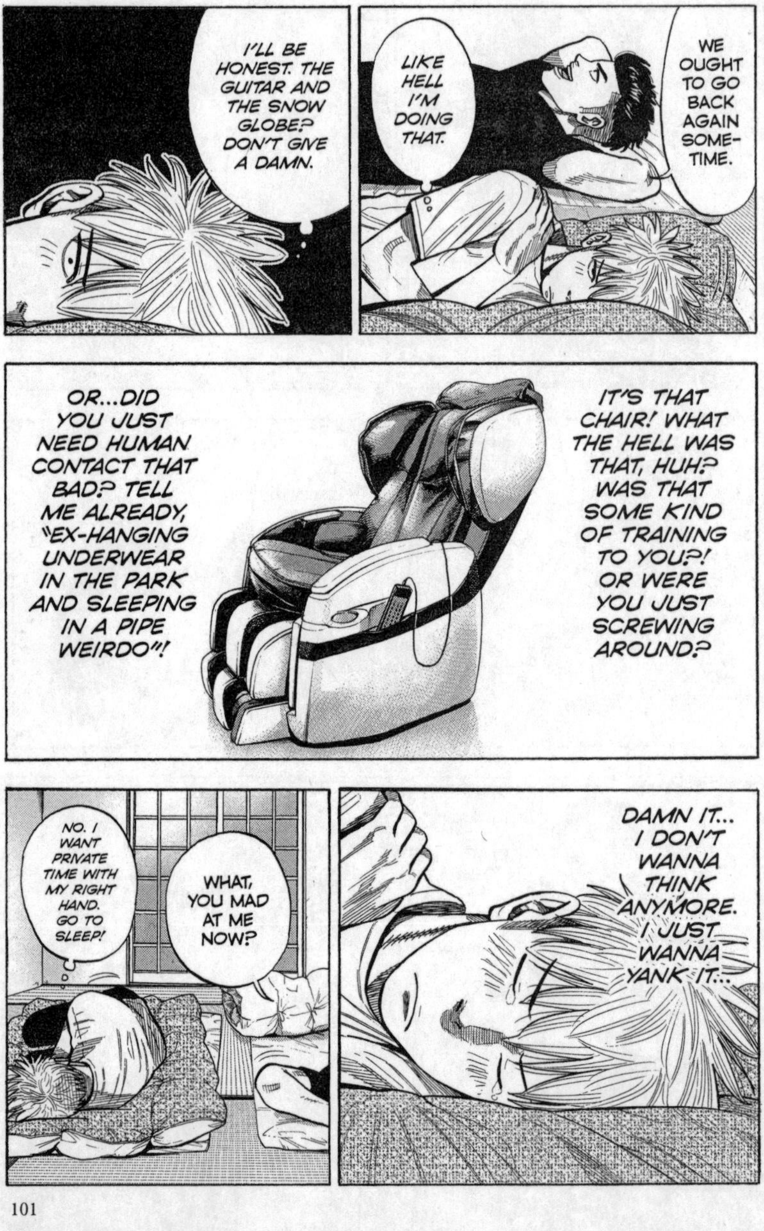
WE OUGHT TO GO BACK AGAIN SOME-TIME.
LIKE HELL I'M DOING THAT.
I'LL BE HONEST. THE GUITAR AND THE SNOW GLOBE? DON'T GIVE A DAMN.
IT'S THAT CHAIR! WHAT THE HELL WAS THAT, HUH? WAS THAT SOME KIND OF TRAINING TO YOU?! OR WERE YOU JUST SCREWING AROUND?
OR...DID YOU JUST NEED HUMAN CONTACT THAT BAD? TELL ME ALREADY, "EX-HANGING UNDERWEAR IN THE PARK AND SLEEPING IN A PIPE WEIRDO"!
DAMN IT... I DON'T WANNA THINK ANYMORE. I JUST WANNA YANK IT...
WHAT, YOU MAD AT ME NOW?
NO. I WANT PRIVATE TIME WITH MY RIGHT HAND. GO TO SLEEP!

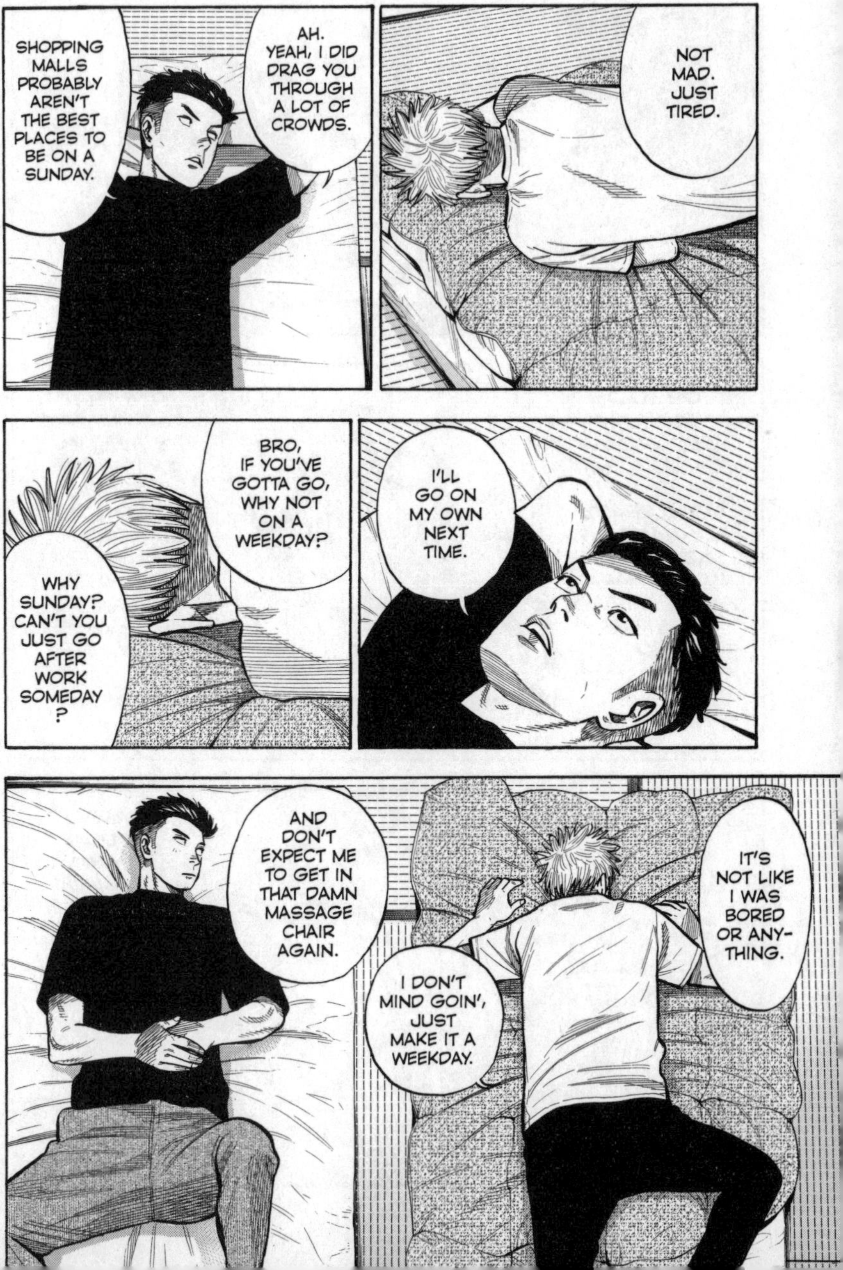
NOT MAD. JUST TIRED.
AH. YEAH, I DID DRAG YOU THROUGH A LOT OF CROWDS.
SHOPPING MALLS PROBABLY AREN'T THE BEST PLACES TO BE ON A SUNDAY.
I'LL GO ON MY OWN NEXT TIME.
BRO, IF YOU'VE GOTTA GO, WHY NOT ON A WEEKDAY?
WHY SUNDAY? CAN'T YOU JUST GO AFTER WORK SOMEDAY?
IT'S NOT LIKE I WAS BORED OR ANY-THING.
I DON'T MIND GOIN', JUST MAKE IT A WEEKDAY.
AND DON'T EXPECT ME TO GET IN THAT DAMN MASSAGE CHAIR AGAIN.

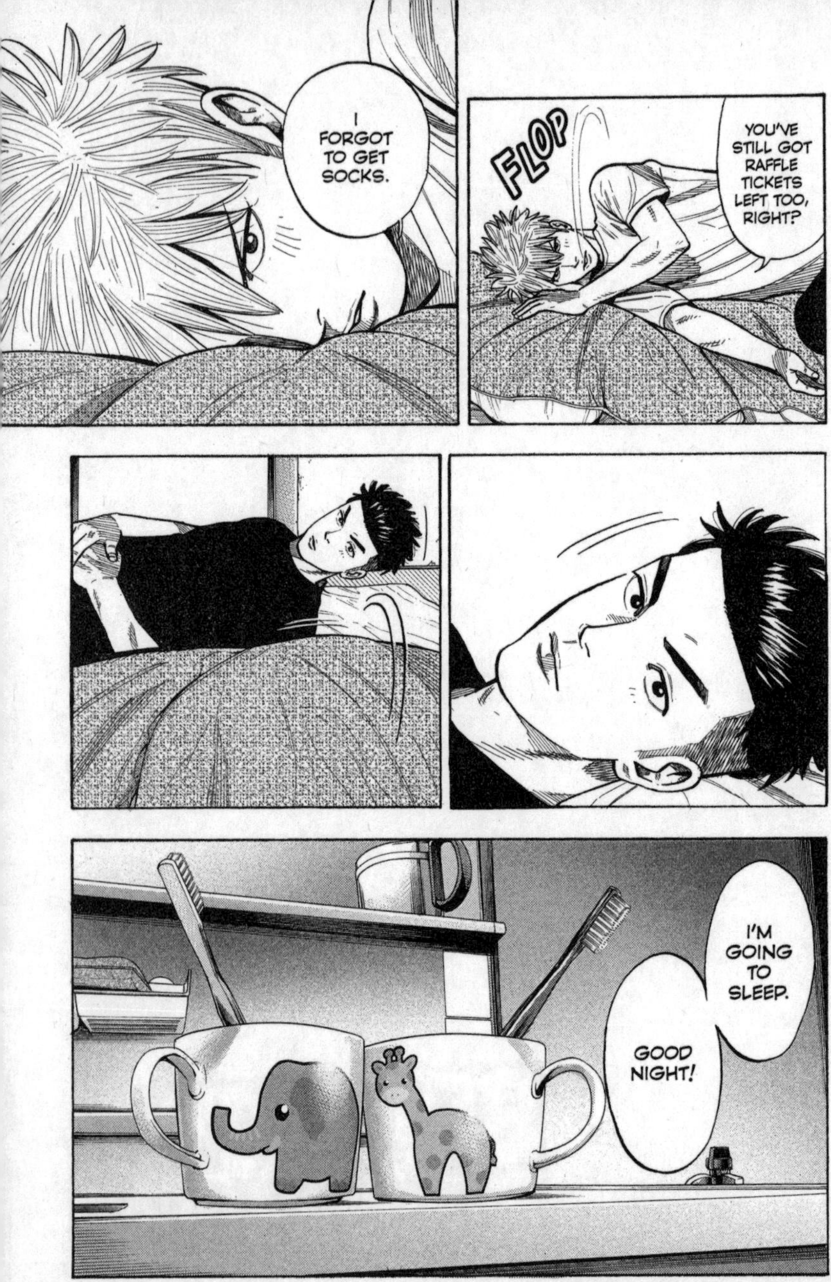
YOU'VE STILL GOT RAFFLE TICKETS LEFT TOO, RIGHT?
FLOP
I FORGOT TO GET SOCKS.
I'M GOING TO SLEEP.
GOOD NIGHT!

BAD BOYS
HAPPY HOME

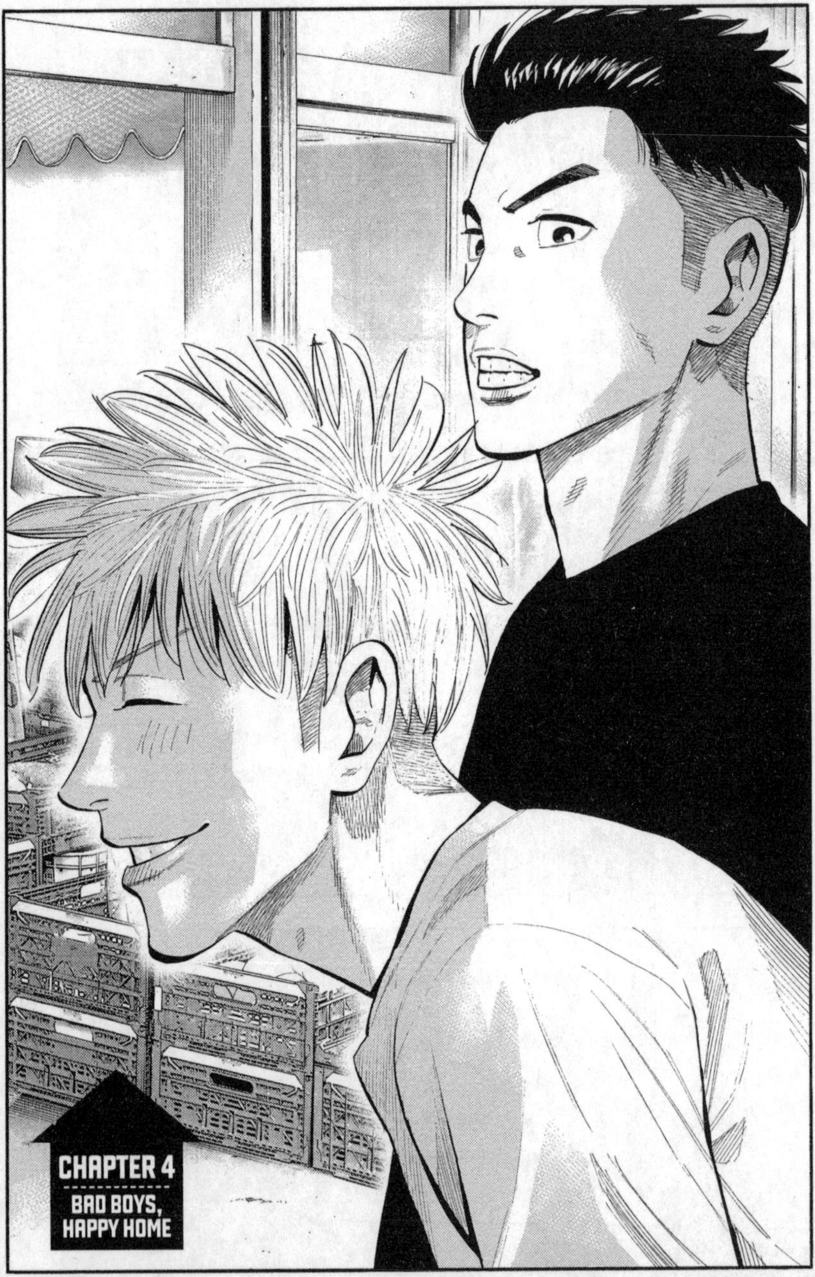
CHAPTER 4
BAD BOYS,
HAPPY HOME

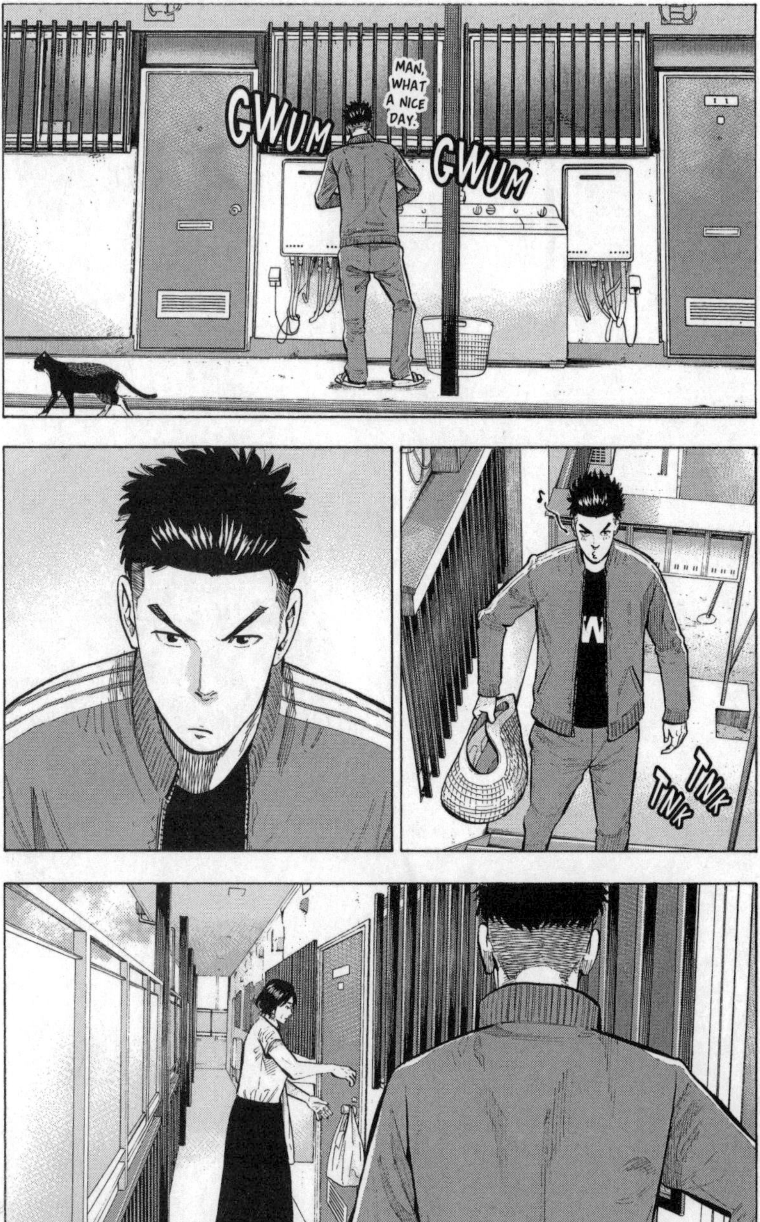
MAN, WHAT A NICE DAY.
GWUM
GWUM
TNK
TNK

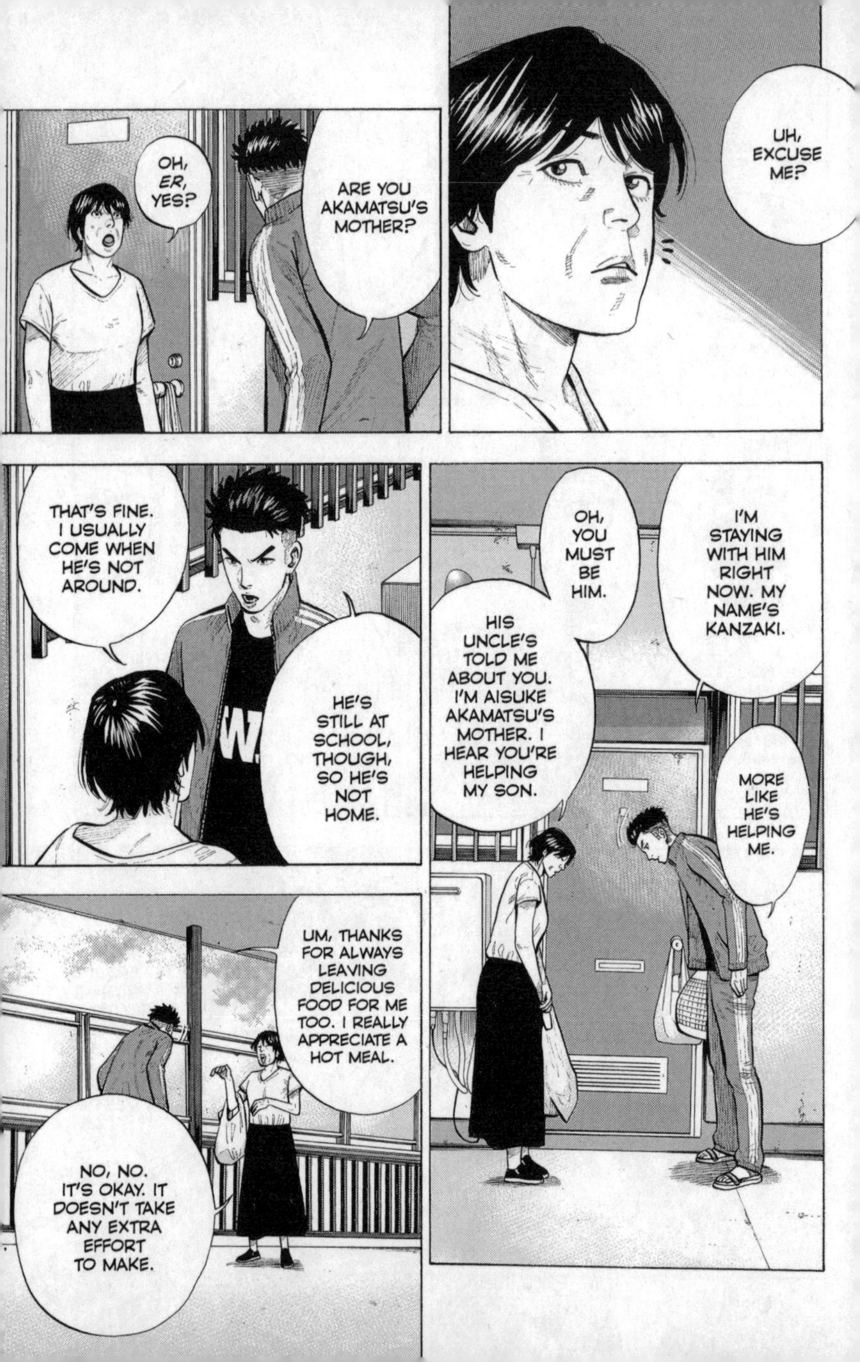
UH, EXCUSE ME?
ARE YOU AKAMATSU'S MOTHER?
OH, ER, YES?
I'M STAYING WITH HIM RIGHT NOW. MY NAME'S KANZAKI.
OH, YOU MUST BE HIM.
HIS UNCLE'S TOLD ME ABOUT YOU. I'M AISUKE AKAMATSU'S MOTHER. I HEAR YOU'RE HELPING MY SON.
MORE LIKE HE'S HELPING ME.
HE'S STILL AT SCHOOL, THOUGH, SO HE'S NOT HOME.
THAT'S FINE. I USUALLY COME WHEN HE'S NOT AROUND.
UM, THANKS FOR ALWAYS LEAVING DELICIOUS FOOD FOR ME TOO. I REALLY APPRECIATE A HOT MEAL.
NO, NO. IT'S OKAY. IT DOESN'T TAKE ANY EXTRA EFFORT TO MAKE.

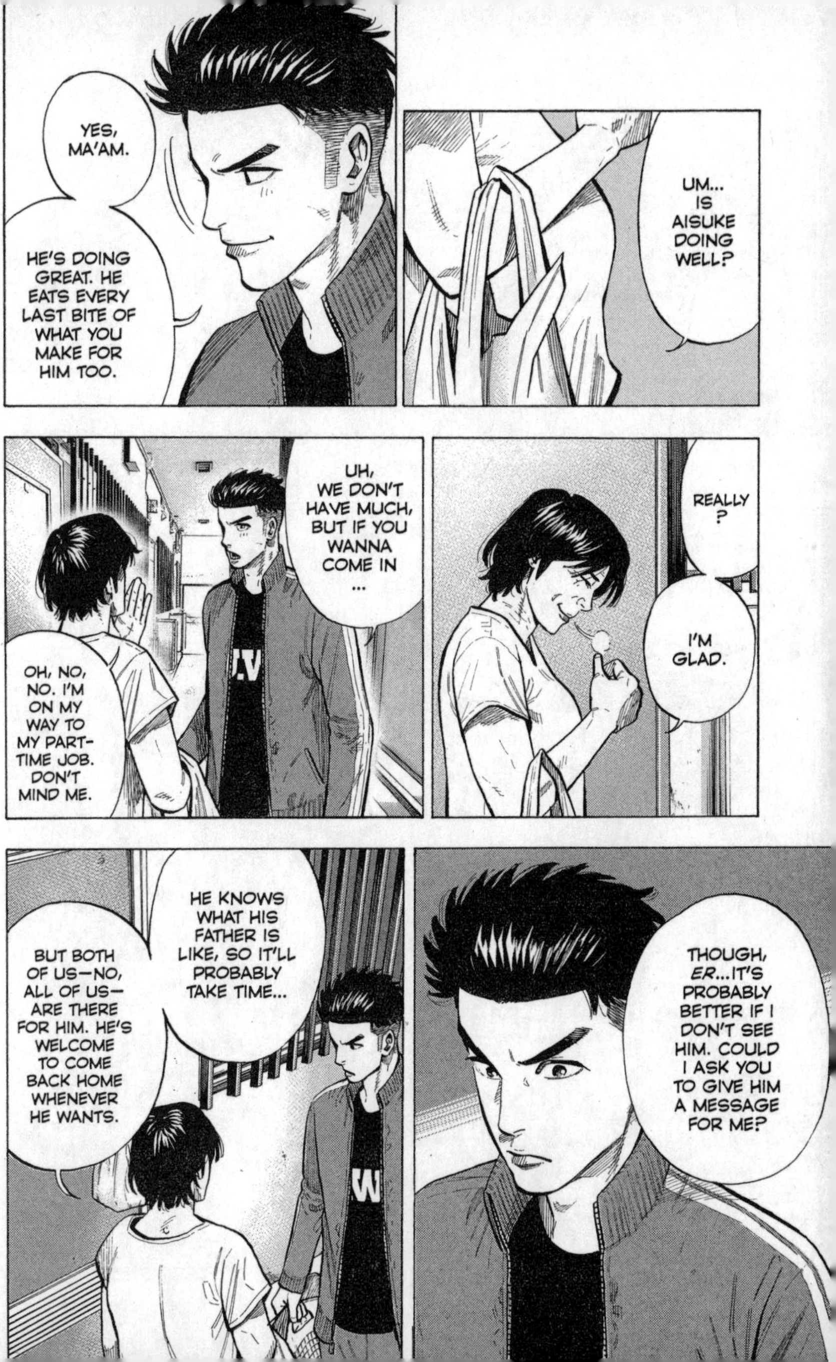
UM... IS AISUKE DOING WELL?
YES, MA'AM.
HE'S DOING GREAT. HE EATS EVERY LAST BITE OF WHAT YOU MAKE FOR HIM TOO.
REALLY?
I'M GLAD.
UH, WE DON'T HAVE MUCH, BUT IF YOU WANNA COME IN ...
OH, NO, NO. I'M ON MY WAY TO MY PART-TIME JOB. DON'T MIND ME.
THOUGH, *ER*...IT'S PROBABLY BETTER IF I DON'T SEE HIM. COULD I ASK YOU TO GIVE HIM A MESSAGE FOR ME?
HE KNOWS WHAT HIS FATHER IS LIKE, SO IT'LL PROBABLY TAKE TIME...
BUT BOTH OF US—NO, ALL OF US—ARE THERE FOR HIM. HE'S WELCOME TO COME BACK HOME WHENEVER HE WANTS.

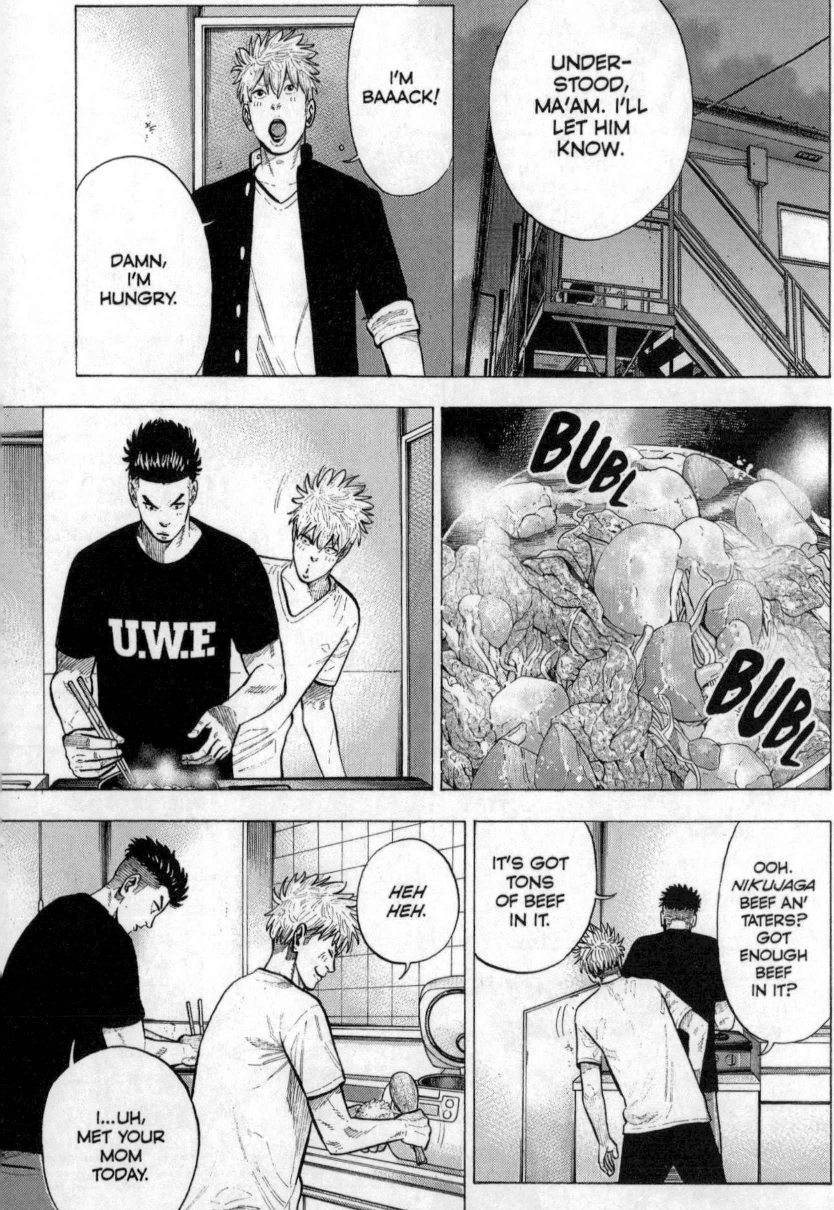
UNDER-STOOD, MA'AM. I'LL LET HIM KNOW.
I'M BAAACK!
DAMN, I'M HUNGRY.
BUBL
BUBL
U.W.F.
OOH. *NIKUJAGA* BEEF AN' TATERS? GOT ENOUGH BEEF IN IT?
IT'S GOT TONS OF BEEF IN IT.
HEH HEH.
I...UH, MET YOUR MOM TODAY.

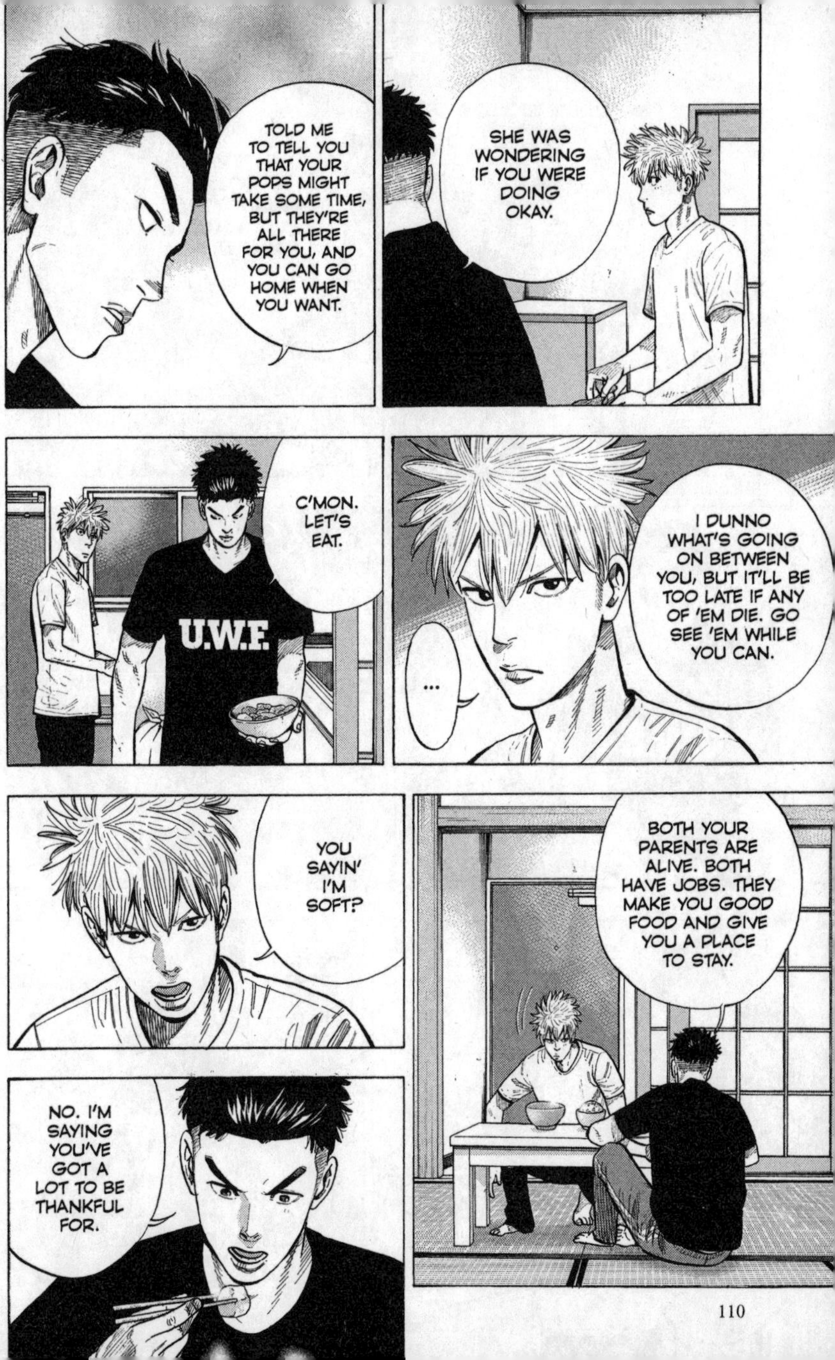
SHE WAS WONDERING IF YOU WERE DOING OKAY.
TOLD ME TO TELL YOU THAT YOUR POPS MIGHT TAKE SOME TIME, BUT THEY'RE ALL THERE FOR YOU, AND YOU CAN GO HOME WHEN YOU WANT.
I DUNNO WHAT'S GOING ON BETWEEN YOU, BUT IT'LL BE TOO LATE IF ANY OF 'EM DIE. GO SEE 'EM WHILE YOU CAN.
...
C'MON. LET'S EAT.
U.W.F.
BOTH YOUR PARENTS ARE ALIVE. BOTH HAVE JOBS. THEY MAKE YOU GOOD FOOD AND GIVE YOU A PLACE TO STAY.
YOU SAYIN' I'M SOFT?
NO. I'M SAYING YOU'VE GOT A LOT TO BE THANKFUL FOR.

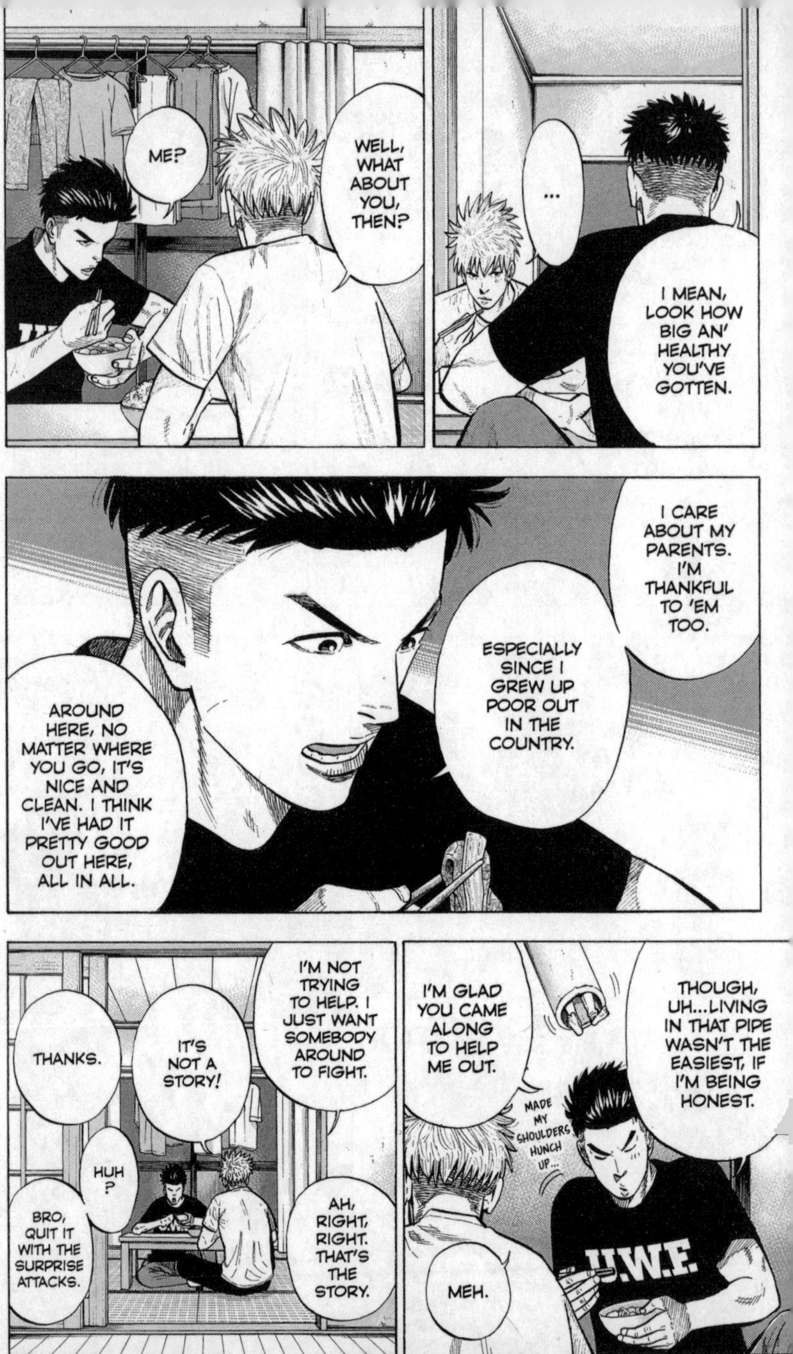
...
I MEAN, LOOK HOW BIG AN' HEALTHY YOU'VE GOTTEN.
WELL, WHAT ABOUT YOU, THEN?
ME?
I CARE ABOUT MY PARENTS. I'M THANKFUL TO 'EM TOO.
ESPECIALLY SINCE I GREW UP POOR OUT IN THE COUNTRY.
AROUND HERE, NO MATTER WHERE YOU GO, IT'S NICE AND CLEAN. I THINK I'VE HAD IT PRETTY GOOD OUT HERE, ALL IN ALL.
THOUGH, UH...LIVING IN THAT PIPE WASN'T THE EASIEST, IF I'M BEING HONEST.
MADE MY SHOULDERS HUNCH UP...
I'M GLAD YOU CAME ALONG TO HELP ME OUT.
MEH.
I'M NOT TRYING TO HELP. I JUST WANT SOMEBODY AROUND TO FIGHT.
AH, RIGHT, RIGHT. THAT'S THE STORY.
IT'S NOT A STORY!
THANKS.
HUH?
BRO, QUIT IT WITH THE SURPRISE ATTACKS.

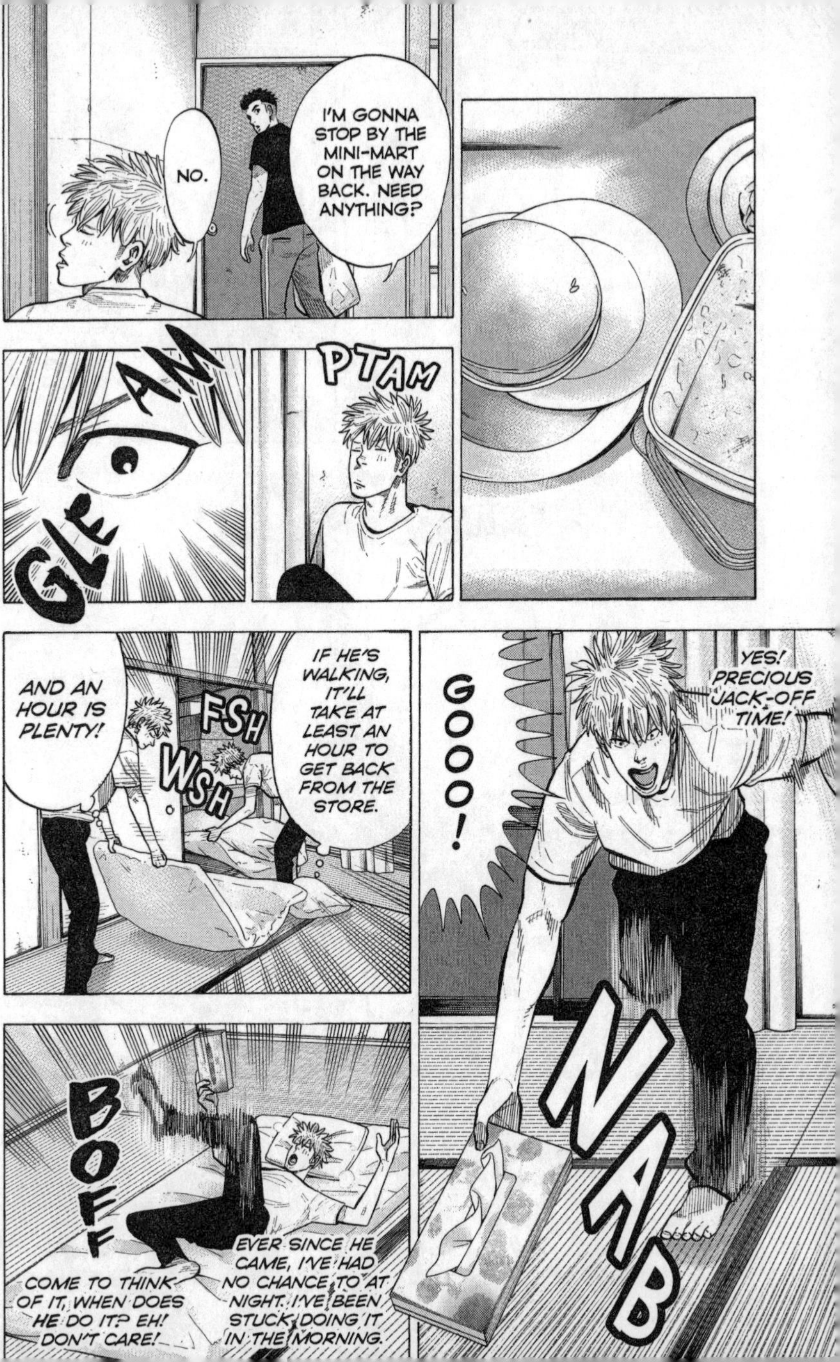
I'M GONNA STOP BY THE MINI-MART ON THE WAY BACK. NEED ANYTHING?
NO.
PTAM
GLEAM
YES! PRECIOUS JACK-OFF TIME!
GOOOO!
NAB
IF HE'S WALKING, IT'LL TAKE AT LEAST AN HOUR TO GET BACK FROM THE STORE.
AND AN HOUR IS PLENTY!
FSH
WSH
BOFF
EVER SINCE HE CAME, I'VE HAD NO CHANCE TO AT NIGHT. I'VE BEEN STUCK DOING IT IN THE MORNING.
COME TO THINK OF IT, WHEN DOES HE DO IT? EH! DON'T CARE!

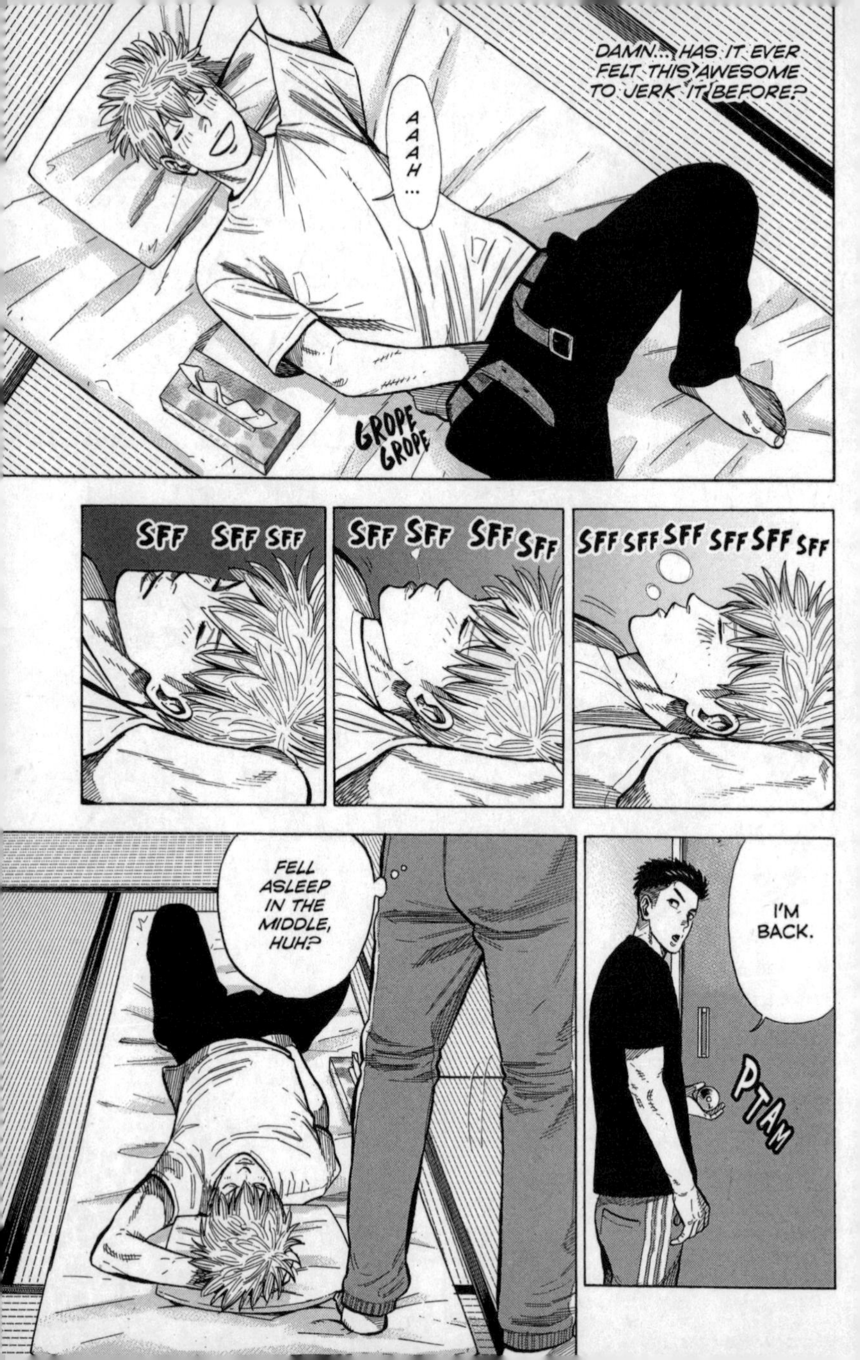
DAMN... HAS IT EVER FELT THIS AWESOME TO JERK IT BEFORE?
AAAH...
GROPE GROPE
SFF SFF SFF SFF SFF SFF
SFF SFF SFF SFF
SFF SFF SFF
I'M BACK.
PTAM
FELL ASLEEP IN THE MIDDLE, HUH?

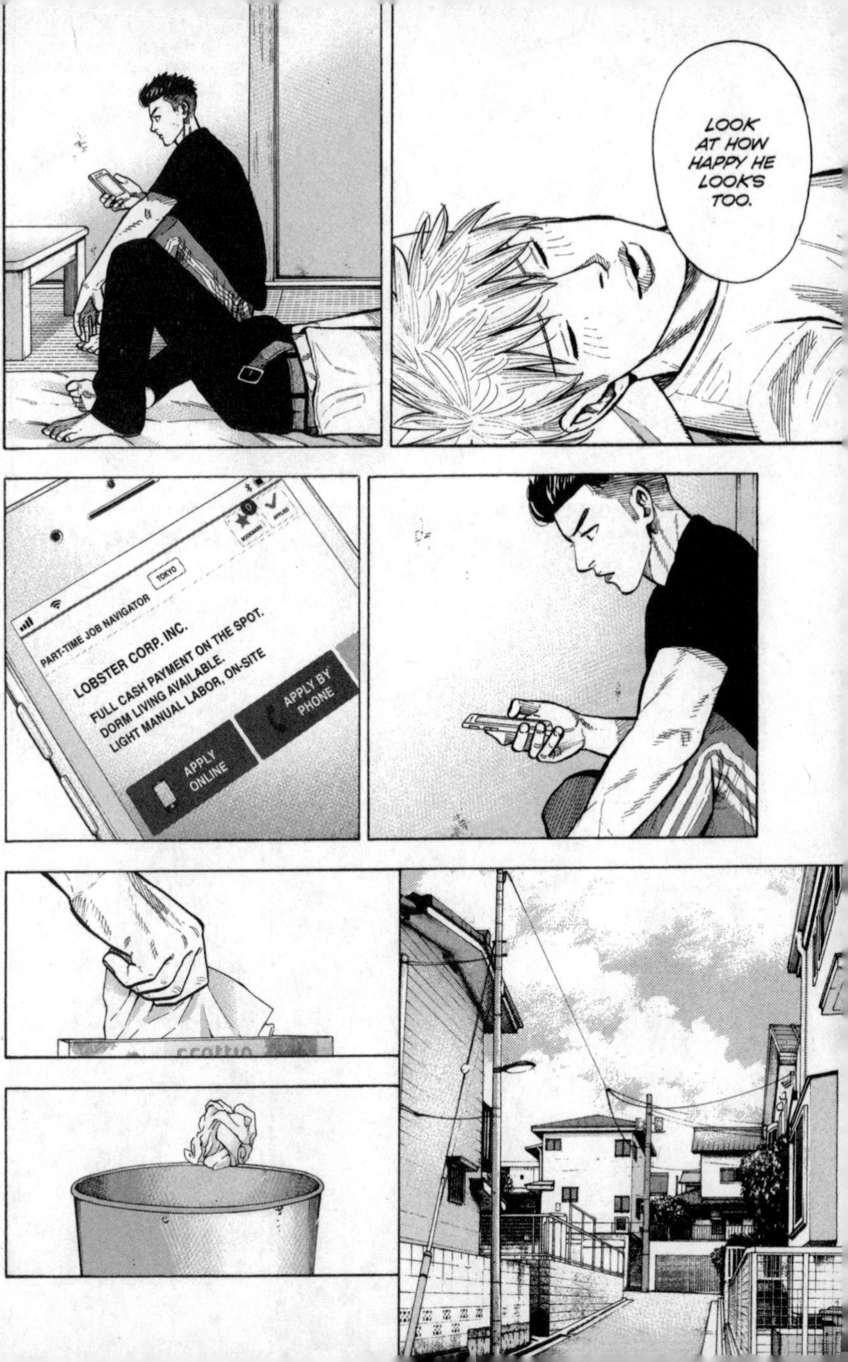
LOOK AT HOW HAPPY HE LOOKS TOO.
PART-TIME JOB NAVIGATOR
TOKYO
LOBSTER CORP. INC.
FULL CASH PAYMENT ON THE SPOT.
DORM LIVING AVAILABLE.
LIGHT MANUAL LABOR, ON-SITE
APPLY BY PHONE
APPLY ONLINE

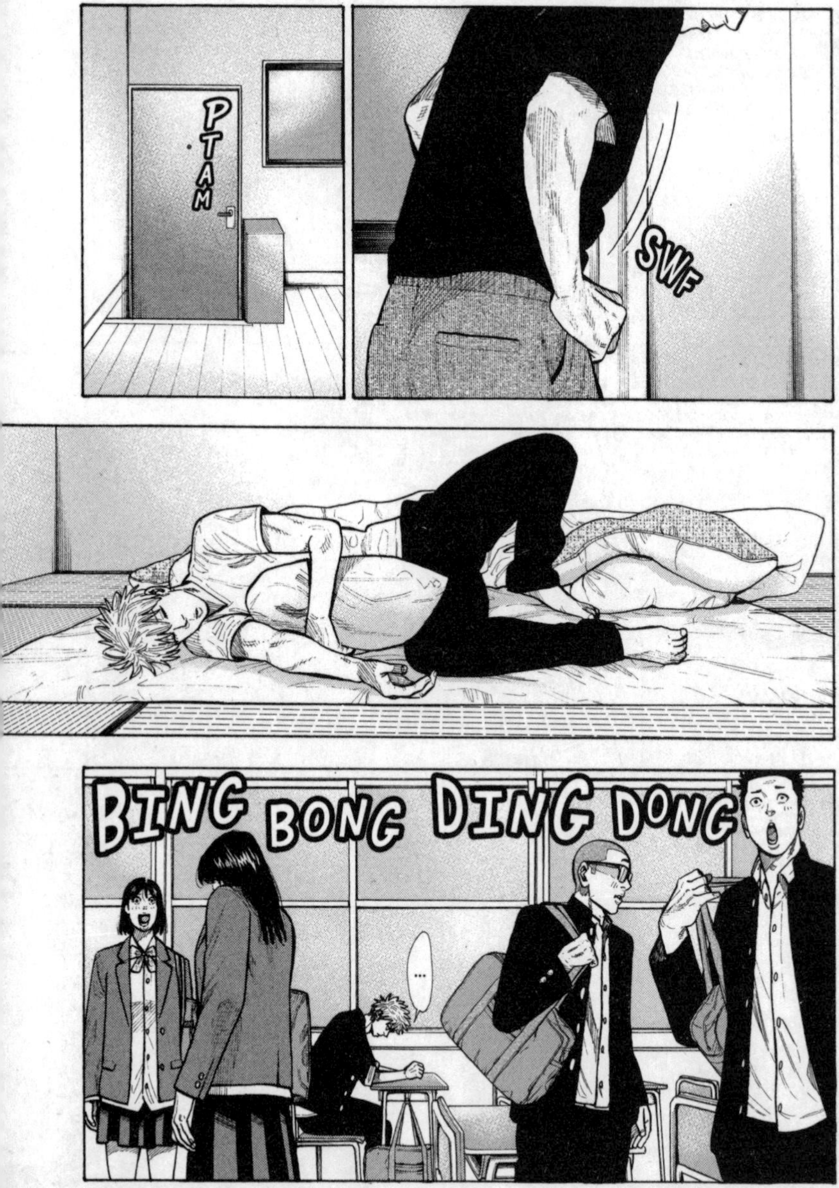
SWF
PTAM
BING BONG DING DONG
...

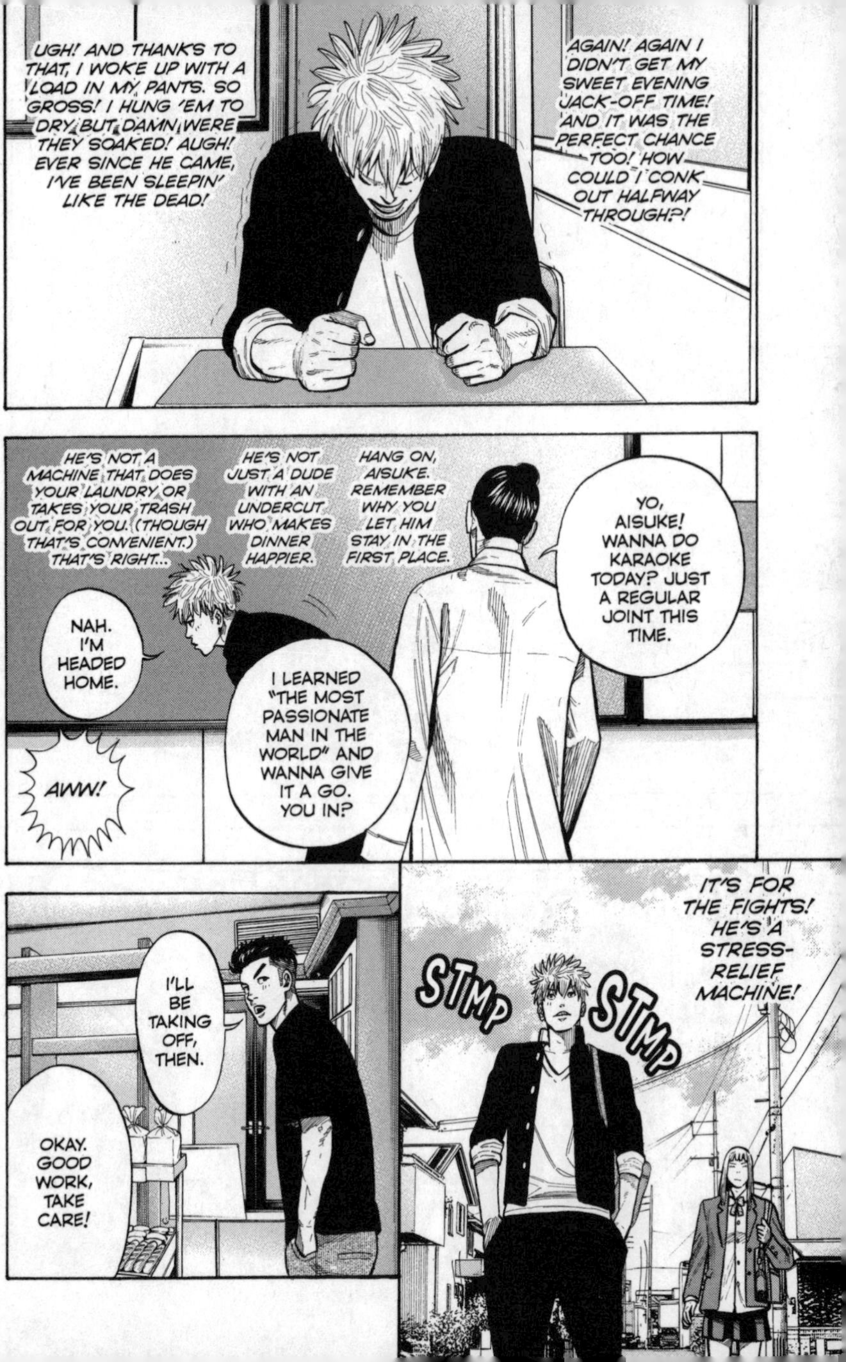
AGAIN! AGAIN I DIDN'T GET MY SWEET EVENING JACK-OFF TIME! AND IT WAS THE PERFECT CHANCE TOO! HOW COULD I CONK OUT HALFWAY THROUGH?!
UGH! AND THANKS TO THAT, I WOKE UP WITH A LOAD IN MY PANTS. SO GROSS! I HUNG 'EM TO DRY, BUT DAMN, WERE THEY SOAKED! AUGH! EVER SINCE HE CAME, I'VE BEEN SLEEPIN' LIKE THE DEAD!
YO, AISUKE! WANNA DO KARAOKE TODAY? JUST A REGULAR JOINT THIS TIME.
HANG ON, AISUKE. REMEMBER WHY YOU LET HIM STAY IN THE FIRST PLACE.
HE'S NOT JUST A DUDE WITH AN UNDERCUT WHO MAKES DINNER HAPPIER.
HE'S NOT A MACHINE THAT DOES YOUR LAUNDRY OR TAKES YOUR TRASH OUT FOR YOU. (THOUGH THAT'S CONVENIENT.) THAT'S RIGHT...
I LEARNED "THE MOST PASSIONATE MAN IN THE WORLD" AND WANNA GIVE IT A GO. YOU IN?
NAH. I'M HEADED HOME.
AWW!
IT'S FOR THE FIGHTS! HE'S A STRESS-RELIEF MACHINE!
STMP
STMP
I'LL BE TAKING OFF, THEN.
OKAY. GOOD WORK, TAKE CARE!

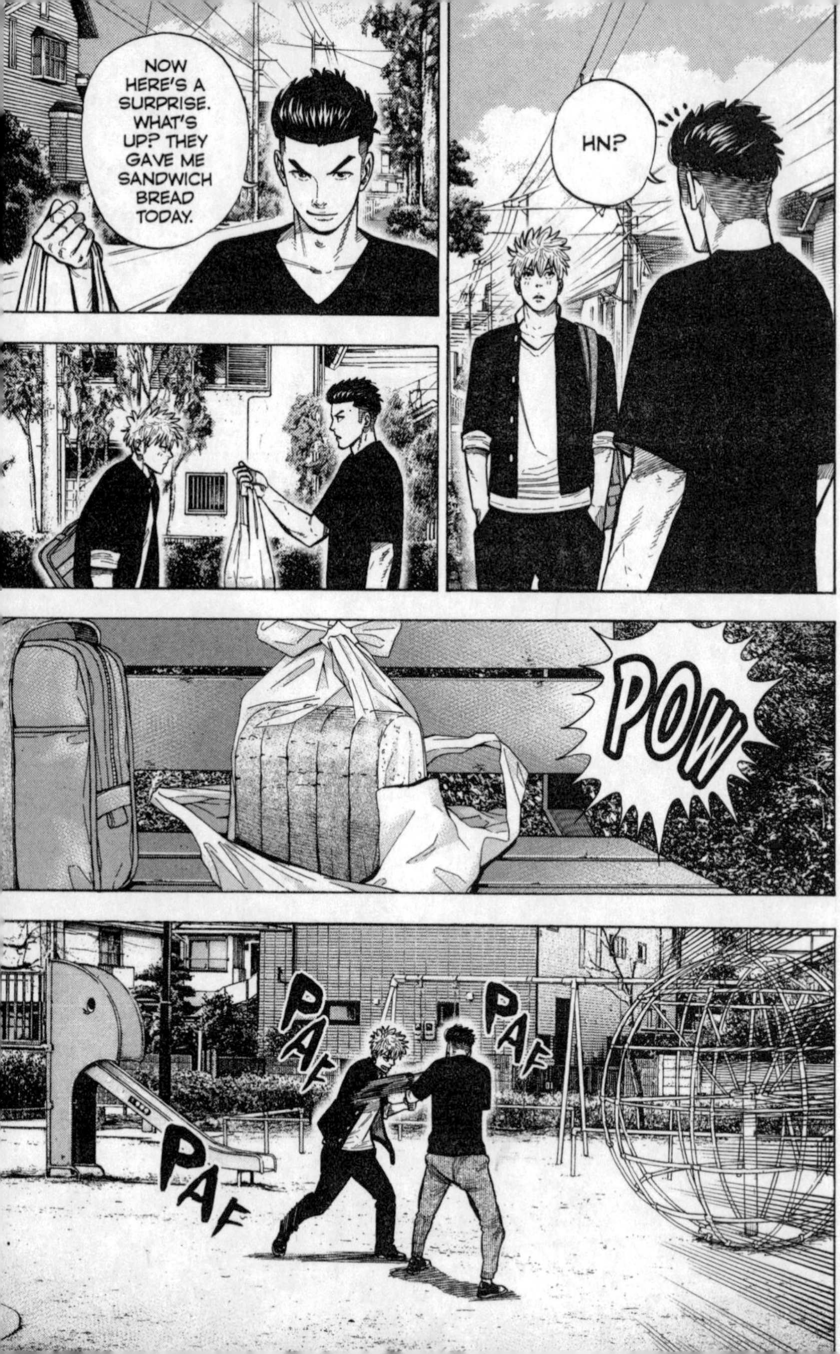
HN?
NOW HERE'S A SURPRISE. WHAT'S UP? THEY GAVE ME SANDWICH BREAD TODAY.
POW
PAF
PAF
PAF

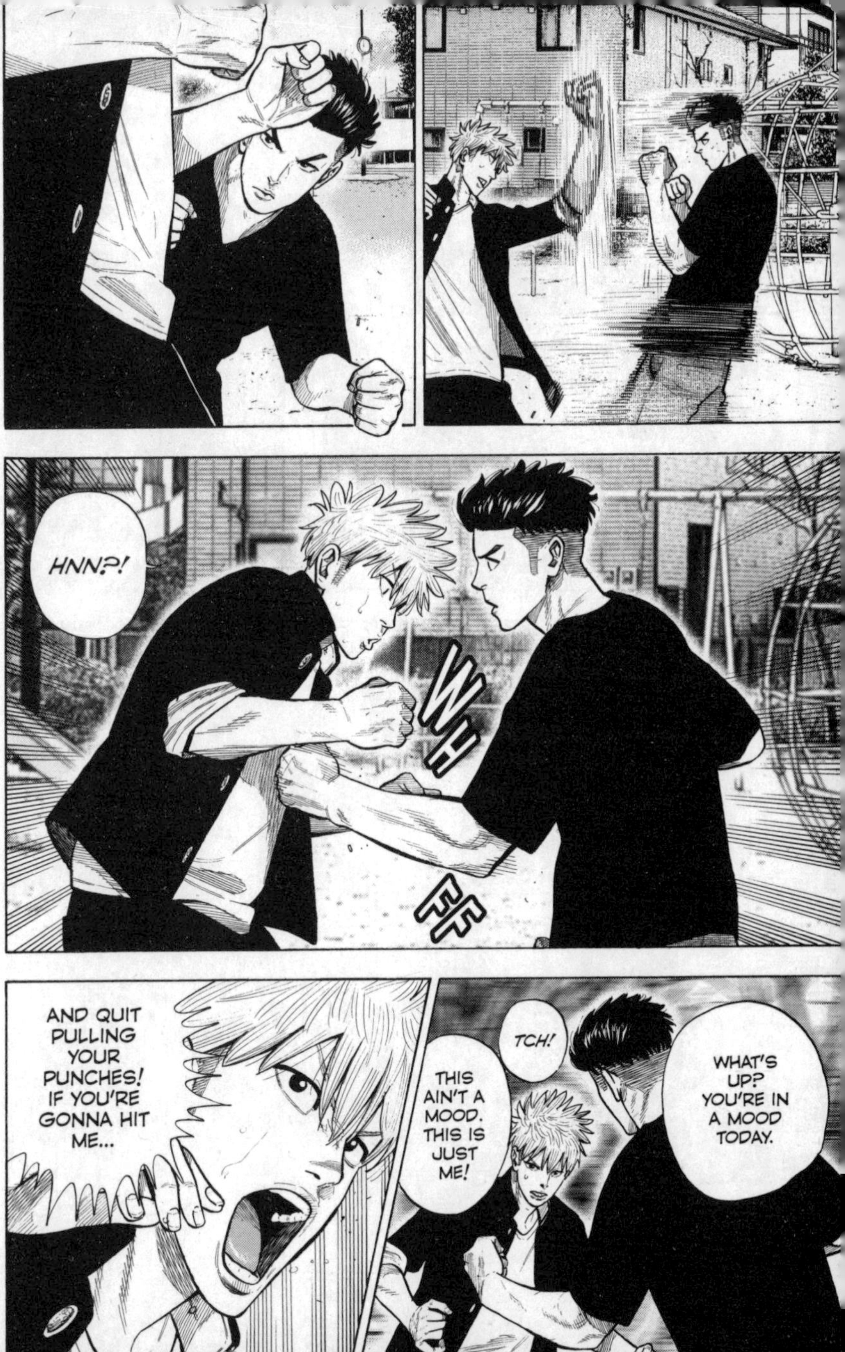
HNN?!
WHFF
WHAT'S UP? YOU'RE IN A MOOD TODAY.
TCH!
THIS AIN'T A MOOD. THIS IS JUST ME!
AND QUIT PULLING YOUR PUNCHES! IF YOU'RE GONNA HIT ME...

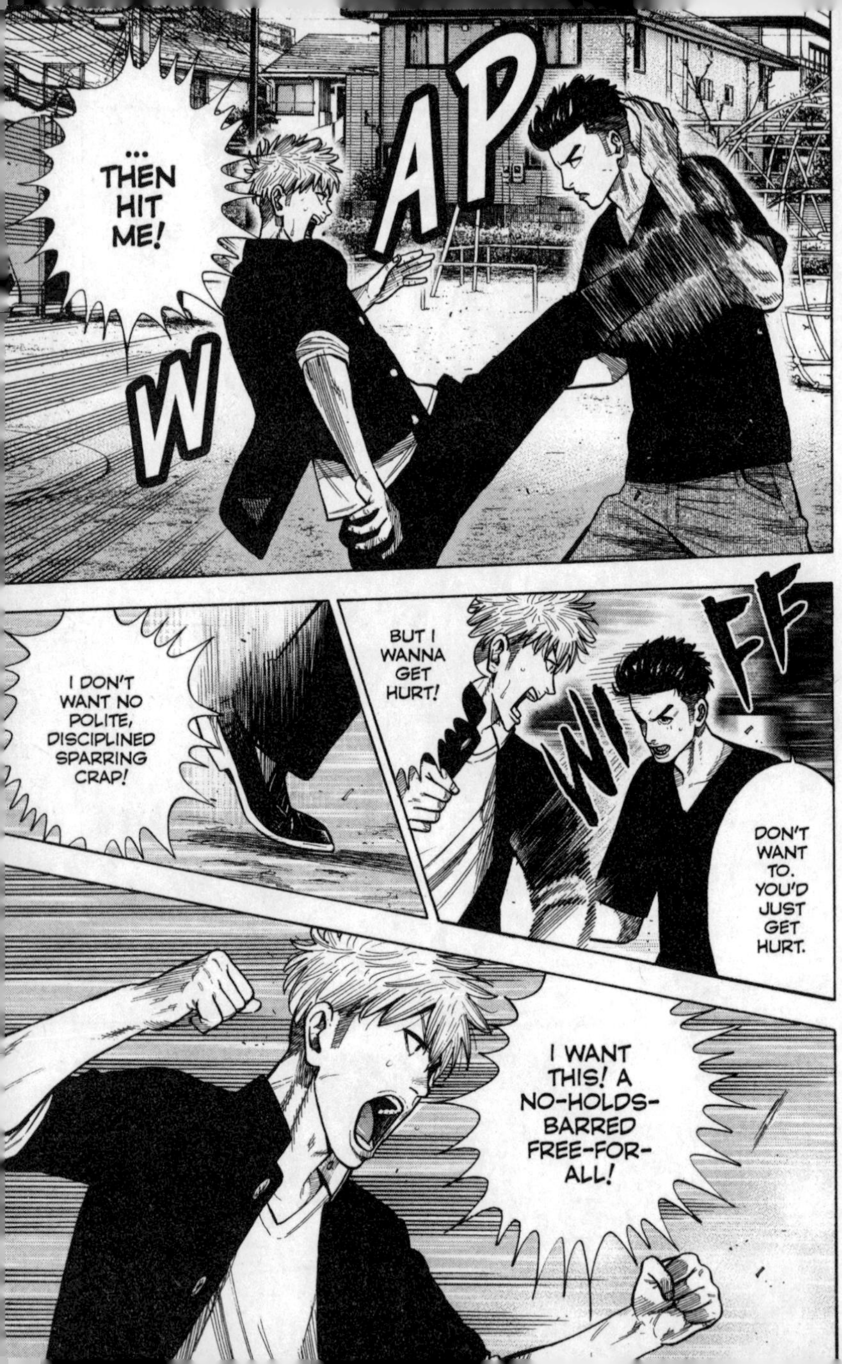
AP
...THEN HIT ME!
W
FF
WI
DON'T WANT TO. YOU'D JUST GET HURT.
BUT I WANNA GET HURT!
I DON'T WANT NO POLITE, DISCIPLINED SPARRING CRAP!
I WANT THIS! A NO-HOLDS-BARRED FREE-FOR-ALL!

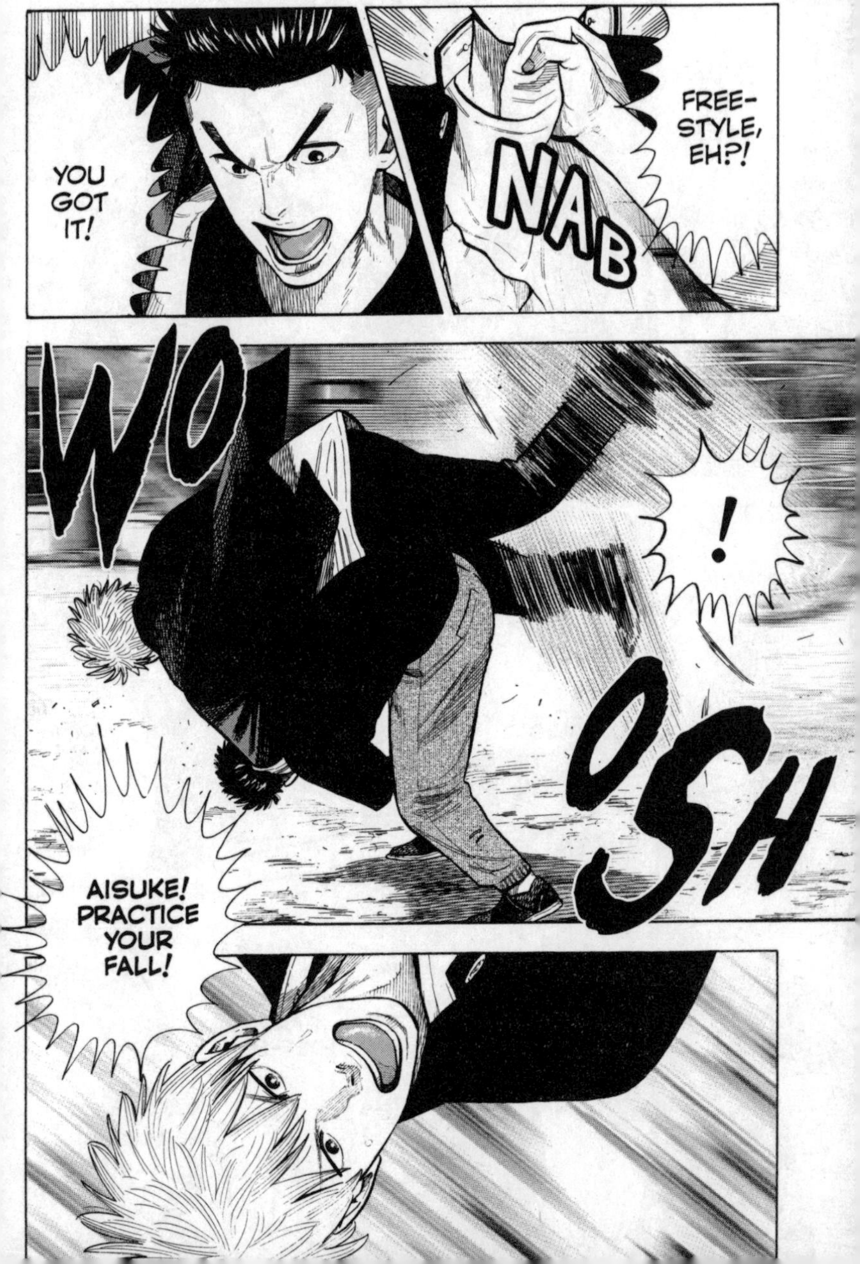
FREE-STYLE, EH?!
NAB
YOU GOT IT!
WOOSH
!
AISUKE! PRACTICE YOUR FALL!

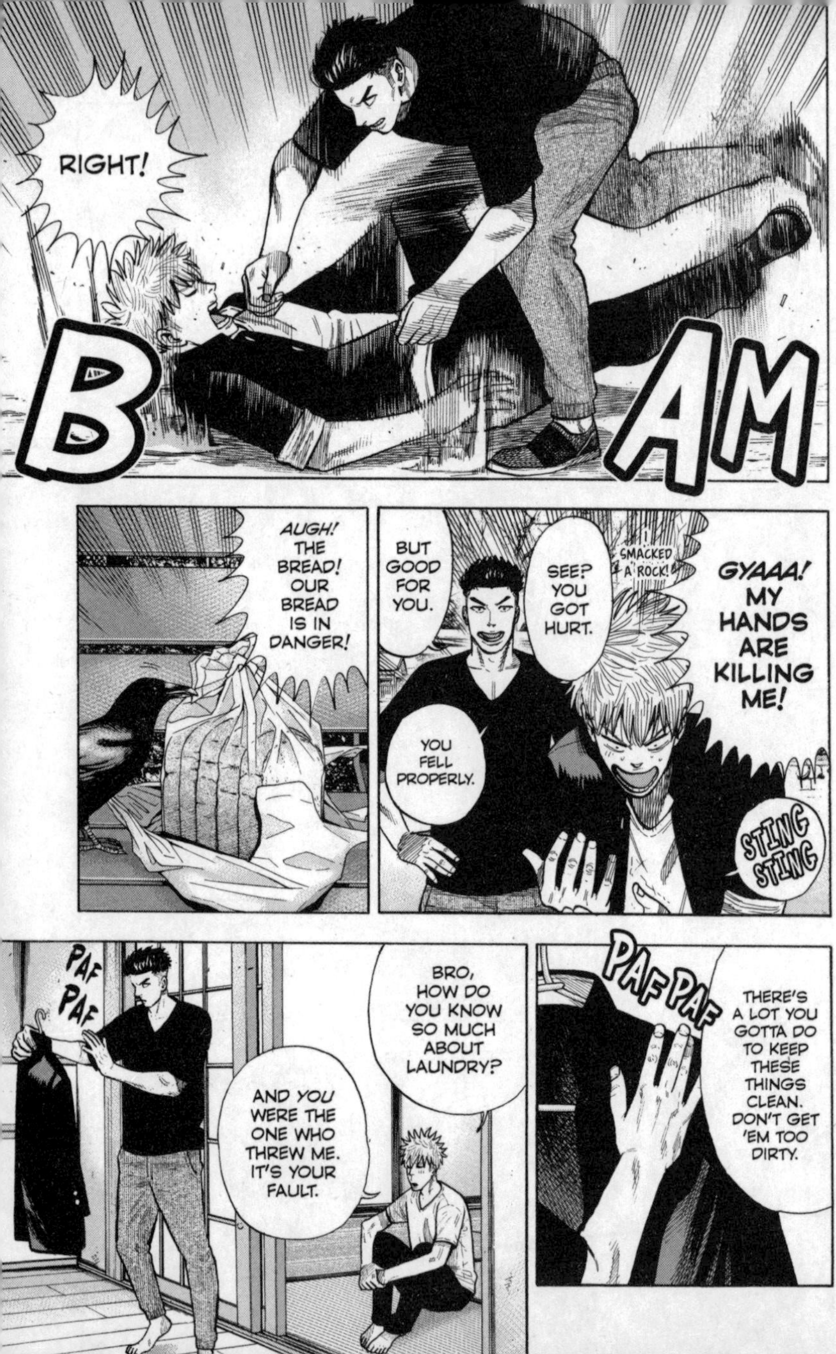
RIGHT!
BAM
GYAAA! MY HANDS ARE KILLING ME!
I SMACKED A ROCK!
SEE? YOU GOT HURT.
BUT GOOD FOR YOU.
YOU FELL PROPERLY.
STING STING
AUGH! THE BREAD! OUR BREAD IS IN DANGER!
PAF PAF
THERE'S A LOT YOU GOTTA DO TO KEEP THESE THINGS CLEAN. DON'T GET 'EM TOO DIRTY.
BRO, HOW DO YOU KNOW SO MUCH ABOUT LAUNDRY?
AND YOU WERE THE ONE WHO THREW ME. IT'S YOUR FAULT.
PAF PAF

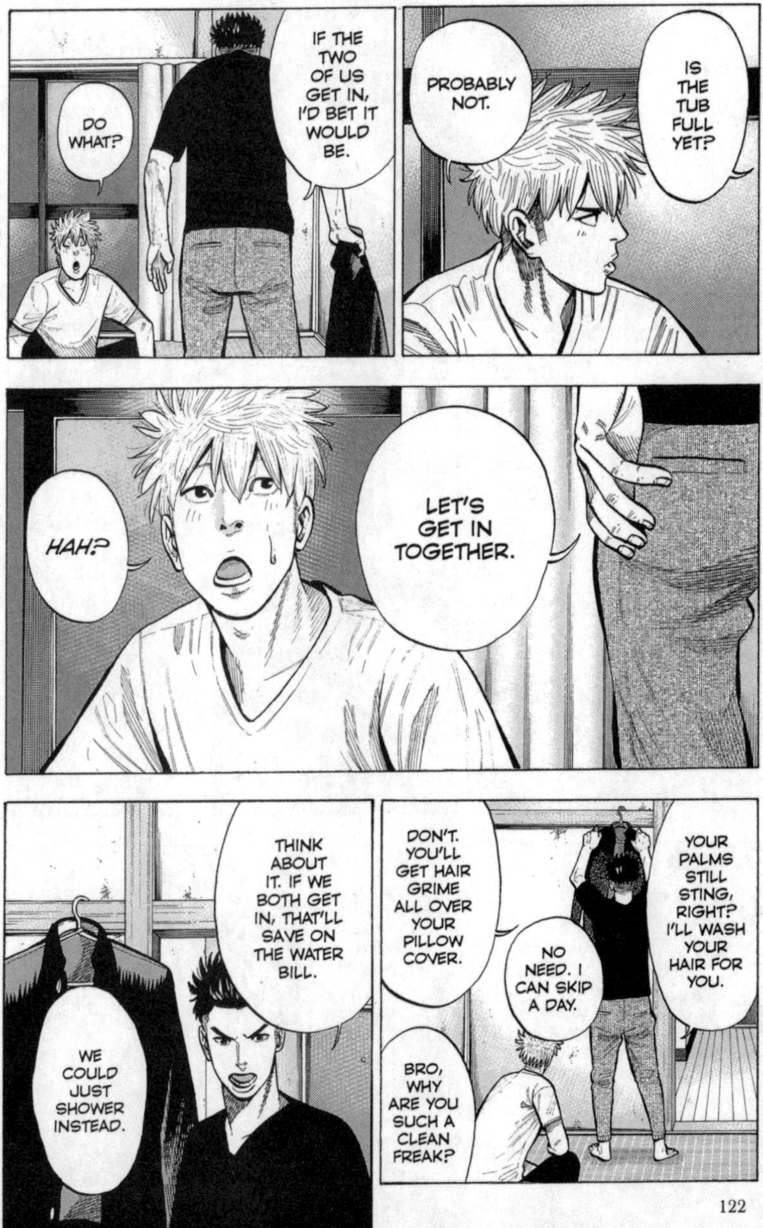
IS THE TUB FULL YET?
PROBABLY NOT.
IF THE TWO OF US GET IN, I'D BET IT WOULD BE.
DO WHAT?
LET'S GET IN TOGETHER.
HAH?
YOUR PALMS STILL STING, RIGHT? I'LL WASH YOUR HAIR FOR YOU.
NO NEED. I CAN SKIP A DAY.
DON'T. YOU'LL GET HAIR GRIME ALL OVER YOUR PILLOW COVER.
BRO, WHY ARE YOU SUCH A CLEAN FREAK?
THINK ABOUT IT. IF WE BOTH GET IN, THAT'LL SAVE ON THE WATER BILL.
WE COULD JUST SHOWER INSTEAD.

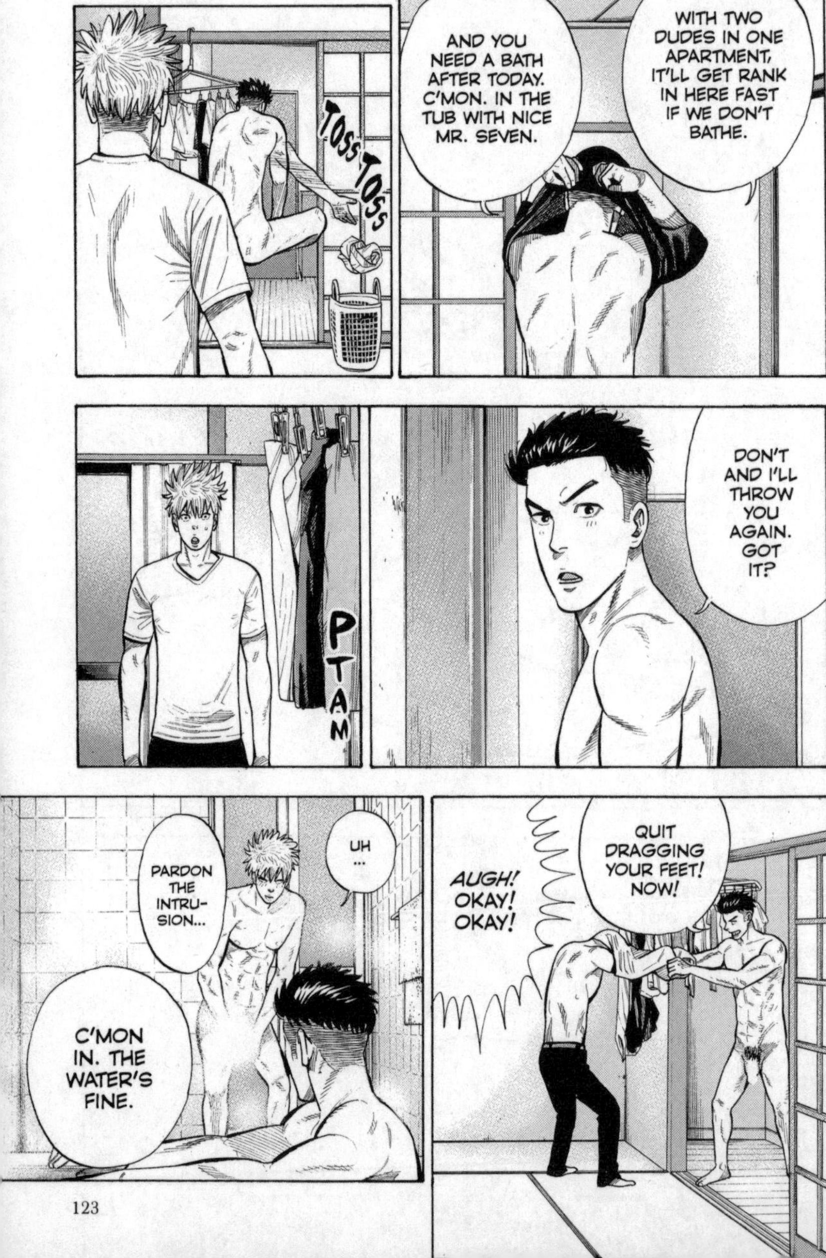
WITH TWO DUDES IN ONE APARTMENT, IT'LL GET RANK IN HERE FAST IF WE DON'T BATHE.
AND YOU NEED A BATH AFTER TODAY. C'MON. IN THE TUB WITH NICE MR. SEVEN.
TOSS TOSS
DON'T AND I'LL THROW YOU AGAIN. GOT IT?
PTAM
QUIT DRAGGING YOUR FEET! NOW!
AUGH! OKAY! OKAY!
UH ...
PARDON THE INTRU-SION...
C'MON IN. THE WATER'S FINE.

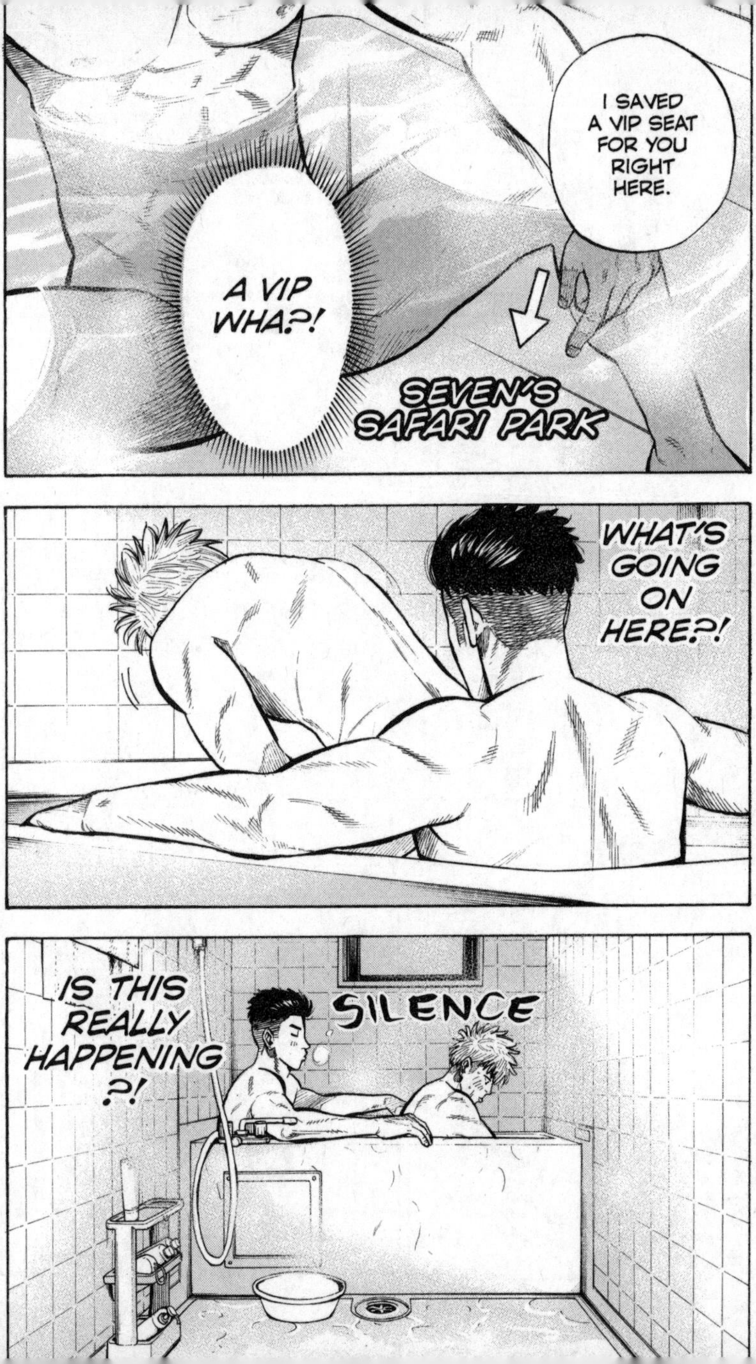
I SAVED A VIP SEAT FOR YOU RIGHT HERE.
A VIP WHA?!
SEVEN'S SAFARI PARK
WHAT'S GOING ON HERE?!
SILENCE
IS THIS REALLY HAPPENING?!

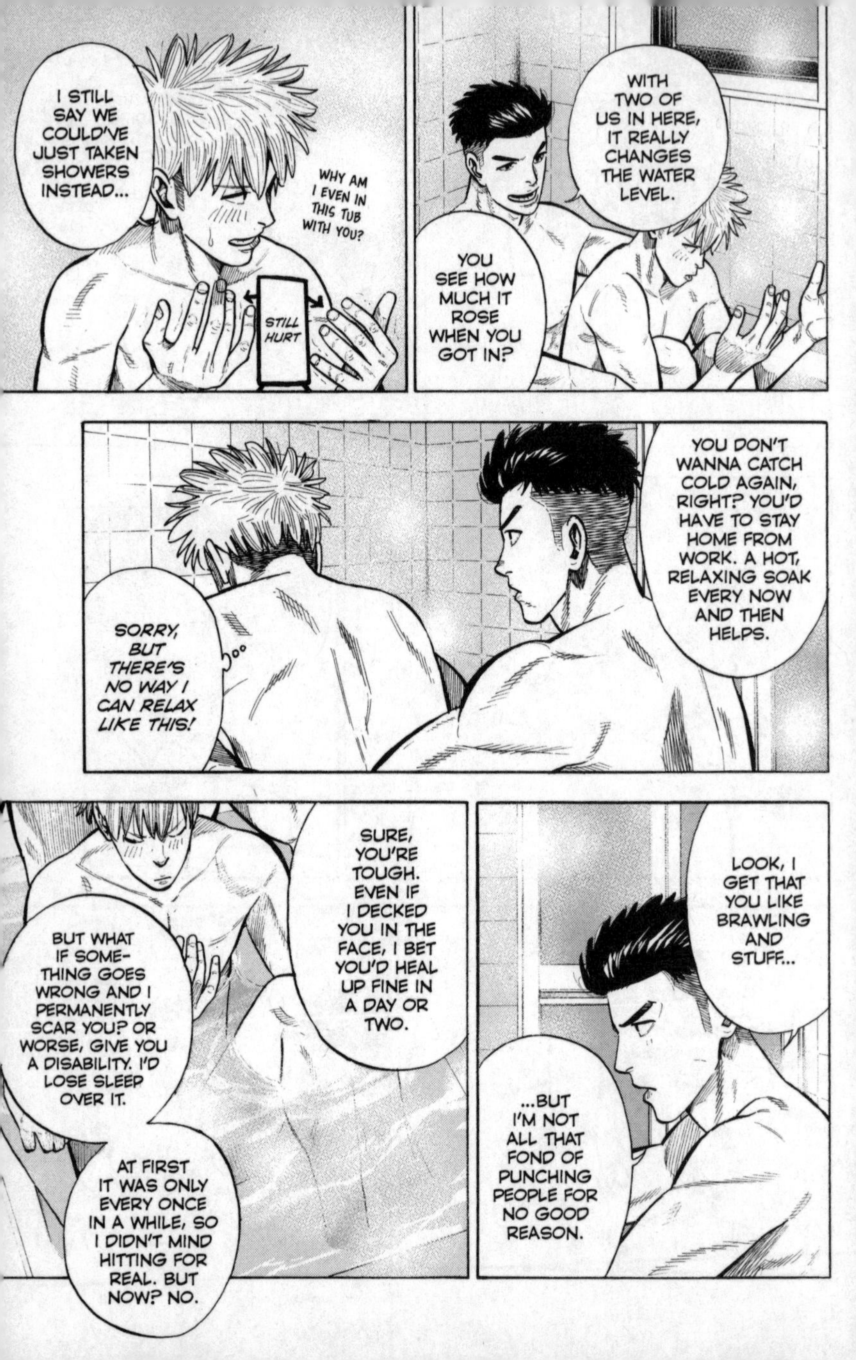
WITH TWO OF US IN HERE, IT REALLY CHANGES THE WATER LEVEL.
YOU SEE HOW MUCH IT ROSE WHEN YOU GOT IN?
I STILL SAY WE COULD'VE JUST TAKEN SHOWERS INSTEAD...
WHY AM I EVEN IN THIS TUB WITH YOU?
STILL HURT
YOU DON'T WANNA CATCH COLD AGAIN, RIGHT? YOU'D HAVE TO STAY HOME FROM WORK. A HOT, RELAXING SOAK EVERY NOW AND THEN HELPS.
SORRY, BUT THERE'S NO WAY I CAN RELAX LIKE THIS!
LOOK, I GET THAT YOU LIKE BRAWLING AND STUFF...
...BUT I'M NOT ALL THAT FOND OF PUNCHING PEOPLE FOR NO GOOD REASON.
SURE, YOU'RE TOUGH. EVEN IF I DECKED YOU IN THE FACE, I BET YOU'D HEAL UP FINE IN A DAY OR TWO.
BUT WHAT IF SOME-THING GOES WRONG AND I PERMANENTLY SCAR YOU? OR WORSE, GIVE YOU A DISABILITY. I'D LOSE SLEEP OVER IT.
AT FIRST IT WAS ONLY EVERY ONCE IN A WHILE, SO I DIDN'T MIND HITTING FOR REAL. BUT NOW? NO.

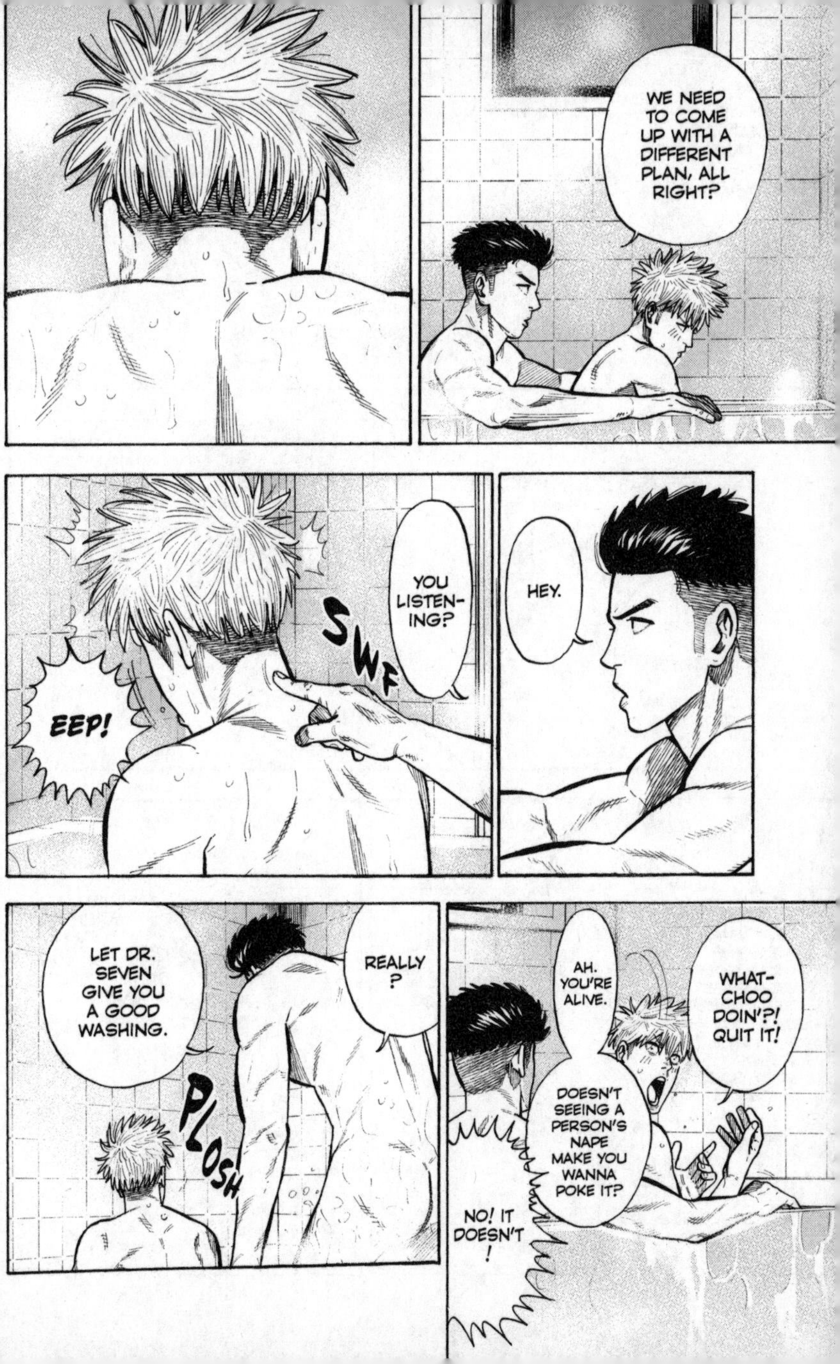
WE NEED TO COME UP WITH A DIFFERENT PLAN, ALL RIGHT?
HEY.
YOU LISTENING?
SWF
EEP!
WHAT-CHOO DOIN'?! QUIT IT!
AH. YOU'RE ALIVE.
DOESN'T SEEING A PERSON'S NAPE MAKE YOU WANNA POKE IT?
NO! IT DOESN'T!
REALLY?
LET DR. SEVEN GIVE YOU A GOOD WASHING.
PLOSH

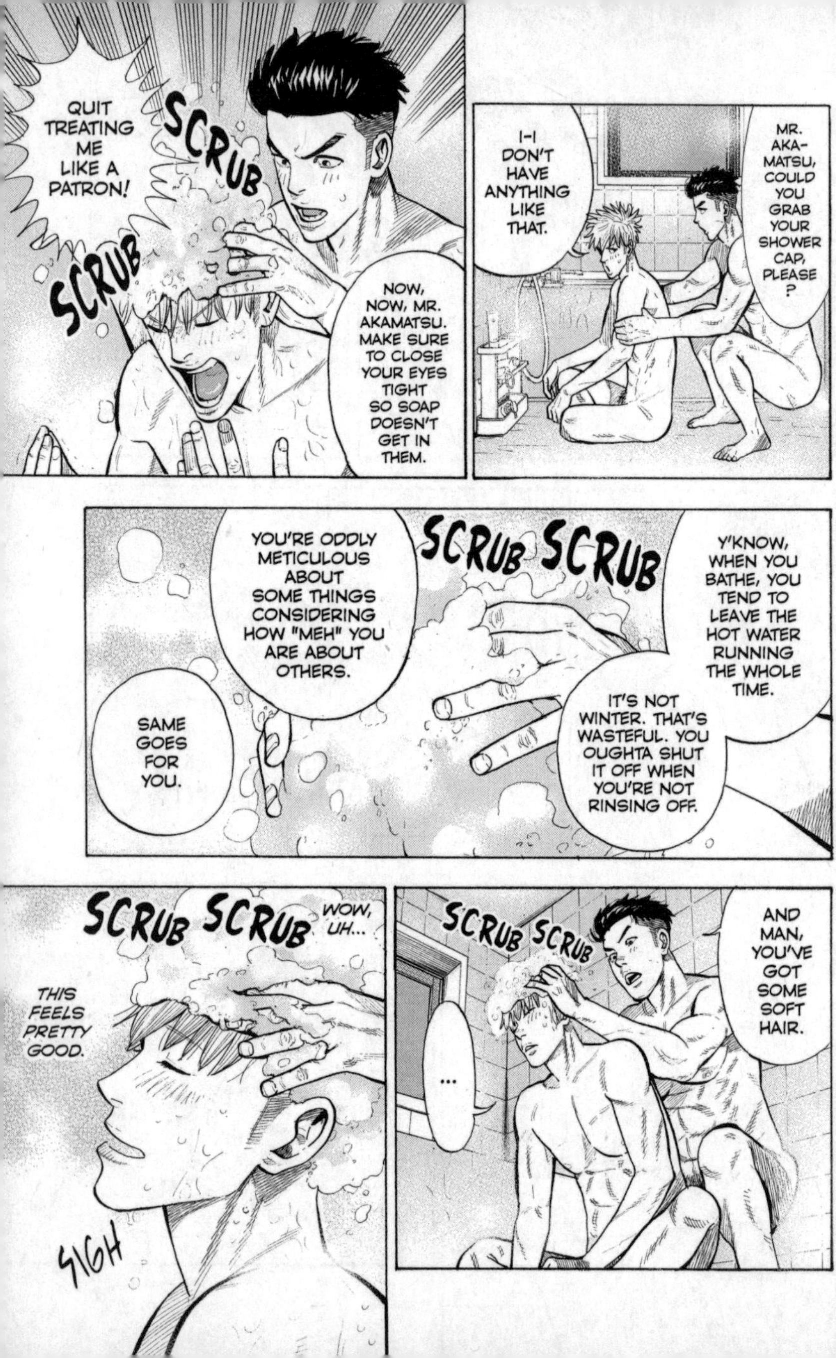

MR. AKA-MATSU, COULD YOU GRAB YOUR SHOWER CAP, PLEASE?
I-I DON'T HAVE ANYTHING LIKE THAT.
SCRUB
NOW, NOW, MR. AKAMATSU. MAKE SURE TO CLOSE YOUR EYES TIGHT SO SOAP DOESN'T GET IN THEM.
QUIT TREATING ME LIKE A PATRON!
SCRUB
Y'KNOW, WHEN YOU BATHE, YOU TEND TO LEAVE THE HOT WATER RUNNING THE WHOLE TIME.
SCRUB SCRUB
IT'S NOT WINTER. THAT'S WASTEFUL. YOU OUGHTA SHUT IT OFF WHEN YOU'RE NOT RINSING OFF.
YOU'RE ODDLY METICULOUS ABOUT SOME THINGS CONSIDERING HOW "MEH" YOU ARE ABOUT OTHERS.
SAME GOES FOR YOU.
AND MAN, YOU'VE GOT SOME SOFT HAIR.
SCRUB SCRUB
...
WOW, UH...
SCRUB SCRUB
THIS FEELS PRETTY GOOD.
SIGH

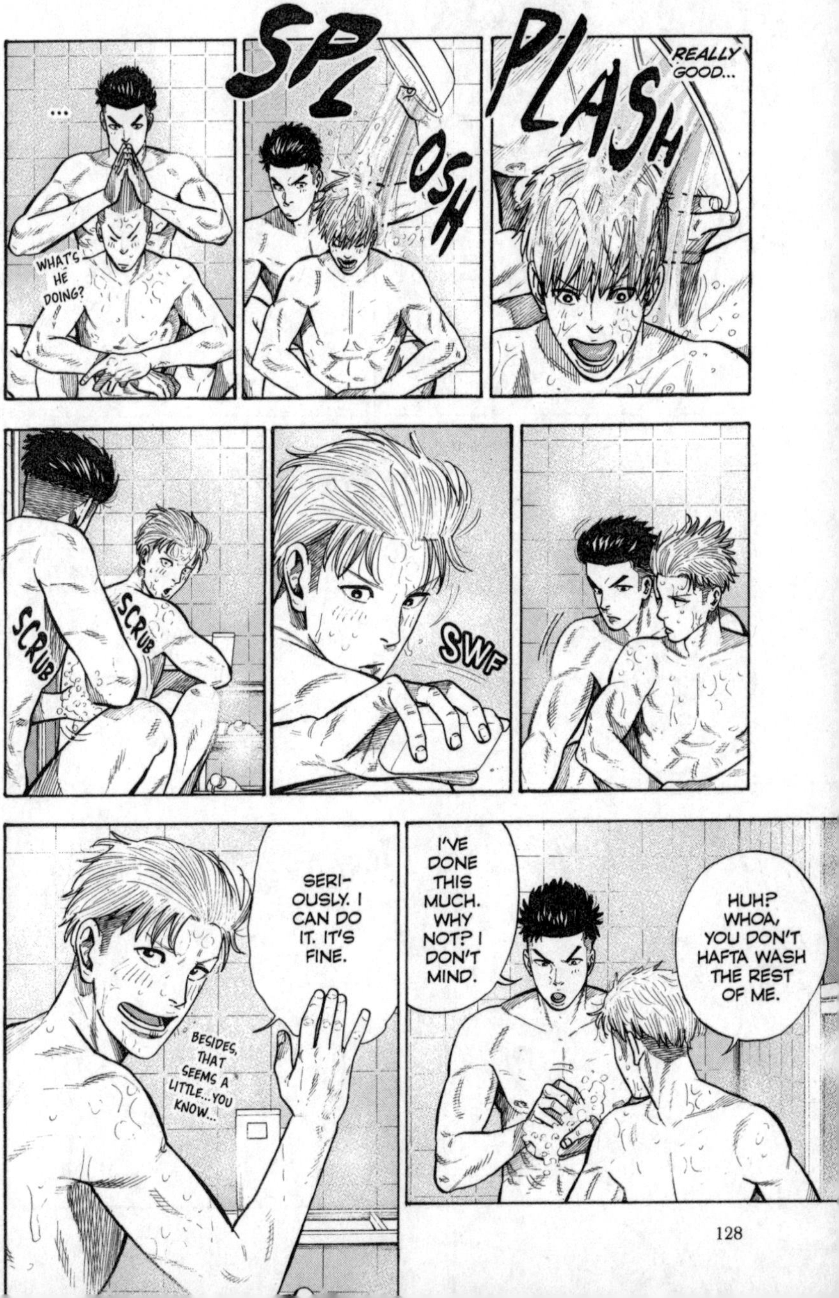
PLASH
REALLY GOOD...
SPLOSH
...
WHAT'S HE DOING?
SWF
SCRUB
SCRUB
HUH? WHOA, YOU DON'T HAFTA WASH THE REST OF ME.
I'VE DONE THIS MUCH. WHY NOT? I DON'T MIND.
SERI-OUSLY. I CAN DO IT. IT'S FINE.
BESIDES, THAT SEEMS A LITTLE...YOU KNOW...

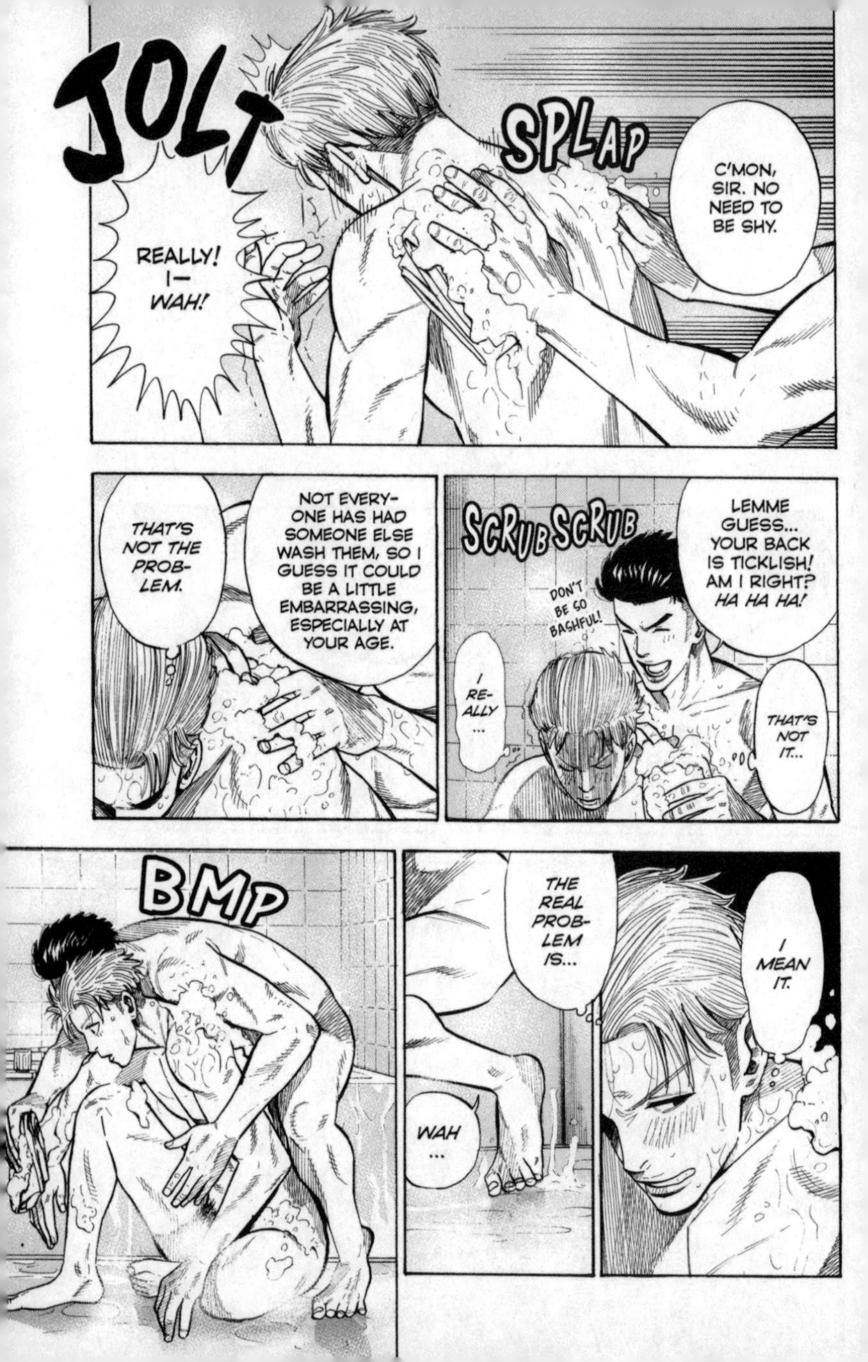
C'MON, SIR. NO NEED TO BE SHY.
SPLAP
JOLT
REALLY! I— WAH!
LEMME GUESS... YOUR BACK IS TICKLISH! AM I RIGHT? HA HA HA!
SCRUB SCRUB
DON'T BE SO BASHFUL!
THAT'S NOT IT...
I REALLY ...
NOT EVERYONE HAS HAD SOMEONE ELSE WASH THEM, SO I GUESS IT COULD BE A LITTLE EMBARRASSING, ESPECIALLY AT YOUR AGE.
THAT'S NOT THE PROBLEM.
I MEAN IT.
THE REAL PROBLEM IS...
WAH ...
BMP

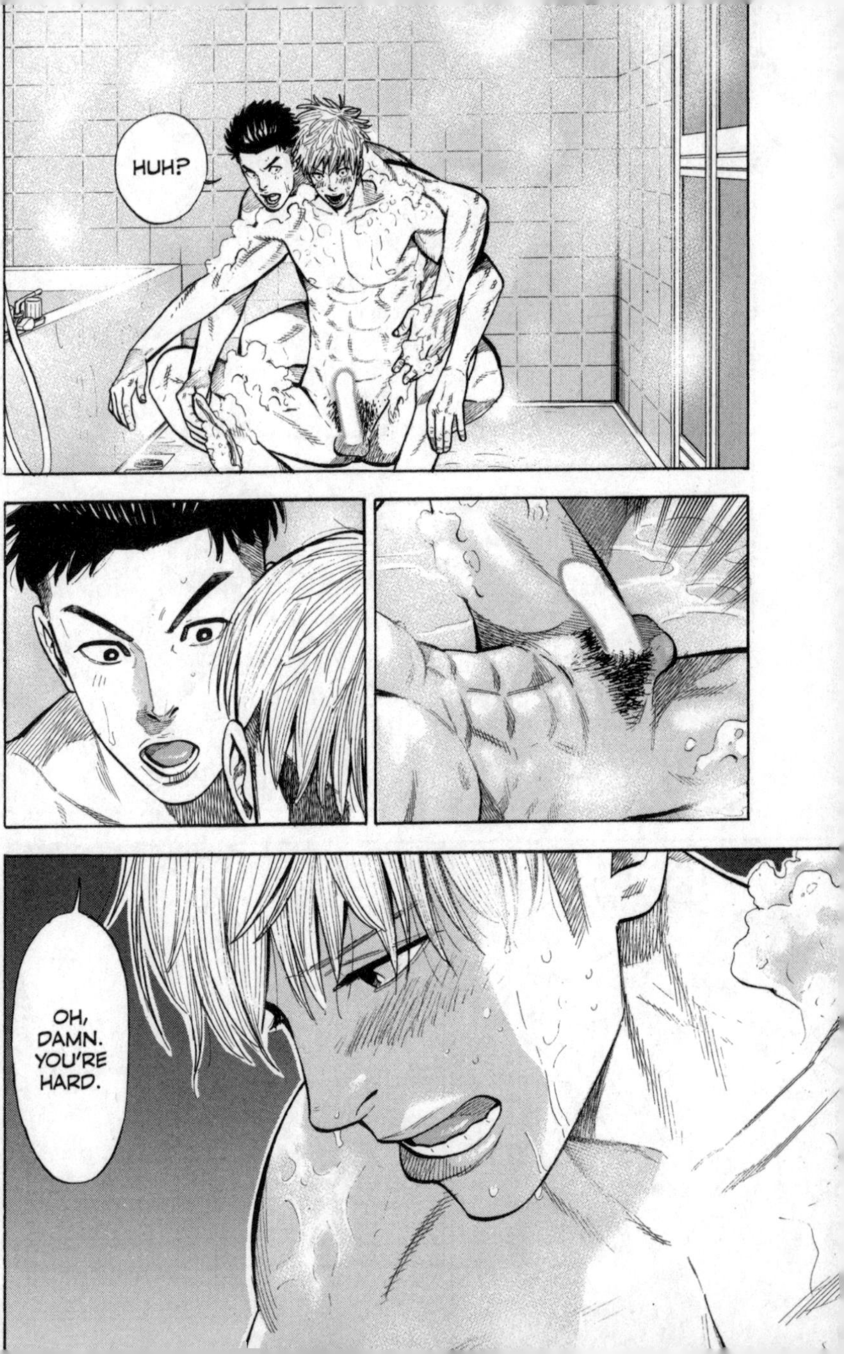
HUH?
OH, DAMN. YOU'RE HARD.

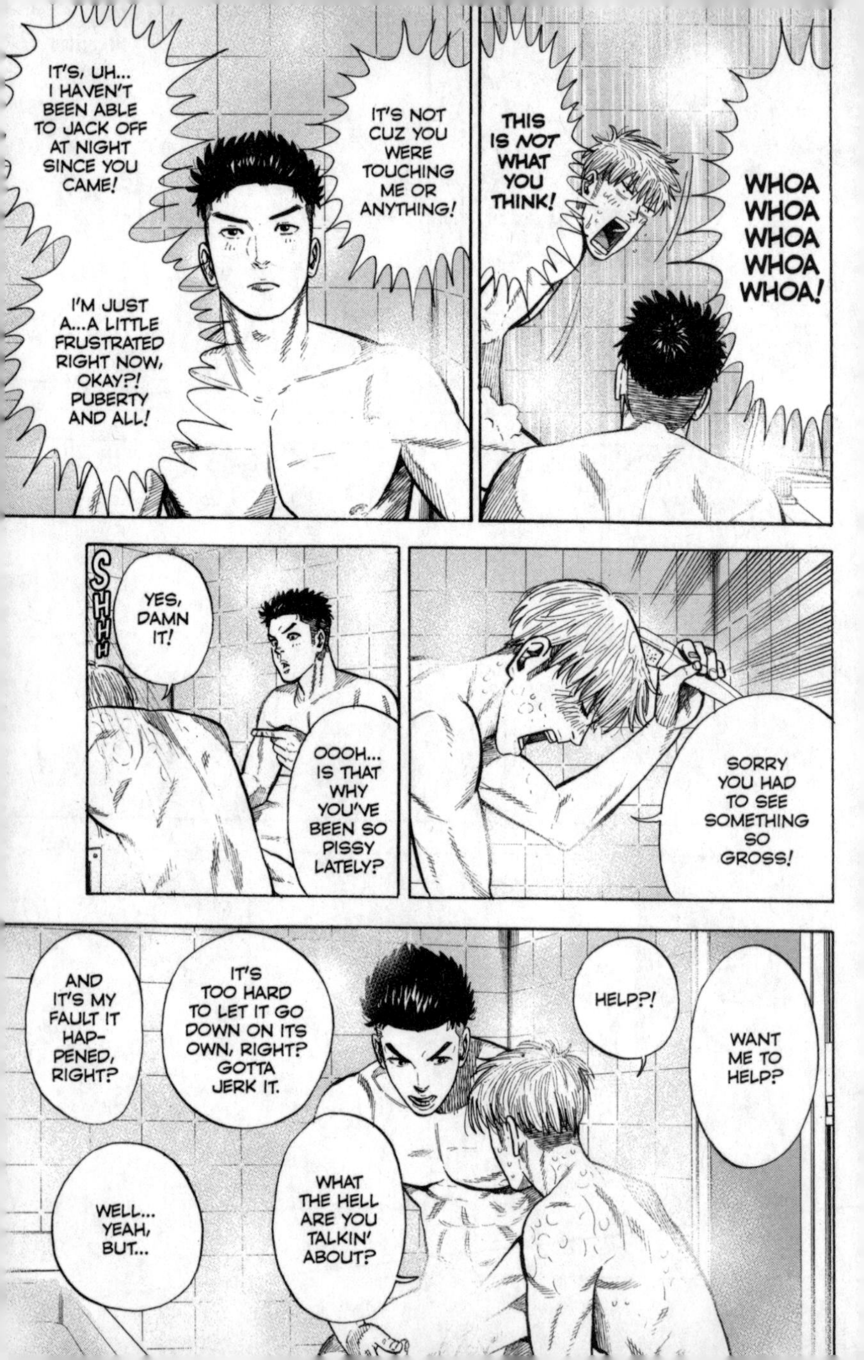
WHOA WHOA WHOA WHOA WHOA!
THIS IS *NOT* WHAT YOU THINK!
IT'S NOT CUZ YOU WERE TOUCHING ME OR ANYTHING!
IT'S, UH... I HAVEN'T BEEN ABLE TO JACK OFF AT NIGHT SINCE YOU CAME!
I'M JUST A...A LITTLE FRUSTRATED RIGHT NOW, OKAY?! PUBERTY AND ALL!
SORRY YOU HAD TO SEE SOMETHING SO GROSS!
OOOH... IS THAT WHY YOU'VE BEEN SO PISSY LATELY?
YES, DAMN IT!
SHHH
WANT ME TO HELP?
HELP?!
IT'S TOO HARD TO LET IT GO DOWN ON ITS OWN, RIGHT? GOTTA JERK IT.
AND IT'S MY FAULT IT HAP-PENED, RIGHT?
WHAT THE HELL ARE YOU TALKIN' ABOUT?
WELL... YEAH, BUT...

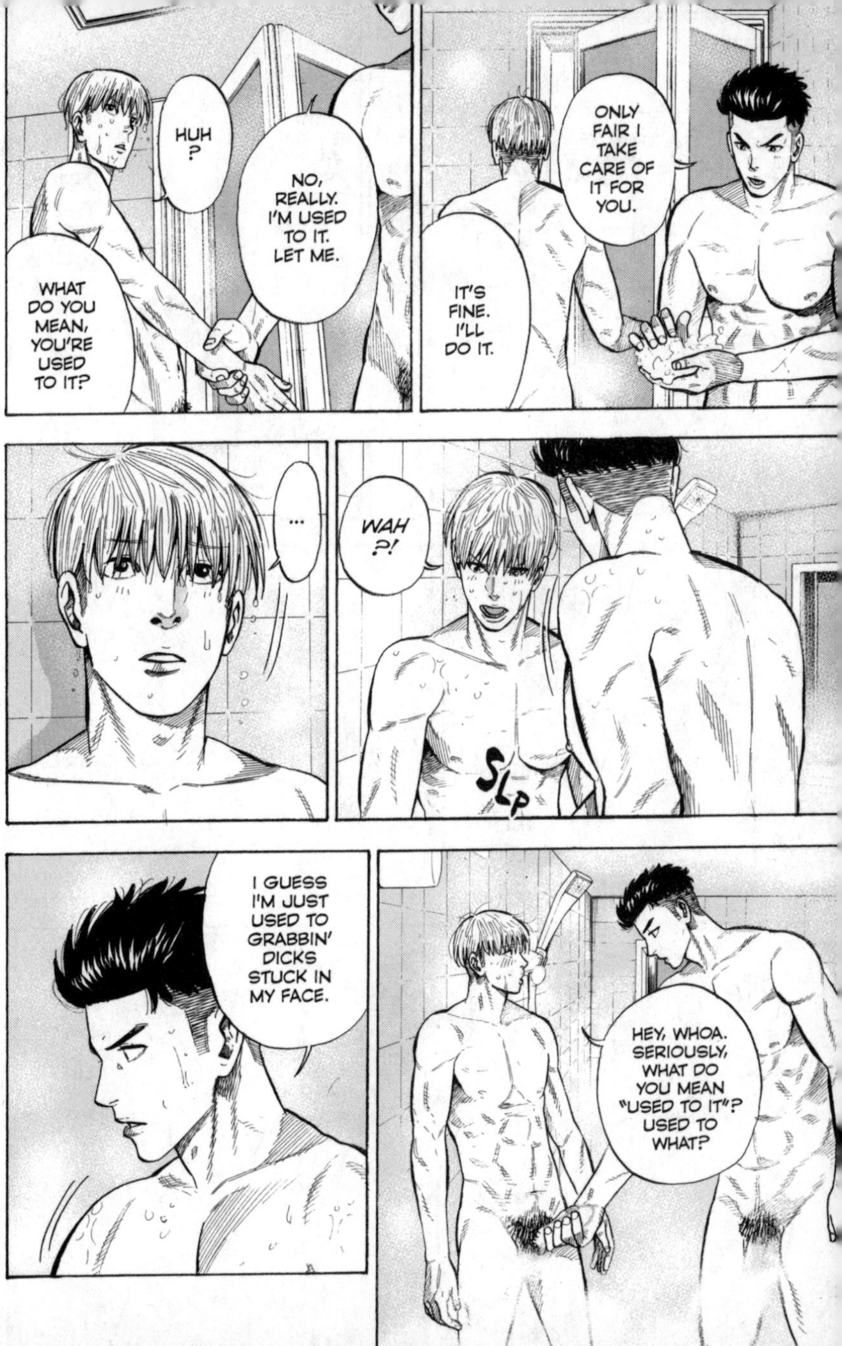
ONLY FAIR I TAKE CARE OF IT FOR YOU.
IT'S FINE. I'LL DO IT.
NO, REALLY. I'M USED TO IT. LET ME.
HUH?
WHAT DO YOU MEAN, YOU'RE USED TO IT?
WAH?!
SLP
...
HEY, WHOA. SERIOUSLY, WHAT DO YOU MEAN "USED TO IT"? USED TO WHAT?
I GUESS I'M JUST USED TO GRABBIN' DICKS STUCK IN MY FACE.

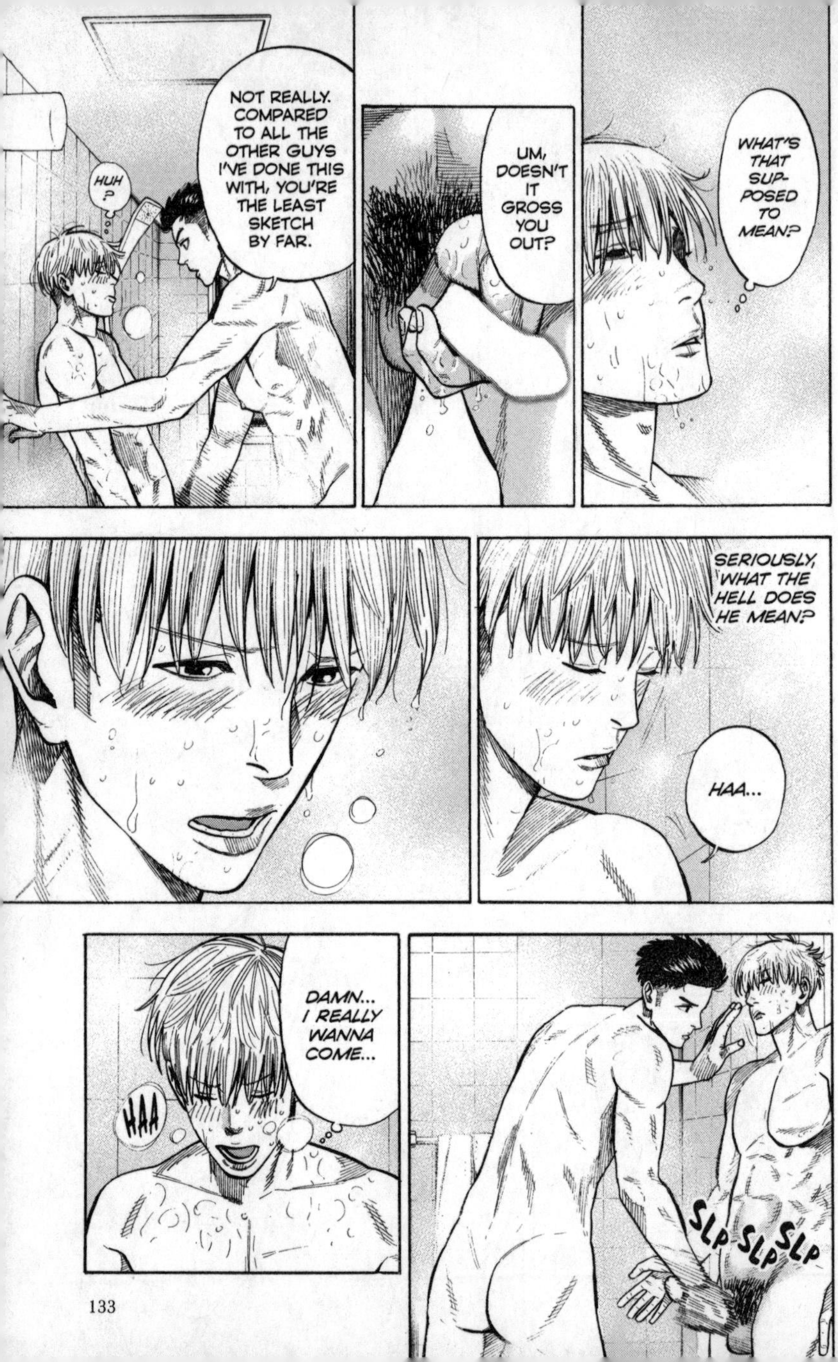
WHAT'S THAT SUP-POSED TO MEAN?
UM, DOESN'T IT GROSS YOU OUT?
NOT REALLY. COMPARED TO ALL THE OTHER GUYS I'VE DONE THIS WITH, YOU'RE THE LEAST SKETCH BY FAR.
HUH?
SERIOUSLY, WHAT THE HELL DOES HE MEAN?
HAA...
SLP SLP SLP
DAMN... I REALLY WANNA COME...
HAA

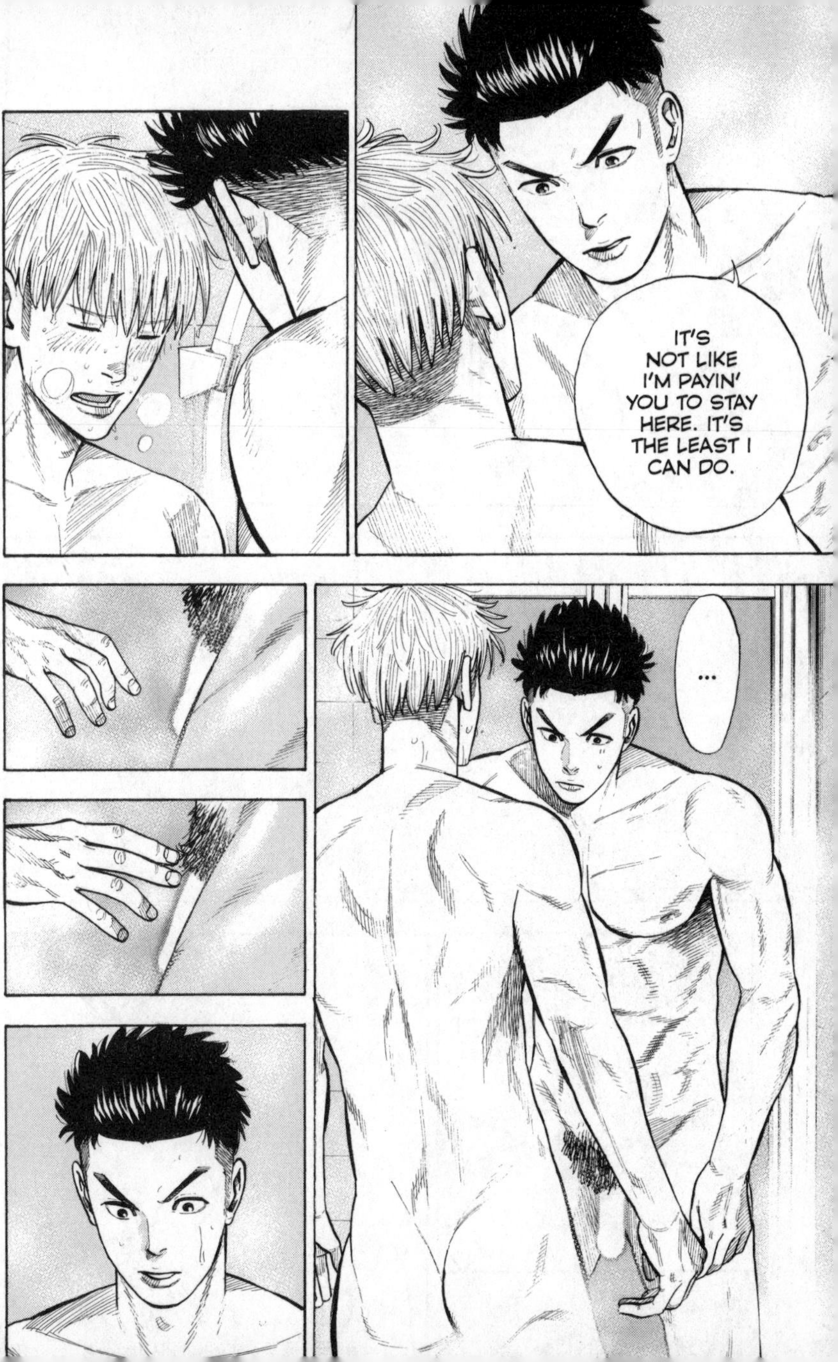
IT'S NOT LIKE I'M PAYIN' YOU TO STAY HERE. IT'S THE LEAST I CAN DO.
...

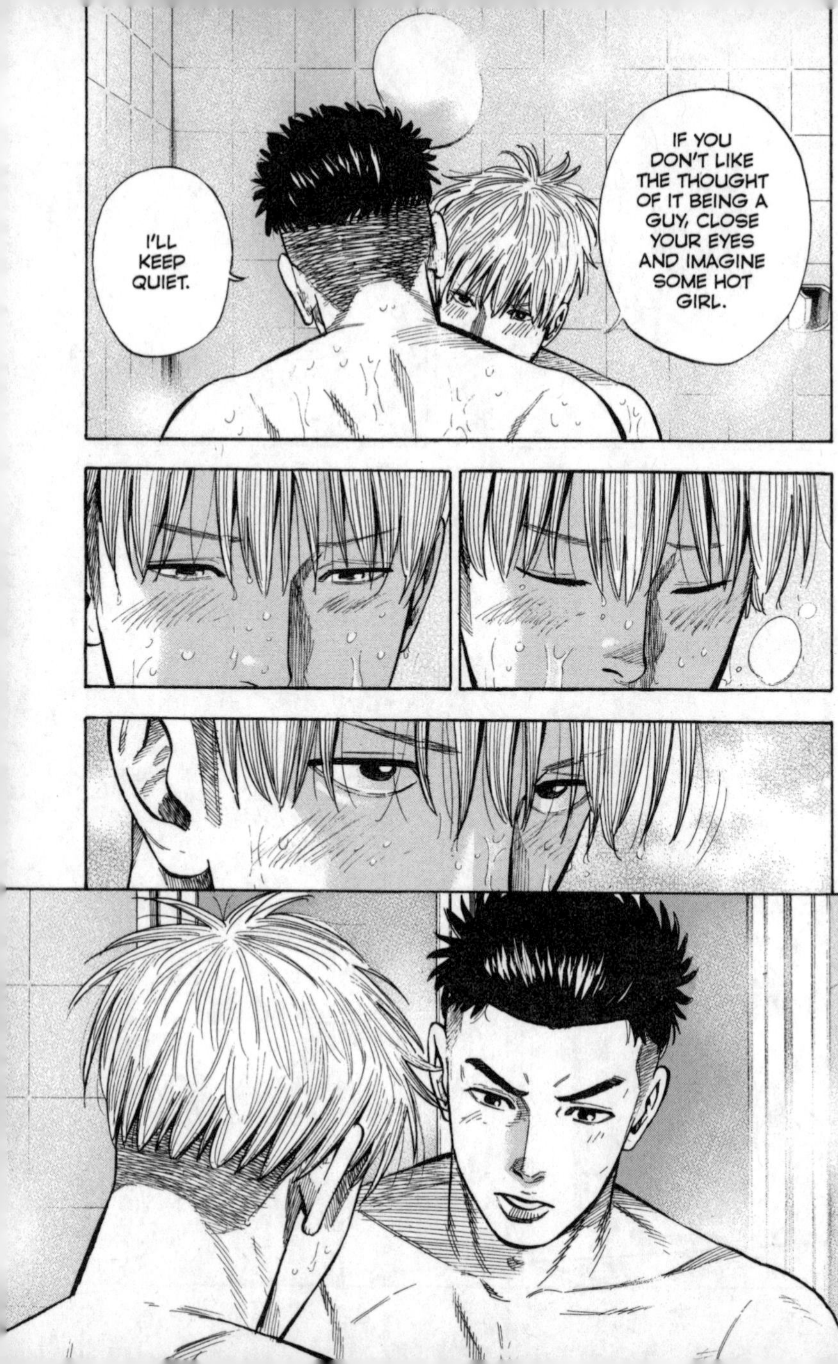
IF YOU DON'T LIKE THE THOUGHT OF IT BEING A GUY, CLOSE YOUR EYES AND IMAGINE SOME HOT GIRL.
I'LL KEEP QUIET.

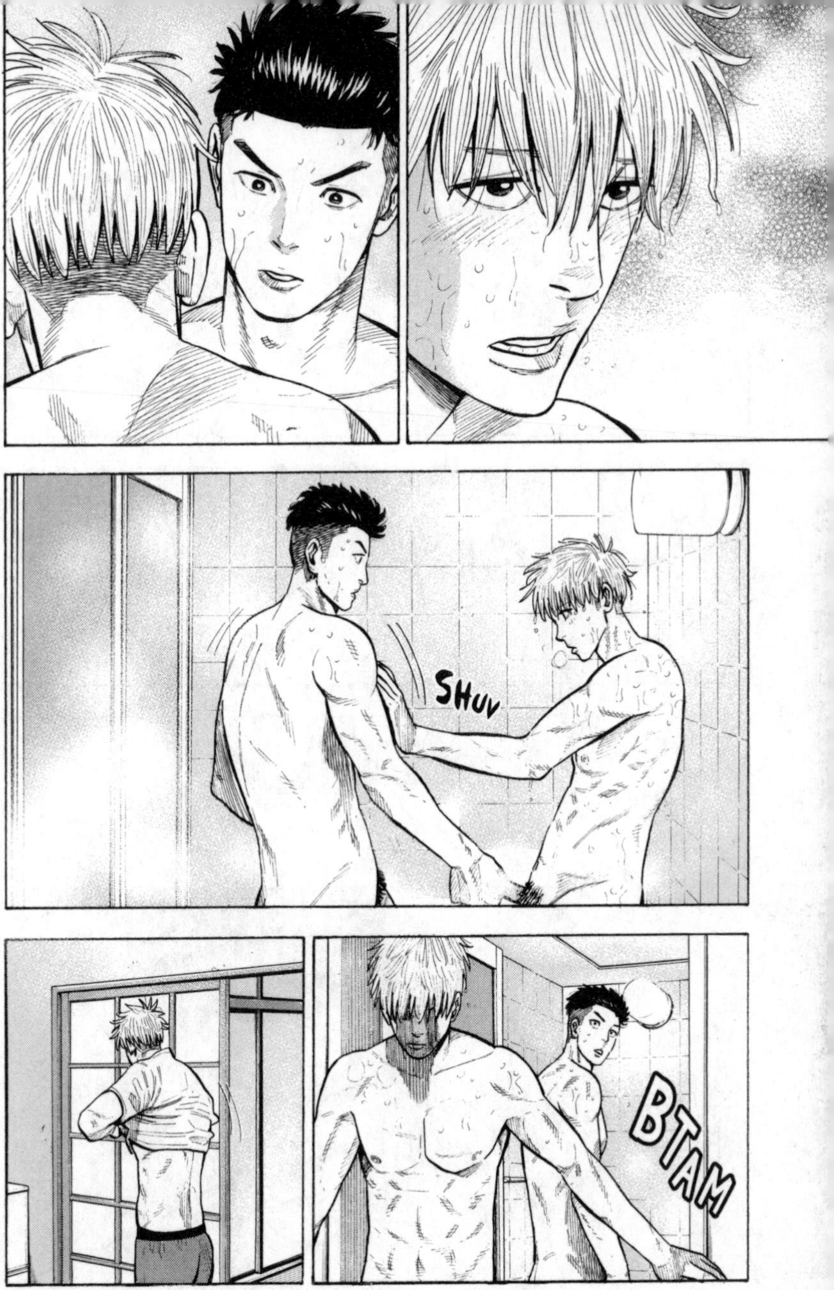
SHUV
BTAM

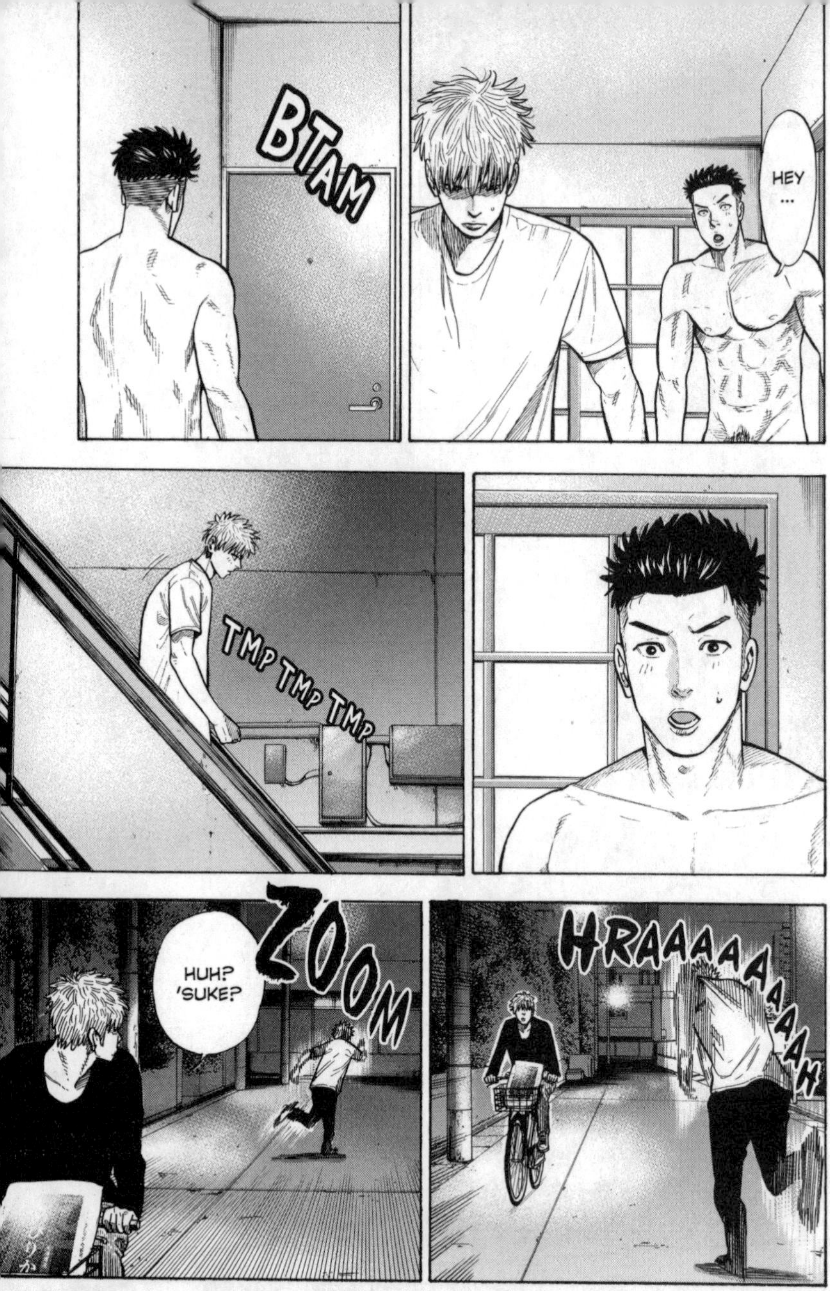
HEY ...
BTAM
TMP TMP TMP
HRAAAAAAAAH
HUH? 'SUKE?
ZOOM

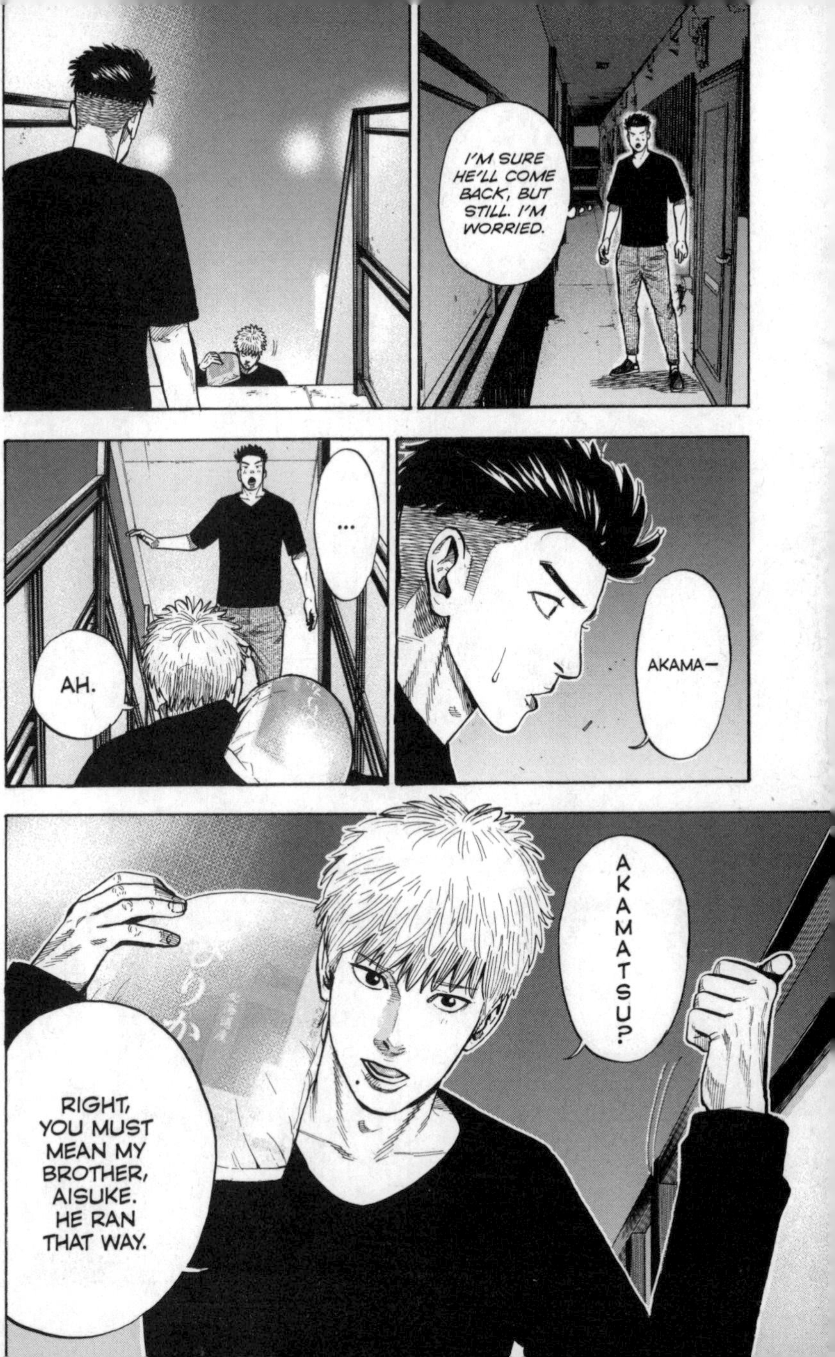
I'M SURE HE'LL COME BACK, BUT STILL. I'M WORRIED.
AKAMA—
...
AH.
AKAMATSU?
RIGHT, YOU MUST MEAN MY BROTHER, AISUKE. HE RAN THAT WAY.

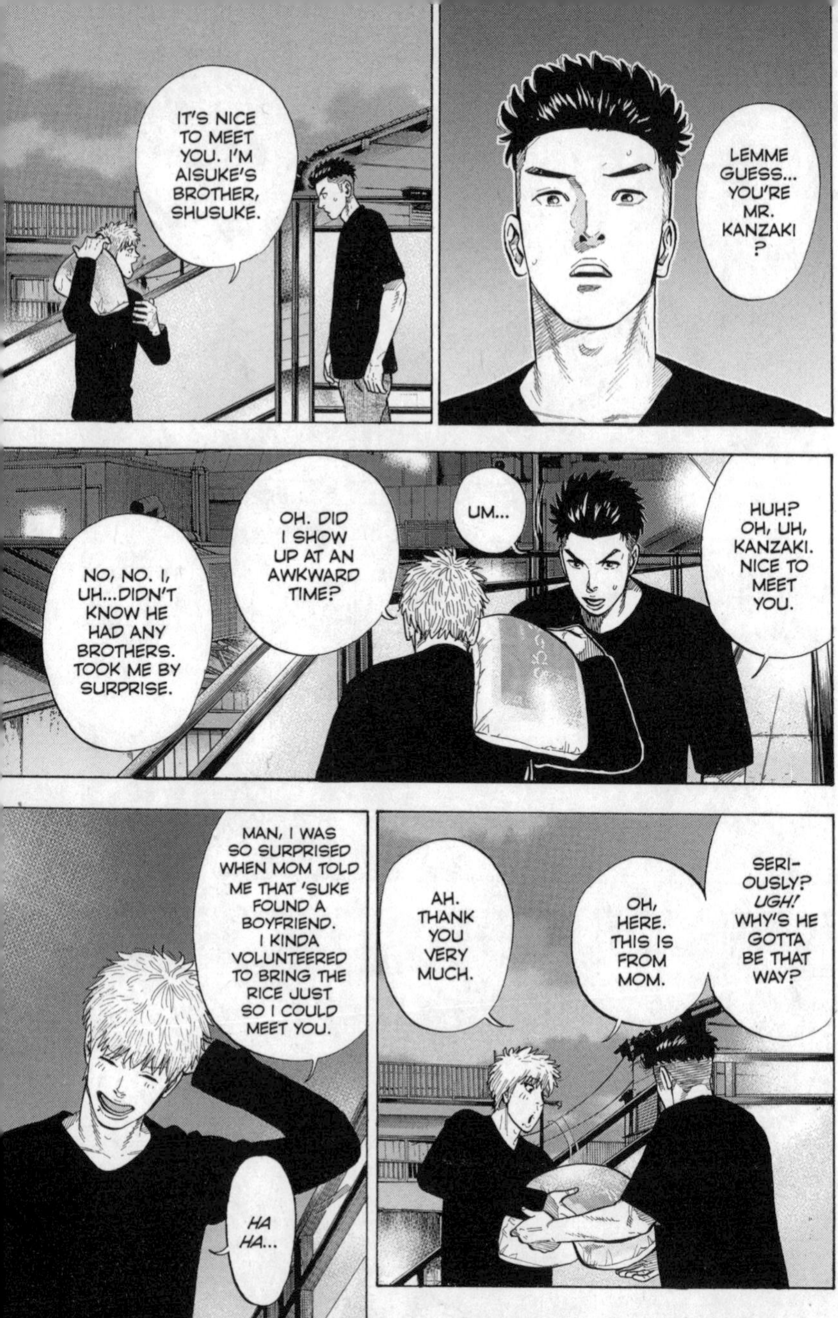
LEMME GUESS... YOU'RE MR. KANZAKI?
IT'S NICE TO MEET YOU. I'M AISUKE'S BROTHER, SHUSUKE.
HUH? OH, UH, KANZAKI. NICE TO MEET YOU.
UM...
OH. DID I SHOW UP AT AN AWKWARD TIME?
NO, NO. I, UH...DIDN'T KNOW HE HAD ANY BROTHERS. TOOK ME BY SURPRISE.
SERI-OUSLY? *UGH!* WHY'S HE GOTTA BE THAT WAY?
OH, HERE. THIS IS FROM MOM.
AH. THANK YOU VERY MUCH.
MAN, I WAS SO SURPRISED WHEN MOM TOLD ME THAT 'SUKE FOUND A BOYFRIEND. I KINDA VOLUNTEERED TO BRING THE RICE JUST SO I COULD MEET YOU.
HA HA...

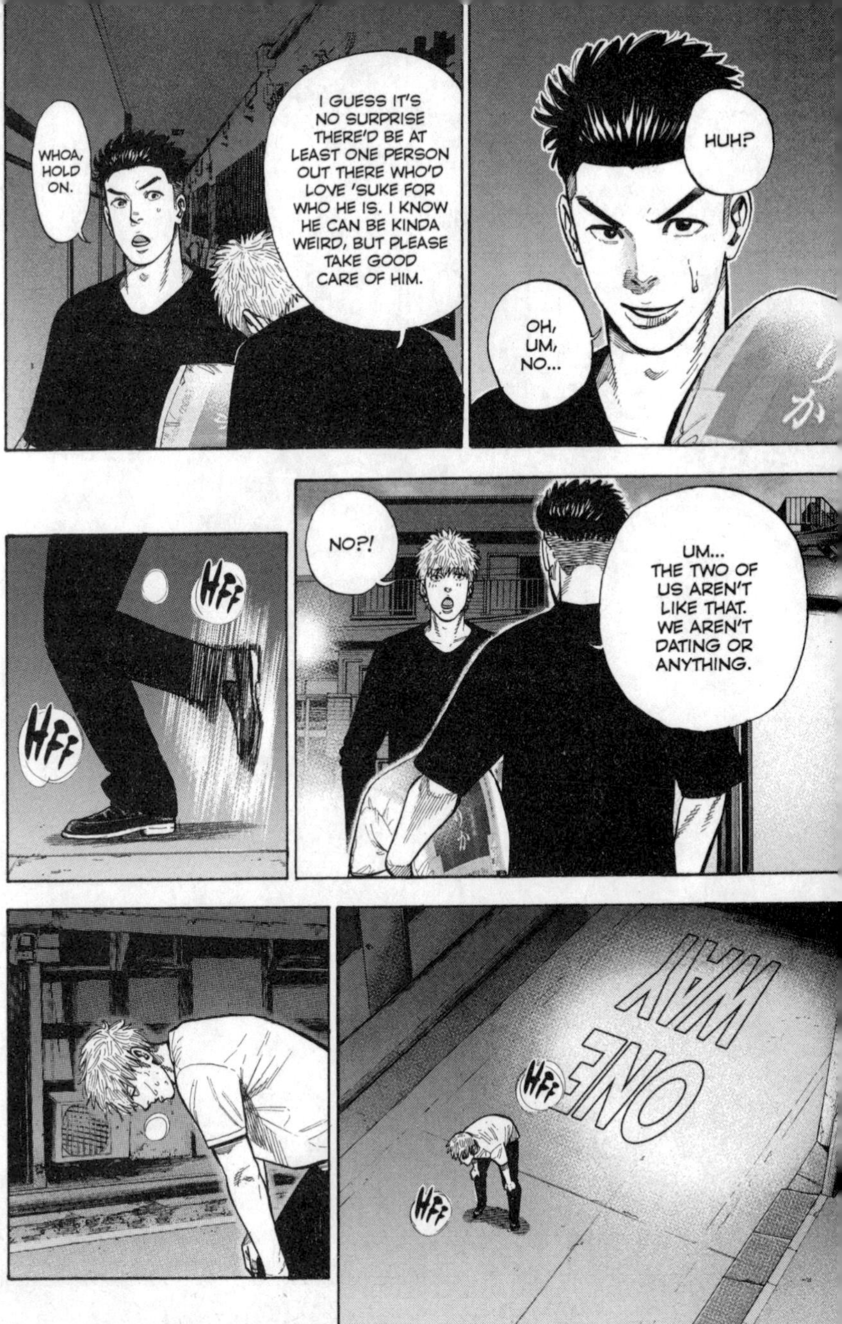

HUH?
OH, UM, NO...
I GUESS IT'S NO SURPRISE THERE'D BE AT LEAST ONE PERSON OUT THERE WHO'D LOVE 'SUKE FOR WHO HE IS. I KNOW HE CAN BE KINDA WEIRD, BUT PLEASE TAKE GOOD CARE OF HIM.
WHOA, HOLD ON.
UM... THE TWO OF US AREN'T LIKE THAT. WE AREN'T DATING OR ANYTHING.
NO?!
HFF
HFF
ONE WAY
HFF
HFF

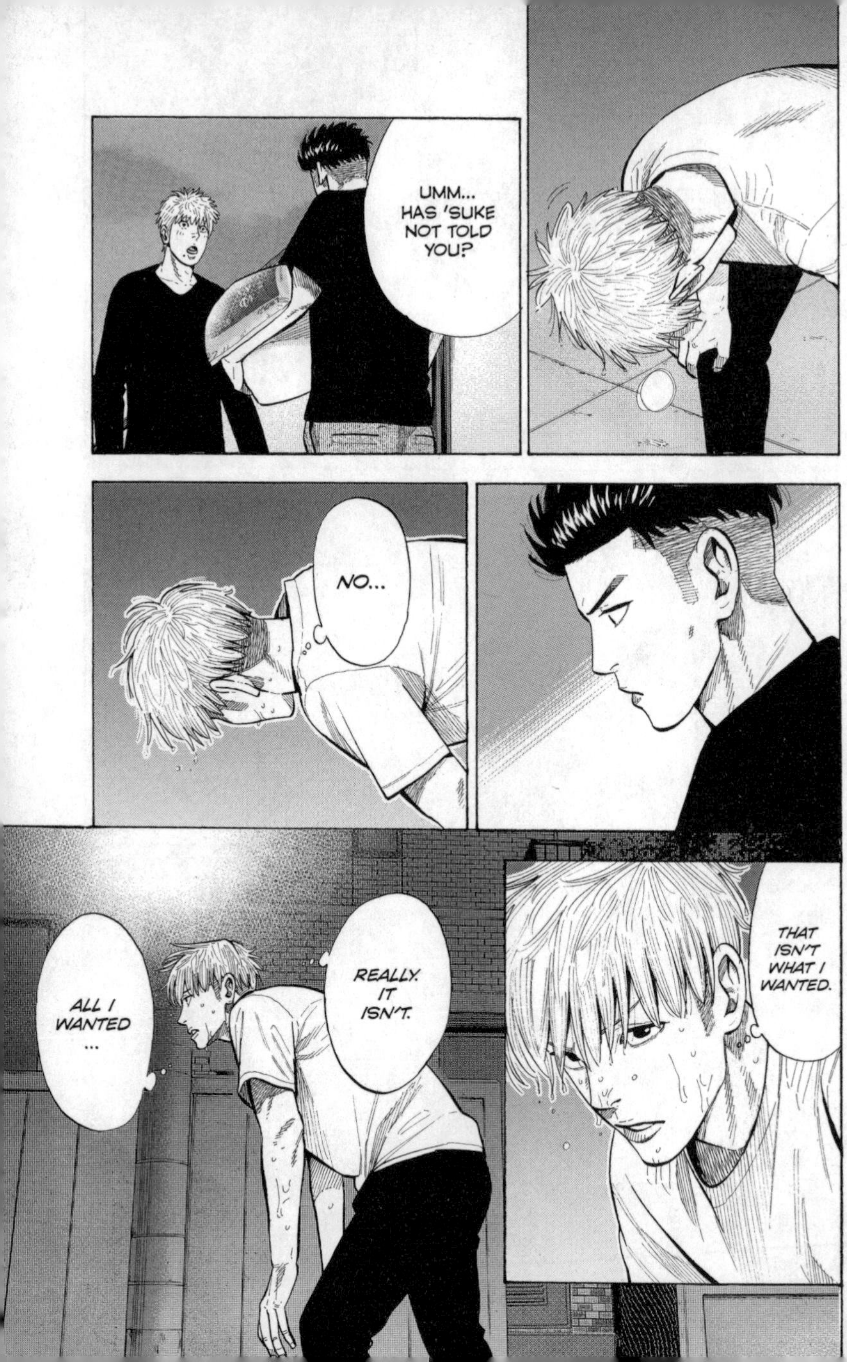
UMM... HAS 'SUKE NOT TOLD YOU?
NO...
THAT ISN'T WHAT I WANTED.
REALLY. IT ISN'T.
ALL I WANTED ...

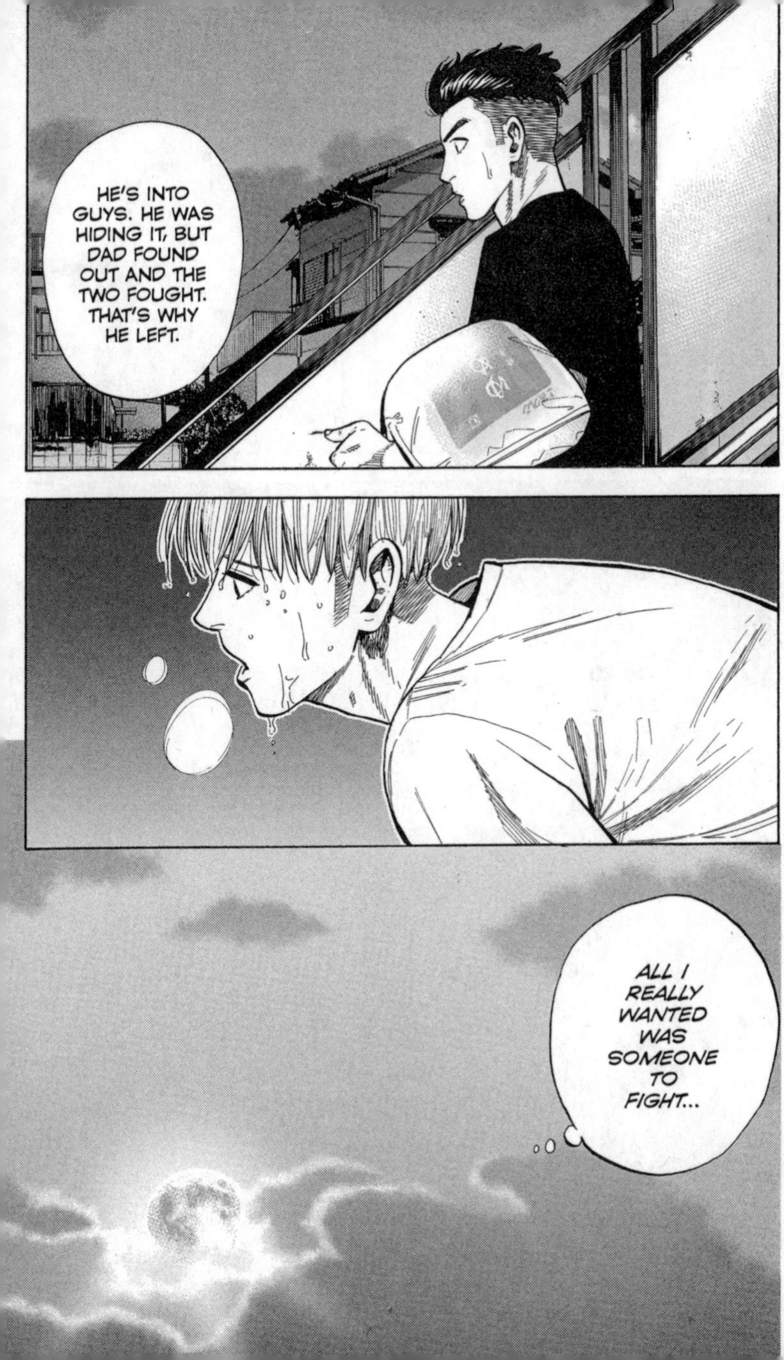
HE'S INTO GUYS. HE WAS HIDING IT, BUT DAD FOUND OUT AND THE TWO FOUGHT. THAT'S WHY HE LEFT.
ALL I REALLY WANTED WAS SOMEONE TO FIGHT...

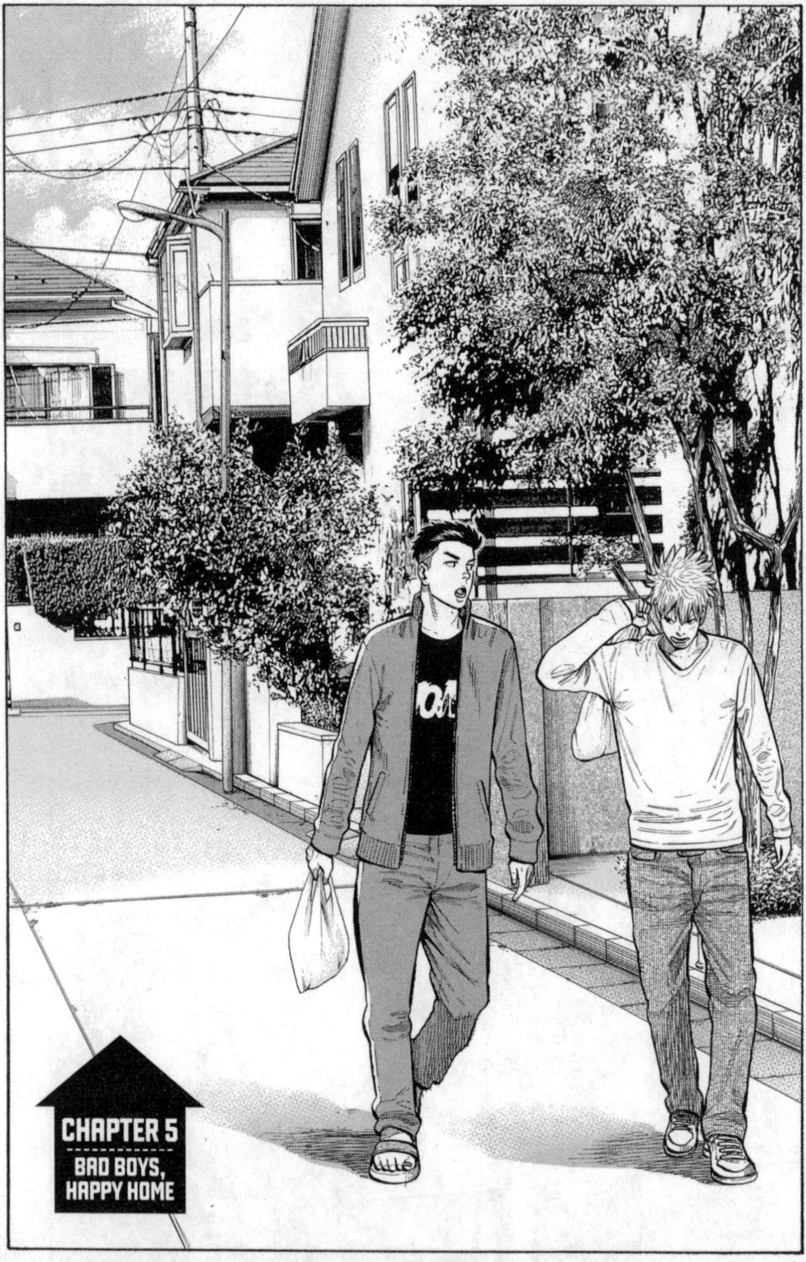
CHAPTER 5
BAD BOYS, HAPPY HOME

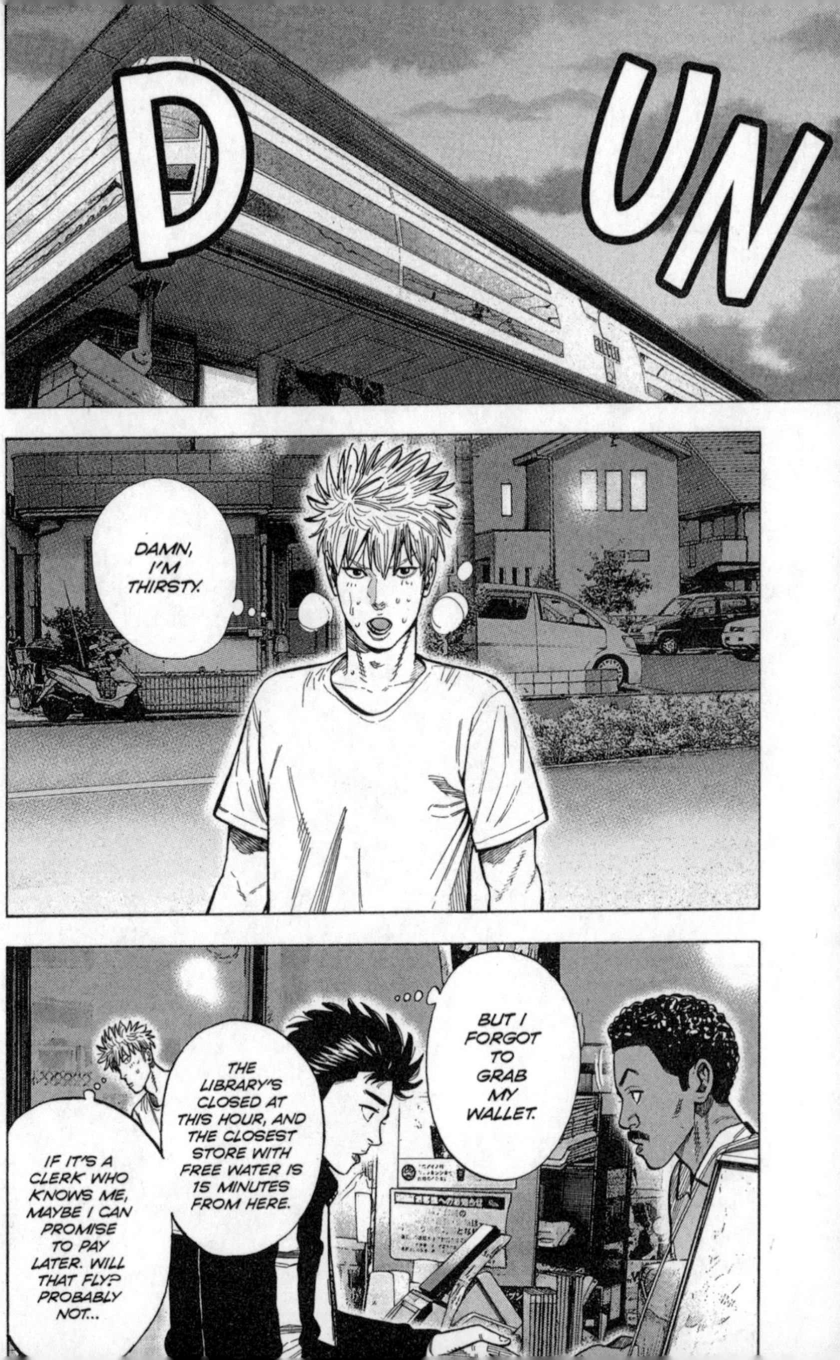
DUN
DAMN, I'M THIRSTY.
BUT I FORGOT TO GRAB MY WALLET.
THE LIBRARY'S CLOSED AT THIS HOUR, AND THE CLOSEST STORE WITH FREE WATER IS 15 MINUTES FROM HERE.
IF IT'S A CLERK WHO KNOWS ME, MAYBE I CAN PROMISE TO PAY LATER. WILL THAT FLY? PROBABLY NOT...

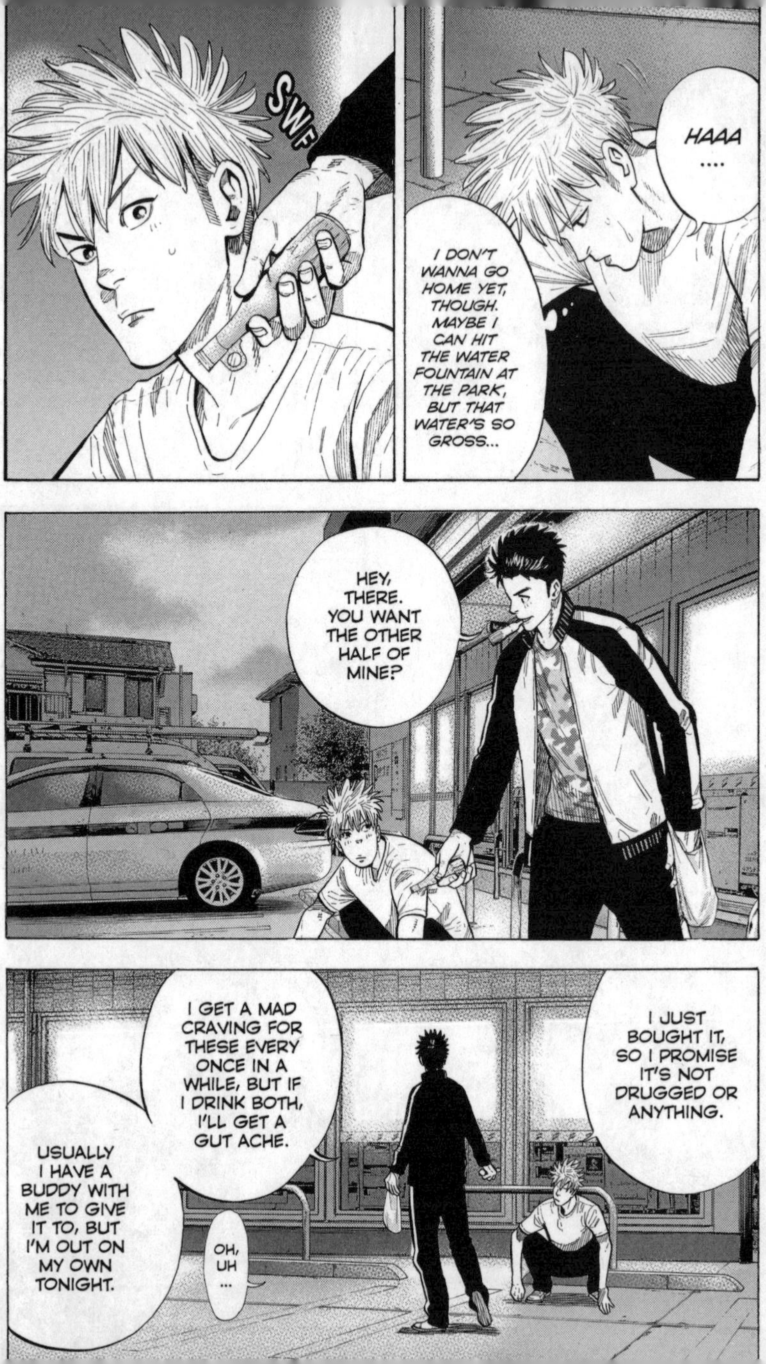
HAAA ....
I DON'T WANNA GO HOME YET, THOUGH. MAYBE I CAN HIT THE WATER FOUNTAIN AT THE PARK, BUT THAT WATER'S SO GROSS...
SWF
HEY, THERE. YOU WANT THE OTHER HALF OF MINE?
I JUST BOUGHT IT, SO I PROMISE IT'S NOT DRUGGED OR ANYTHING.
I GET A MAD CRAVING FOR THESE EVERY ONCE IN A WHILE, BUT IF I DRINK BOTH, I'LL GET A GUT ACHE.
OH, UH ...
USUALLY I HAVE A BUDDY WITH ME TO GIVE IT TO, BUT I'M OUT ON MY OWN TONIGHT.

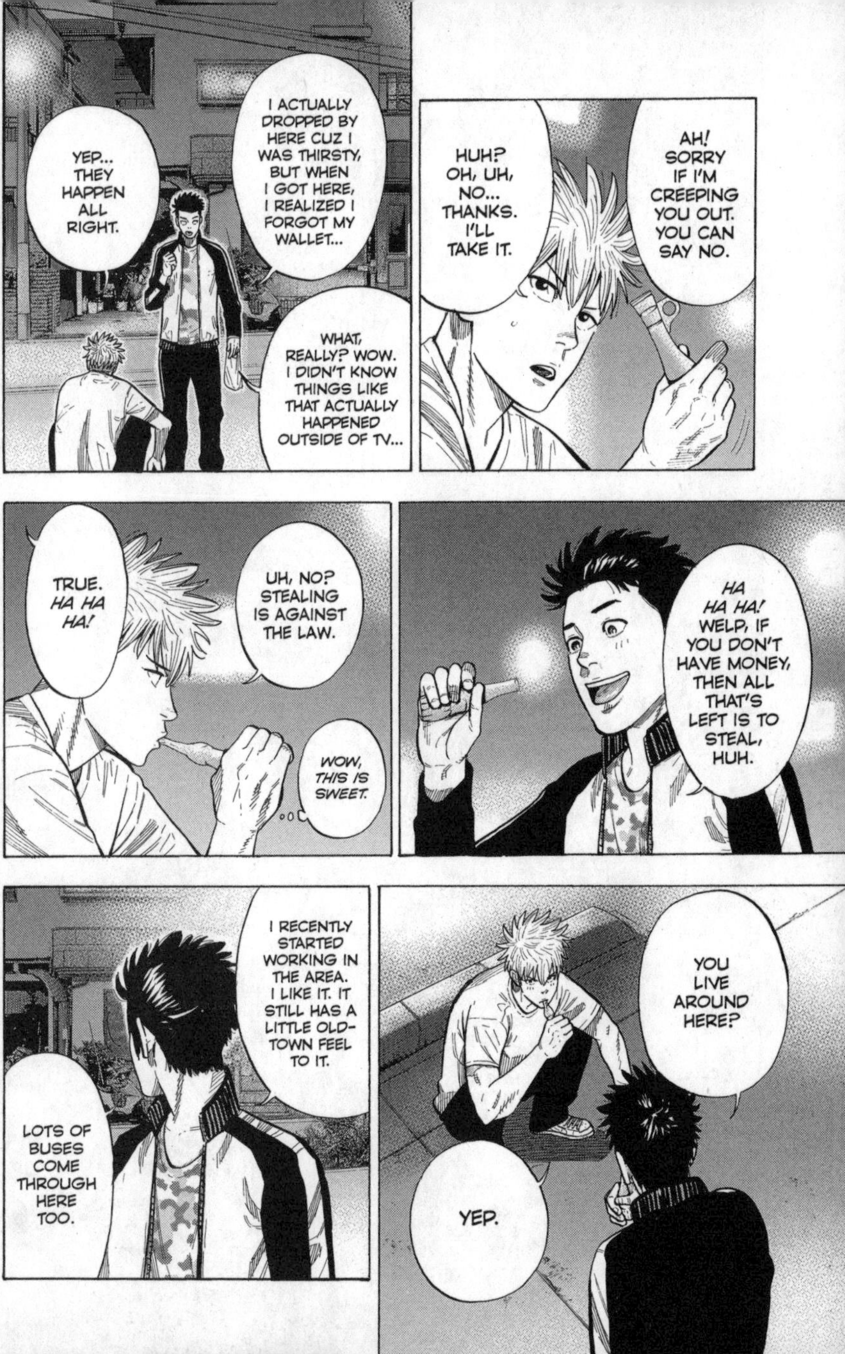
AH! SORRY IF I'M CREEPING YOU OUT. YOU CAN SAY NO.
HUH? OH, UH, NO... THANKS. I'LL TAKE IT.
I ACTUALLY DROPPED BY HERE CUZ I WAS THIRSTY, BUT WHEN I GOT HERE, I REALIZED I FORGOT MY WALLET...
WHAT, REALLY? WOW. I DIDN'T KNOW THINGS LIKE THAT ACTUALLY HAPPENED OUTSIDE OF TV...
YEP... THEY HAPPEN ALL RIGHT.
HA HA HA! WELP, IF YOU DON'T HAVE MONEY, THEN ALL THAT'S LEFT IS TO STEAL, HUH.
UH, NO? STEALING IS AGAINST THE LAW.
TRUE. *HA HA HA!*
WOW, THIS IS SWEET.
YOU LIVE AROUND HERE?
YEP.
I RECENTLY STARTED WORKING IN THE AREA. I LIKE IT. IT STILL HAS A LITTLE OLD-TOWN FEEL TO IT.
LOTS OF BUSES COME THROUGH HERE TOO.

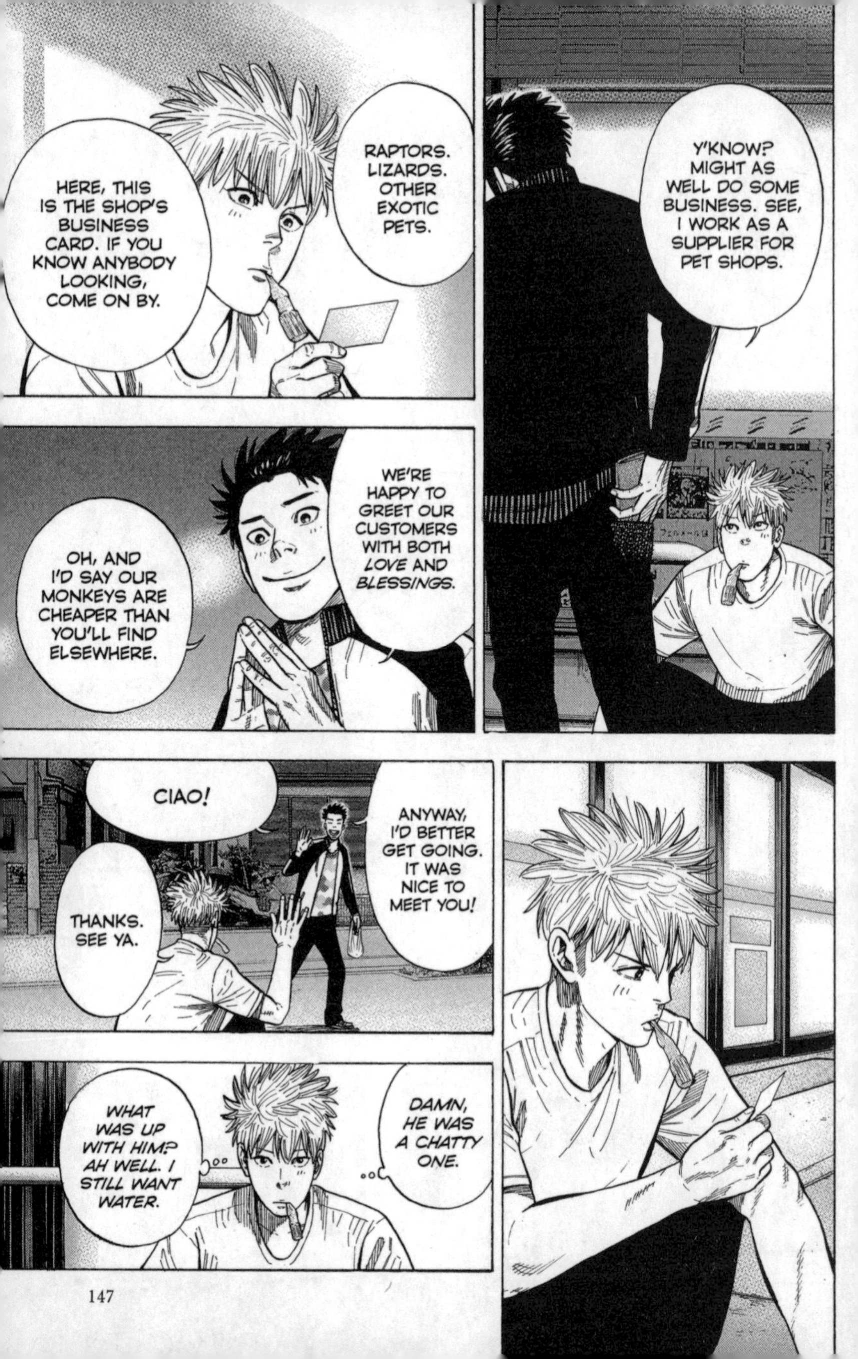
Y'KNOW? MIGHT AS WELL DO SOME BUSINESS. SEE, I WORK AS A SUPPLIER FOR PET SHOPS.
RAPTORS. LIZARDS. OTHER EXOTIC PETS.
HERE, THIS IS THE SHOP'S BUSINESS CARD. IF YOU KNOW ANYBODY LOOKING, COME ON BY.
WE'RE HAPPY TO GREET OUR CUSTOMERS WITH BOTH *LOVE* AND *BLESSINGS*.
OH, AND I'D SAY OUR MONKEYS ARE CHEAPER THAN YOU'LL FIND ELSEWHERE.
ANYWAY, I'D BETTER GET GOING. IT WAS NICE TO MEET YOU!
CIAO!
THANKS. SEE YA.
DAMN, HE WAS A CHATTY ONE.
WHAT WAS UP WITH HIM? AH WELL. I STILL WANT WATER.

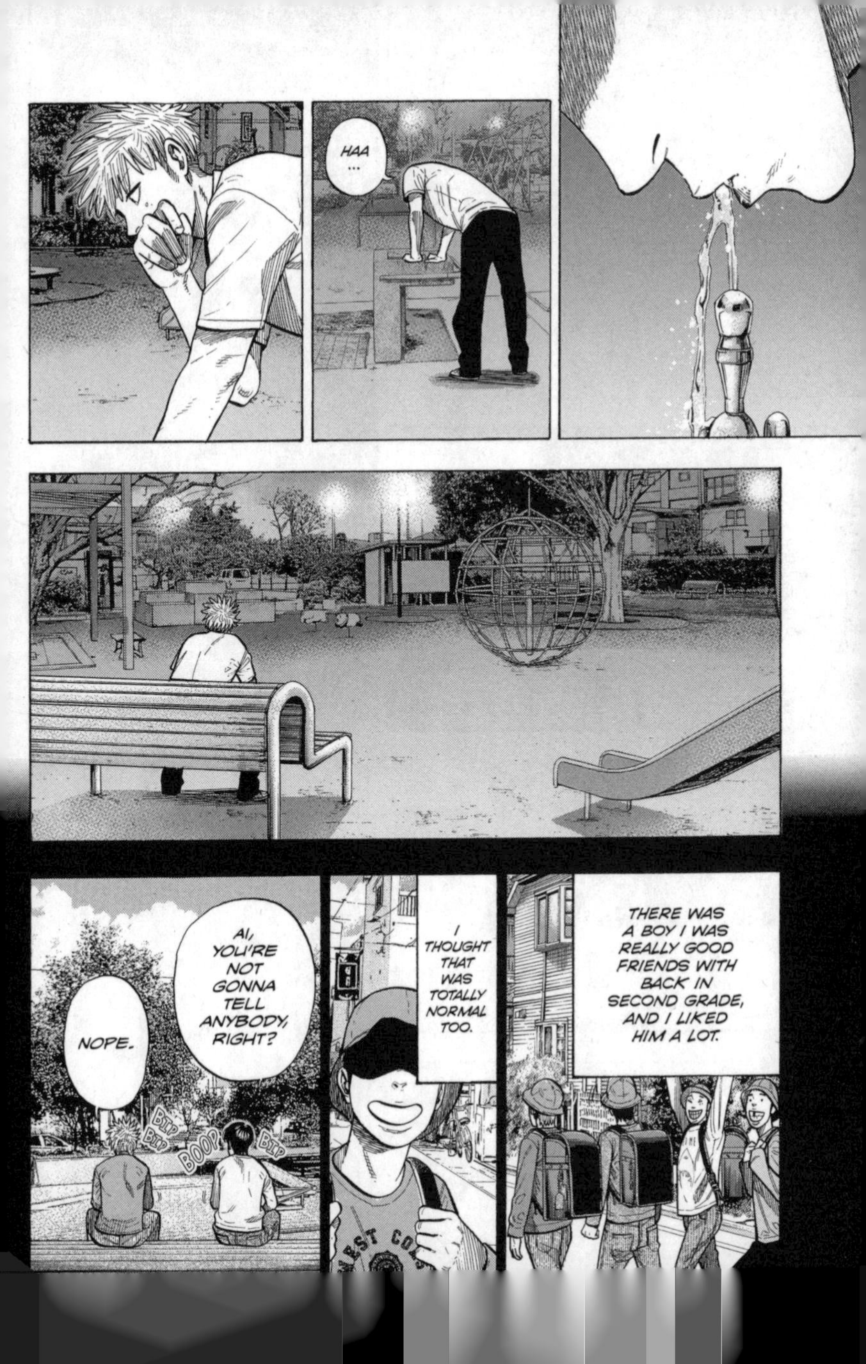
HAA ...
THERE WAS A BOY I WAS REALLY GOOD FRIENDS WITH BACK IN SECOND GRADE, AND I LIKED HIM A LOT.
I THOUGHT THAT WAS TOTALLY NORMAL TOO.
AI, YOU'RE NOT GONNA TELL ANYBODY, RIGHT?
NOPE.
BIP BIP BOOP BIP

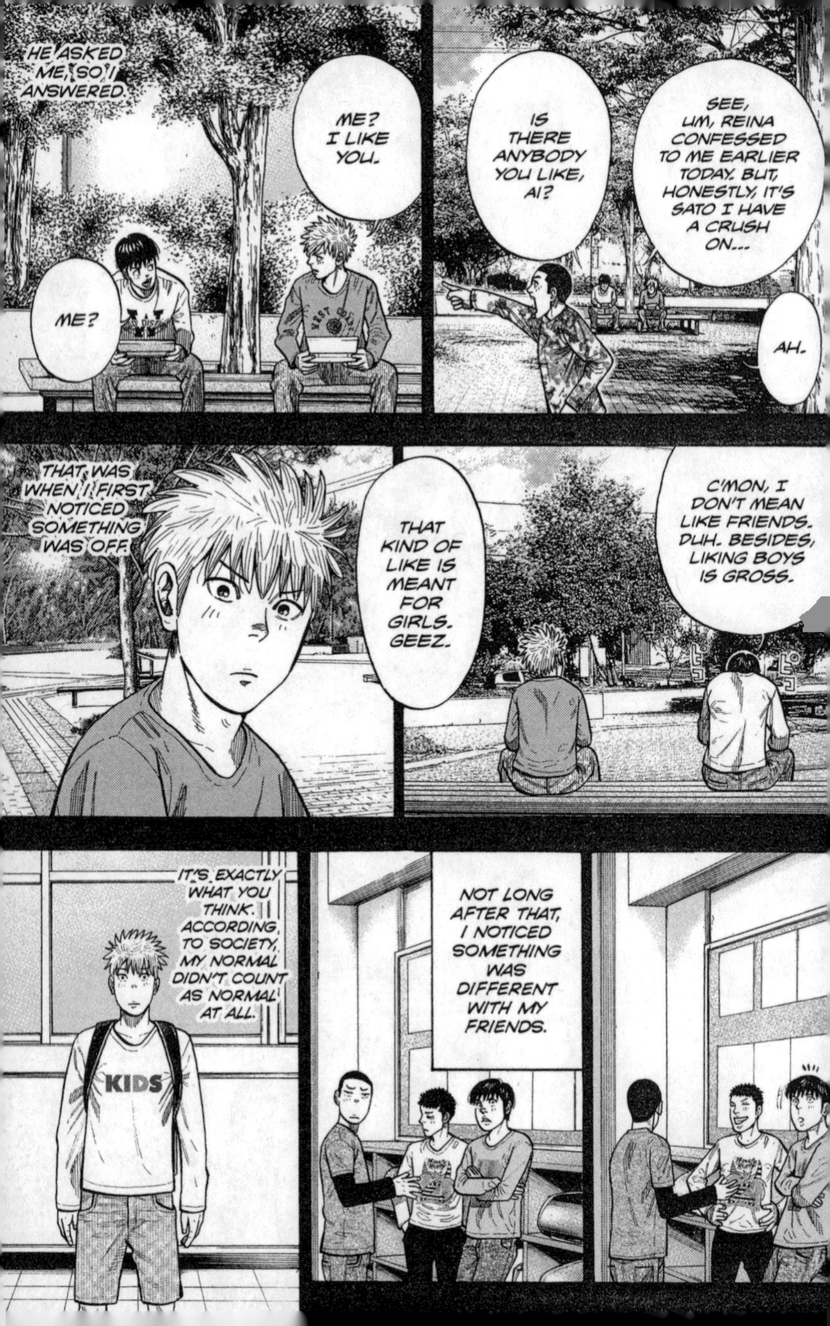

SEE, UM, REINA CONFESSED TO ME EARLIER TODAY. BUT, HONESTLY, IT'S SATO I HAVE A CRUSH ON...
IS THERE ANYBODY YOU LIKE, AI?
AH.
ME? I LIKE YOU.
HE ASKED ME, SO I ANSWERED.
ME?
C'MON, I DON'T MEAN LIKE FRIENDS. DUH. BESIDES, LIKING BOYS IS GROSS.
THAT KIND OF LIKE IS MEANT FOR GIRLS. GEEZ.
THAT WAS WHEN I FIRST NOTICED SOMETHING WAS OFF.
NOT LONG AFTER THAT, I NOTICED SOMETHING WAS DIFFERENT WITH MY FRIENDS.
IT'S EXACTLY WHAT YOU THINK. ACCORDING TO SOCIETY, MY NORMAL DIDN'T COUNT AS NORMAL AT ALL.
KIDS

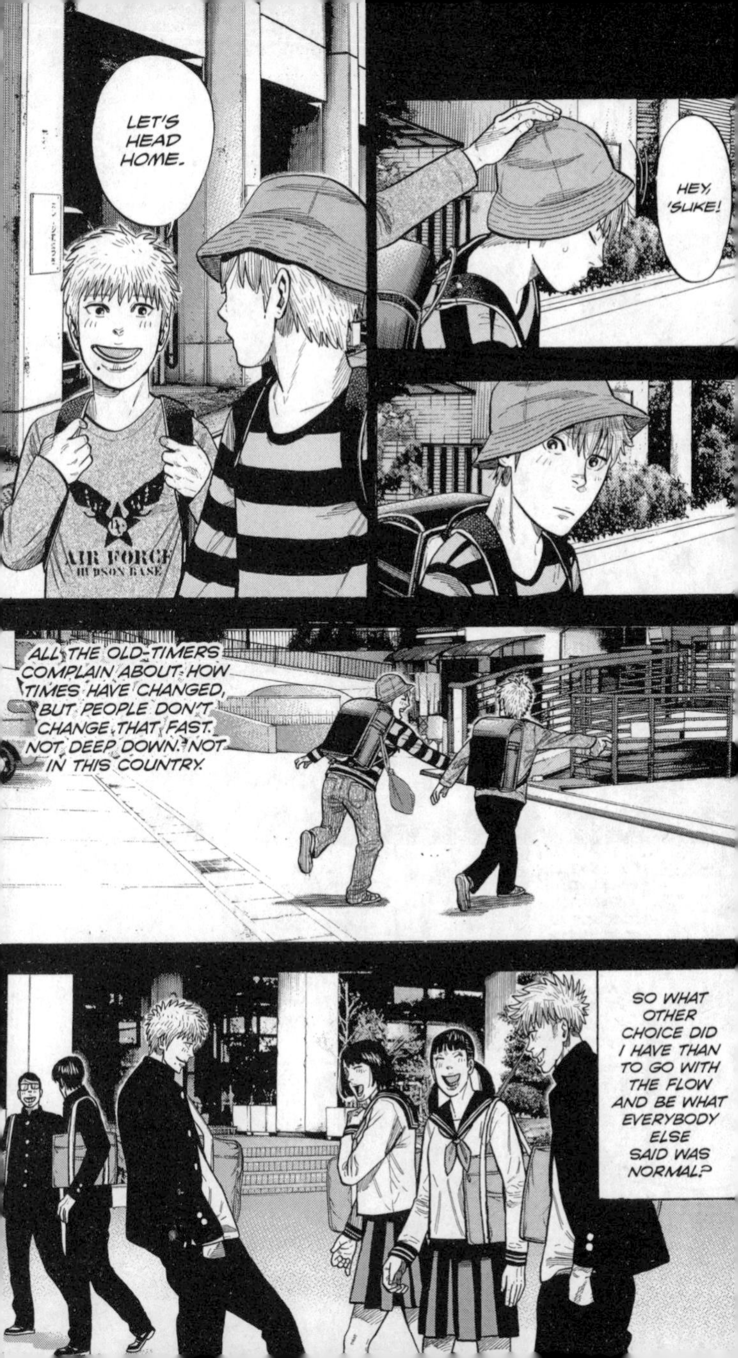
HEY, 'SUKE!
LET'S HEAD HOME.
AIR FORCE
HUDSON BASE
ALL THE OLD-TIMERS COMPLAIN ABOUT HOW TIMES HAVE CHANGED, BUT PEOPLE DON'T CHANGE THAT FAST. NOT DEEP DOWN. NOT IN THIS COUNTRY.
SO WHAT OTHER CHOICE DID I HAVE THAN TO GO WITH THE FLOW AND BE WHAT EVERYBODY ELSE SAID WAS NORMAL?

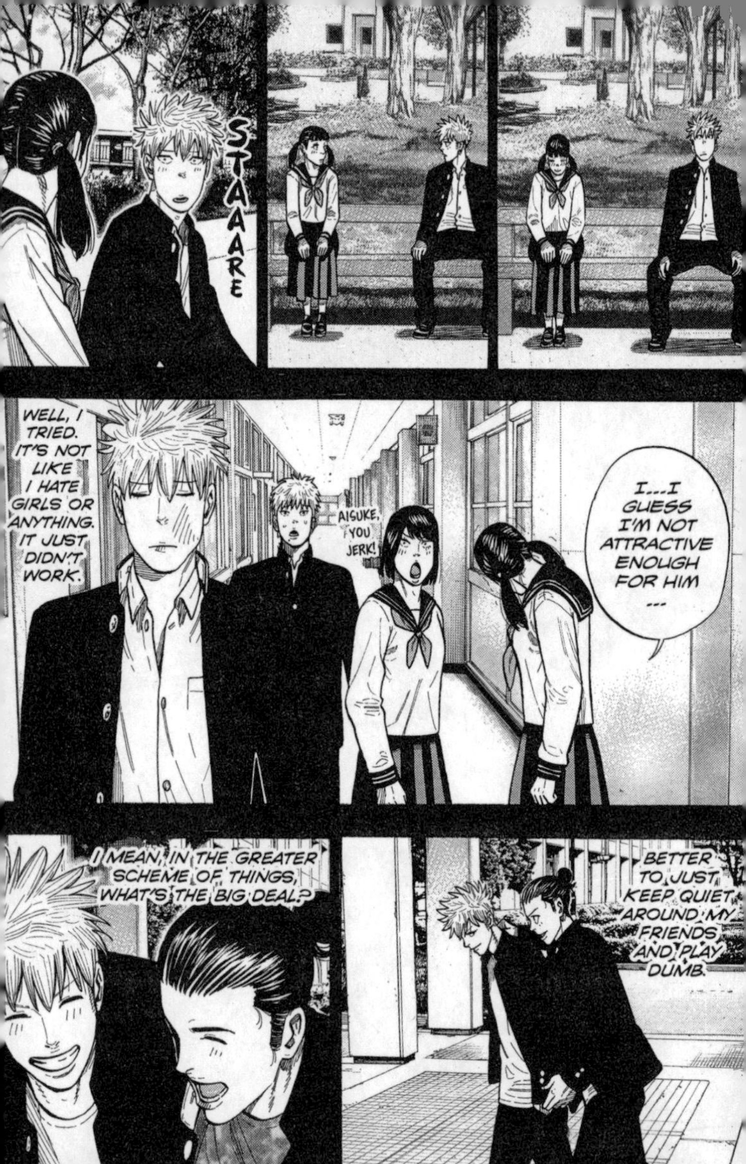
STAAAARE
I...I GUESS I'M NOT ATTRACTIVE ENOUGH FOR HIM ...
AISUKE, YOU JERK!
WELL, I TRIED. IT'S NOT LIKE I HATE GIRLS OR ANYTHING. IT JUST DIDN'T WORK.
BETTER TO JUST KEEP QUIET AROUND MY FRIENDS AND PLAY DUMB.
I MEAN, IN THE GREATER SCHEME OF THINGS, WHAT'S THE BIG DEAL?

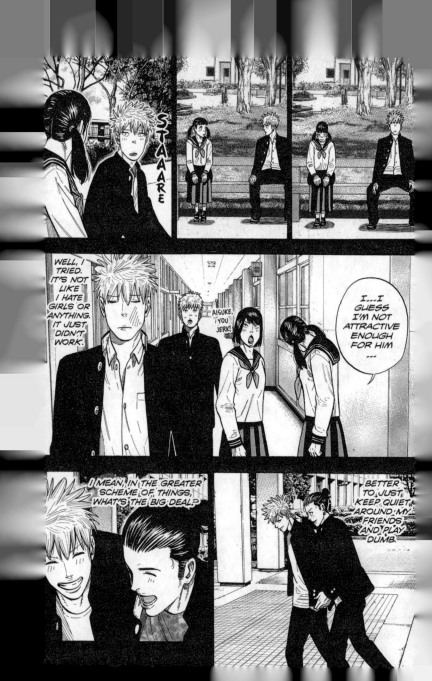

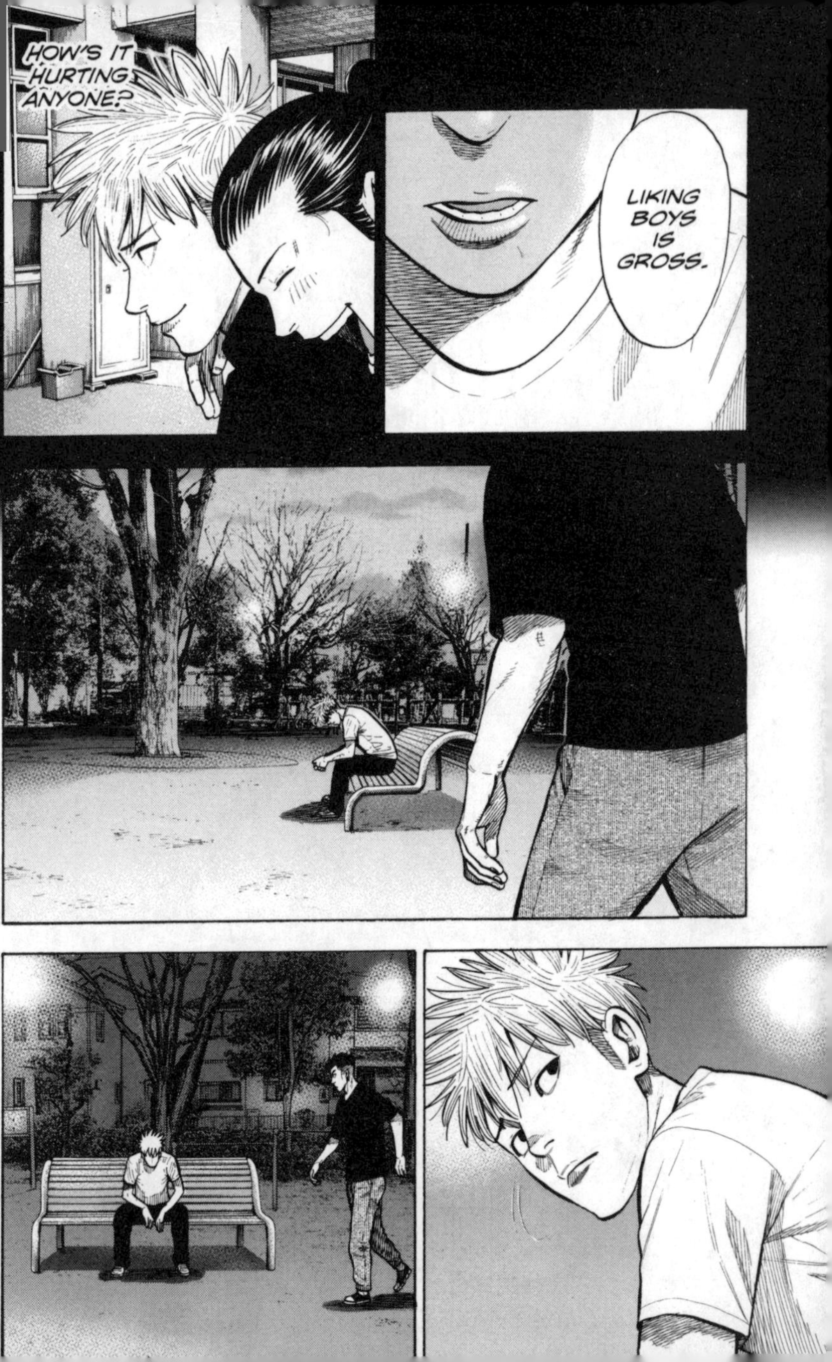
LIKING BOYS IS GROSS.
HOW'S IT HURTING ANYONE?

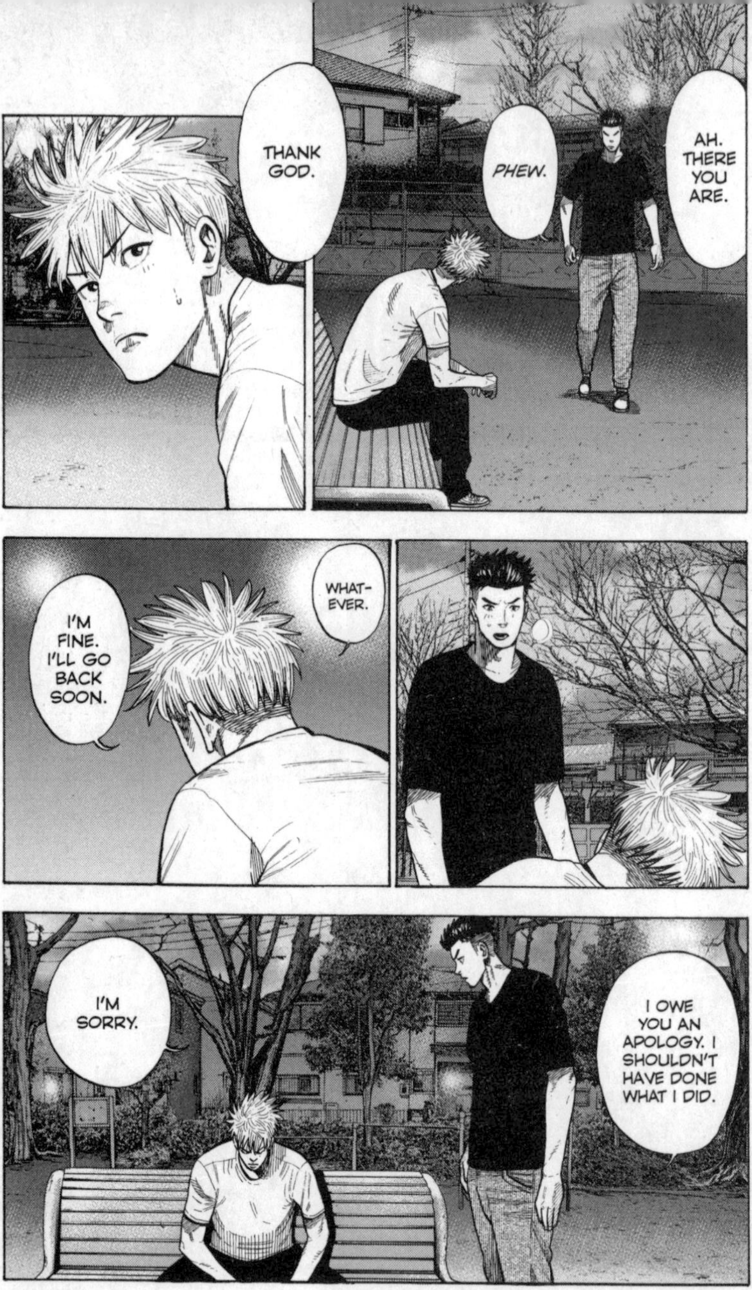
AH. THERE YOU ARE.
PHEW.
THANK GOD.
WHAT-EVER.
I'M FINE. I'LL GO BACK SOON.
I OWE YOU AN APOLOGY. I SHOULDN'T HAVE DONE WHAT I DID.
I'M SORRY.

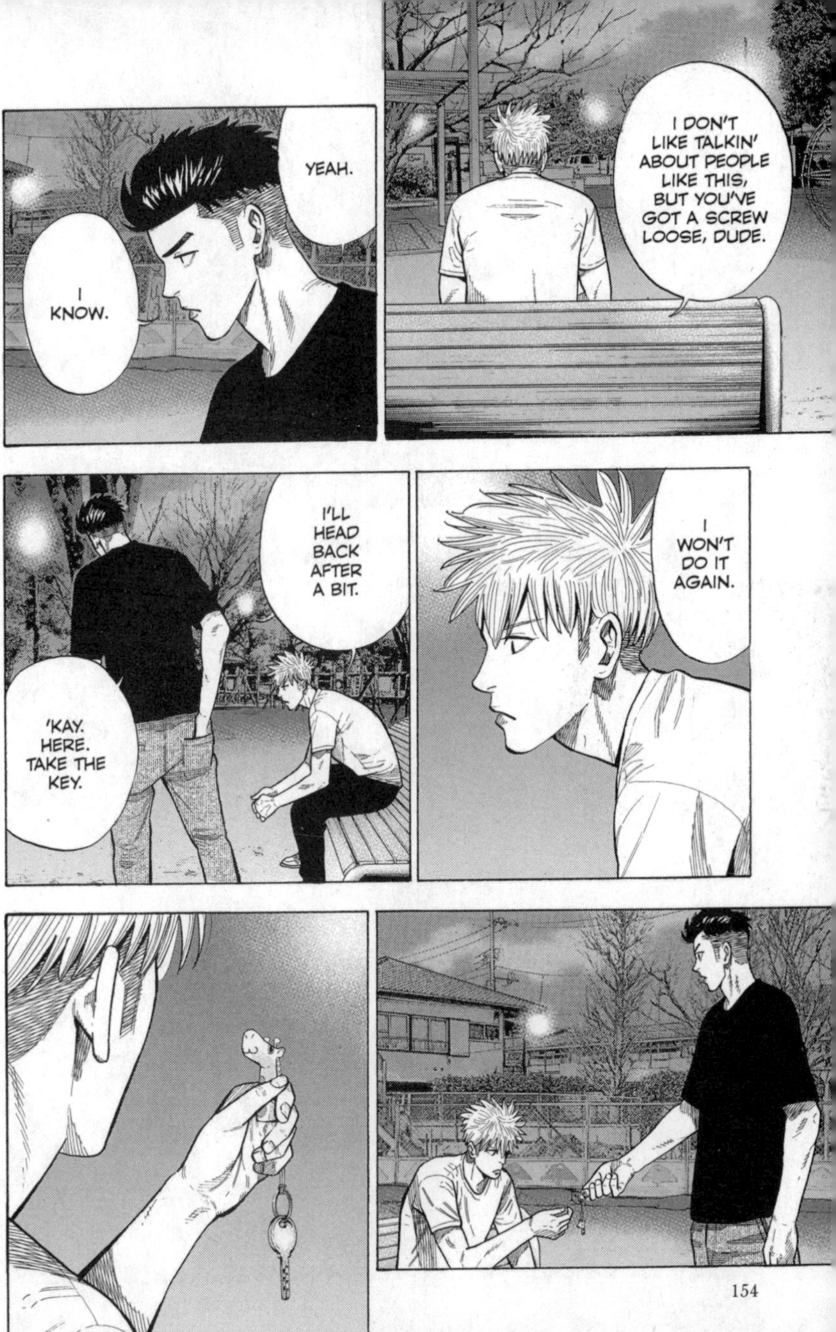
I DON'T LIKE TALKIN' ABOUT PEOPLE LIKE THIS, BUT YOU'VE GOT A SCREW LOOSE, DUDE.
YEAH.
I KNOW.
I WON'T DO IT AGAIN.
I'LL HEAD BACK AFTER A BIT.
'KAY. HERE. TAKE THE KEY.

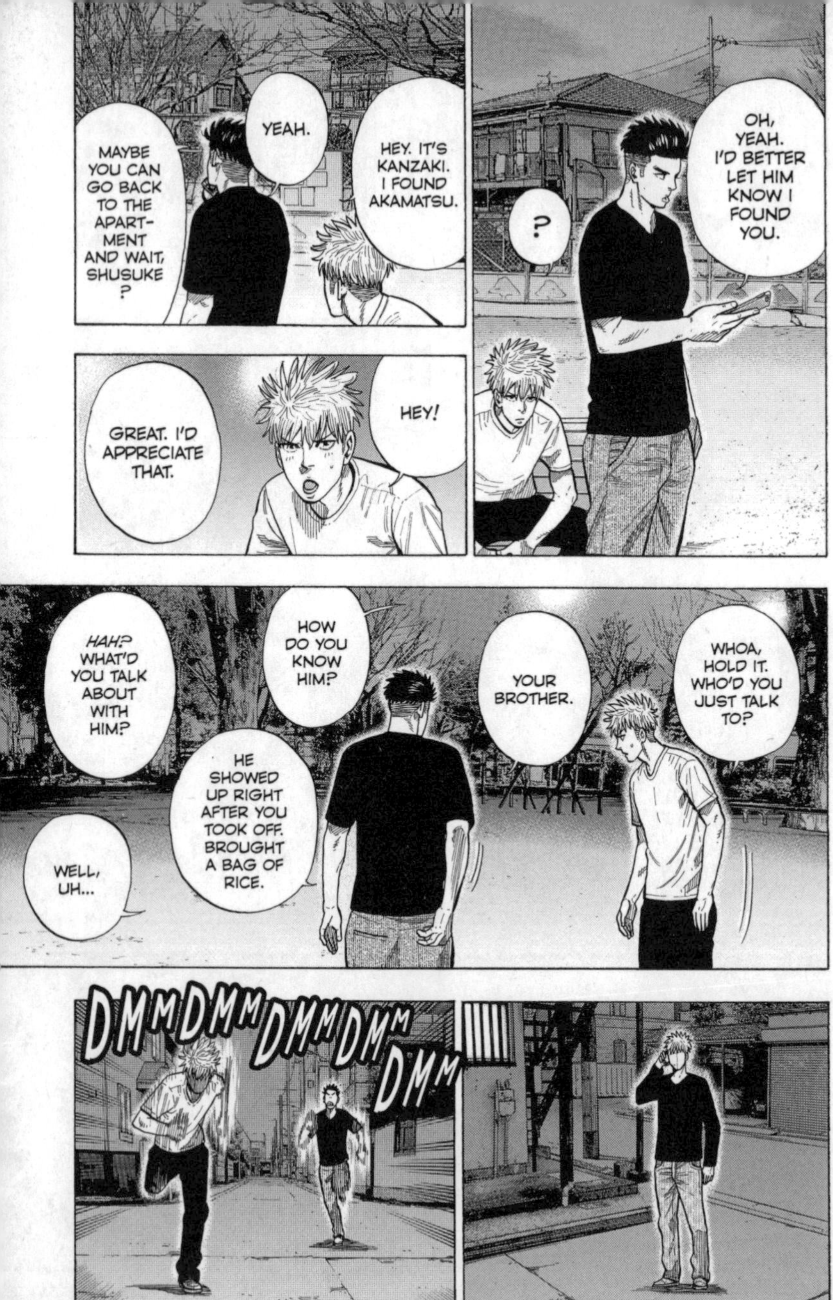
OH, YEAH. I'D BETTER LET HIM KNOW I FOUND YOU.
?
HEY. IT'S KANZAKI. I FOUND AKAMATSU.
YEAH.
MAYBE YOU CAN GO BACK TO THE APARTMENT AND WAIT, SHUSUKE?
HEY!
GREAT. I'D APPRECIATE THAT.
WHOA, HOLD IT. WHO'D YOU JUST TALK TO?
YOUR BROTHER.
HOW DO YOU KNOW HIM?
HAH? WHAT'D YOU TALK ABOUT WITH HIM?
HE SHOWED UP RIGHT AFTER YOU TOOK OFF. BROUGHT A BAG OF RICE.
WELL, UH...
DMMDMMDMMDMMDMM

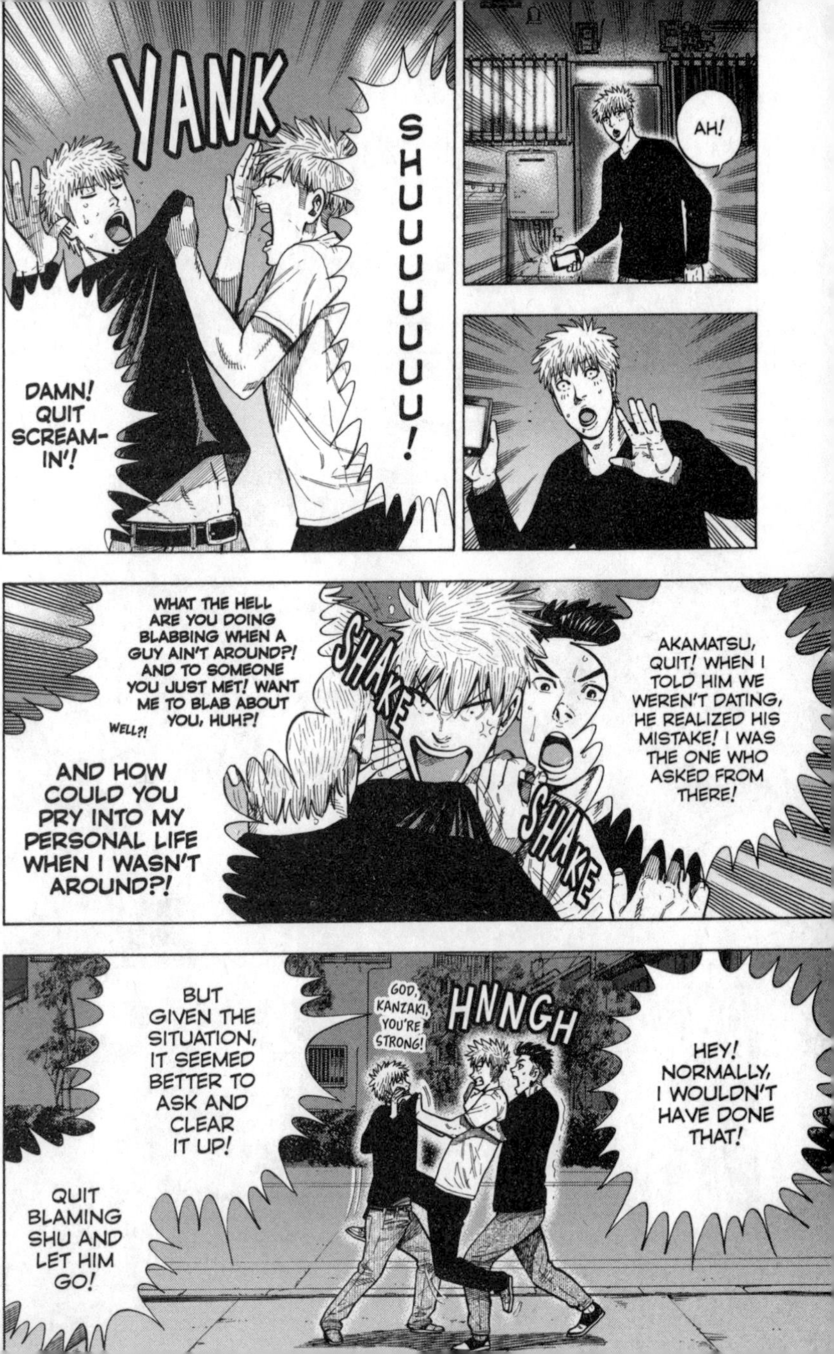
AH!
SHUUUUUUUU!
YANK
DAMN! QUIT SCREAM-IN'!
AKAMATSU, QUIT! WHEN I TOLD HIM WE WEREN'T DATING, HE REALIZED HIS MISTAKE! I WAS THE ONE WHO ASKED FROM THERE!
SHAKE
WHAT THE HELL ARE YOU DOING BLABBING WHEN A GUY AIN'T AROUND?! AND TO SOMEONE YOU JUST MET! WANT ME TO BLAB ABOUT YOU, HUH?!
WELL?!
AND HOW COULD YOU PRY INTO MY PERSONAL LIFE WHEN I WASN'T AROUND?!
SHAKE
HEY! NORMALLY, I WOULDN'T HAVE DONE THAT!
HNNGH
GOD, KANZAKI, YOU'RE STRONG!
BUT GIVEN THE SITUATION, IT SEEMED BETTER TO ASK AND CLEAR IT UP!
QUIT BLAMING SHU AND LET HIM GO!

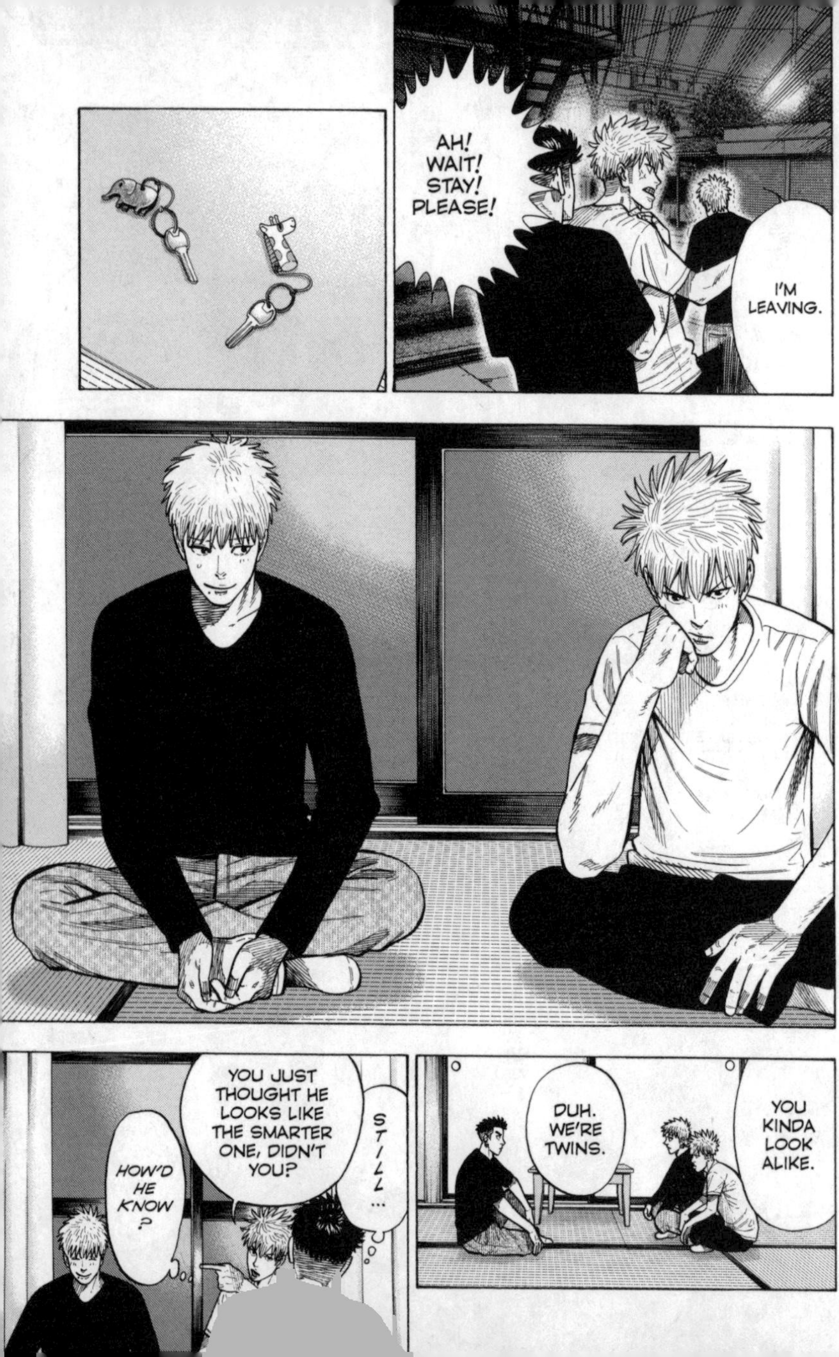
I'M LEAVING.
AH! WAIT! STAY! PLEASE!
YOU KINDA LOOK ALIKE.
DUH. WE'RE TWINS.
STILL...
YOU JUST THOUGHT HE LOOKS LIKE THE SMARTER ONE, DIDN'T YOU?
HOW'D HE KNOW?

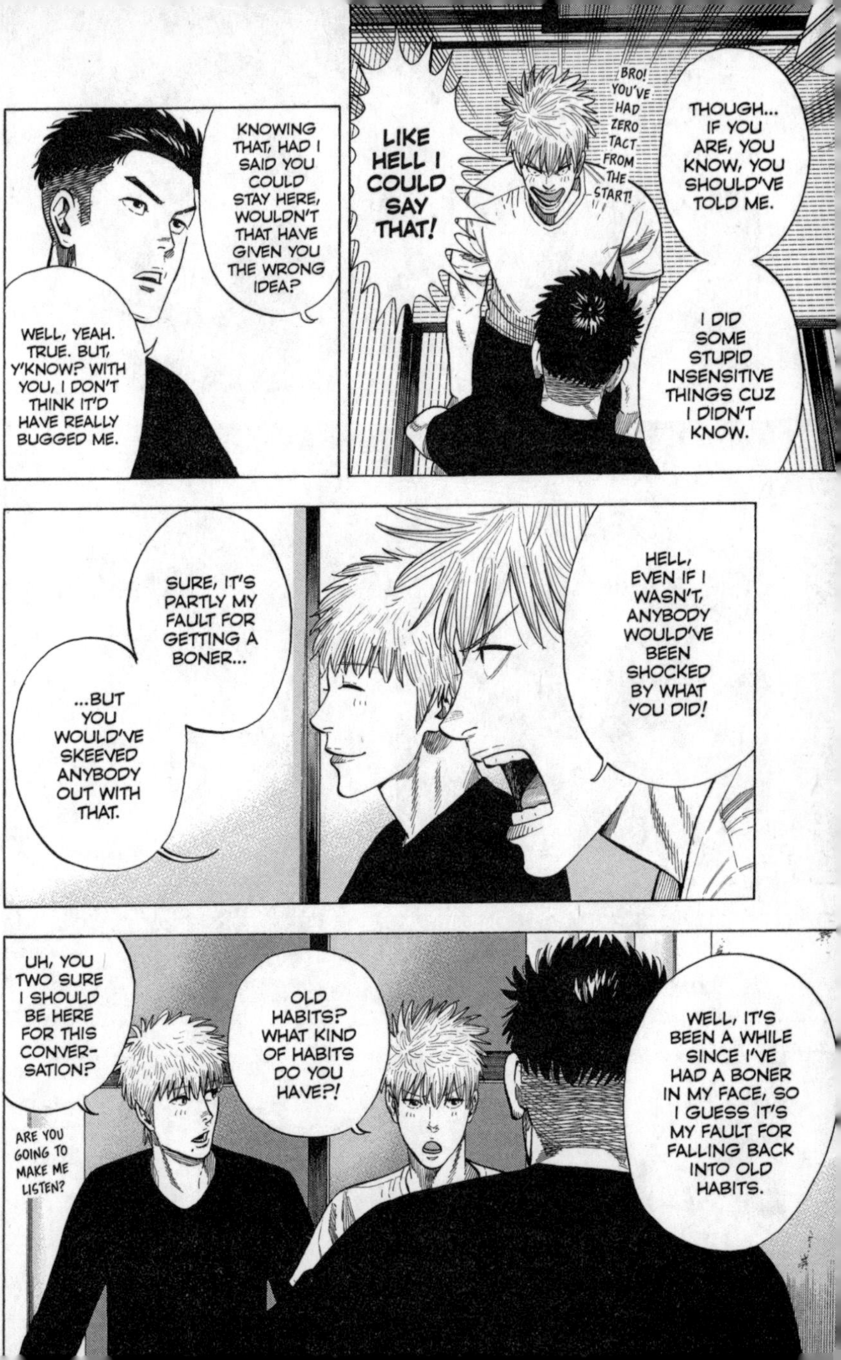
THOUGH... IF YOU ARE, YOU KNOW, YOU SHOULD'VE TOLD ME.
I DID SOME STUPID INSENSITIVE THINGS CUZ I DIDN'T KNOW.
LIKE HELL I COULD SAY THAT!
BRO! YOU'VE HAD ZERO TACT FROM THE START!
KNOWING THAT, HAD I SAID YOU COULD STAY HERE, WOULDN'T THAT HAVE GIVEN YOU THE WRONG IDEA?
WELL, YEAH. TRUE. BUT, Y'KNOW? WITH YOU, I DON'T THINK IT'D HAVE REALLY BUGGED ME.
HELL, EVEN IF I WASN'T, ANYBODY WOULD'VE BEEN SHOCKED BY WHAT YOU DID!
SURE, IT'S PARTLY MY FAULT FOR GETTING A BONER...
...BUT YOU WOULD'VE SKEEVED ANYBODY OUT WITH THAT.
WELL, IT'S BEEN A WHILE SINCE I'VE HAD A BONER IN MY FACE, SO I GUESS IT'S MY FAULT FOR FALLING BACK INTO OLD HABITS.
OLD HABITS? WHAT KIND OF HABITS DO YOU HAVE?!
UH, YOU TWO SURE I SHOULD BE HERE FOR THIS CONVER-SATION?
ARE YOU GOING TO MAKE ME LISTEN?

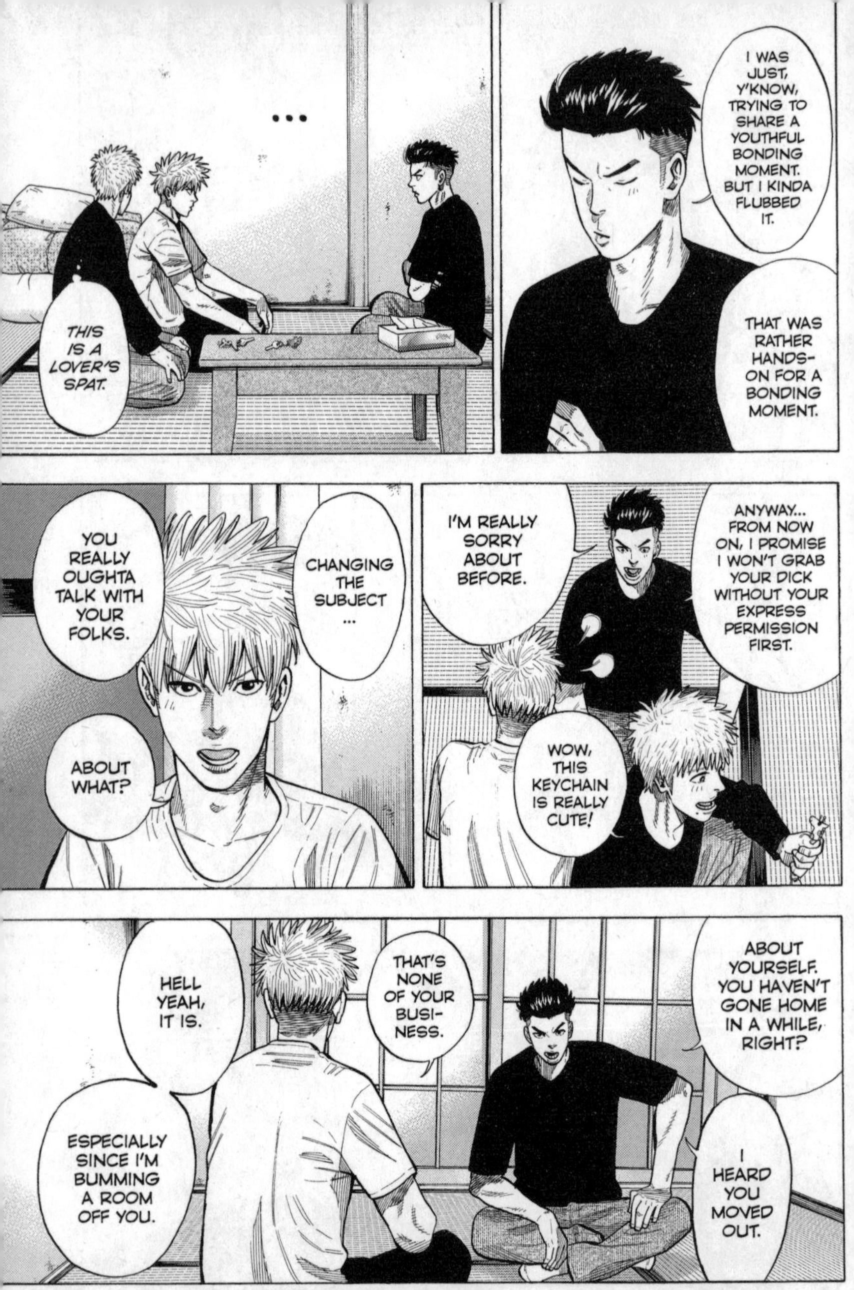
I WAS JUST, Y'KNOW, TRYING TO SHARE A YOUTHFUL BONDING MOMENT. BUT I KINDA FLUBBED IT.
THAT WAS RATHER HANDS-ON FOR A BONDING MOMENT.
...
THIS IS A LOVER'S SPAT.
ANYWAY... FROM NOW ON, I PROMISE I WON'T GRAB YOUR DICK WITHOUT YOUR EXPRESS PERMISSION FIRST.
I'M REALLY SORRY ABOUT BEFORE.
WOW, THIS KEYCHAIN IS REALLY CUTE!
CHANGING THE SUBJECT ...
YOU REALLY OUGHTA TALK WITH YOUR FOLKS.
ABOUT WHAT?
ABOUT YOURSELF. YOU HAVEN'T GONE HOME IN A WHILE, RIGHT?
I HEARD YOU MOVED OUT.
THAT'S NONE OF YOUR BUSI-NESS.
HELL YEAH, IT IS.
ESPECIALLY SINCE I'M BUMMING A ROOM OFF YOU.

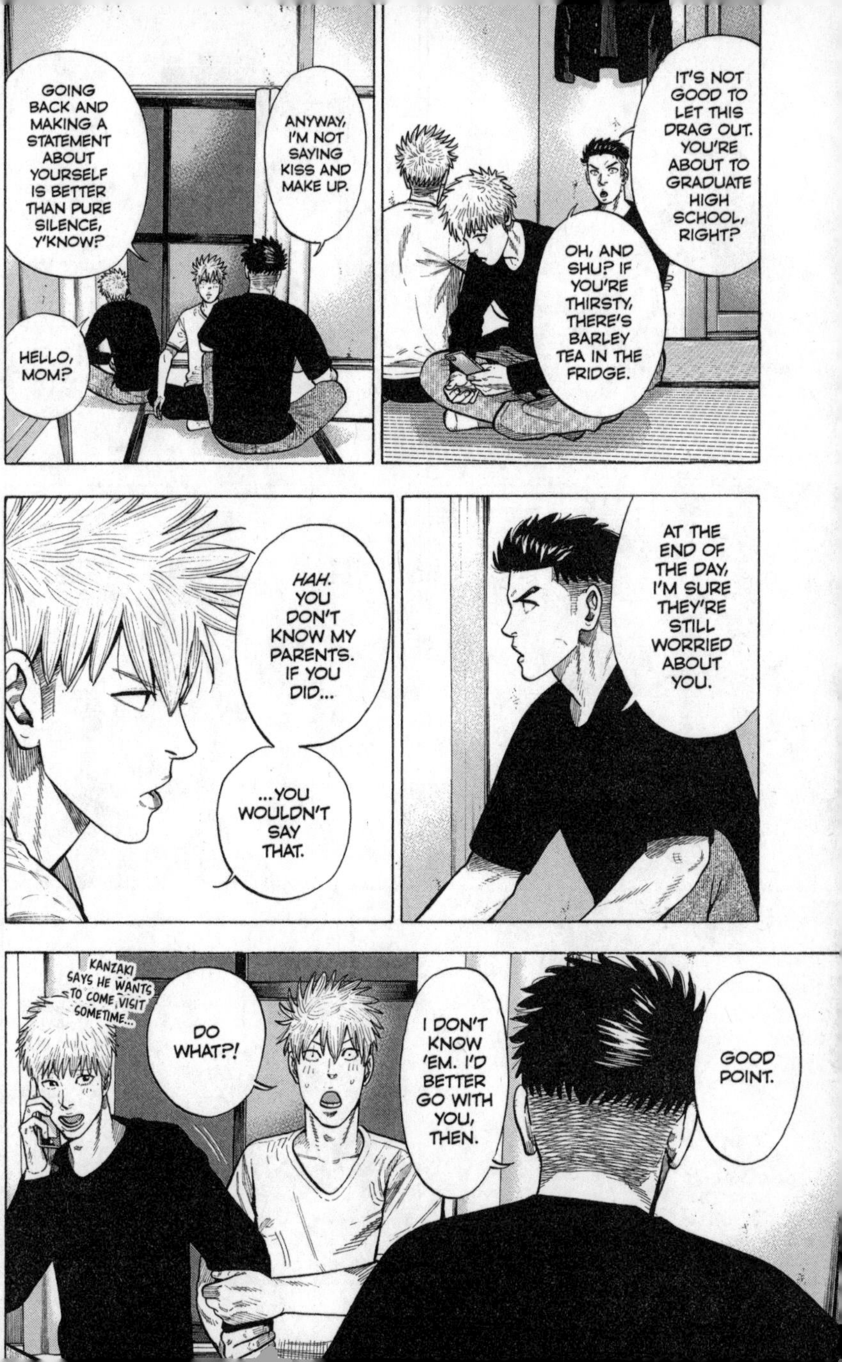
IT'S NOT GOOD TO LET THIS DRAG OUT. YOU'RE ABOUT TO GRADUATE HIGH SCHOOL, RIGHT?
OH, AND SHU? IF YOU'RE THIRSTY, THERE'S BARLEY TEA IN THE FRIDGE.
ANYWAY, I'M NOT SAYING KISS AND MAKE UP.
GOING BACK AND MAKING A STATEMENT ABOUT YOURSELF IS BETTER THAN PURE SILENCE, Y'KNOW?
HELLO, MOM?
AT THE END OF THE DAY, I'M SURE THEY'RE STILL WORRIED ABOUT YOU.
HAH. YOU DON'T KNOW MY PARENTS. IF YOU DID...
...YOU WOULDN'T SAY THAT.
GOOD POINT.
I DON'T KNOW 'EM. I'D BETTER GO WITH YOU, THEN.
DO WHAT?!
KANZAKI SAYS HE WANTS TO COME VISIT SOMETIME...

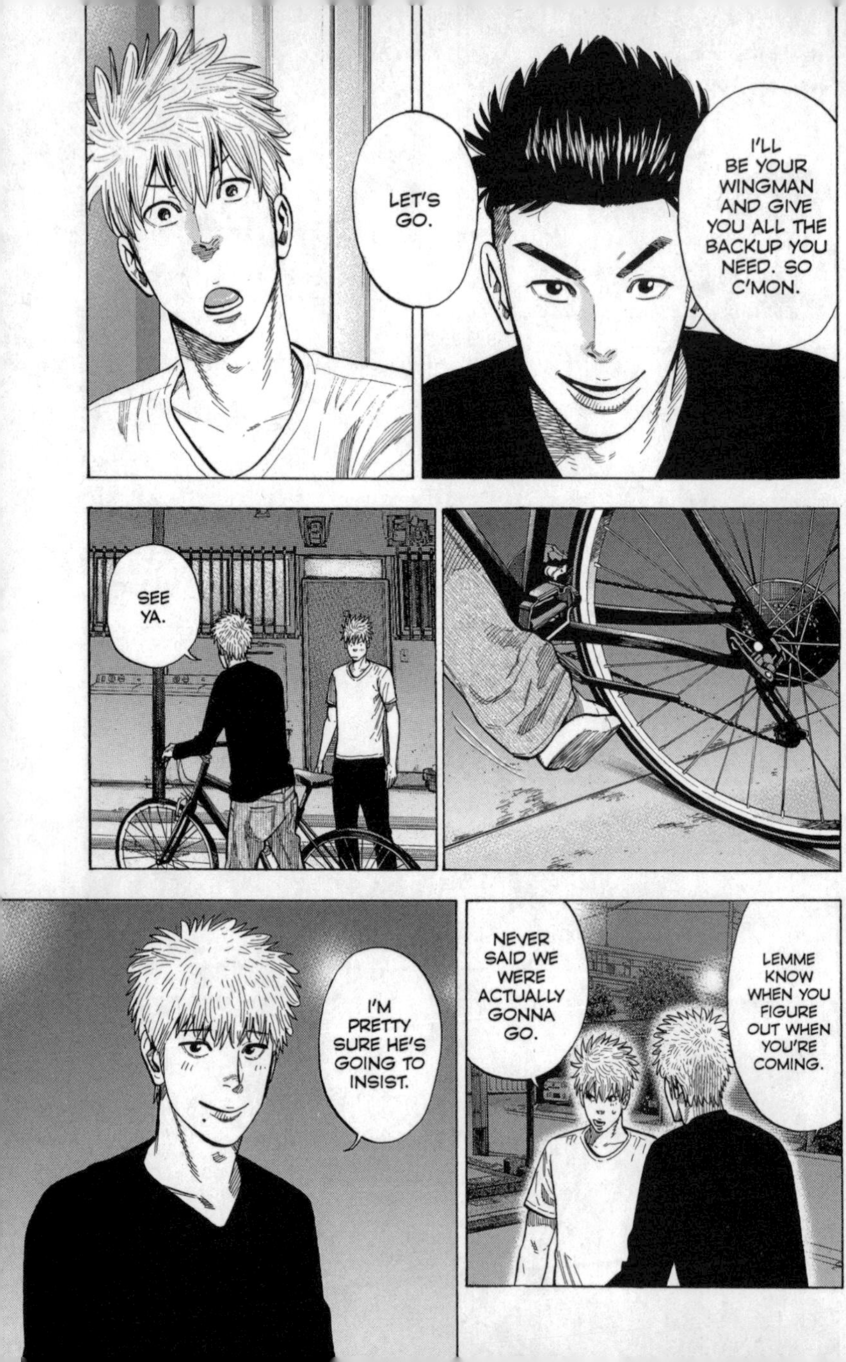
I'LL BE YOUR WINGMAN AND GIVE YOU ALL THE BACKUP YOU NEED. SO C'MON.
LET'S GO.
SEE YA.
LEMME KNOW WHEN YOU FIGURE OUT WHEN YOU'RE COMING.
NEVER SAID WE WERE ACTUALLY GONNA GO.
I'M PRETTY SURE HE'S GOING TO INSIST.

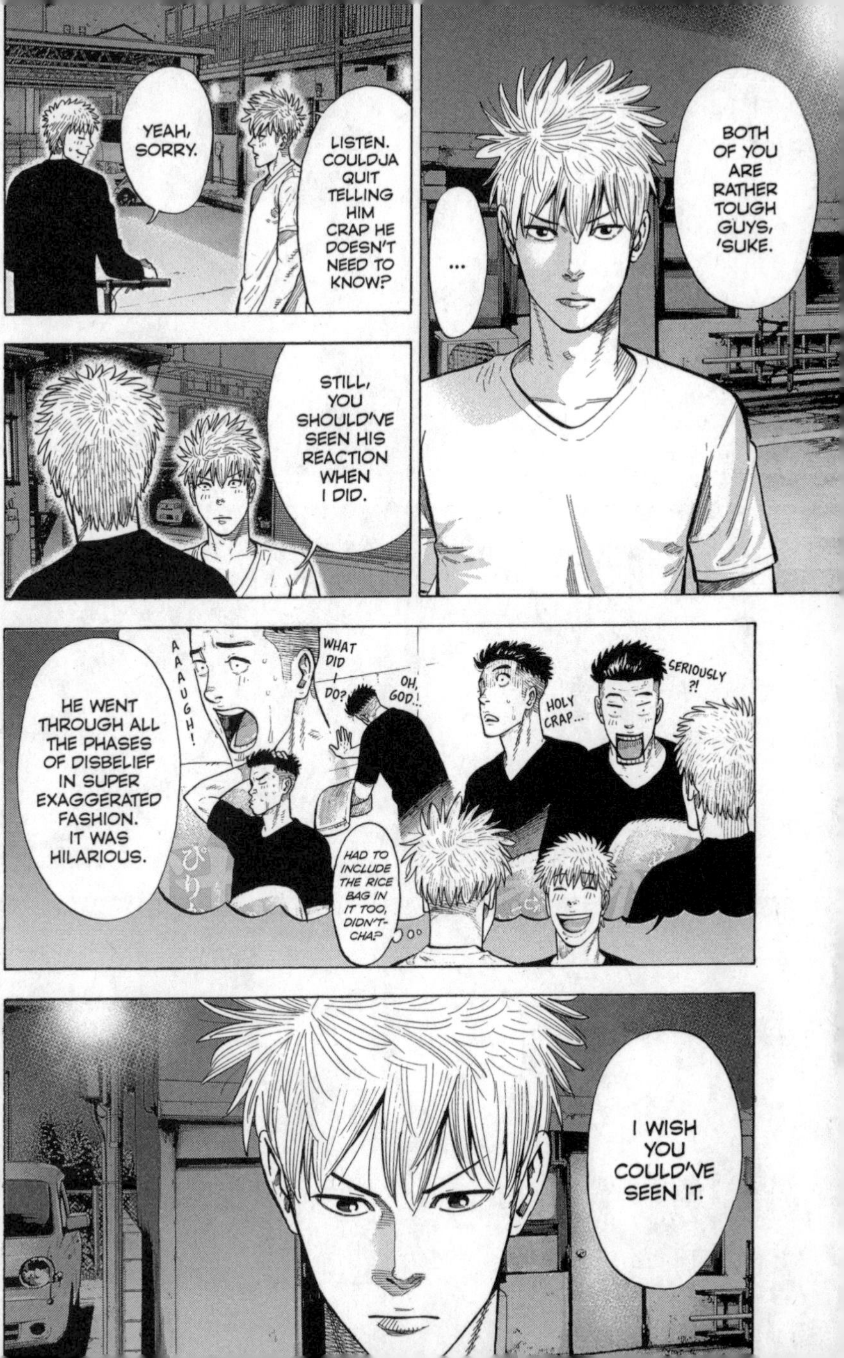
BOTH OF YOU ARE RATHER TOUGH GUYS, 'SUKE.
...
LISTEN. COULDJA QUIT TELLING HIM CRAP HE DOESN'T NEED TO KNOW?
YEAH, SORRY.
STILL, YOU SHOULD'VE SEEN HIS REACTION WHEN I DID.
SERIOUSLY ?!
HOLY CRAP...
OH, GOD...
WHAT DID I DO?
AAAAUGH!
HE WENT THROUGH ALL THE PHASES OF DISBELIEF IN SUPER EXAGGERATED FASHION. IT WAS HILARIOUS.
HAD TO INCLUDE THE RICE BAG IN IT TOO, DIDN'T-CHA?
I WISH YOU COULD'VE SEEN IT.

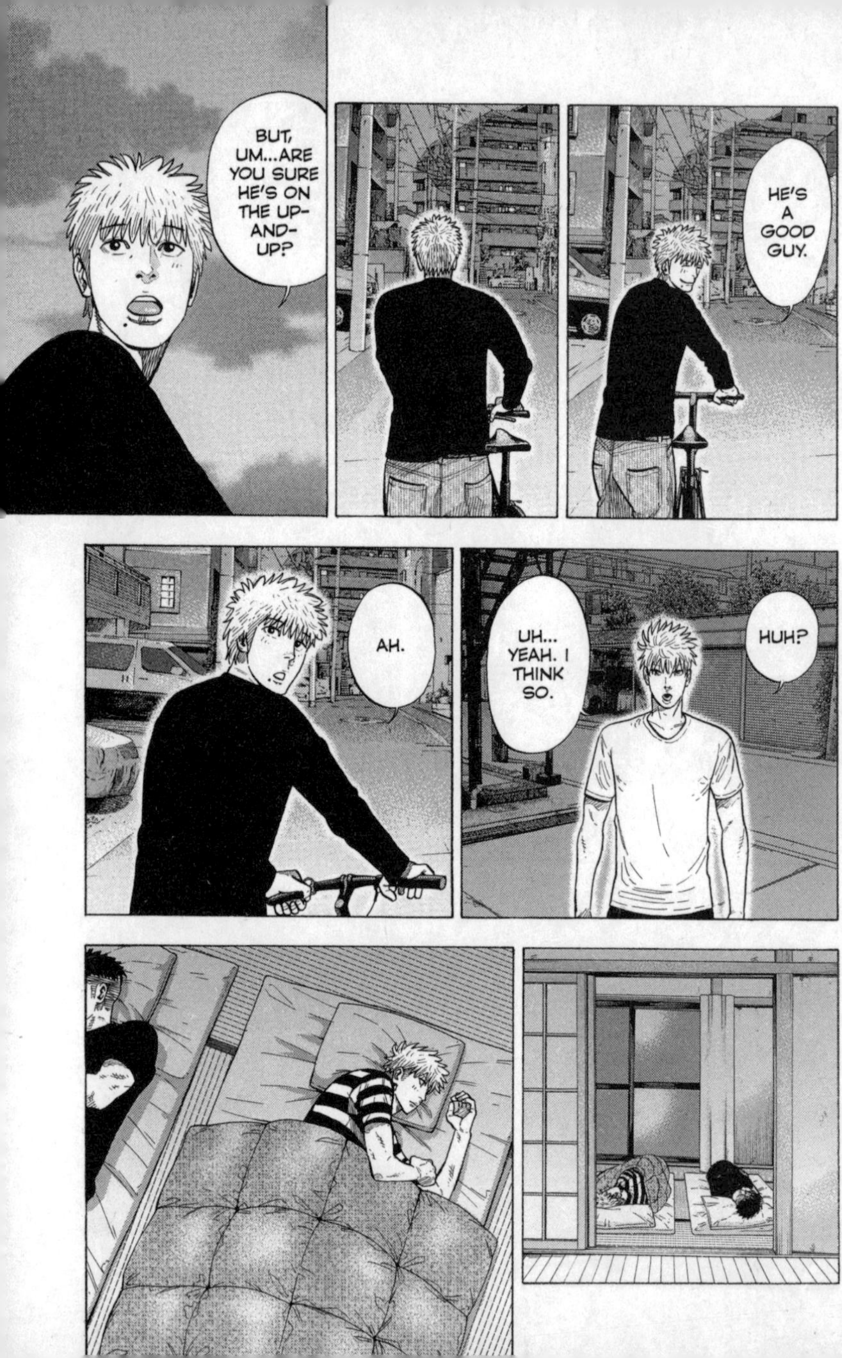
HE'S A GOOD GUY.
BUT, UM...ARE YOU SURE HE'S ON THE UP-AND-UP?
HUH?
UH... YEAH. I THINK SO.
AH.

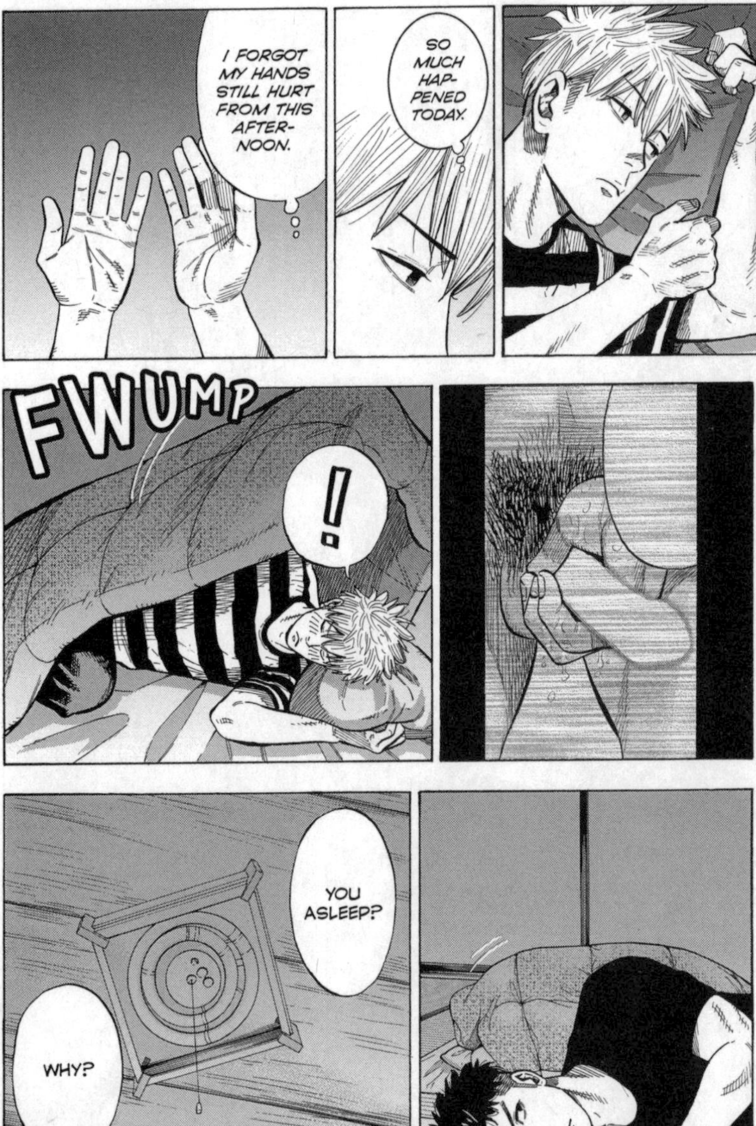
SO MUCH HAPPENED TODAY.
I FORGOT MY HANDS STILL HURT FROM THIS AFTERNOON.
FWUMP
!
YOU ASLEEP?
WHY?

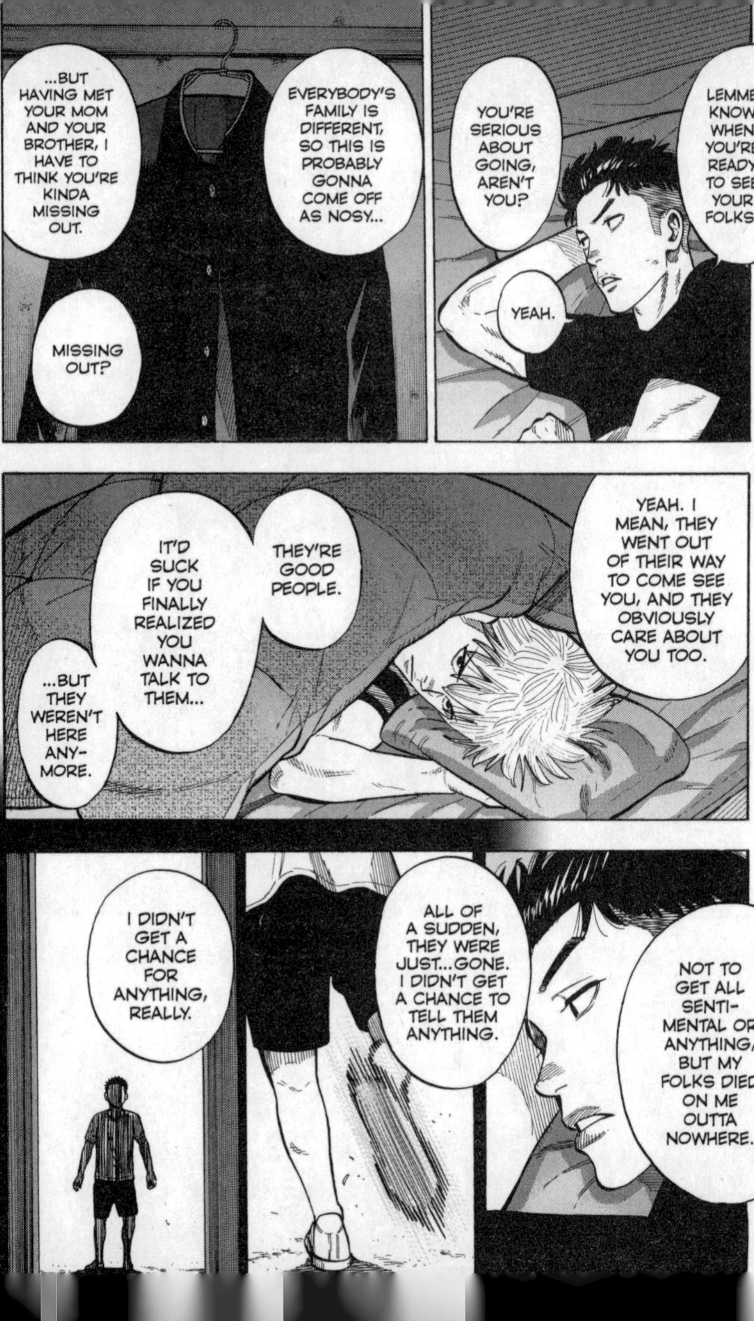
LEMME KNOW WHEN YOU'RE READY TO SEE YOUR FOLKS.
YOU'RE SERIOUS ABOUT GOING, AREN'T YOU?
YEAH.
EVERYBODY'S FAMILY IS DIFFERENT, SO THIS IS PROBABLY GONNA COME OFF AS NOSY...
...BUT HAVING MET YOUR MOM AND YOUR BROTHER, I HAVE TO THINK YOU'RE KINDA MISSING OUT.
MISSING OUT?
YEAH. I MEAN, THEY WENT OUT OF THEIR WAY TO COME SEE YOU, AND THEY OBVIOUSLY CARE ABOUT YOU TOO.
THEY'RE GOOD PEOPLE.
IT'D SUCK IF YOU FINALLY REALIZED YOU WANNA TALK TO THEM...
...BUT THEY WEREN'T HERE ANY-MORE.
NOT TO GET ALL SENTI-MENTAL OR ANYTHING, BUT MY FOLKS DIED ON ME OUTTA NOWHERE.
ALL OF A SUDDEN, THEY WERE JUST...GONE. I DIDN'T GET A CHANCE TO TELL THEM ANYTHING.
I DIDN'T GET A CHANCE FOR ANYTHING, REALLY.

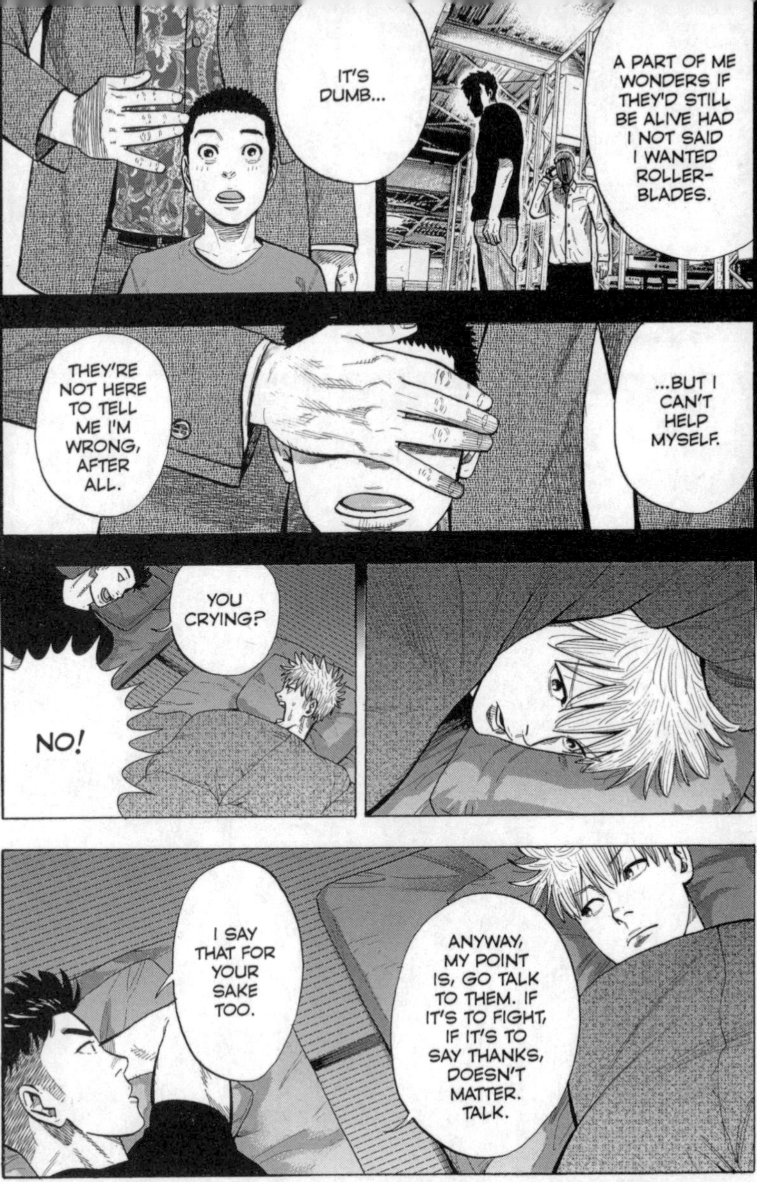
A PART OF ME WONDERS IF THEY'D STILL BE ALIVE HAD I NOT SAID I WANTED ROLLER-BLADES.
IT'S DUMB...
...BUT I CAN'T HELP MYSELF.
THEY'RE NOT HERE TO TELL ME I'M WRONG, AFTER ALL.
YOU CRYING?
NO!
ANYWAY, MY POINT IS, GO TALK TO THEM. IF IT'S TO FIGHT, IF IT'S TO SAY THANKS, DOESN'T MATTER. TALK.
I SAY THAT FOR YOUR SAKE TOO.

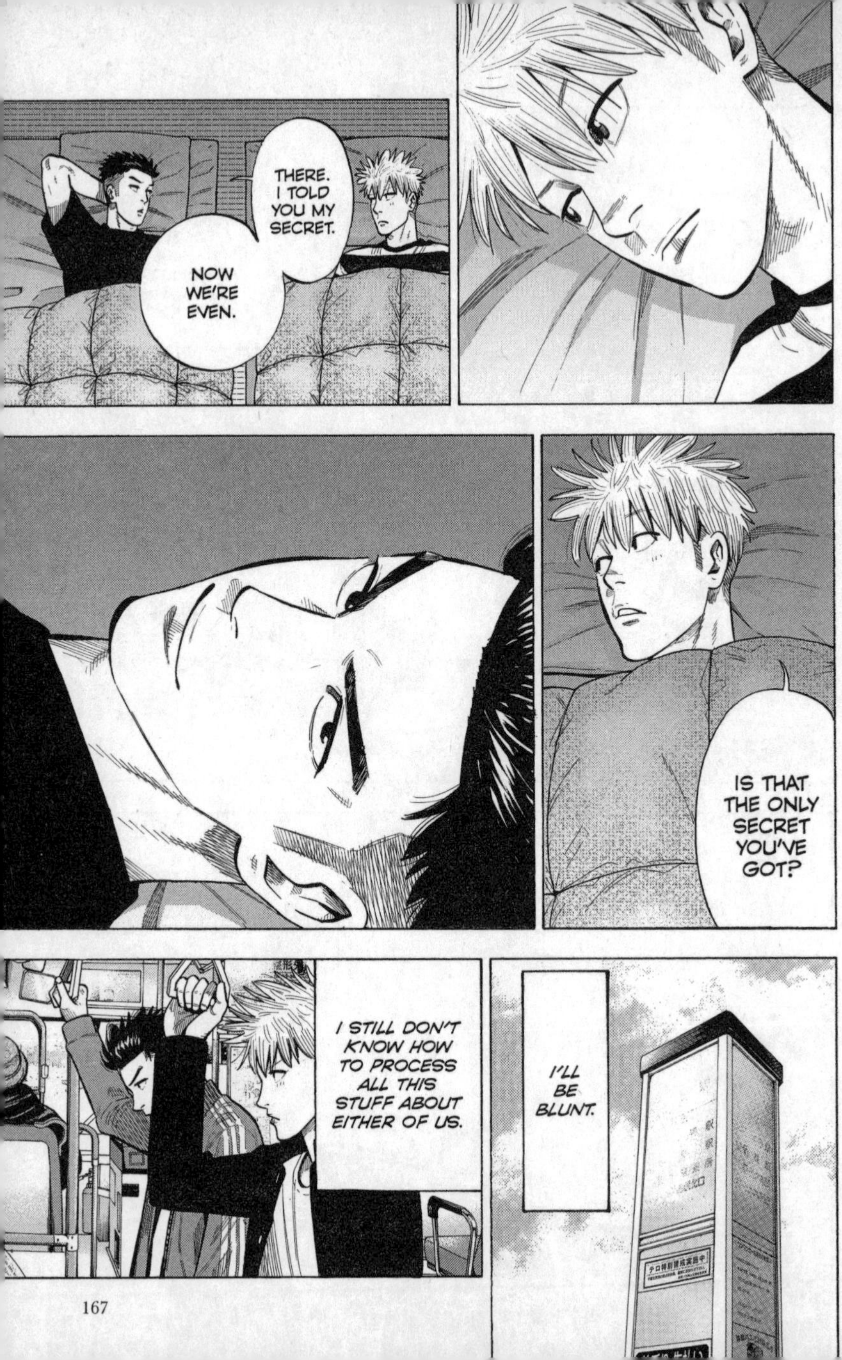
THERE. I TOLD YOU MY SECRET.
NOW WE'RE EVEN.
IS THAT THE ONLY SECRET YOU'VE GOT?
I'LL BE BLUNT.
I STILL DON'T KNOW HOW TO PROCESS ALL THIS STUFF ABOUT EITHER OF US.

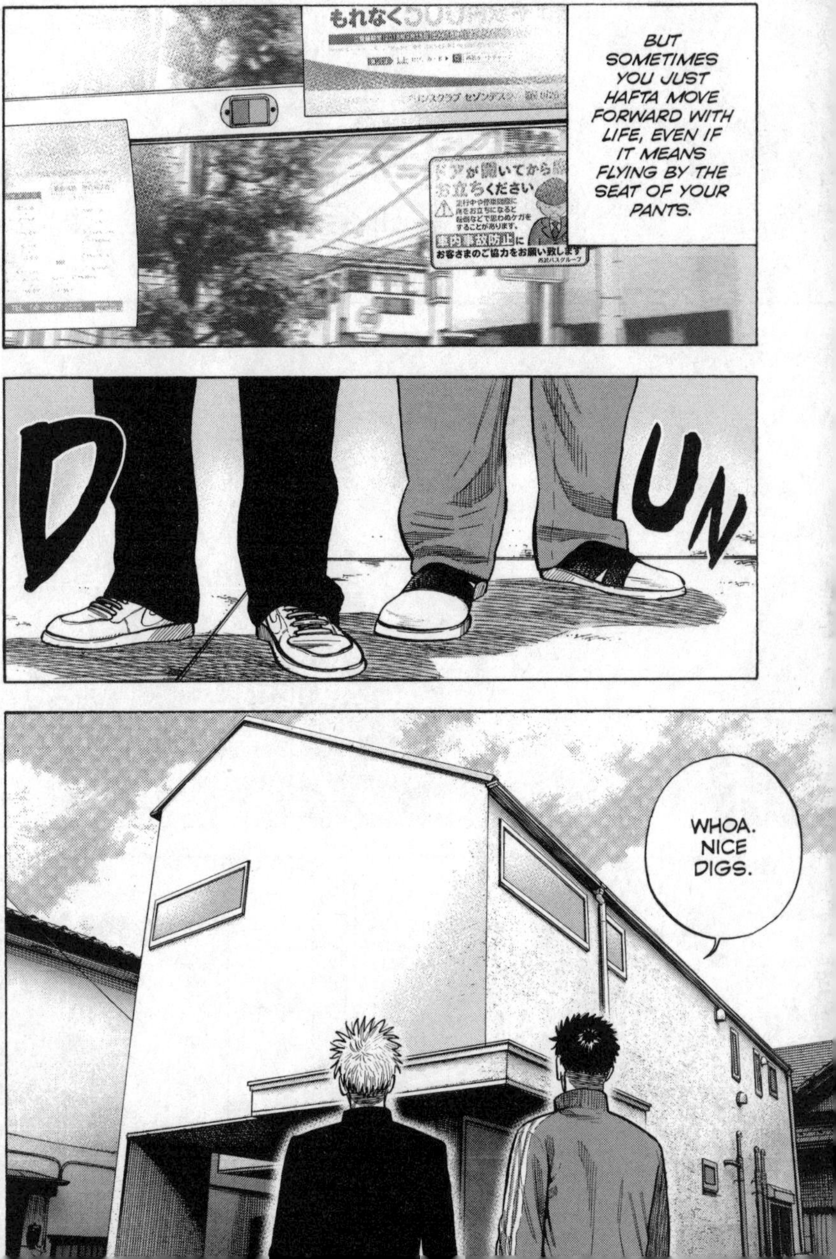
BUT SOMETIMES YOU JUST HAFTA MOVE FORWARD WITH LIFE, EVEN IF IT MEANS FLYING BY THE SEAT OF YOUR PANTS.
お立ちください
車内事故防止に
お客さまのご協力をお願い致します
D UN
WHOA. NICE DIGS.

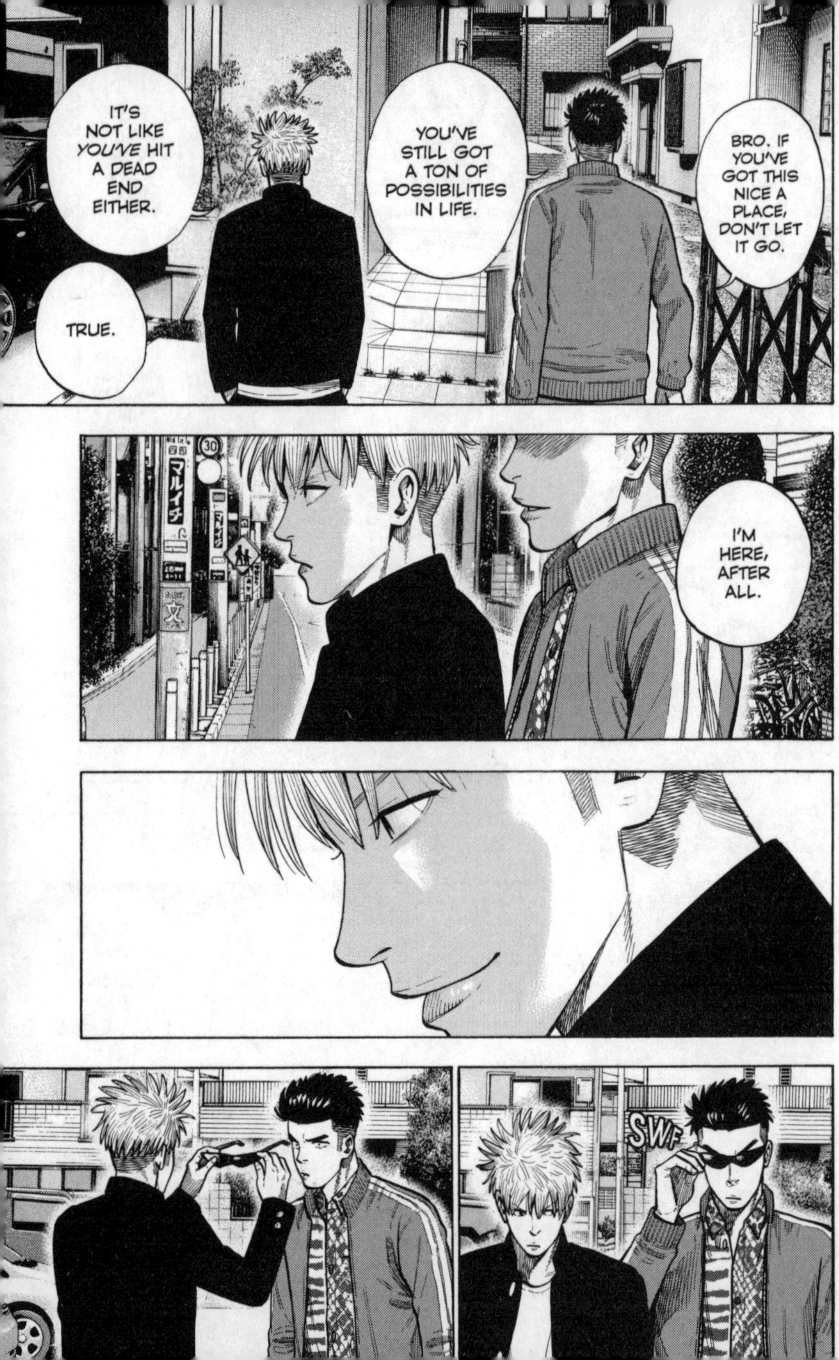
BRO. IF YOU'VE GOT THIS NICE A PLACE, DON'T LET IT GO.
YOU'VE STILL GOT A TON OF POSSIBILITIES IN LIFE.
IT'S NOT LIKE *YOU'VE* HIT A DEAD END EITHER.
TRUE.
I'M HERE, AFTER ALL.
マルイチ
SWF

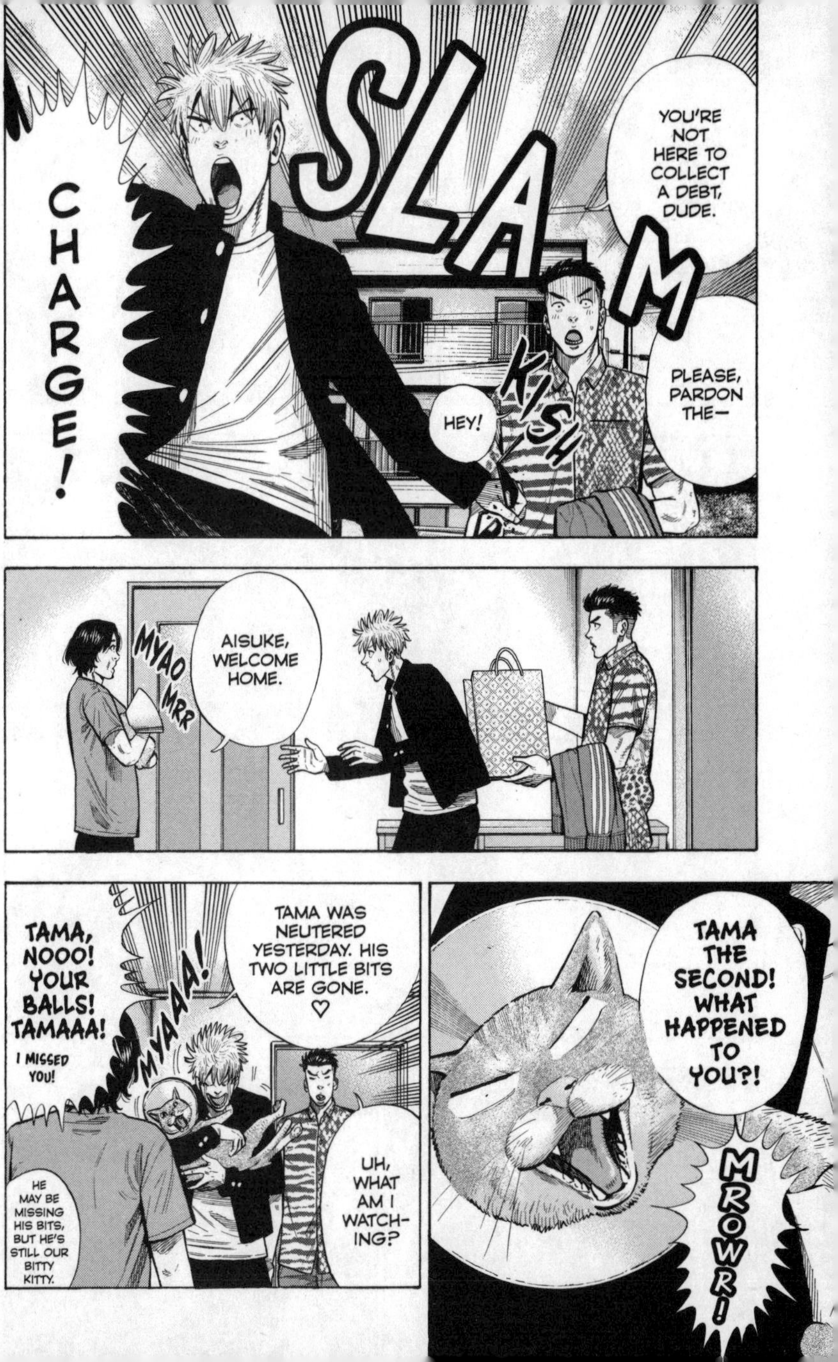
YOU'RE NOT HERE TO COLLECT A DEBT, DUDE.
PLEASE, PARDON THE—
SLAM
KISH
HEY!
CHARGE!
AISUKE, WELCOME HOME.
MYAO MRR
TAMA THE SECOND! WHAT HAPPENED TO YOU?!
MROWR!
TAMA WAS NEUTERED YESTERDAY. HIS TWO LITTLE BITS ARE GONE. ♡
MYAAA!
TAMA, NOOO! YOUR BALLS! TAMAAA!
I MISSED YOU!
UH, WHAT AM I WATCHING?
HE MAY BE MISSING HIS BITS, BUT HE'S STILL OUR BITTY KITTY.

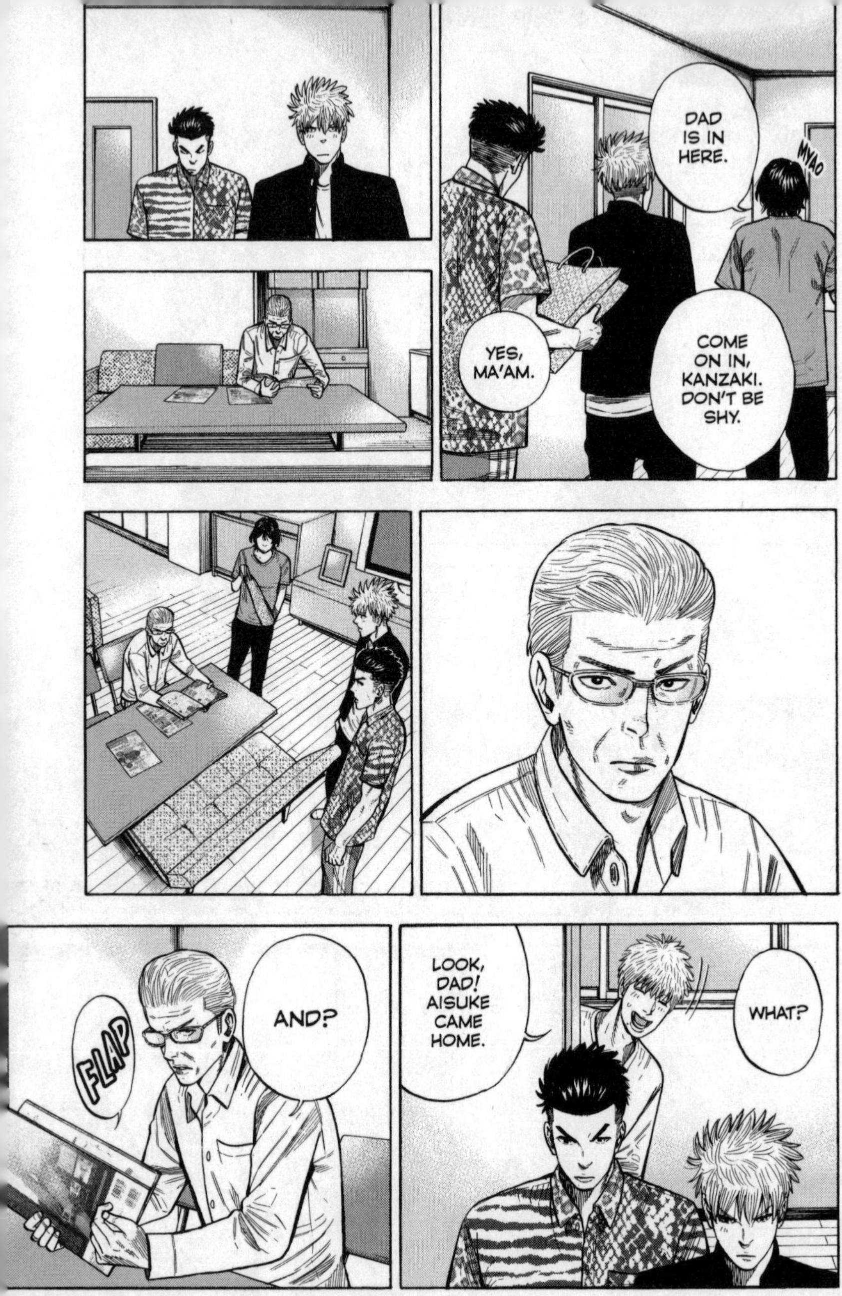
DAD IS IN HERE.
MYAO
COME ON IN, KANZAKI. DON'T BE SHY.
YES, MA'AM.
WHAT?
LOOK, DAD! AISUKE CAME HOME.
AND?
FLAP

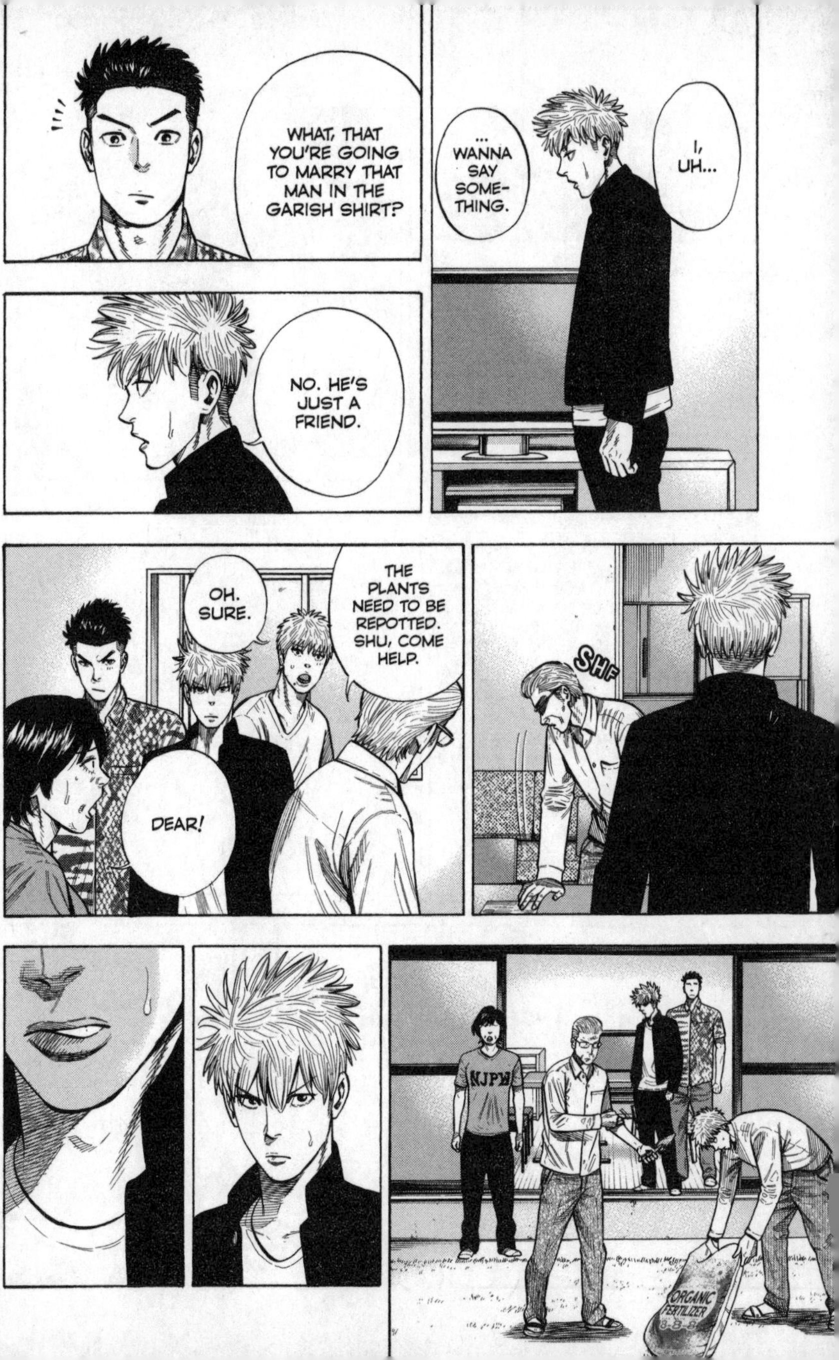
I, UH...
... WANNA SAY SOME-THING.
WHAT, THAT YOU'RE GOING TO MARRY THAT MAN IN THE GARISH SHIRT?
NO. HE'S JUST A FRIEND.
SHF
THE PLANTS NEED TO BE REPOTTED. SHU, COME HELP.
OH. SURE.
DEAR!
NJPW
ORGANIC FERTILIZER
8-8-8

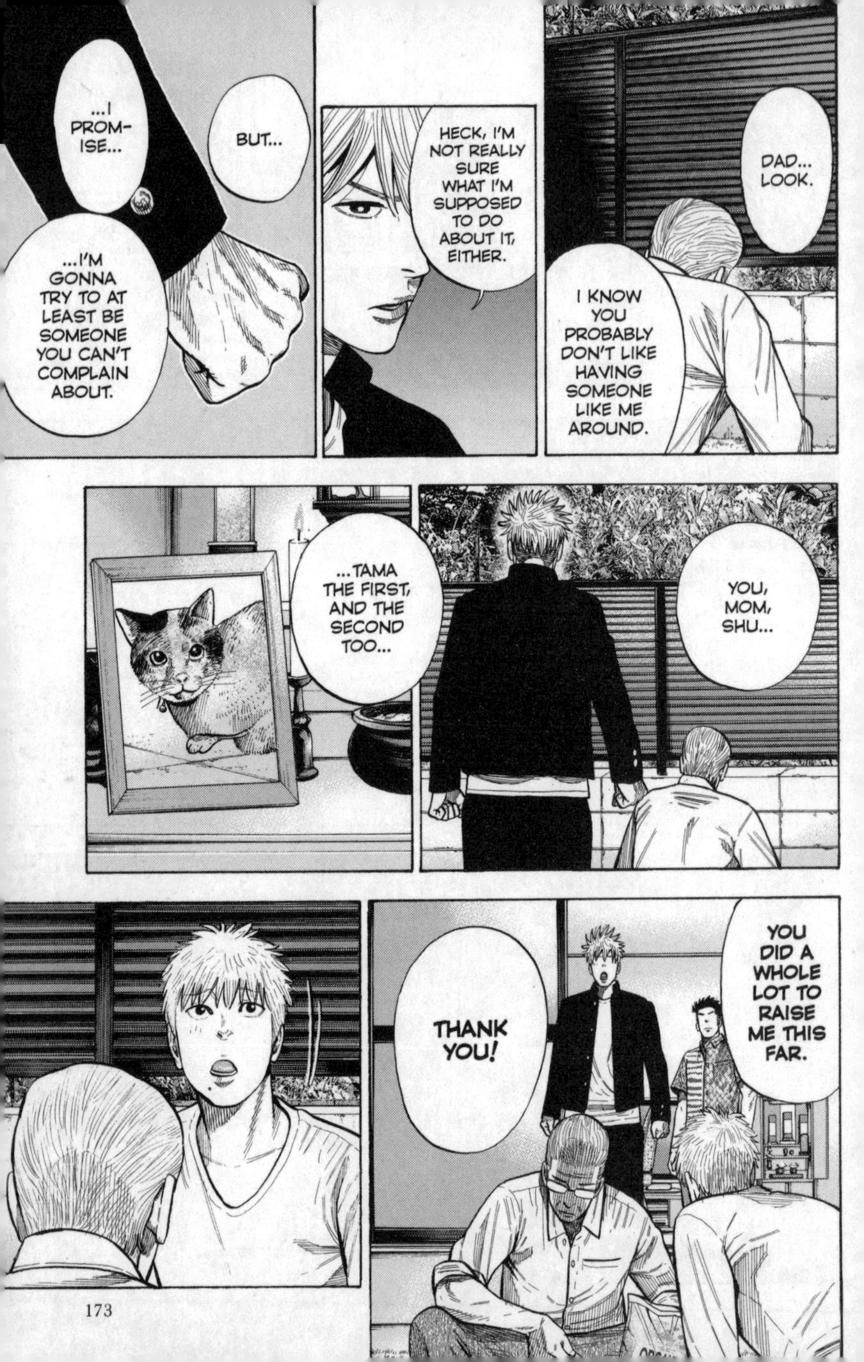
DAD... LOOK.
I KNOW YOU PROBABLY DON'T LIKE HAVING SOMEONE LIKE ME AROUND.
HECK, I'M NOT REALLY SURE WHAT I'M SUPPOSED TO DO ABOUT IT, EITHER.
BUT...
...I PROMISE...
...I'M GONNA TRY TO AT LEAST BE SOMEONE YOU CAN'T COMPLAIN ABOUT.
YOU, MOM, SHU...
...TAMA THE FIRST, AND THE SECOND TOO...
YOU DID A WHOLE LOT TO RAISE ME THIS FAR.
THANK YOU!

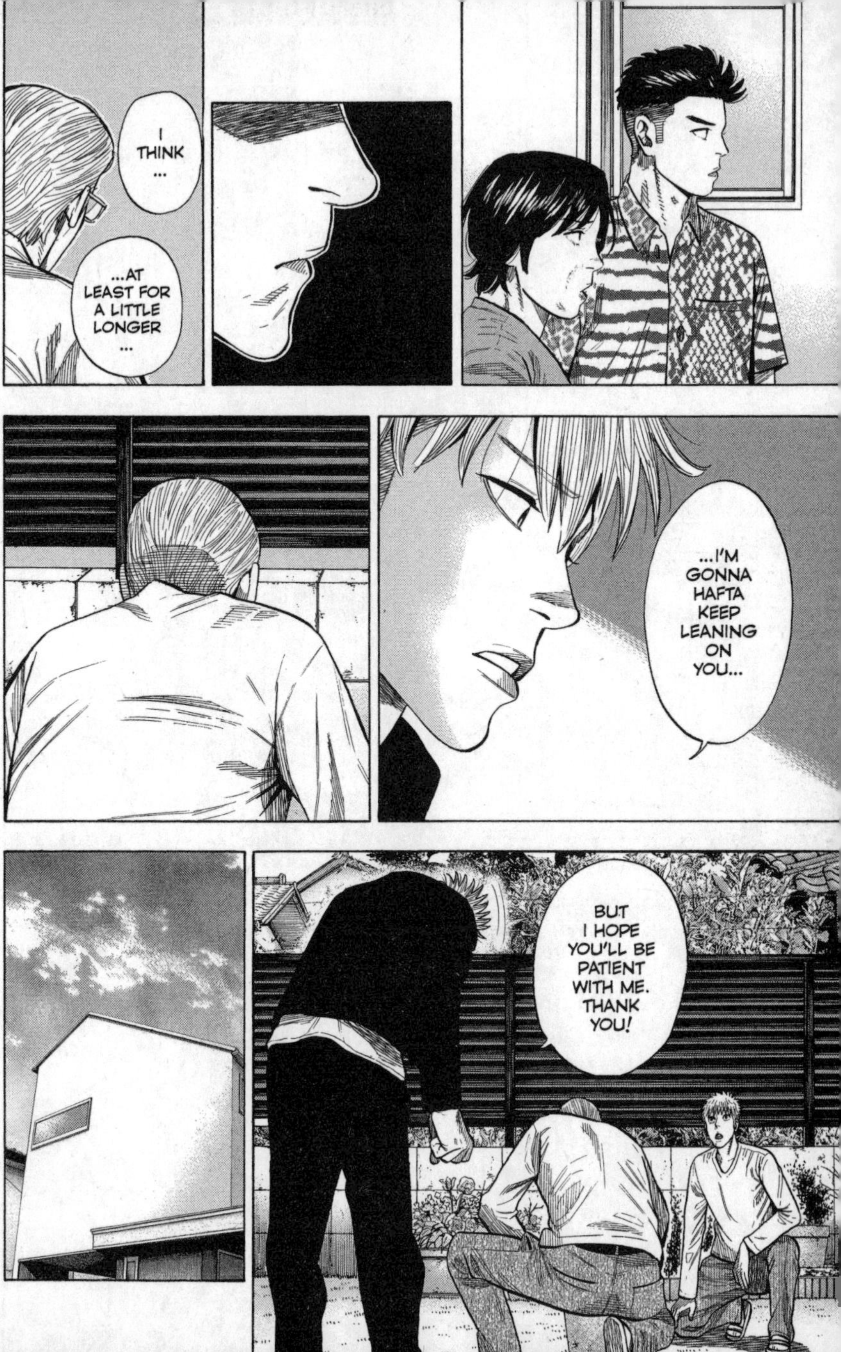
I THINK ...
...AT LEAST FOR A LITTLE LONGER ...
...I'M GONNA HAFTA KEEP LEANING ON YOU...
BUT I HOPE YOU'LL BE PATIENT WITH ME. THANK YOU!

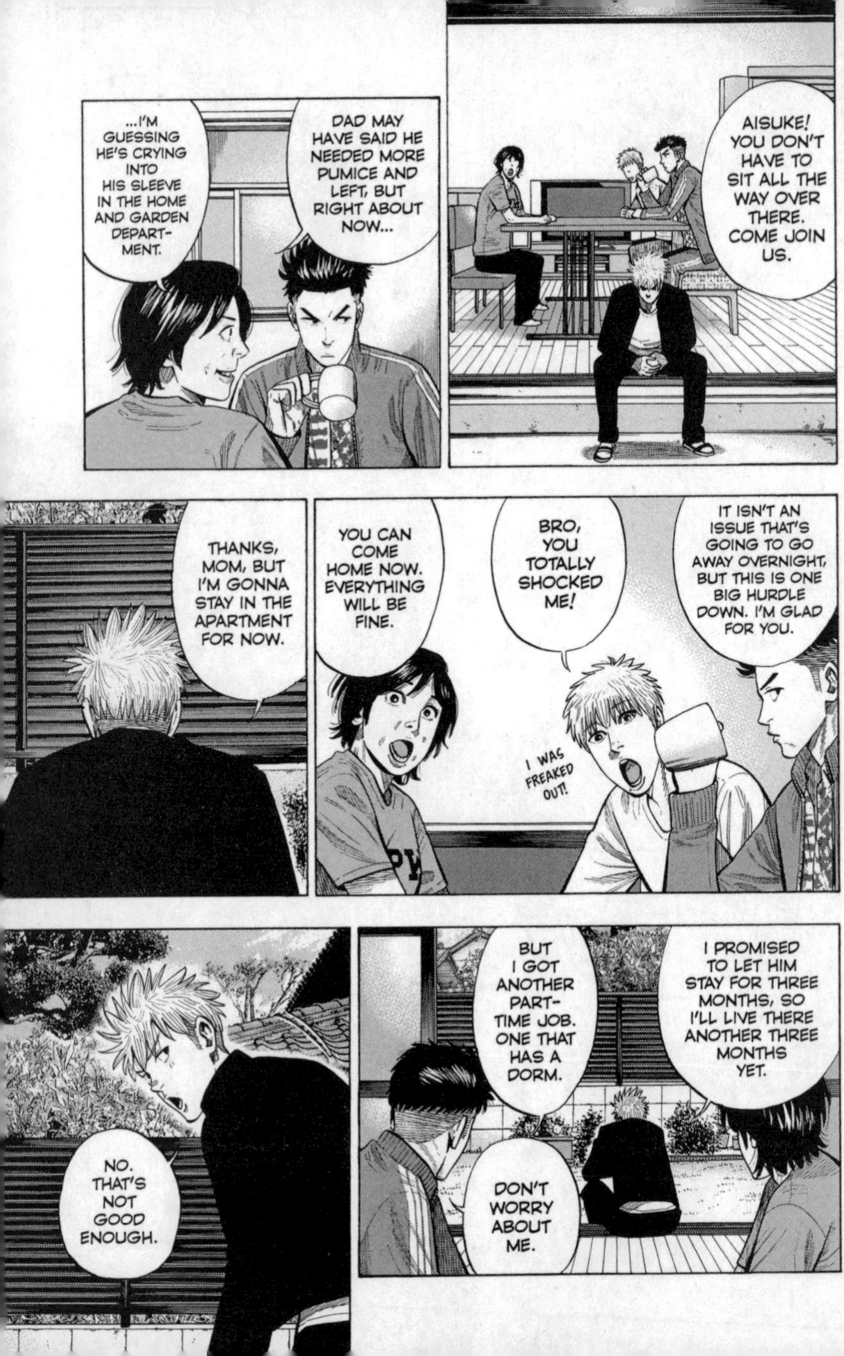
AISUKE! YOU DON'T HAVE TO SIT ALL THE WAY OVER THERE. COME JOIN US.
DAD MAY HAVE SAID HE NEEDED MORE PUMICE AND LEFT, BUT RIGHT ABOUT NOW...
...I'M GUESSING HE'S CRYING INTO HIS SLEEVE IN THE HOME AND GARDEN DEPART-MENT.
IT ISN'T AN ISSUE THAT'S GOING TO GO AWAY OVERNIGHT, BUT THIS IS ONE BIG HURDLE DOWN. I'M GLAD FOR YOU.
BRO, YOU TOTALLY SHOCKED ME!
I WAS FREAKED OUT!
YOU CAN COME HOME NOW. EVERYTHING WILL BE FINE.
THANKS, MOM, BUT I'M GONNA STAY IN THE APARTMENT FOR NOW.
I PROMISED TO LET HIM STAY FOR THREE MONTHS, SO I'LL LIVE THERE ANOTHER THREE MONTHS YET.
BUT I GOT ANOTHER PART-TIME JOB. ONE THAT HAS A DORM.
DON'T WORRY ABOUT ME.
NO. THAT'S NOT GOOD ENOUGH.

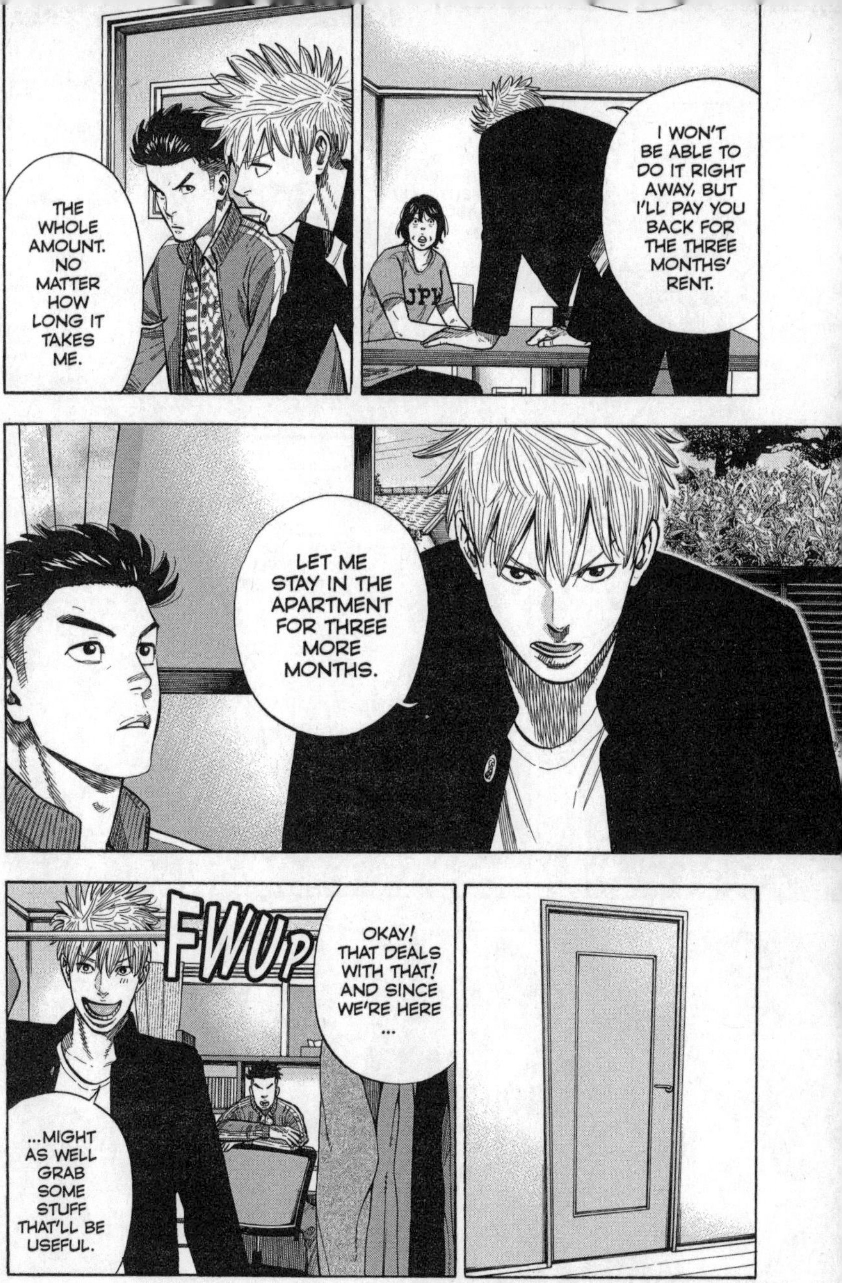
I WON'T BE ABLE TO DO IT RIGHT AWAY, BUT I'LL PAY YOU BACK FOR THE THREE MONTHS' RENT.
THE WHOLE AMOUNT. NO MATTER HOW LONG IT TAKES ME.
LET ME STAY IN THE APARTMENT FOR THREE MORE MONTHS.
OKAY! THAT DEALS WITH THAT! AND SINCE WE'RE HERE ...
FWUP
...MIGHT AS WELL GRAB SOME STUFF THAT'LL BE USEFUL.

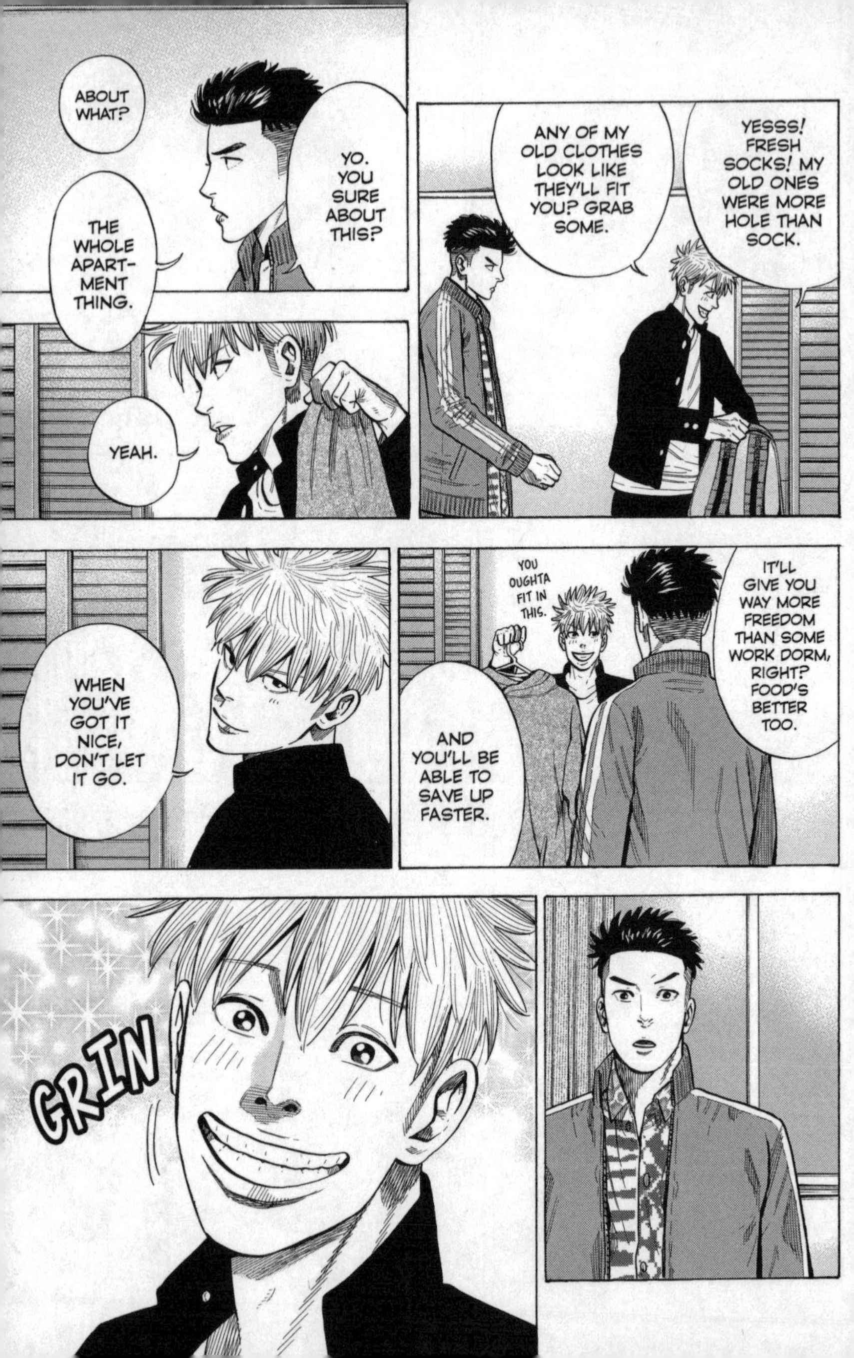
YESSS! FRESH SOCKS! MY OLD ONES WERE MORE HOLE THAN SOCK.
ANY OF MY OLD CLOTHES LOOK LIKE THEY'LL FIT YOU? GRAB SOME.
YO. YOU SURE ABOUT THIS?
ABOUT WHAT?
THE WHOLE APART- MENT THING.
YEAH.
IT'LL GIVE YOU WAY MORE FREEDOM THAN SOME WORK DORM, RIGHT? FOOD'S BETTER TOO.
YOU OUGHTA FIT IN THIS.
AND YOU'LL BE ABLE TO SAVE UP FASTER.
WHEN YOU'VE GOT IT NICE, DON'T LET IT GO.
GRIN

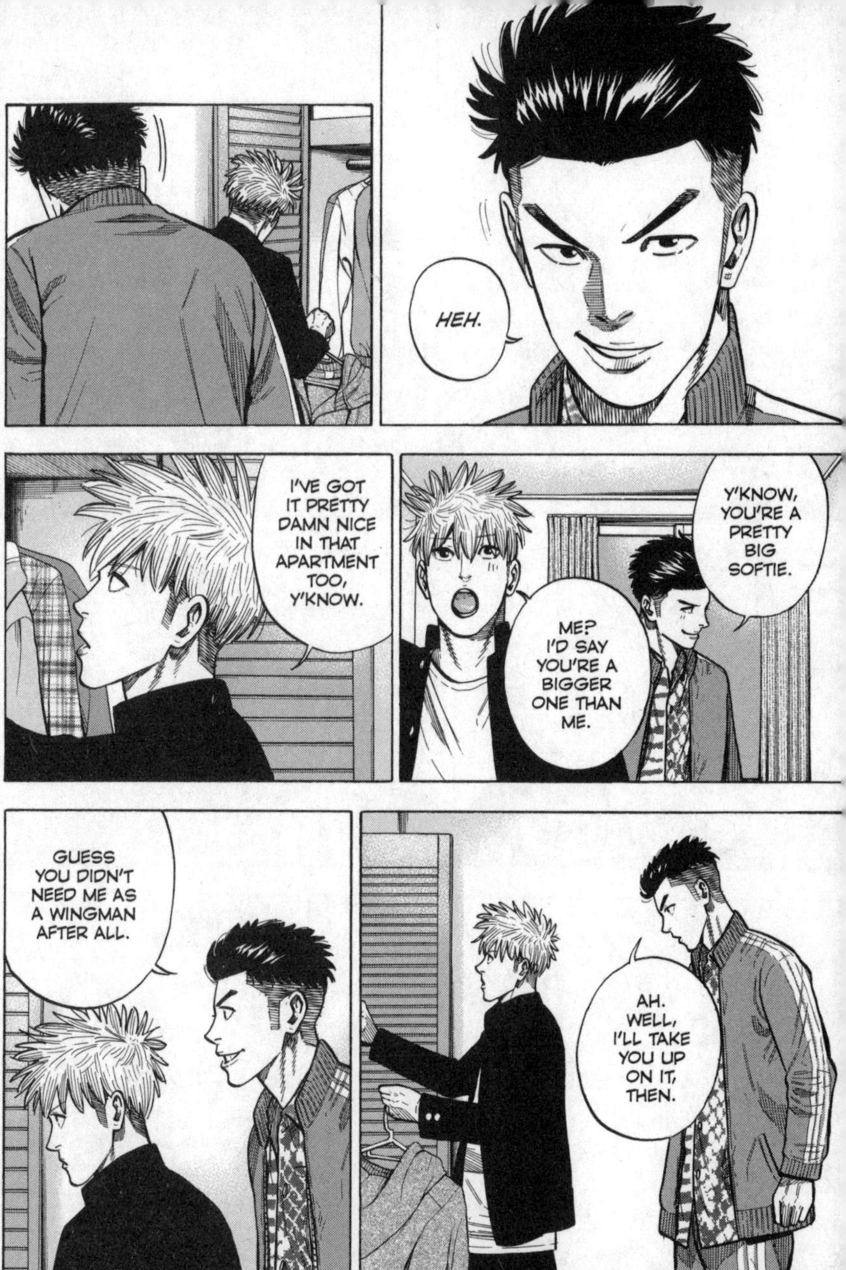
HEH.
Y'KNOW, YOU'RE A PRETTY BIG SOFTIE.
ME? I'D SAY YOU'RE A BIGGER ONE THAN ME.
I'VE GOT IT PRETTY DAMN NICE IN THAT APARTMENT TOO, Y'KNOW.
AH. WELL, I'LL TAKE YOU UP ON IT, THEN.
GUESS YOU DIDN'T NEED ME AS A WINGMAN AFTER ALL.

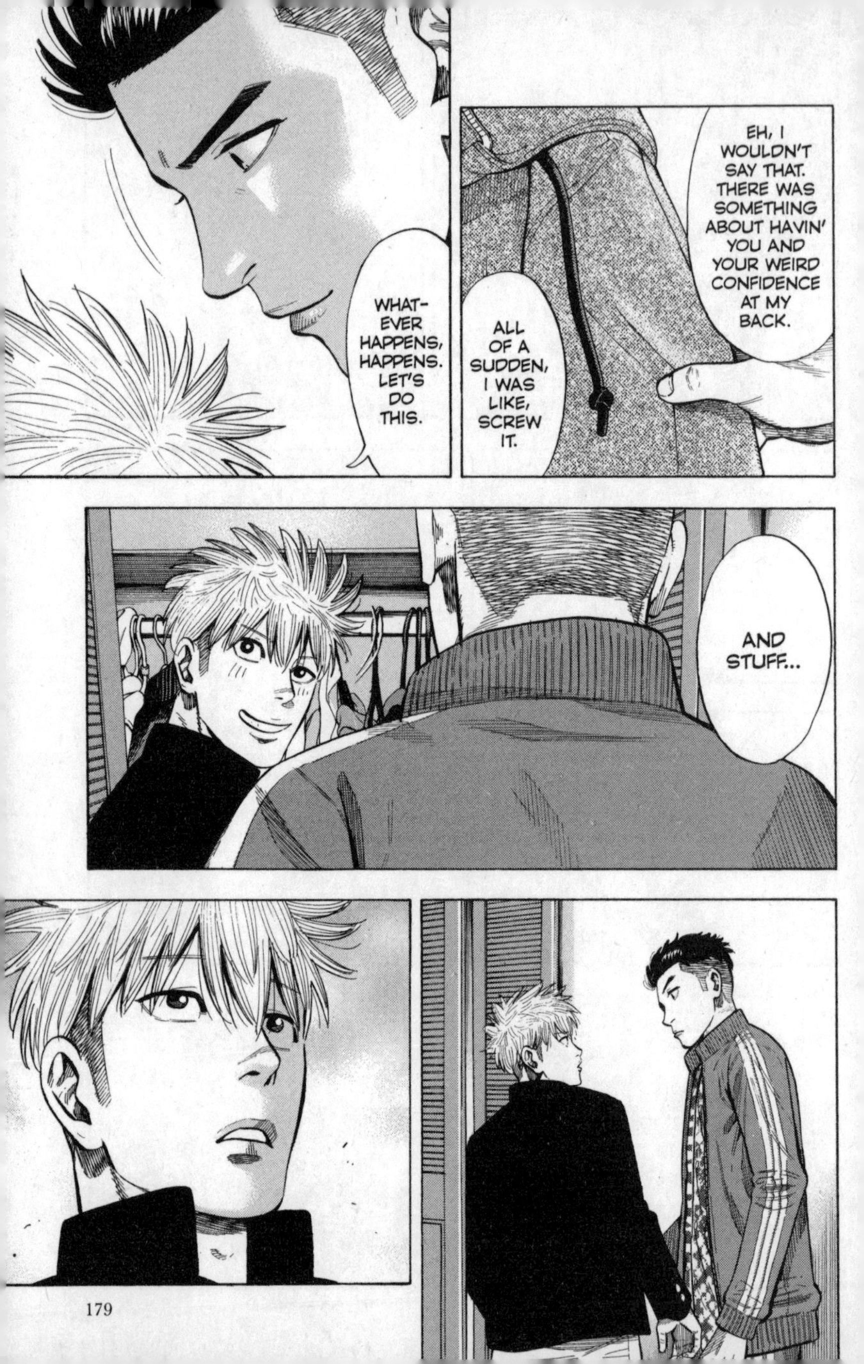
EH, I WOULDN'T SAY THAT. THERE WAS SOMETHING ABOUT HAVIN' YOU AND YOUR WEIRD CONFIDENCE AT MY BACK.
ALL OF A SUDDEN, I WAS LIKE, SCREW IT.
WHATEVER HAPPENS, HAPPENS. LET'S DO THIS.
AND STUFF...

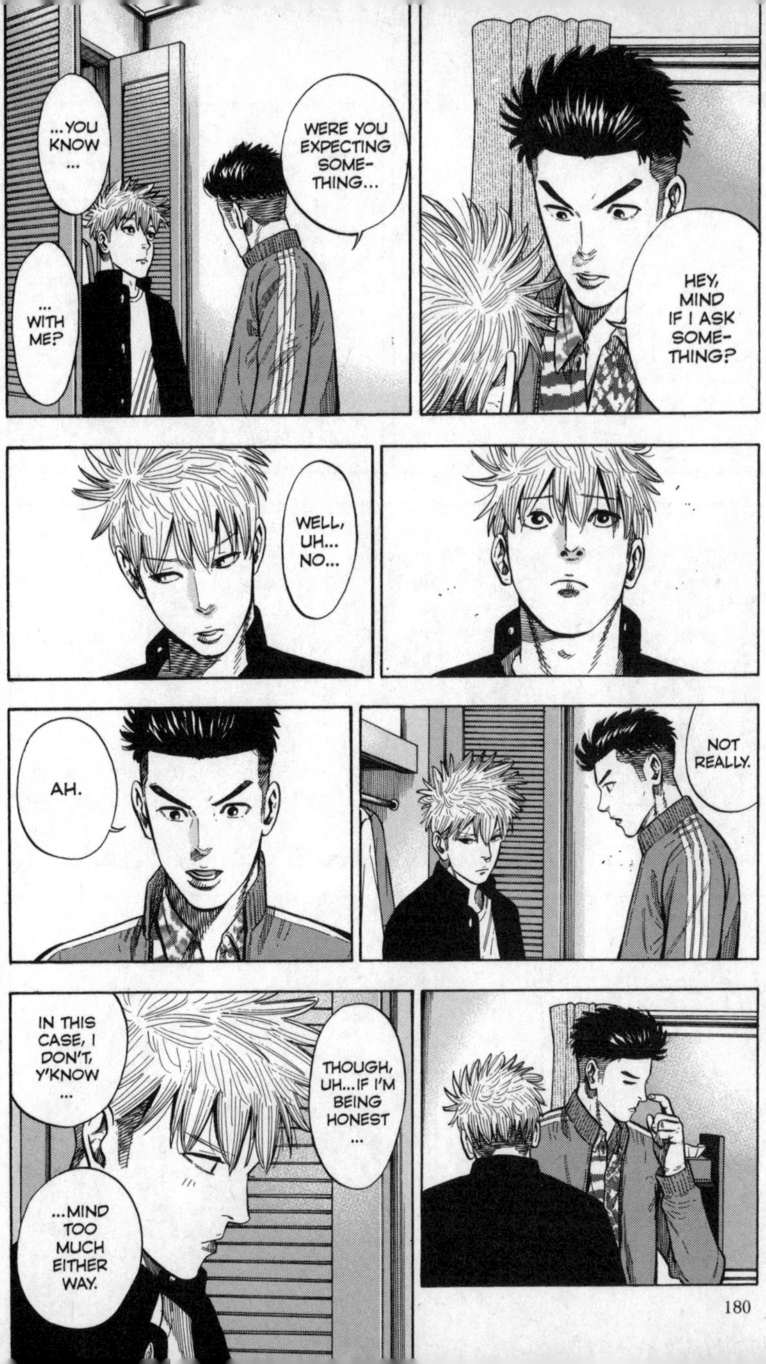
HEY, MIND IF I ASK SOMETHING?
WERE YOU EXPECTING SOMETHING...
...YOU KNOW ...
... WITH ME?
WELL, UH... NO...
NOT REALLY.
AH.
THOUGH, UH...IF I'M BEING HONEST ...
IN THIS CASE, I DON'T, Y'KNOW ...
...MIND TOO MUCH EITHER WAY.

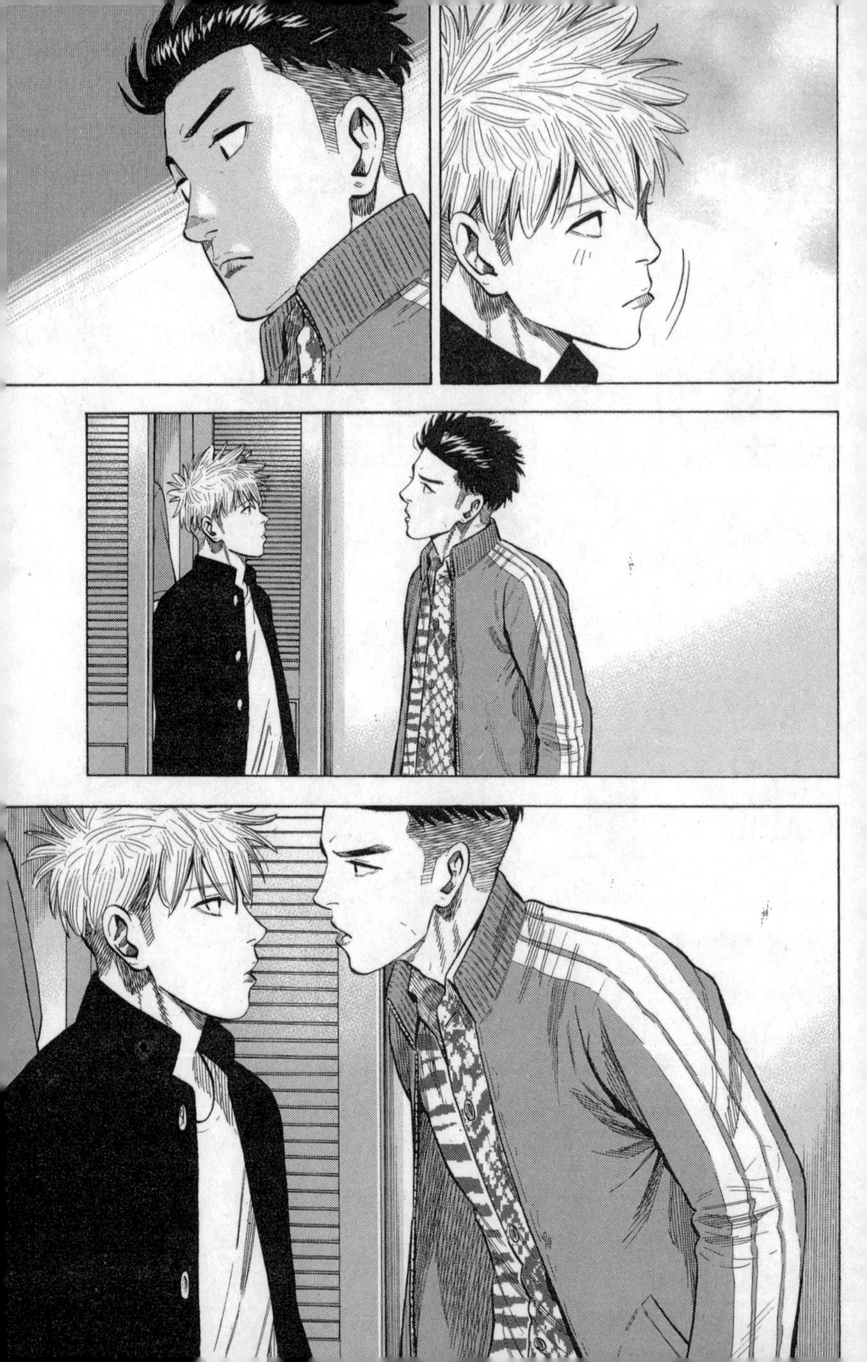

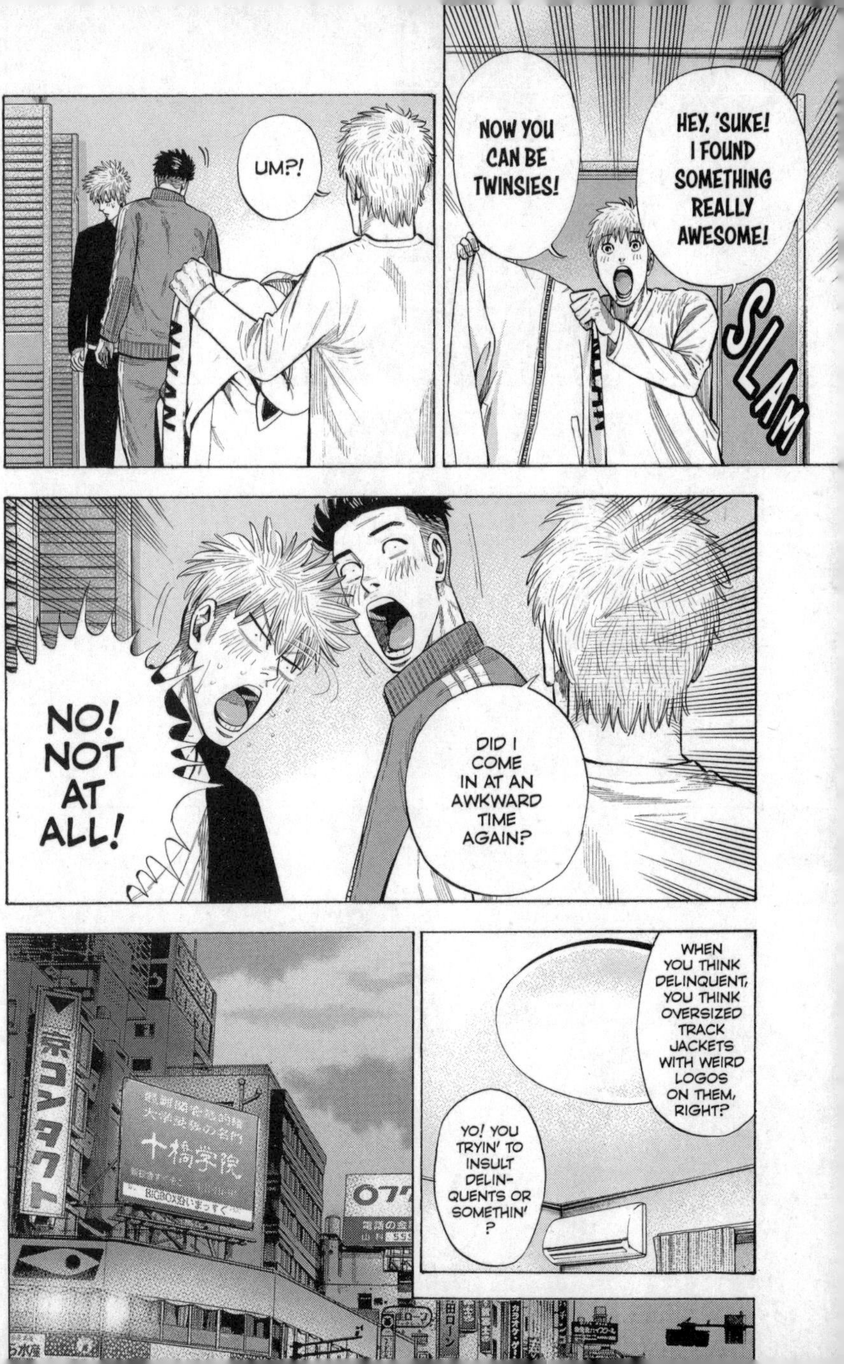
HEY, 'SUKE! I FOUND SOMETHING REALLY AWESOME!
NOW YOU CAN BE TWINSIES!
SLAM
UM?!
DID I COME IN AT AN AWKWARD TIME AGAIN?
NO! NOT AT ALL!
WHEN YOU THINK DELINQUENT, YOU THINK OVERSIZED TRACK JACKETS WITH WEIRD LOGOS ON THEM, RIGHT?
YO! YOU TRYIN' TO INSULT DELIN-QUENTS OR SOMETHIN'?
十橋学院

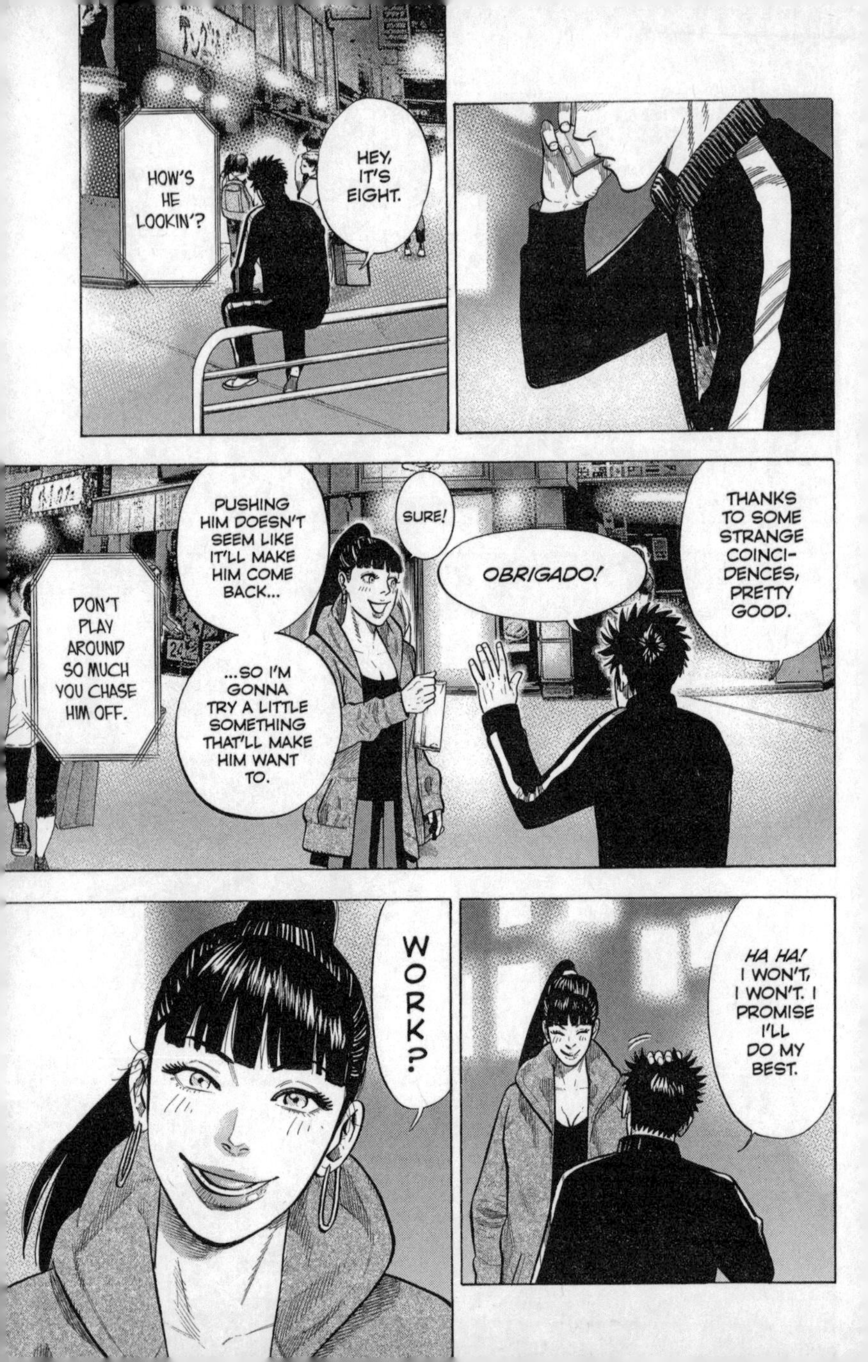
HEY, IT'S EIGHT.
HOW'S HE LOOKIN'?
THANKS TO SOME STRANGE COINCIDENCES, PRETTY GOOD.
OBRIGADO!
SURE!
PUSHING HIM DOESN'T SEEM LIKE IT'LL MAKE HIM COME BACK...
...SO I'M GONNA TRY A LITTLE SOMETHING THAT'LL MAKE HIM WANT TO.
DON'T PLAY AROUND SO MUCH YOU CHASE HIM OFF.
HA HA! I WON'T, I WON'T. I PROMISE I'LL DO MY BEST.
WORK?

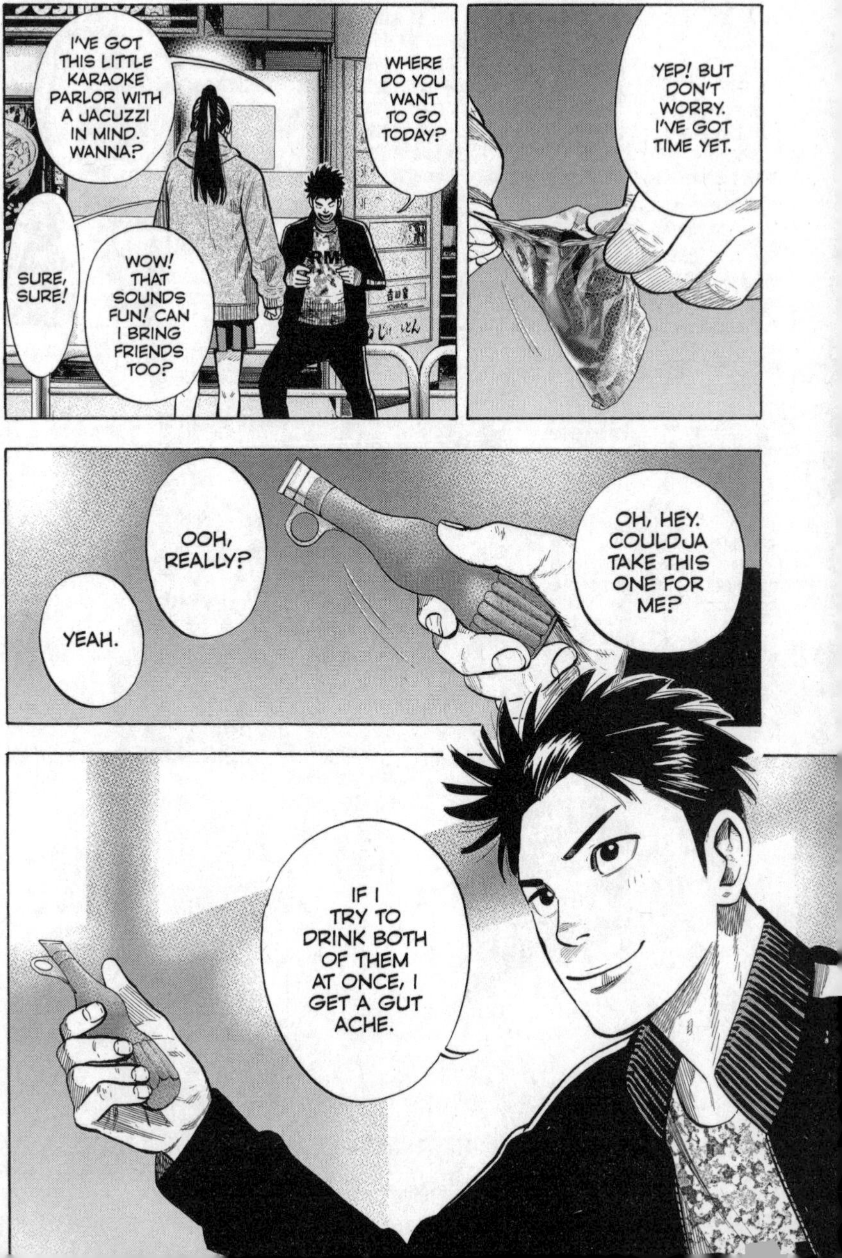
YEP! BUT DON'T WORRY. I'VE GOT TIME YET.
WHERE DO YOU WANT TO GO TODAY?
I'VE GOT THIS LITTLE KARAOKE PARLOR WITH A JACUZZI IN MIND. WANNA?
WOW! THAT SOUNDS FUN! CAN I BRING FRIENDS TOO?
SURE, SURE!
OH, HEY. COULDJA TAKE THIS ONE FOR ME?
OOH, REALLY?
YEAH.
IF I TRY TO DRINK BOTH OF THEM AT ONCE, I GET A GUT ACHE.

I'M SHOOWA, ORIGINAL CREATOR AND STORYBOARD WRITER. WHEN I SUBMITTED THE IDEA FOR THIS STORY, I HAD NO IDEA I'D BE ALLOWED TO CONTINUE WORKING ON IT IN SUCH A BIG CAPACITY. BUT MR. OKUJIMA WARMLY AGREED TO HAVE ME, SO I HAD THE PRIVILEGE OF WORKING TOGETHER WITH HIM. THIS IS THE FIRST TIME I'VE WORKED ON A PROJECT WHERE SOMEONE ELSE TOOK OVER THE ART DUTIES AFTER I FINISHED THE STORYBOARDS. LOOKING AT THE FINISHED MANGA PAGES WAS SO MUCH FUN. IN SOME PLACES, THERE WERE HAPPY ACCIDENTS WHERE I'D BE LIKE, "OH, SO YOU WENT WITH THAT EXPRESSION THERE," AND IN OTHERS, IT WOULD BE EVEN COOLER OR CUTER THAN I EXPECTED. THERE WERE SO MANY I LOVED I COULDN'T NAME THEM ALL. AND MOST OF ALL, THE ART IS JUST SO GREAT! READING A BL STORY WITH ART THIS GREAT IS AWESOME, AND I HOPE YOU'LL JOIN ME!

I'D ALSO BE HONORED IF YOU WOULD CONTINUE TO WARMLY WATCH OVER THESE TWO CHARACTERS. MR. OKUJIMA, THANK YOU SO MUCH FOR MAKING THEM SUCH CHARMING PEOPLE! I'M SO GLAD IT'S YOU I GOT TO WORK WITH!

I STILL HAVE SO MUCH TO LEARN, BUT I'M HONORED TO BE WORKING ON THIS PROJECT. I HAVE NOTHING BUT MY MOST PROFUSE GRATITUDE FOR MR. OKUJIMA AND ALL HIS LOVE AND PASSION, FOR HIS CAPABLE ASSISTANTS, FOR OUR EDITOR, WHO UNDERSTANDS *MOE* EVEN BETTER THAN I AND WHO SOMETIMES SAYS THE CRAZIEST THINGS, AND TO EVERYONE WHO READ (AND BOUGHT!) THIS VOLUME. THANK YOU SO VERY MUCH! YOU CAN CONTINUE TO FOLLOW THEIR STORY IN THE NEXT VOLUME!

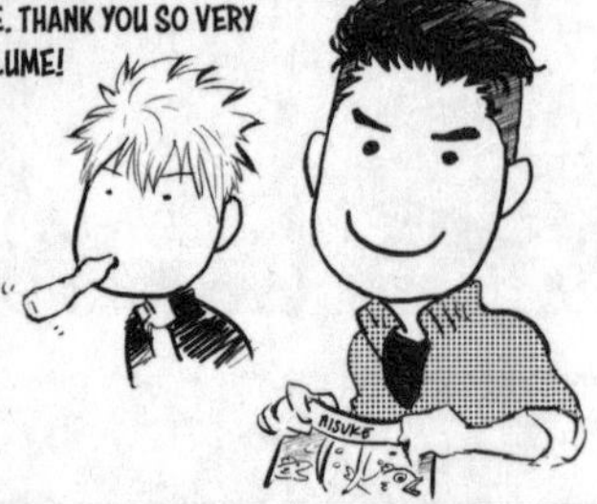
RISUKE

THANK YOU VERY MUCH!

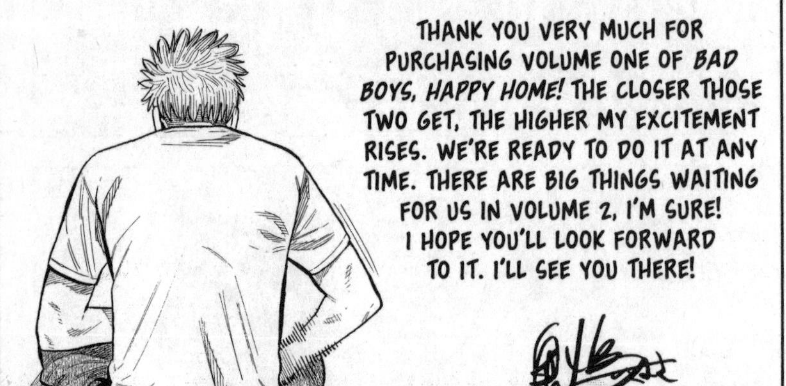

THANK YOU VERY MUCH FOR PURCHASING VOLUME ONE OF *BAD BOYS, HAPPY HOME!* THE CLOSER THOSE TWO GET, THE HIGHER MY EXCITEMENT RISES. WE'RE READY TO DO IT AT ANY TIME. THERE ARE BIG THINGS WAITING FOR US IN VOLUME 2, I'M SURE! I HOPE YOU'LL LOOK FORWARD TO IT. I'LL SEE YOU THERE!

HIROMASA OKUJIMA

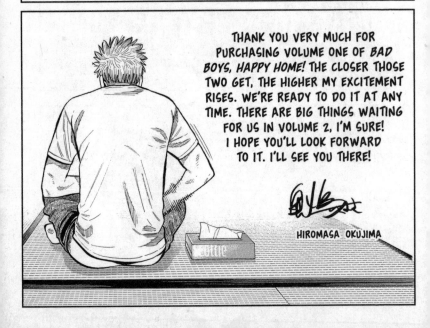

BONUS STORY

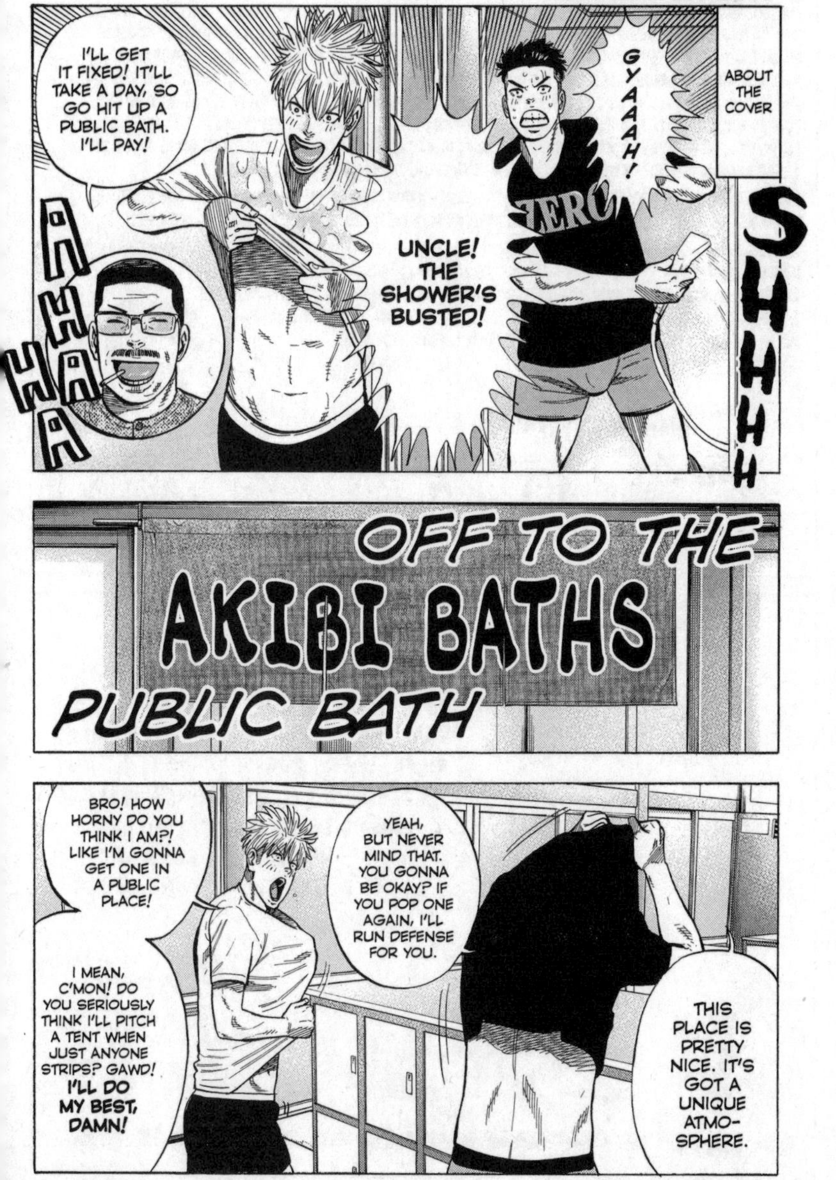
ABOUT THE COVER
SHHHHH
GYAAAH!
UNCLE! THE SHOWER'S BUSTED!
I'LL GET IT FIXED! IT'LL TAKE A DAY, SO GO HIT UP A PUBLIC BATH. I'LL PAY!
AHAHAHA
OFF TO THE
AKIBI BATHS
PUBLIC BATH
THIS PLACE IS PRETTY NICE. IT'S GOT A UNIQUE ATMO-SPHERE.
YEAH, BUT NEVER MIND THAT. YOU GONNA BE OKAY? IF YOU POP ONE AGAIN, I'LL RUN DEFENSE FOR YOU.
BRO! HOW HORNY DO YOU THINK I AM?! LIKE I'M GONNA GET ONE IN A PUBLIC PLACE!
I MEAN, C'MON! DO YOU SERIOUSLY THINK I'LL PITCH A TENT WHEN JUST ANYONE STRIPS? GAWD! **I'LL DO MY BEST, DAMN!**

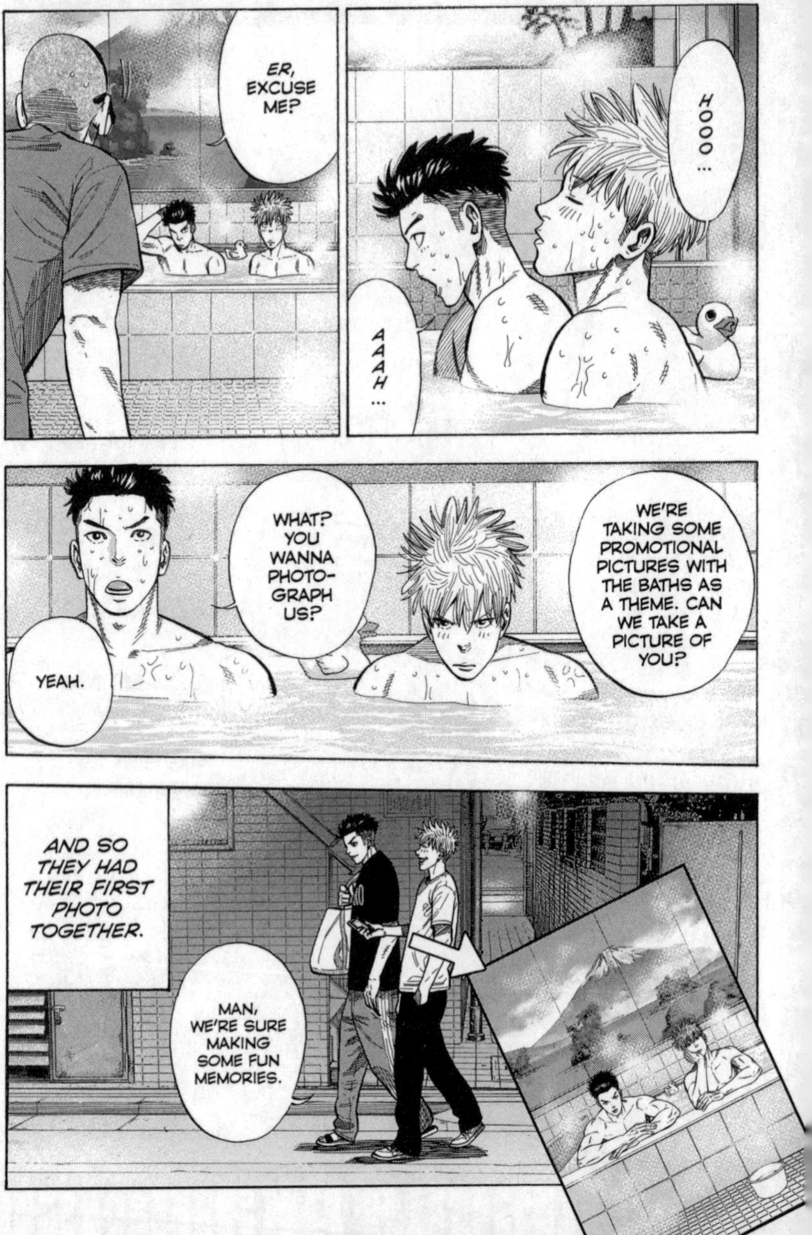
HOOO...
AAAH...
ER, EXCUSE ME?
WE'RE TAKING SOME PROMOTIONAL PICTURES WITH THE BATHS AS A THEME. CAN WE TAKE A PICTURE OF YOU?
WHAT? YOU WANNA PHOTO-GRAPH US?
YEAH.
AND SO THEY HAD THEIR FIRST PHOTO TOGETHER.
MAN, WE'RE SURE MAKING SOME FUN MEMORIES.

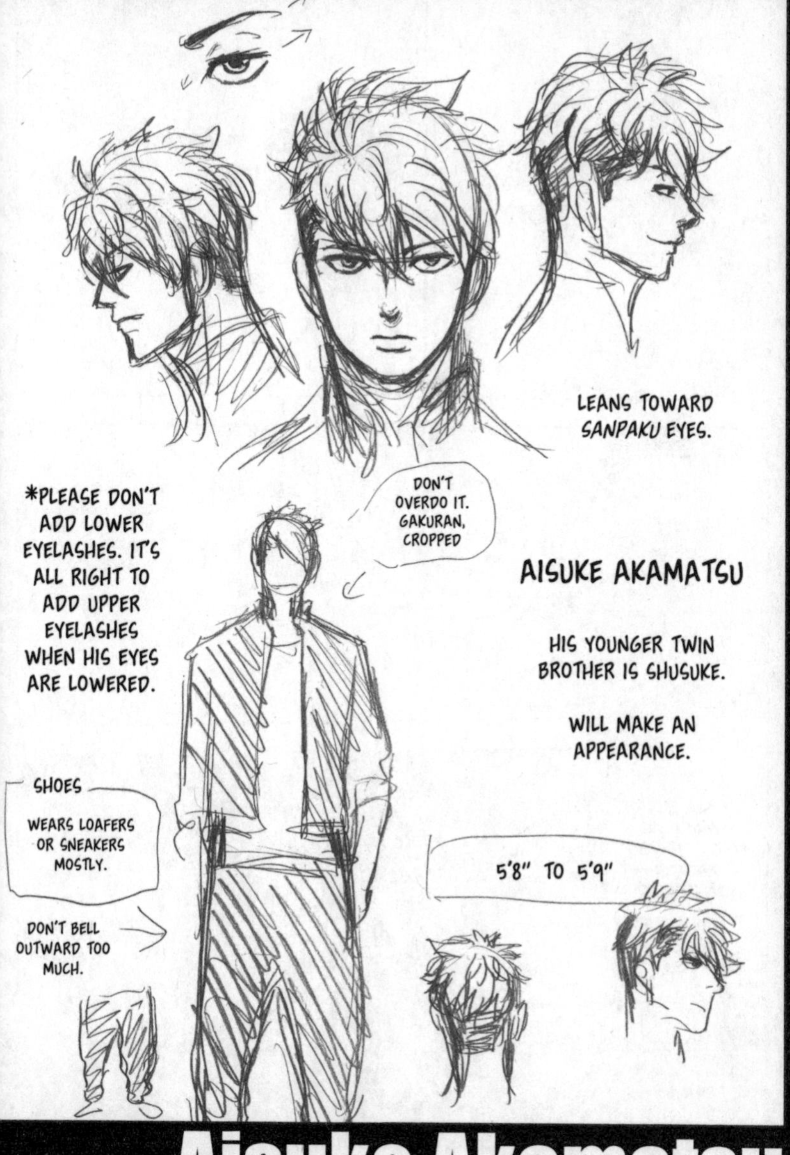
LEANS TOWARD SANPAKU EYES.
DON'T OVERDO IT. GAKURAN, CROPPED
*PLEASE DON'T ADD LOWER EYELASHES. IT'S ALL RIGHT TO ADD UPPER EYELASHES WHEN HIS EYES ARE LOWERED.
AISUKE AKAMATSU
HIS YOUNGER TWIN BROTHER IS SHUSUKE.
WILL MAKE AN APPEARANCE.
SHOES
WEARS LOAFERS OR SNEAKERS MOSTLY.
DON'T BELL OUTWARD TOO MUCH.
5'8" TO 5'9"

Aisuke Akamatsu

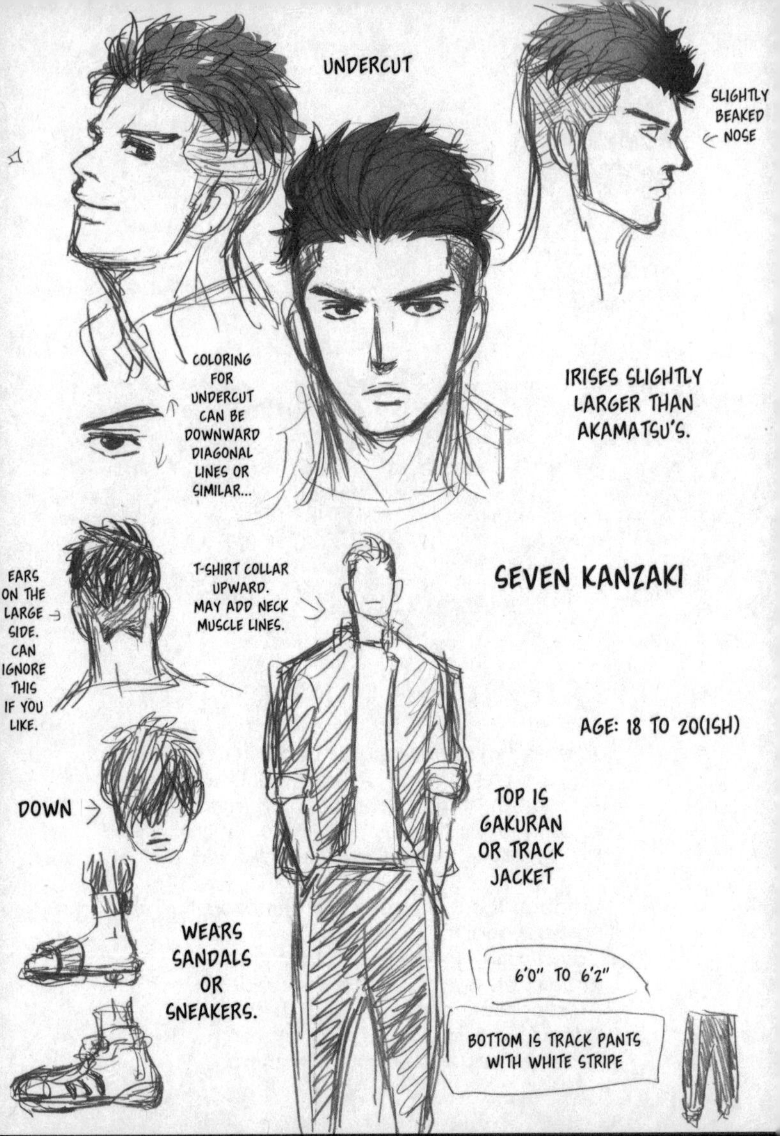
UNDERCUT
SLIGHTLY BEAKED NOSE
COLORING FOR UNDERCUT CAN BE DOWNWARD DIAGONAL LINES OR SIMILAR...
IRISES SLIGHTLY LARGER THAN AKAMATSU'S.
EARS ON THE LARGE SIDE. CAN IGNORE THIS IF YOU LIKE.
T-SHIRT COLLAR UPWARD. MAY ADD NECK MUSCLE LINES.
SEVEN KANZAKI
AGE: 18 TO 20(ISH)
DOWN
TOP IS GAKURAN OR TRACK JACKET
WEARS SANDALS OR SNEAKERS.
6'0" TO 6'2"
BOTTOM IS TRACK PANTS WITH WHITE STRIPE

Seven Kanzaki

BAD BOYS. HAPPY HOME V1/END

SHOOWA
I'm SHOOWA, a newbie author at joint projects. I hope you enjoy it!

Hiromasa Okujima
I'm Okujima, a newbie BL manga artist. I'm super excited that my experience living together with a friend has come in handy here. Hope you like it!

About the Creators

Bad Boys, Happy Home may be **SHOOWA**'s first English-language release, but she's also been published internationally in both French and Korean. You can find out more about her on her Twitter page, **@shoowa**.

Although this is **Hiromasa Okujima**'s first professional foray into boys' love, he's created many shonen and seinen manga. Some of his hobbies include martial arts and collecting secondhand clothing. You can find out more about him on his Twitter page, **@HiromasaOkujima**.

Bad Boys, Happy Home

Volume 1
SuBLime Manga Edition

Story by **SHOOWA**
Art by **Hiromasa Okujima**

Translation—**Adrienne Beck**
Touch-Up Art and Lettering—**Deborah Fisher**
Cover and Graphic Design—**Julian [JR] Robinson**
Editor—**Jennifer LeBlanc**

DOUSEI YANKEE AKAMATSU SEVEN Volume 1
© 2019 SHOOWA/HIROMASA OKUJIMA
First published in Japan in 2019 by Akita Publishing Co., Ltd., Tokyo
English translation rights arranged with Akita Publishing Co., Ltd.
through Tuttle-Mori Agency, Inc., Tokyo

AKITA SHOTEN since 1948

Printed in the U.S.A.

Published by SuBLime Manga
P.O. Box 77010
San Francisco, CA 94107

10 9 8 7 6 5 4 3 2 1
First printing, July 2021

PARENTAL ADVISORY
BAD BOYS, HAPPY HOME is rated M for Mature and is recommended for mature readers. This volume contains graphic imagery, mature themes, and cute guys cohabitating.

www.SuBLimeManga.com

Escape Journey

Story and Art by
OGERETSU TANAKA

Naoto and Taichi's first try at love during their high school days crashed and burned. Years later the two unexpectedly reunite on their first day of college. Tumultuous love often burns hot, and the glowing embers of their previous relationship reignite into a second try at love!

Complete Series

Escape Journey

OGERETSU TANAKA

1

When a playboy falls for a nerd,
chemistry results in … on!

D… Cruel

Story and Art by Yonezou Nekota

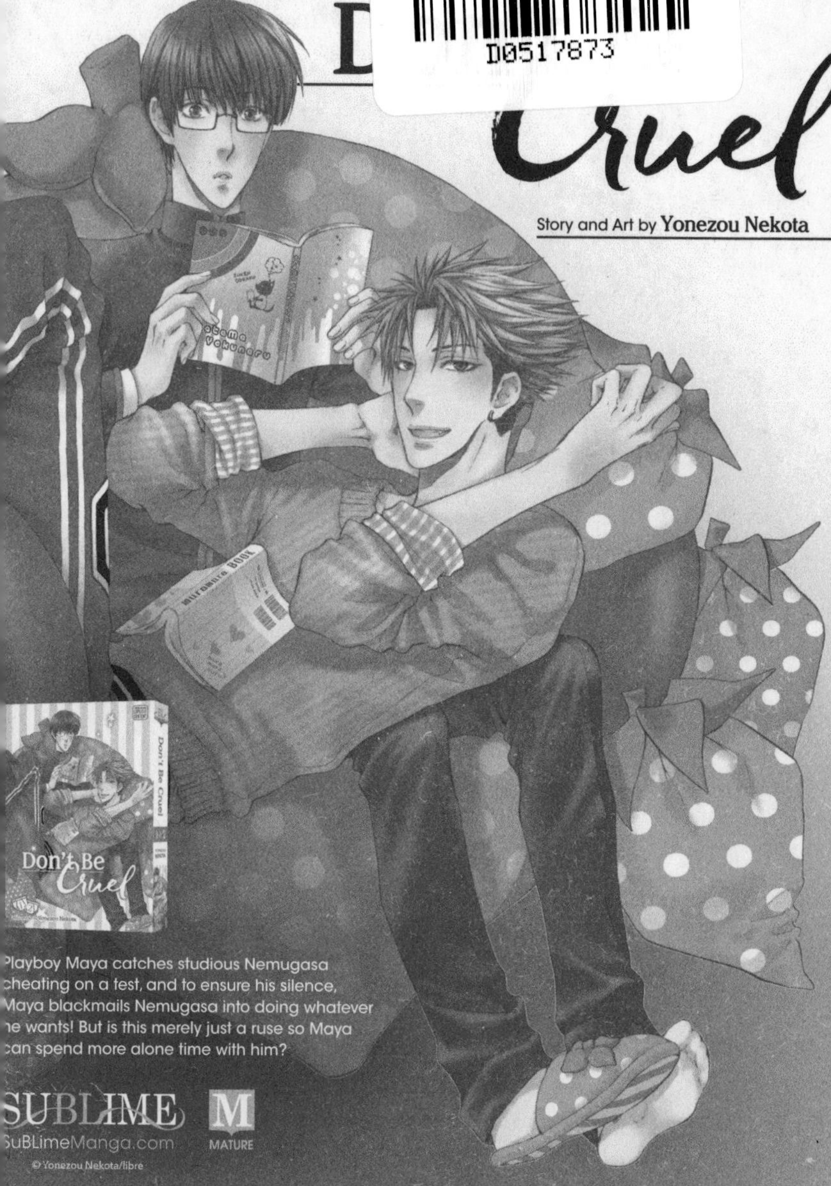
Don't Be Cruel
Don't Be Cruel

Playboy Maya catches studious Nemugasa cheating on a test, and to ensure his silence, Maya blackmails Nemugasa into doing whatever he wants! But is this merely just a ruse so Maya can spend more alone time with him?